QUEER FAITH

SEXUAL CULTURES

General Editors: Ann Pellegrini, Tavia Nyong'o, and Joshua Chambers-Letson
Founding Editors: José Esteban Muñoz and Ann Pellegrini

Titles in the series include:

Queer Faith

Reading Promiscuity and Race in the
Secular Love Tradition

Melissa E. Sanchez

NEW YORK UNIVERSITY PRESS

New York

NEW YORK UNIVERSITY PRESS
New York
www.nyupress.org

References to Internet websites (URLs) were accurate at the time of writing. Neither the author nor New York University Press is responsible for URLs that may have expired or changed since the manuscript was prepared.

Library of Congress Cataloging-in-Publication Data
Names: Sanchez, Melissa E., author.
Title: Queer faith : reading promiscuity and race in the secular love tradition / Melissa E. Sanchez.
Description: New York : NYU Press, 2019. | Includes bibliographical references and index.
Identifiers: LCCN 2018043757| ISBN 9781479871872 (hbk : alk. paper) | ISBN 9781479840861 (pbk : alk. paper)
Subjects: LCSH: Queer theory. | Religion—Philosophy. | Promiscuity. | Sexual minorities.
Classification: LCC HQ75.15 .S25 2019 | DDC 306.7601—dc23
LC record available at https://lccn.loc.gov/2018043757

New York University Press books are printed on acid-free paper, and their binding materials are chosen for strength and durability. We strive to use environmentally responsible suppliers and materials to the greatest extent possible in publishing our books.

Manufactured in the United States of America

10 9 8 7 6 5 4 3 2 1

Also available as an ebook

For Quincy

CONTENTS

A NOTE ON TRANSLATIONS

Because the writings of Paul, Augustine, Luther, Calvin, and Petrarch have been available in multiple editions and languages, each situated in its own historical moment, determining which text to quote is already an interpretive decision.

For biblical passages, throughout this book I have settled on the imperfect solution of using the translations that best approximate the readers I discuss. For the first chapter, I chose the Douay-Rheims version (DRB), along with the Vulgate (V) on which it is based, on the premise that this approximates the Latin that Augustine (who was not a fluent reader of Greek) and Petrarch would have read and the Catholic tradition through which Petrarch would have understood Paul. In the following chapters, I use the 1576 Geneva translation (GB) because this would have been the English version available to and preferred by the English authors I consider, most of whom composed the poems I discuss before the King James translation (KJB) appeared in 1611. Throughout these chapters, I continue to cite the Vulgate, as well as the King James translation, when these versions differ significantly from the Geneva and provide additional information. When biblical passages appear within quotations from other sources, I leave them as they are translated in that source.

In my discussion of Petrarch, I have included all poems in both English and Italian. For Augustine, Luther, Calvin, Montaigne, Freud, and Lacan, I work primarily with the English translations; I include the original Latin, German, or French only when those languages' differences or nuances inform my reading.

Introduction

No Past? Theology, Race, and Queer Theory's
Authorized Genealogies

Like a Prayer

This book exhumes a dead metaphor—the comparison of secular love to religious faith—in order to examine the unexpectedly queer affordances of its theological vehicle. In the modern West, the description of secular desire through a Christian lexicon of prayer, conversion, salvation, redemption, confession, sacrifice, revelation, and ecstasy is so pervasive that it is scarcely noticeable. We need look no farther than contemporary popular music, ranging from bad to brilliant, in which examples abound: just a few obvious instances are George Michael's "Faith," Madonna's "Like a Prayer," REM's "Losing My Religion," Melissa Ethridge's "Angels Would Fall," Beyonce's "All Night," John Legend's "Made to Love," Lady Gaga's "Judas."[1] These lyrics cite a tradition formalized by Dante and the troubadours, diffused into European discourse by Francesco Petrarch and his Renaissance imitators, and central to such standbys of modern wedding recital as Elizabeth Barrett Browning's vow that "I love thee with a love I seemed to lose / With my lost saints."[2] True love, as distinct from lust or infatuation, resembles religious faith in structure but is directed at love objects who are in the world rather than saints or deities beyond it. Taken straight, this tradition would seem to supply ideological grounding for many of the compulsory normativities that queer theory has critiqued: monogamy, singular identity, self-sovereignty, and self-disclosure.

But what if religious discourse instead offers a script for theorizing promiscuity? My central proposal in this book is that if we linger over the secular religion of monogamous love, we can appreciate the deep affinities between queerness and faith across the temporal, national,

and generic borders that both queer theory and early modern studies too often take for granted. Throughout, I build on Carla Freccero's
astute observation that "a critical genealogy of one of heterosexuality's
most powerful discourses, the love song, demonstrates, proleptically,
the queerness at the heart of heteronormative culture."[3] The particular
strand of this genealogy that I examine is the Pauline theology of the
divided will, which I treat as a neglected resource for queer theoriza-
tions of desire and subjectivity. Because Christianity has been so widely
invoked to justify discrimination and violence against sexual minorities, that proposition would appear counterintuitive at best. In light of
the long history of religious hostility to sodomy, homosexuality, adultery, promiscuity, and gender nonconformity, it makes sense that queer
theory would give biblical and theological writing no quarter. Religion
has done, and continues to do, untold damage to queer life. Particularly
given the alarming and seemingly inexorable ascendency of the religious
Right in US politics, shouldn't queer theorists be calling for *increased*
secularization, rather than inviting theological discourse into our own
archives and genealogies?

To the contrary, I argue that when we dismiss the queer potential of
religious writing on the grounds that this is not how it is understood by
most practicing Christians, we grant that it is off-limits to those who
do not believe. We thereby make theology sacred in the dual sense of
that term explored by Giorgio Agamben: both consecrated and cursed,
barred from human contact insofar as it has been sacrificed to the gods
(even if we don't believe in them).[4] Instead, I suggest that we *profane*
theology, bringing it into contact with the creaturely world through use
and play. As numerous queer theologians, religious studies scholars,
queer and psychoanalytic theorists, and early modernists have observed,
taken on its own terms, a good deal of biblical and theological writing
troubles normative views of intimacy and attachment.[5] The result is that,
Richard Rambuss demonstrates, "Christianity's own myths, institutions,
and cultural expressions offer too many transit points to the ecstatic,
the excessive, the transgressive, the erotic to be allowed to serve tenably
in . . . a censorious capacity, to be cast as a force field for the proscription
of desire and its ever-wanton vagaries." I would add that the "(orthodox)
perversities" that Rambuss has identified in Christianity are present not
only in spontaneous moments of devotional ecstasy.[6] They are also part

of theology, understood as a systematic attempt to theorize belief, and of secular discourses of love. And because theology is itself a human invention, the metaphoric transport between sacred faith and secular love works both ways. It is not only that discourses of secular eroticism adopt religious idioms but also that theological writing deploys human desires and attachments to figure the relation between creature and creator. The sacred and the profane are mutually dependent and mutually disruptive.

I focus in this book on the secular legacy of the Pauline Epistles, whose soteriological elevation of faith over works, feelings over acts, guides the thought of Saint Augustine, Martin Luther, and John Calvin. Through Augustine, Pauline theology also shapes the lyrics of Francesco Petrarch, whose interminable pining and petulance affords a model for the secular love tradition that I examine in the writing of William Shakespeare, Edmund Spenser, Philip Sidney, Mary Wroth, John Milton, and John Donne. This long and unruly genealogy, I propose, allows us to examine eroticism in a more complex and capacious sense than oppositions between monogamy and promiscuity, or normativity and transgression, can accommodate. Rather than depict love as eternal, the translation of religious fervor into secular eroticism registers with unusual precision the theological conviction that human desire and subjectivity are fundamentally promiscuous, a word I use not only in its sexual sense, but also in its more expansive designation of all that is errant, disorderly, flexible, and indiscriminate.

Central to Pauline theology is the view that faithlessness is not only inevitable, but also indispensable to salvation. It is in its failures and struggles that faith escapes becoming just one more work, one more mechanical ritual. Indeed, Paul's conceptual system is premised on the view that the human will is inherently divided and obscure, and therefore congenitally incapable of fulfilling that first and most merciless of divine commands: *Love me. Only me.* The value of the crucifixion rests on humanity's inability to offer eternal, exclusive, and unambivalent devotion and thereby to *earn* salvation on its own. Faced with frailty and failure, the human creature accepts the need for divine grace. Accordingly, far from assuming the possibility of happy fidelity often trumpeted by the modern evangelical Right, premodern Christian thought is obsessed with humanity's salutary faithlessness and self-opacity. Paul, Augustine, Luther, and Calvin offer a theory of subjectivity centered on the recognition that what we know and tell of ourselves is unreliable, opaque, and partial: as I discuss at greater length in chapter 2, Lacan observes that what Pauline theology calls "sin" diagnoses the ambivalence and aggression that psychoanalysis has located at the core of desire.[7] Devotion pulsates with doubt and distraction, the experience of which reminds humanity that grace is amazing because no one deserves it, but everyone can hope for it. In this, it is like secular love.

Intimacy, in this Christian schema, is premised not on an enduring commitment that guarantees a predictable future, but on a recursive temporality of broken vows, shifted attention, and renewed zeal. The resulting ethics of promiscuity, as I discuss in chapters 1, 2, and 5, requires a humbling awareness that the love we receive as well as that which we feel can be *only* charitable, never merited. We have blind spots that will catch us unaware; we will make compromises that will appear as such only in retrospect; our most deeply felt affections are potentially poisonous, cruel, and self-serving. In short, we are neither innocent nor invulnerable—whatever our hopes and intentions, we will inflict as well as suffer pain and disappointment. Paul, and the theologians and poets who take him seriously, know that Nietzsche is right: *ressentiment* saturates morality, and generosity can become its own form of aggression. As I will argue throughout this book, this theological, and especially Protestant, conviction of human depravity surprisingly offers a model of relationality that, premised as it is on a view of love as a matter of (always partial) charity and forgiveness, also offers a striking departure from normative definitions of romance based on self-knowledge, mutual desert, and lifelong fidelity.

Treating theology as a theoretical resource for examining secular desire, intimacy, and subjectivity can expand queer theory's authorized genealogies and objects of study in several ways. First, amidst ongoing debates about the definition, utility, and purview of queer theory, attending to the queerness of premodern theology and poetry unsettles an acquired, unquestioned habit of mind that sees promiscuity and monogamy, obedience and transgression, as opposites. Ironically, a sexual radicalism that assumes that promiscuity frees us from repressive commitment and dreary vanilla sex may affirm neoliberal ideals of autonomy, privacy, and accumulation (of partners, of experiences, of goods). The profiles and preferences of app-based cruising or the acquisition of the tools and techniques of BDSM, for instance, illustrate what Kathryn Lofton has said of the "religion" of modern consumerism more generally: they can "forge new kinds of sectarian allegiance and new forms of obedience" to dominant structures of race and class.[8] Although I critique commitment as a potentially discriminatory and damaging ideal, I avoid treating monogamy as the problem and promiscuity as the solution. Instead, I trace the long, intricate, and contradictory genealogies of these secular concepts as they collaborate with gendered, racial, national, and socioeconomic taxonomies.

The second affordance of the theological and poetic tradition I study is its perspective on the presecular and premodern roots of what Sharon Holland has called "the erotic life of racism."[9] Because religion is so explicitly central to both past conceptions of race and current neoracisms, attending to the theological concepts that shape secular eroticism illuminates a long history in which race and sexuality are mutually constituted. Poetic and theological writing concerned with the vexed relation between body and soul, works and faith, what one does and who one is, allows us to see the relation of acts and identities as inseparable from a genealogy of racialized sexuality and thereby challenges the imagination of a single, universalized queer subject. The secular lyrics I study, written at a time when the cultural dominance of companionate bourgeois marriage was not yet inevitable, often register a racialized sense of the contrast between the sincerity and freedom claimed for Christian (and especially Protestant) believers and the unregenerate hypocrisy and servitude of religious and racial others. This association of freedom (from history, from necessity) with authenticity makes both mainstream morality *and* queer promiscuity differently accessible for differently racialized bodies and souls. As I discuss at length in chapters 2 and 3, numerous women of color and queer of color scholars have shown how racial hierarchies are sustained by attaching unique respectability and morality to monogamous marriage and treating alternate forms of intimacy and kinship as evidence of a pathological failure of self-regulation. Yet ideals of promiscuity also enact their own taxonomies of segregation, devaluation, and omission. As Holland has argued, "In many ways, mainstream queer theory wants to leave history behind," because recalling the long history of racial, ethnic, and colonial subjugation and violence that conditions erotic fantasy and preference is "entirely disruptive to a theoretical project invested in the autonomy of . . . erotic preference."[10] I extend Holland's call for locating queer subjectivity in "a *transhistorical* view of time" to account for the conjoined categories of religion, race, and sexuality before modernity.[11] As I show in chapters 2 and 4, the alternatives to laborious monogamy found in premodern theological and poetic writing frequently depend on the figuration of formal—and therefore hypocritical rather than heartfelt— allegiance through improvised racial categories. At the same time, these lyrics are structured by a theological conviction of the impossibility of the lucid rationality and firm self-possession that classical philosophy had long deemed evidence of fitness for liberty. In stressing the failures of the classical values of self-knowledge and self-determination, Pauline theology and its poetic legacy open on a theoretical level an ethics of relationality suppressed by the material history of slavery and colonialism.

Finally, in turning to biblical, patristic, and early modern writing and cultural history, I join the many medieval and early modern scholars who have sought to rethink queer theory's archive to include premodern materials usually understood as outside the temporal and identitarian boundaries of modern queer studies.[12] What Eve Kosofsky Sedgwick described as the Great Paradigm Shift is also a secularization of both sexuality and race. According to this narrative, the theological category of sin is succeeded by those of crime, illness, and identity; ethnoreligious categories of Christians, Jews, Saracens, Moors, heathens, and pagans are succeeded by racial distinctions based on visual differences of skin color and phenotype. As Jonathan Goldberg has insisted, "The model of supersession and revelation—enlightenment—is always committed to a forgetting or obliteration."[13] Such a model obscures its own historicity: no less than modern definitions of "race" and "sexuality," both historical periods and present definitions of the religious and the secular were nineteenth-century inventions. When we read beyond modern and secular boundaries to engage with premodern analyses of faith and subjectivity, we can appreciate that many "traditions" invoked by rightwing politics and opposed by queer scholars are themselves a product of selective memory and citation.

I take Pauline theology as my object of analysis because it is so central to what Lauren Berlant and Michael Warner call a "fantasized mainstream" in US secular culture.[14] I treat theology, and the erotic poetry it shaped, as archives that are, to borrow Goldberg's words, "contributions to queer theory that do not appear under that rubric."[15] Although this book engages with and at times contextualizes the writings of the past, and although it draws on a number of pathbreaking histories and gene-alogies of sexuality, its goals are primarily theoretical rather than his-torical. In reevaluating writing that has been habitually dismissed, queer theory as a field can challenge both the normative culture that theology and love poetry are assumed to undergird and its own orthodoxies as a field. We can start by taking a closer look at the religious foundations of secularism itself.

Have We Ever Been Secular?

As Mark Jordan aptly notes, "Queer theorists have trouble paying enough attention to queer religion—especially if the religion is Christian and the theorists Anglo-American."[16] From the perspective of intellectual and political history, this exclusion of theology from queer theory is odd. Intellectually, in L. O. Aranye Fradenburg's succinct description of the relationship between courtly love and psychoanalysis, Christian theol-ogy is part of the genealogy of psychoanalysis and poststructuralism, and "for this reason it is also part of contemporary theory."[17] Thinkers who have been central to queer theory's conceptual frameworks—perhaps most prominently, Freud, Lacan, Foucault, and Derrida—consistently engage with biblical and theological sources to examine desire and subjectivity. Politically, before the late 1970s, as Janet Jakobsen and Ann Pellegrini remind us, there is a "rich history of progressive move-ments for African American civil rights that were grounded in the Black Church, the movements for economic justice grounded in the Catholic worker movements in the United States and Catholic base communities in Central America, the long-standing tradition of Jewish progressive politics, and the Quaker movements on behalf of abolition and against war."[18] To this list we can add Mormon polygamy, Spiritualist gender nonconformity, and first-wave feminism.[19] Historically, religiosity has prompted radical as well as reactionary responses to the dominant order.

The evacuation of theology from queer theory may have been less an inevitable development than a result of the specific cultural and historical moment in which queer theory consolidated itself as a field.

Queer theory is only one instance of Lawrence Buell's observation that in late-twentieth-century literary and cultural studies more generally, "religiocentric frames of explanation started to go out of fashion at about the same time evangelical Christianity began to seize control of public culture to a degree unprecedented since colonial times."[20] The institutionalization of the field that would come to be known as queer theory began in the 1980s, which was also the decade in which religious culture in the United States saw a sea change. Cold War distinctions that deemed the United States the site of individual religious choice and freedom as against the state-mandated atheism and conformity of the Soviet Union had paved the way for a conceptual conjunction of Christianity, capitalism, and democracy that would flourish with the "prosperity gospel" of mass-mediated Christianity in the 1980s.[21] The year of the first National March on Washington for Lesbian and Gay Rights, 1979, was also a banner year for white evangelicalism in the United States: Jerry Falwell founded the Moral Majority as a political action committee and Pat Robertson released an "Action Plan for the 1980s," the goal of which was to incite "a profound moral revival" by harnessing the "awesome power of the media."[22] In the 1980s and 1990s, a politically reactionary evangelical Christianity was fostered through megachurches, political action committees, Christian amusement parks and youth groups, and televised broadcasts of religious programming.[23] The spread of white evangelical Christianity abetted the US government's deadly inaction in response to the HIV/AIDS pandemic—we might think of Billy Graham's malicious claim that HIV was God's way of punishing America for tolerating homosexuals. At the same time, an ascendant discourse of "family values" put the nail in the coffin of the Equal Rights Amendment and forged a new link between Protestant Christianity and opposition to contraception and abortion. During the Clinton, Bush, and Obama administrations, faith-based charities, businesses, and organizations habitually defended discriminatory policies under the banner of religious freedom. Most recently, the rhetoric and policies of the Trump-Pence administration have accentuated the ease with which claims of sincerely held religious belief provide cover for attacks on women, immigrants, and racial, ethnic, and sexual minorities.

Given that the rise of right-wing evangelicalism was coterminous with that of queer theory, it is unsurprising that the field tends to regard

Christianity with suspicion, if not hostility. Yet in treating secularization as a prerequisite of queer politics, the field of queer theory also risks perpetuating what Jakobsen and Pellegrini describe as "the Enlightenment progress narrative, which forecasts the continuous and inevitable expansion of freedom" that is "often told as the legitimating narrative of American life."[24] Secularization is usually understood as an accumulation of what Charles Taylor calls "subtraction stories," the gradual liberation from erroneous belief and practice that has accompanied the arrival of modern secularity.[25] In Linell Cady's evaluation, the "story of secularization narrates the triumph of empiricism over superstition, reason over faith, and the emancipation of all spheres—science, knowledge, the market, the state—from the oppressive and authoritarian 'yoke of religion.'"[26] Trust in secularization as the path to a "disenchanted" state of rationality and freedom is based on a definition of "religion" as individual belief that must be kept separate from the public, political, and economic life of modern democracy.[27] Yet this particular distinction between religiosity and secularity is itself a Christian one. It was initiated by the Pauline denial of the soteriological significance of ceremony, circumcision, and dietary laws; taken up by the Latin Church to proclaim the unique sincerity of Christian devotion as against Judaic, Muslim, and pagan ritual and custom; and significantly expanded by the Protestant Reformers' denunciation of Catholic sacraments as mere superstitions.[28]

Christian norms continue to haunt secular culture in part because, as Tracy Fessenden puts it, "a Protestant conception of religion" determines the "meanings of both the religious and the secular."[29] While it is empirically true that organized religion's formal role in the state has been restricted in modern Western societies, from French *laïcité* to the US separation of church and state, it is also true that Christian perspectives and practices still inform everyday life and state politics in a myriad of norms so taken for granted that their credal basis has been rendered all but invisible.[30] In the twentieth and twenty-first centuries, the privatization of belief has allowed modern secular states and national cultures to be structured according to Christian norms. The free exercise of Christian belief receives staunch legal protection, even when it involves overt discrimination against sexual and racial minorities, while non-Christian religious identities and practices are treated as mere pretext for illegal, dangerous, or culturally marginal activities and ways of being.[31] Christianity's productive invisibility itself depends on a suppression of the historicity of the concepts of the religious and the secular. The adjective "secular" originally designated those clergy who lived, preached, and ministered in the present, temporary, visible world designated by the Latin *saeculum* (age, lifetime, or generation). By contrast, "religious" clergy retreated into monasteries to worship an eternal and invisible deity. The Protestant Reformation was the beginning of secularization in the sense that it argued for the transfer of political, legal, economic, and cultural institutions from religious to secular basis and jurisdiction. This change sought not to exclude religious experience from everyday life but to integrate them. Protestant reformers rejected monastic seclusion as hypocritical and superstitious—a misguided substitution of works for faith, external conformity for internal sincerity. As against secularity as an epistemic category, "secularism" as an ideology names the nineteenth-century doctrine of the separation of religion and politics, a separation made possible by the Protestant definition of religion as private belief that, unlike embodied ritual or custom, could be sustained without public display or enactment.[32]

Accordingly, postsecular scholars maintain that, in Talal Asad's laconic formulation, "the 'religious' and the 'secular' are not essentially fixed categories."[33] Within literary and cultural studies, Peter Coviello and Jared Hickman have argued that by "naming and provincializing the animating master narrative of the secular"—seeing it as a product of the Western university's particular geographical and historical location—we can reconsider an equation of secularization with freedom and progress that can be complicit with doctrines of Western superiority and American exceptionalism.[34] I would add that this postsecular perspective might have affinities with a *pre*secular one. Rather than situating our present moment as "after" secularism in the sense that religion has returned to Western culture, politics, or academia, postsecularism reckons with the possibility that we have never been as secular as we thought we were.[35] Presecular writing can attune us to modes of thought that do not assume the possibility of progress, disenchantment, or liberation (this allies them with posthuman and new materialist theory, as I demonstrate in chapter 5). Premodern theology and poetry abjure humanist ideals of autonomous choice or prudential commitment in favor of a Pauline and Protestant mindset that, in Alan Sinfield's apt assessment, "thrived on irrationality."[36] Recognizing that mainstream secular discourses of desire are in fact Christian in structure if not in content allows us to notice the perversity and abjection that infuse "our" ostensibly modern world. This also allows us to rethink the association of theology with normative morality, on the one hand, and of queerness with modernity and liberation, on the other.

The Freedom of a Christian versus Babylonian Captivity

From the early days of the Protestant Reformation, the conceptual nexus of faith, freedom, and authenticity was framed in overlapping geographic and racialized terms. The titles of two of Luther's influential 1520 tracts, "The Babylonian Captivity of the Church" and "The Freedom of a Christian," sum up the goal of reform as a rejection of Catholic sacramental works, the rote fulfilment of which encourages resentment and hypocrisy, in favor of trust in God's grace, which inspires love and gratitude. And even as Luther deemed the "black devil" of visible, carnal sin *less* dangerous than the "white devil" of secret, spiritual sin, this metaphor depended on a long history of depicting the devil as black, on the one hand, and dark-skinned persons as excessively libidinous, on the other.[37] Indeed, one early justification of chattel slavery, inherited from Aristotle and fused with Christianity, was that it was merely an outer confirmation of an inner condition, a collapse of figurative and actual enslavement that naturalized the institution itself.[38] Both the forced labor of Indigenous Americans and the African slave trade were justified on religious as well as racial grounds, and through the middle of the eighteenth century the religious differentiation of "Christians" and "Strangers" determined the lawfulness of enslavement.[39] Legal distinctions between Christians and strangers were themselves understood in hereditary terms, as is evident in the decrees of colonial legislatures that "conversion did not alter the status of those *descended* from pagan lands."[40] Insofar as Christianity became a grounds for claiming citizenship, what we can see as a Protestant American version of Spain's pure blood laws served to shore up a longstanding association of "true religion with enlightenment, with whiteness" against the leveling threats of Christian conversion and fellowship.[41] New World emphasis on skin color did not so much replace as supplement Old World religious groupings.[42]

By attending to the religious dimension of racial differentiation, we can appreciate the extent to which Protestant notions of faith and authenticity continue to inform ostensibly secular understandings of both normativity and queerness as racialized constructs. Too often, the term "race" has been deemed anachronistic by scholars who maintain that before the eighteenth century it meant something more like what we now call "ethnicity": a cultural or religious attribution that was unstable and acquired rather than biologically fixed. Because, this argument goes, race was understood in fluid terms and lacked a coherent pseudoscientific rationale, premodern discourses of race, color, blood, or blackness are distinct from the rigid and discriminatory logic of modern, genetic views of race.[43] Charges of anachronism enable an omission that Kim F. Hall critiqued over two decades ago: "Dismissing the term 'race' altogether or imposing absolute historical boundaries between early modern and contemporary constructions may allow us not to think about race either in Renaissance texts or in our classrooms. More specifically, it serves to perpetuate white privilege in Renaissance studies, the luxury of *not* thinking about race—hence duplicating racism in writing and professional relations."[44] I would add that the view that race is a modern concept is limiting to scholars of modernity as well, for it obscures a longer history of race that precedes the era of large-scale European colonization and American slavery.[45] Confining the definition of racism to systematic color-based differentiation occludes more diffuse forms of racism built on class, religious, linguistic, and stylistic stereotypes, and thereby allows bias to be excused as observation of cultural differences rather than racist discrimination—in the present as well as the past.

This anxiety about anachronism, as Hall, writing with Peter Erickson, has more recently argued, disavows the archival discoveries and theoretical sophistication achieved by scholars examining early modern race and racism.[46] For decades, scholars of medieval and early modern worlds have contested the view that race is a modern invention, the product of colonialism, Atlantic slavery, and pseudoscientific taxonomies. This body of work has established that (1) a recognizably modern racial discrimination is fully evident by the thirteenth century; (2) the European trade in African slaves began in the fifteenth century; (3) the

English knew of this trade from the beginning and participated in it from at least the mid-sixteenth century; (4) the early modern English population included far more nonwhite and non-Christian persons than has previously been estimated; (5) differences in skin color were accounted for in terms of climatic, humoral, and imprintation theory that at that time had the same pseudobiological status as eighteenth- and nineteenth-century eugenics, phrenology, physiognomy, and forensic anthropometry, all of which once were deemed legitimate modern science but have since been wholly discredited.[47] Race, before the eighteenth century as after it, was viewed as somatic as well as cultural, and racialist thought was instrumental in shaping the modern political and economic abuses often thought to have produced it.

Drawing on the work of Ania Loomba, Ayanna Thompson, and Geraldine Heng, I argue that when we encourage the study of race in the early modern period on the grounds that it had many of the somatic and pseudoscientific meanings usually understood in its modern usage, we endow *modern* racialization and racism with a precision, intelligibility, and stability that they do not in reality have.[48] Examining race's volatile cultural and religious constructedness *also* is critical to contesting modern racism. The work of early modern scholars illuminates the longer history of the critical race theory argument that race is a dynamic and shifting social and cultural construct, not a meaningful physical or genetic characteristic.[49] Then as now, physical attributes acquire valuation and meaning with regard to fantasies about religion, language, national origin, class and economic status, domestic arrangements, and sexual disposition and practice. This historical perspective is necessary to challenging a modern neoracism that thrives by denying that it is "racism," properly speaking, at all. Étienne Balibar has observed of discrimination based on nonassimilation to dominant religious and cultural identities that "*culture can also function like a nature*, and it can in particular function as a way of locking individuals and groups a priori into a genealogy, into a determination that is immutable and intangible in origin."[50] Contrasting cultural and biological justifications for racism, Balibar insists, does nothing to change its discriminatory structure and effects, and may in fact rationalize them.

Attention to historical moments when race, always a promiscuous construct, was explicitly intertwined with religion can be instrumental in allowing us to recognize past and present racisms that cannot be pinned to prejudice against particular phenotypes. In Geraldine Heng's words, "A political hermeneutics of religion—so much in play again today—enabled the positing of fundamental human differences in biopolitical and culturalist ways to create strategic essentialisms demarcating human kinds and populations."[51] Leerom Medovoi offers a helpful conceptualization of premodern *and* modern racism as operating along two axes, those of color and faith. Dogma-line racialization, for Medovoi, supplements and interacts with a more familiar color-line racialization based on descent or phenotype. Dogma-line racism is a "racism of the soul" that can be traced back to the consolidation of Christian European identity through the Crusades and that "maps populations along the other side of Cartesian modernity's mind/body split, in primary reference to mind rather than body, ideology rather than corporality, according to theologies, creeds, beliefs, faiths, and ideas, rather than their color, face, hair, blood, and origin."[52] Medovoi's most prominent examples are modern Islamaphobia and anti-Semitism, but he argues that dogma-line racism is itself a secularized theology in which "Jews and Muslims become prototypes for the abnormality of analogized secular religiosities that over time came to include dogmas ranging from socialism to anarchism to black power to feminism."[53] Medovoi's work on twenty-first-century dogma-line racism, like Balibar's writings on contemporary neoracism, helps to crystalize the political urgency of understanding race as more than a simple binary in which the past is divided from the present, religious from secular culture, and racism is reduced to prejudice against those who are visibly "not white." What Roland Greene has said about European responses to Indigenous Americans in early modern colonial writing also describes modern racial distinctions based on the "one-drop rule," Islamaphobia, anti-Semitism, and past and present hysteria about East Asian and Latin American immigration: "racial 'color' . . . exists as much in the minds of observers as in physical fact."[54] For Medovoi, the difficulty of defining just which combination of skin tone, eye color, hair texture, facial features, body type, dress, and comportment allows someone to "look" white brings dogma- and color-line racism together. The two axes of racism converge to "retroactively read the telltale signs on the racial body for what should have been noticed in the first place," even as the search for somatic evidence of hidden danger is "animated by the fear that the moment of recognition may come too late or not all" since "the body can successfully disguise the disloyalty it contains."[55]

Questions of sexual excess and repression have long been central to the formation of racial distinctions, and this book examines how theological concepts of faith and grace complicate conjoined racial and sexual categories.[56] As I discuss in chapters 2, 3, and 4, tracing the Pauline logics that still shape Western secular views of love and commitment can provide us a surprising challenge to the innocence of the respectable, monogamous, procreative marriage associated with Christian thought. At the same time, the assumptions of authenticity and emancipation that have shaped queer endorsements of promiscuity may themselves derive from a Pauline distinction between hypocritical conformity and sincere desire. Several queer and feminist studies of the collaboration between narratives of secularization, modernization, and sexual liberation have demonstrated that when queer and feminist theorists assume that secularization is necessary to gender equality and sexual freedom, they unwittingly accept what Jasbir Puar describes as Western "sexual exceptionalism" that perpetuates distinctions between archaic and repressive religiosity and modern and liberatory secularity.[57] As Puar contends, in this queer paradigm "'Freedom from norms' resonates with liberal humanism's authorization of the fully self-possessed speaking subject" and "relies on a normative notion of deviance, always defined in relation to normativity, often universalizing."[58]

Given that sexual exceptionalism incorporates a secularist ideal that itself derives from Christian tradition, I propose that one response is to look more closely at the theological discourses from which Christian family values rhetoric claims authority and which queer anti-identitarian rhetorics purport to reject. Analyzed on its own terms, Christian faith refuses the reassuring distinctions between transgression and normativity, emancipation and repression, that have shaped queer as well as normative associations of erotic choice with modernity, secularization, and whiteness.

This Book

The following five chapters examine how premodern theology and poetry strikingly contest modern assumptions—both in their explicit proclamation by believers and in their secular iterations—about what Christian writing has to say about desire, sex, commitment, selfhood, and ethics. Considering the topics of faith, monogamy, procreative marriage, adultery, and erotic accountability, each chapter treats lyric poetry as a hinge articulating theological convictions of humanity's innate promiscuity with psychoanalytic and queer assessments of opaque and fragmented subjectivity. This poetry makes visible an ethos of promiscuity that—distinct from a libertine ethos of individual entitlement—practices a humbling awareness of our own propensity to guile, aggression, and self-deceit. This ethos does not enjoin a cynical dismissal of intellectual consistency or social justice, but suggests a consciousness of how easily and often we fall short of these goals. In relinquishing a belief in our own wholeness or harmlessness, we might become more open to unbidden encounters with similarly imperfect others.[59] We might also come to practice the ongoing efforts of ethical self-formation that Foucault called *askesis*.[60]

This book builds on much that has gone before in studies of the relations among theology, early modern literature, gender, sexuality, race, and colonialism. Along with the accounts of secularism, race, and religion discussed in the sections above, two fields from which this project has drawn considerable inspiration are political theology and queer theology. The first of these, political theology, resists strict periodization and contextualization, and, as Julia Lupton writes, treats the "religious turn" in early modern studies as "the chance for a return to theory."[61] As Lupton and Graham Hammill summarize it, this body of scholarship has sought to "identify the exchanges, pacts, and contests that obtain between religious and political life, especially the use of sacred narratives, motifs, and liturgical forms to establish, legitimate, and reflect upon the sovereignty of monarchs, corporations, and parliaments."[62] The second field I engage, queer theology, contests the tendency among both the Christian Right and queer theorists to focus on those biblical "texts of terror" condemning homosexuality, adultery, masturbation, promiscuity, and gender deviance.[63] Queer theology instead brings together philological, historical, and theoretical methods of reading to illuminate the complexity of biblical and theological representations of gender, sexuality, and kinship.[64] At its most optimistic, queer theology has proclaimed, in Andy Buechal's words, that "*all good theology has always been queer,* even if this way of describing it is new. Christian practice and belief have always been somewhat bizarre."[65] Other queer theologians have stressed the imperfect fit between queer and Christian identity, however, and urged extensive disciplinary self-critique for a field that, as Susannah Cornwall observes, "always stands in a difficult relationship to the ecclesiastical *and* academic mainstream."[66]

My readings of secular love lyrics bring together political theology's attention to, in Lupton and Hammill's words, "the status of theology as an operative fiction" with queer theology's insight that, as Cornwall writes, "the ambiguity of the Christian tradition means that . . . it is neither queer nor anti-queer: or rather, it is both."[67] This is hardly news, of course, to scholars whose work has illuminated the strangeness of early modern religious verse, which is more likely to describe promiscuous attachments and agonized apostasy than serene devotion.[68] My contribution to this body of thought is to consider how the fundamentally anxious theology of Paul, Augustine, and their Protestant heirs shapes the obsessive self-inventories of lovers of worldly as well as divine objects. Both formally and thematically, Renaissance sonnet sequences and poetic collections manifest the oscillations of love through cycles of resentment, aggression, appetite, appeal, gratitude, humiliation, and forgiveness. This maelstrom of desires emerges from the "Protestant paradox" diagnosed by Constance Furey: even as the Reformation elevated individual faith over communal ritual, the very turn from works to grace constructed the self as vulnerable and dependent on God and community, and therefore a matter of interactive poesis, "the crafted fragment of thought" that is not sui generis but responsive and, to that degree, relational.[69] Poetic disjunctions between sound and sense, metrical and grammatical units, semiotic and syntactic events, as well as the interruptions, silences, juxtapositions, and opacities that exist between one poem and another, all register the fragmentary, incoherent nature of desire and subjectivity—the propensity to confuse and delude self no less than other, the difficulty of collating event with intensity of reaction. And as the lyric "I," like its theological counterpart, aspires to the inclusiveness of the "we," it also reveals the divisions and incoherencies of this relational and communal construct.

Moreover, as Roland Greene has shown, before "lyric largely disappears from the spheres of society and politics and into the dead end of a discrete literary culture," it is a key medium for the socialization of gendered, racial, and colonial relations that hinge on the ethical dilemmas of desire and unrequitedness.[70] While early modern love poetry has not been a continuous object of analysis for contemporary queer, feminist, or critical race theory, it has appeared in some of the seminal work in these fields: we might think of Eve Sedgewick's theory of the homosocial triangulation of desire in Shakespeare's sonnets; Barbara Johnson's excavation of the Petrarchan legacy of "muteness envy" in modern cinema and politics; Fred Moten's analysis of Amiri Baraka's "Dark Lady of the Sonnets" in light of the technological apparatus within which Shakespeare sexualizes racial difference; or José Esteban Muñoz's discussion of male vulnerability in Shakespeare's sonnets and modern art.[71] I return throughout this book to the formal manifestations of secular love poetry's resistance to optimistic ideals of the permanence or perfectibility of desire. I thereby practice what Elizabeth Freeman describes as "close readings of the past for the odd detail, the unintelligible or resistant moment" in order to "treat these texts and their formal work as theories of their own, interventions upon both critical theory and historiography."[72] To restate the beginning of this chapter, close reading revivifies dead metaphors and permits them to disrupt and derange the routines of modern life.

In chapter 1, "The Queerness of Christian Faith," I analyze the theological roots of secular understandings of erotic temporality and fidelity. I begin with the Pauline Epistles, in which the radical humiliation that manifests divine love is necessarily beyond human capacity. I then turn to Saint Augustine's conviction that the divided human will renders confession incomplete and conversion provisional. Based on the premise that as a human creature he can always change, Augustine's depiction of faith as a result of miraculous passion is cause for optimism as well as anxiety about who he will be in the future. Salvation for Augustine inheres in the consequent realization that professions of faith are in fact ambivalent prayers for it. Finally, I trace the centrality of Pauline and Augustinian theology to the structure of fidelity in Petrarch's secular lyrics, which limn in excruciating detail the "mille rivolte"—the thousand turns, revolts, and returns—of his competing attachments to Laura, God, and his own worldly ambition. These poems confront a fragmented self incapable of the conviction and fidelity to which it desperately aspires but does not entirely want.

In chapter 2, "The Color of Monogamy," I examine how an ideal of monogamy helps sustain intersecting gendered and racial hierarchies. Women of color feminism has long censured the association of female sexual respectability with whiteness and social privilege, but this work generally dates the advent of that association to the establishment of modern slavery and colonialism. Shakespeare's sonnets, however, register the development of a fiction of somatic, heritable whiteness as a correlate of respectable sexuality, one disseminated in classical discourses celebrating male friendship and in imperial allegories of sexual conquest. Yet in their depiction of a three-way affair between the poet, a "fair" young man, and a "black" mistress, the sonnets conspicuously fail to cordon off rational and mutual "fair" male friendship from the humiliating enslavement of "black" female appetite. Instead, drawing on the Pauline theory of sin and grace that influenced thinkers from Luther to Lacan, the sonnets dissolve the oppositions ostensibly embodied by the poet's "two loves"—agency and passivity, mastery and submission, fidelity and promiscuity, purity and pollution—to imagine intimacies beyond the couple.

Chapter 3, "The Shame of Conjugal Sex," traces the effects of Pauline and Augustinian soteriology on Protestant views of marriage. The Protestant Reformation is conventionally understood as elevating conjugal love above the lifelong celibacy idealized by the Catholic Church. But this redemptive vision of companionate marriage overlooks a key argument of leading reformers like Luther and Calvin: both deemed marriage superior to celibacy not because marriage sanctifies shameful creaturely desires, but because it publicly acknowledges them. This view of marriage as humbling confession of impurity runs counter to the modern ideals assumed by the US Supreme Court in *Obergefell v. Hodges*, which affirmed the constitutional right to marriage for all couples. In *Obergefell*, the majority claims that marriage is a unique expression of love, while the dissent insists that it is a sanctuary for the family values threatened by promiscuous queers and welfare queens. Both arguments work to excise the irrational lust whose administration Protestant writers, following Paul, deemed the institution's chief aim. Anxiety that nuptial sex shares the excess and indignity of fornication structures the gendered, sexual, and racial fantasies of Shakespeare's sonnets and Spenser's *Amoretti* and *Epithalamion*. When Shakespeare's procreation sonnets cast poetry as a reproductive technology free of the contamination of lust, they valorize not only same-sex desire but also the preservation of specifically "fair"—white—life and culture. Spenser, by contrast, reveals that the ideal of chaste romance generates sadomasochistic fantasies that naturalize white male rapacity and racialize female innocence.

Chapter 4, "The Optimism of Infidelity: Divorce and Adultery," argues that whereas in modern thought secularism appears the only route to challenging lifelong monogamous marriage, the early modern writers John Milton, Philip Sidney, and Mary Wroth base their endorsement of divorce and adultery on the Pauline distinction between duty and love, letter and spirit, that infuses faith itself with a salutary faithlessness. Milton's divorce pamphlets and Sidney's and Wroth's adulterous sonnet sequences presume that any given commitment may turn out to be a mistake, so intimacy is inevitably provisional. In their emphasis on interiority, these writers participate in a cultural project of privatizing love, which scholars have rightly seen as an ideological foundation of heteronormativity, capitalism, and neoliberalism. Yet by taking this privatization to its logical extreme, they provide grounds for removing intimacy from institutional regulation and reward altogether. These writings are useful to modern queer thought not just as positive models, but also because they alert us to the exclusions upon which freedom may be premised. Sidney, Wroth, and Milton are part of the longer history that precedes and conditions present queer associations of secularism with Western reason and modernity, religion with superstitious and oppressive non-Western cultures. The ideal of sexual liberation, no less than those of monogamy and marriage, has its own racialized genealogy.

Chapter 5, "On Erotic Accountability," focuses on lyrics written from the point of view of the unfaithful lover. I argue that the theological concepts of charity, forgiveness, and confession can inform secular discussions of erotic accountability: What do we owe those whom we love and those who love us, particularly when those categories do not converge? Understanding accountability in the dual senses of responsibility and narration illuminated by Judith Butler, I consider how aesthetic creation—the struggle to tell a coherent story of the self and its desires—constitutes an unattainable ethical obligation. I focus on the devotional and libertine lyrics of John Donne, who, like Augustine, Luther, and Calvin before him, represents confession not as a Foucauldian act of truth, but as an imaginative, aestheticized acknowledgment of guilt *in potentia*. Donne's attention to the entanglement of matter and spirit resists the ideals of romance and rationality that have often been deemed the signal characteristics of "human" sexuality; instead, he writes from the perspective of a being coopted by foreign forces within and without. Counterintuitively, Donne is at his most religious when he defends promiscuous, impermanent, and impure intimacies. For the indiscriminate desire that Donne's speakers pursue is not only the contrary of singular devotion but also a secular approximation of divine forgiveness and *caritas*, the arbitrary yet generous love for imperfect creatures regardless of merit.

I conclude with a coda in which I examine some implications of Pauline theology for recent debates about periodization, affect, and reading. Here, I observe that the figure of the scholar whose work is spurred by love rather than professional aspiration, submission to texts rather than mastery over them, reparative rather than paranoid approaches, offers a paradigm for scholarly commitments that are not defined in terms of traditional periodization. Yet I recognize that an endorsement of amateurism and attachment might be a secular version of the Pauline hierarchy of faith and love over works and rewards—and therefore itself quite consonant with a longstanding view of literary study as a "secular vocation."[73] Rather than treat this theological resonance as a reason to dismiss the possibility that different orientations to reading can reinvent institutional norms, I explore what the persistence of this Pauline structure can tell us about our ways of inhabiting academia. By pursing this framework to its logical conclusion, I propose that a revaluation of promiscuity—with all of its implications of infidelity and instrumentality, distraction and play—may encourage scholarship that resists ideals of scholarly mastery and commitment that tend to reinforce the institutionalization of queer theory's archive as modern and secular.

I close this introduction with a reflection on the value of scholarly dialogue from Lee Edelman and Lauren Berlant's *Sex, or the Unbearable*. At the end of this book, Edelman comments that "except as a rhetorical gesture . . . we can't renounce persuasion. But that doesn't make agreement the point toward which we ought to tend. . . . The shaping of our claims in terms of various rhetorics of persuasion . . . solicits, in this context, resistance, counterargument, and the teasing out of thought that allows us . . . to rework our ideas as they pass through the filter of the other."[74] This offers a useful summary of the interchange that I endeavor to stage in following chapters between conceptual systems and scholarly conversations often considered incongruent, if not mutually incompatible. By passing these writings "through the filter[s] of the other," I try to reassess many of the academic boundaries—of method, historical period, and institutional organization—that currently shape field formations and interpretive protocols. My reading of these materials tends to be opportunistic rather than systematic, evocative rather than exhaustive. In committing to such promiscuous reading, I hope to find new pasts in the present—and new futures in the past.

1

The Queerness of Christian Faith

Things Unseen

It is hard to dissociate the concept of love from some definition of faith: sincerity, trust, perseverance, loyalty, commitment. Understood in terms of either monogamy or the belief in things unseen that characterizes religious thought, "faith" seems an inherently straight concept, one that excludes the experimentation with and destabilization of identity usually associated with queerness. To be sure, the modern Christian Right has relentlessly coupled "faith" with the heteronormative nuclear "family." Faith in God is verified by the formation of and devotion to a family; identity as a spouse and parent functions as a badge of morality, respectability, and legal entitlement. Because "faith and family" has become such a catchphrase, it has been easy to forget not only that the definition and cultural significance of "family" has varied throughout Western Christian history, but also that within biblical, patristic, and Reform writings, "faith" is neither sure nor stable, nor is it dependably satisfying or pleasurable.

Quite the opposite. The experience of faith is one of experimentation, frustration, damage, and reluctance. In the theological as in the vernacular meaning, "faith" is both objective and subjective. Belief and believability are mutually reinforcing: we are faithful not only because we trust, but also because we are trustworthy.[1] Once we stop believing, once we turn away from someone, whatever the reason, the purity of our own faith—the extent to which our promises and loyalties are to be credited—comes into question. In its objective sense, faith is the ultimate sign of love, for it entails making oneself vulnerable to another, trusting in something that, by definition, cannot be proven—that, however much we accept the truism that love hurts, we will, on balance, gain more than we lose. The more intense the love, the more intense the faith, the more intense the demand for faith in return, the greater the danger of heartbreak or disillusion. To practice faith is to doubt much of what we see and to believe in what we don't, to believe that behind the faulty creatures we embrace and the broken world we encounter there is goodness and redemption.

Faith would not be faith without such risk, but with this risk comes the battle against our own faithlessness. This orientation to the unseen and unverifiable involves the possibility that we may be wrong. We may be duped, betrayed, used, let down. Or we may just get bored. Keeping the faith means battling self-protective suspicion, fear, anger, and testing. It also requires us to face our propensity to distraction and seduction, the possibility that we may find ourselves tired of or repulsed by someone who once seemed irresistible. The human lover (and, as Paul and Augustine assiduously remind us, the obedient Christian subject is above all a lover) is congenitally incapable of sustaining the whole-hearted trust, concentration, and self-forgetting that defines absolute faith. Absorption gives way to distraction, fascination to boredom, attraction to repulsion, certainty to doubt. We have neither the stamina nor the attention span to hold a pose of rapt adoration.

Faithful love, in other words, entails work on the self. It cannot be directed toward a future outcome. To the extent that faith (or love) demands reciprocity or reward, it is instrumental, finite, and ultimately self-serving. True love, by contrast, proclaims itself in a tenacity and patience focused only on persevering in what Alain Badiou aptly calls the "grueling work" of the present moment.[2] If love is pure and selfless, we don't get anything out of it. The logical end of this proposition appears in stark relief in the seventeenth-century cult of "pure love" described by Leo Bersani, which endorsed the "impossible supposition" that true believers were those who would continue to worship God even after they were condemned to hell.[3] The paradigmatic expression of a love that desacralizes all else in the world—including the self's own needs, interests, and desires—is not mutuality but unrequitedness. Finding secular expression in any number of romances and melodramas, this noble ideal of selfless love, in fact, mimics the position of a Christian God, who inexplicably loves creatures who can never repay or deserve his affection.

In the vicissitudes of feeling that faith struggles to stabilize is also a confrontation with a self that is never transparent or predicable. To strive for faith is to approach the self and its motives with suspicion. Self-abnegation can be a form of self-promotion. Because faith entails not only our credence but also our credibility, its exercise endows us with the ability to convince, to persuade others to believe our vows and testimony. The sincerest claims of integrity and selflessness are themselves rhetorical insofar as they pursue moral authority for the future that cannot be empirically validated in the present. The temporal dimension of faith—a present feeling about a future that does not yet exist and that we cannot *know* will come to pass—entails the hazard of treating the present as instrumental. To exercise faith, one must resist straining toward its own supersession and fulfillment in a future in which belief is replaced by vindication. Rather than belief in and desire for a future in which the present has become the past, faith in the theological sense is rooted in the present. To adapt a venerable biblical pun, we believe only as long as we do not "know."

Because faith cannot by definition be based on empirical fact, it is a form of fantasy about ourselves and our objects of desire. This fantasy recombines the fragments of our reality that we deem meaningful into truths that are bearable. Faith, in short, turns out to be a profoundly queer concept, one that disrupts stable understandings of desire, identification, and subjectivity.[4] A view of faith as inherently elusive and perverse is at the heart of Paul's Epistles and Augustine's *Confessions*. Because the pursuit of faith is already a second-order desire—a desire to feel a particular way—it pulsates with infidelity. In this chapter, I first trace the contradictions of faith as they were so influentially articulated by two formidable saints, Paul and Augustine. For these anguished converts, it is only the experience of infidelity that keeps us faithful, for it reminds us that grace is, to state the obvious, gratuitous. We are no more entitled to divine grace than to human love. I then turn to the secular love poetry of one of Augustine's most celebrated fans, Francisco Petrarch. In ruthlessly adapting the logic and structure of religious devotion to secular eroticism, Petrarch places infidelity at the heart of the discourse of romantic love that he was so instrumental in founding. Situating Petrarchan love in a theological genealogy defamiliarizes the romantic conventions we have ceased to notice and makes their perversity and their poignancy newly remarkable.

Paulus = "Small"

In the Pauline Epistles, the pursuit of faith is a struggle with the limits of imagination and desire as much as will and integrity. It is also a struggle with the limitations of language and figuration. When we practice faith (and faith is always practice, never perfection), we try to follow the example of Jesus Christ, who "emptied [*exinanivit*] himself, taking the form of a servant [*formam servi accipiens*]. . . . He humbled himself, becoming obedient unto death, even unto the death of the cross" (V/DR, Phil. 2:7–8).[5] Paul announces his own imitation of Christ's evacuation of self in naming himself *Paulus, servus Jesus Christi*, "servant/slave of Christ" (V/DR, Rom. 1:1). Paul's self-divestiture appears not only in the epitaph *servus Jesus Christi* but also in the change of proper name from Saulos to Paulos. As Giorgio Agamben reminds us,

> Saulos is in fact a regal name, and the man who bore this name surpassed all Israelites, not only in beauty, but also in stature (1 Sam. 9:2; this is why, in the Koran, Saul is called *Talut*, the highest). The substitution of *sigma* by *pi* therefore signifies no less than the passage from the real to the insignificant, from grandeur to smallness—*paulus* in Latin means "small, of little significance," and in 1 Corinthians 15:9 Paul defines himself as "the least [*elachistos*] of the apostles."[6]

In becoming "Paul," the man formerly known as Saul confesses that he was never truly great or powerful—never really "Saul"—to begin with. As human creature, he was always small and insignificant, whatever his worldly stature. To wholeheartedly embrace the role of Christ's servant in imitation of Christ's own humiliation is to empty oneself of will and ego in favor of a servitude that is meaningful only insofar as it is unrewarded. The erotic dimension of this humiliation has not escaped critical notice: as Graham Hammill and Jonathan Goldberg point out, Caravaggio's and Tintoretto's renderings of Paul's conversion accentuate the fleshly intensity of giving in to God.[7]

Such obedience strives to dissolves the hierarchies upon which the concept of submission depends. The true obedience of faith is promiscuous in that it dispels our ability to discern where human will ends and divine will begins. At its logical extreme, Christian faith is the end of individual selfhood. To be a member of Christ's body, given earthly form in the Church, is to relinquish not just power or status, but all individuation. The most famous statement of Christian indifference appears in Paul's Letter to the Galatians: "There is neither Jew nor Greek: there is neither bond nor free: there is neither male nor female. For you are all one in Christ Jesus" (V/DR, Gal. 3:28). Once "all" become "one" in a corporate Christianity, earthly identity, allegiance, and hierarchy cease to exist. The egoism of uniqueness gives way to the emptying out of selfhood, the diminution of ego, that is faith. In Christian devotion, as Virginia Burras, Mark Jordan, and Karmen MacKendrick point out, obedience and selflessness cease to signify in the usual sense as "mastery and submission meet (and dissolve) at their limits."[8]

But the loss of self that is the logical end of faith cannot be complete in the world because that would obviate the very hierarchy of creator and creature that gives deity's sacrifice and humanity's obedience meaning. The wondrous mortification of Christ, if imitated exactly, would reverse the descent of God into human weakness. Humanity would achieve divine perfection expressed in an inhuman control of the will—an absolute command over the self that approximates divine omnipotence. In order to avoid what Burras, Jordan, and MacKendrick aptly describe as the "paradoxical arrogance" betrayed "in the notion of kneeling before humility in a subtly surpassing imitation of divine submission," a gap must always persist between (human) copy and (divine) original.[9] The aspiration to perfect faith must remain thwarted, human and divine will separate. If they are identical, the prayer that "*thy* will be done" is indistinguishable from "*my* will be done"; obedience is no different from omnipotence. The pride and doubt that adulterate human faith are necessary in that they remind us that we are not God, that whatever faith we achieve is itself a divine gift. If we are to remain properly grateful—that is, if we are to understand our relationship to deity correctly— "We must resist even the temptation to be untempted," as Burras, Jordan, and MacKendrick point out. "The ease of non-desire is not an option. . . . There is no merit in not resisting, no submission without a trace of the desire to dominate."[10] Although, as Amy Hollywood observes, "The potential danger of mysticism is that it turns one too completely away from the cares of this world," such rapture also circumvents the need for faith by moving the mystic beyond its struggles.[11] For ecstasy, Badiou argues, is itself a form of knowledge: the unspeakable miracle confirms that belief is justified. Pauline faith, by contrast, can only be declared, never proven, and so resists claims to mastery.[12] In order to obey, the believer must remain a distinct—and potentially intractable—subject.

Put in Pauline terms, we must remember that we are small not only in the sense of our individual insignificance as part of an imagined *corpus Christi* but also in the sense that we are *mean*: distrustful, bitter, stingy, envious. We are small to the extent that we want to be bigger, both grander and more magnanimous. In imitating Christ's self-abnegating love, we strive to be biggest of all. Understood on the level of our vertical relation to deity, our confrontation with worldly difference and hierarchy, desire and disappointment, saves us from ourselves by reminding us just how small we are. Understood on the level of our lateral relation to others, our habitual disobedience to the commandment to love similarly compels us to confront the opacity and deviousness of our own desires.

The necessary failure of any imitation of Christ stems not only from the limitations of human will but also from those of human imagination and language. When Paul directs us to emulate divine love, he also concedes that we can have no direct knowledge of the original we are copying. So he models spiritual faith on *human* relations of power: master-slave, father-child, and most importantly for my argument, husband-wife. Modern mainstream Christianity has proceeded as though these worldly hierarchies are themselves either justified or mitigated by the divine order they catachrestically figure.[13] In the case of marriage, for instance, monogamy and gendered hierarchy are justified by their analogy to Christ's loving rule of his Bride, the church. This union between divine head and ecclesiastical body is itself patterned on the human institution it is said to at once justify and transcend. Divine love is accommodated to human understanding via comparison to a worldly institution that, through its very status as analogy, acquires spiritual value and coercive force. This inversion of vehicle and tenor, original and copy, exposes the smallness of a human mind that cannot think beyond itself. As a result, Slavoj Žižek observes, we must imagine God as a "lacking, vulnerable being," for only such an entity is capable of love: "Perhaps the true achievement of Christianity is to elevate a loving (imperfect) Being to the place of God, that is, of ultimate perfection."[14] The entire point of a Pauline view of grace is that humanity is *not like*

Christ. We can never achieve the absolute commitment, expressed in self-sacrifice, that he models. If we could, we would not need Christ or his resurrection. We could redeem ourselves.

Nowhere is the difficulty of this humiliation more apparent than in the biblical text that has traditionally provided Christian justifications for the monogamous and hierarchical union of man and woman: chapter 5 of Paul's Letter to the Ephesians.[15] Here, Paul repeatedly invokes voluntary obedience to earthly powers as a manifestation of love for God even as he redefines obedience itself. True faith, he maintains, inheres in wholehearted love, not formal obedience:

> Be ye therefore followers [*imitatores*] of God, as [*sicut*] most dear children [*filii carissimus*]. And walk in love [*in dilectione*], as [*sicut*] Christ also hath loved us [*dilexit nos*], and hath delivered [*tradidit semetipsum*] himself for us, an oblation [*oblationem*] and a sacrifice [*hostiam*] to God for an odor of sweetness [*suavitatis*]. (V/DR, Eph. 5:1–2)

To follow God *as if* we were the most cherished of children is to follow him "in love," not out of mere duty. As the Vulgate renders it, obedience is a form of emulation, "like"—*sicut*—that of a beloved child. This initial *sicut* (like, as, in the manner of) is the first of the many similes in Ephesians 5. To follow God *as* most dear children, to lovingly obey, is to perform an *imitatio Christi*. It is, in Badiou's terms, to decline the Father's discourse of mastery and to take up the son's submission and passivity.[16]

But Paul's figural logic folds back on itself: the model for faithful love is not Christ's obedient relation to God but his generous relation to *us*. We are to love God as he, in the person of Christ, has loved us. This is an impossible command. We are not capable of either debasing ourselves as the Messiah did in becoming human or of loving those whom we know in advance cannot requite or warrant our love. To further complicate matters, the Vulgate's *dilectione/dilexit* accentuates the reciprocal pleasure of this love. Divine self-surrender takes the form of a double exchange that is at the same time a double betrayal. In becoming human, Christ trades his divinity for our humanity, his power for our weakness, his innocence for our sin. His assumption of humanity is also an assumption of debt, a substitution of himself for us in what Augustine calls "the wonderful exchange, the divine business deal, the transaction effected in this world by the heavenly dealer."[17] This second verse of Ephesians 5 amplifies the chapter's initial equation of love, imitation, and obedience to specify that what it means to follow God is to imitate a Christ for whom devotion, pleasure, and self-sacrifice converge. The following verses go on to warn that this selfless love excludes "fornication, and all uncleanness, or covetousness" (DR, Eph. 5:3), "obscenity, or foolish talking, or scurrility" (DR, Eph. 5:4), and drunkenness and luxury (DR, Eph. 5:18). Those activities are "a serving of idols" (DR, Eph. 5:5), sources of pleasure that assert rather than surrender the self insofar as they turn from gratitude to the creator to absorption in the created world. Covetousness (*avaratia*) is coupled with fornication and uncleanness (*immunditia*) because it is a turn from pure devotion to another to the impure pleasures and interests of the self, from giving to taking, from generosity to greed. The lure of the secular is necessary to faith in the eternal because it is in the realization that we have been distracted that we recognize that human love is meretricious even when it would be gratuitous.

In opposition to the self-assertion of the "children of unbelief [*filios diffidentiae*]," those who act like God's dearest children follow him in giving themselves up not only to him but to everyone, "being subject to one another in fear of Christ" (DR, Eph. 5:21). Just as *imitatio Christi* approaches success to the extent that it erases distinctions between self and other, original and copy, so too does worldly love. This play of likeness and difference becomes still more fraught in the final verses of Ephesians 5 when human marriage replaces filial loyalty as a model of delight in subjection. The logic of the passage is intricate, so I quote it in full:

> Let women be subject to their husbands, as [*sicut*] to the Lord. Because the husband is the head of the wife, as [*sicut*] Christ is the head of the church. He is the saviour of his body. Therefore as [*sicut*] the church is subject to Christ, so also let the wives be to their husbands in all things. Husbands, love [*diligite*] your wives, as [*sicut*] Christ also loved [*dilexit*] the church, and delivered [*tradidit*] himself up for it: That [*ut*] he might sanctify it, cleansing it by the laver of water in the word of life: That [*ut*] he might present it to himself a glorious church, not having spot or wrinkle, or any such thing; but that it should be holy and without blemish.

So also ought men to love their wives as [*ut*] their own bodies. He that loveth [*diligit*] his wife loveth [*diligit*] himself. For no man ever hated his own flesh; but nourisheth and cherisheth it, as [*sicut*] also Christ doth the church: Because we are members of his body, of his flesh [*de carne*], and of his bones. For this cause shall a man leave his father and mother, and shall cleave to his wife, and they shall be two in one flesh [*erunt duo in carne una*]. This is a great sacrament [*sacramentum*]; but I speak in Christ and in the church. Nevertheless, let every one of you in particular so love his wife as [*sicut*] himself: and let the wife fear her husband. (V/ DR, Eph. 5:22–33)

Often read as tempering the dour view of 1 Corinthians that marriage is just a step up from burning (7:9; I discuss this at length in chapter 3), historically these final verses of Ephesians 5 have often been taken as evidence of the divine origins of female subordination.[18] It is easy to see why: the passage begins by contracting a more general subjection of "one to another in the fear of God" by all believers into the gendered and heteroerotic hierarchy of the married couple, in which women submit to their husband "as" (*sicut*) the church submits to Christ. However, in drawing attention to its own catachrestic figuration, Ephesians 5 also concedes the kinkiness of the role-play it endorses.

One consequence of the analogy that aligns husbands with Christ, wives with church, is a challenge to the association of masculinity with dominance that the first few verses assert. For the expression of Christ's love for his church is the humiliation of incarnation and crucifixion, without which his resurrection would not be possible. To love one's wife as Christ loved the church is to occupy precisely the role of submission enjoined on the wife in the early verses. As Robert Mills has argued, we cannot speak of the simple "feminization" of Christ, the church, or the human soul. That would merely reverse the quotidian binaries of gender and agency that the crucifixion and resurrection dissolve. We should instead attend to "the degree to which positions of power and power-lessness in Christian discourse are in a state of perpetual circulation, the very *mobility* of which creates spaces for the excessive, transgressive, and perversely erotic."[19] From this perspective, the love commanded of the husband is a love for all that is vulnerable and abject—all that is *un*loveable—in himself. The self-humiliation of faith is conceptually at odds with the masculine domination of worldly marriage. The former acknowledges weakness; the latter asserts strength. Indeed, marriage as such—becoming "one flesh" with another—is a proclamation of the determination to unite with Christ's body. In that figurative context, it is an embrace of the flesh that makes man, whatever his earthly powers, not-God. It is an assumption of smallness.

Ephesians 5 troubles not only the gendered order on which its figuration of marriage relies, but also the monogamous devotion that becoming "one flesh" would seem to require.[20] In the tension between literal and figurative meanings of sexual union, Ephesians 5 converges with 1 Corinthians 7, where celibate devotion to God is preferred to worldly marriage on the ground that marriage is a distraction, whereas celibacy "may give you power to attend upon the Lord, without impediment" (V/DR, 1 Cor. 7:35). Real-world marriage may provide a useful figure for eager submission and self-sacrifice, but the same earthly hierarchies and passions that should offer a pattern of spiritual submission threaten to displace it. The catachresis in which one concept cannot be thought except through the medium of figural language gives way to tautology in which we cannot get outside the conceptual limits established by our points of reference. Accommodation is also limitation. And once we shift from defining the relation of marriage as social contract to defining it as intimate entanglement, the figural meaning of marriage appeals to a human experience in which it is hard to imagine sex entirely free of the uncleanness, covetousness, obscenity, and luxury against which the intervening verses warn.

The penultimate verse of Ephesians 5 seems to recognize this danger when it acknowledges the disruptive potential of its own erotic analogy and warns us to not think too hard about what the vehicle (sexual intercourse) may imply about its tenor (devotion to God). The copulation that in verse 31 is the worldly manifestation of the church's union with Christ ("they shall be two in one flesh") is explicitly barred from thought in verse 32: "This [becoming one flesh] is a great mystery: but I speak concerning Christ and the church." The Geneva Bible glosses verse 32 as "That no man might dream of natural conjunction or knitting of Christ and his Church together (such as the husbands and the wives is) he sheweth that it is secret, to wit, spiritual and such as far differeth from the common capacity of man; as which consisteth by the virtue of the

Spirit, and not of the flesh by faith, and by no natural bond." We cannot, in other words, take seriously the comparison of faith to sex because in the "common capacity of man" sexual specificity threatens (or promises) the same arousal as pornography, directing thought to the organs, positions, and pleasures of consummation. A ready example occurs in John Donne's Holy Sonnet "Show me, dear Christ," in which he begs God not only to reveal but also to share his Bride, the true church:

> Betray, kind husband, thy Spouse to our sights,
> And let mine am'rous soul court thy mild Dove,
> Who is most true and pleasing to thee then
> When she's embraced and open to most men. (11–14)

Donne's ecclesiastical wife swap takes the figural logic of Ephesians 5 to its extreme, conceding that in order to serve as a metaphor for faith, human marriage must be bigamous on the human level (one loves both one's spouse and God) and radically promiscuous on the ecclesiastical level. Nor is this marriage necessarily heterosexual. Because Ephesians places male members of the ecclesiastical body in the structural role of wives relative to Christ, Christian sex, in the sense of both gendered identity and sexual practice, appears rather queer. To understand this union as heterosexual marriage, men must be "like" women; to understand the male members of the Church as male, this must be a same-sex union.[21] Once again, Donne is useful here. As Richard Rambuss demonstrates, "Show me, dear Christ" isn't the only instance of group sex in Donne's devotional poetry. In the Holy Sonnet "Batter my heart, thou three-personed God" Donne speaks in the voice of a male believer begging to be ravished by male Father, Son, and Holy Spirit in a "trinitarian gang bang."[22] Along with George Herbert and other devotional poets, Donne thereby makes especially legible "not only the simultaneously exalted and abjected devotional body, but also the conditions of devotional subjectivity itself—this place where the subject is attenuated between the hyperbole of his or her own agency and longing at one pole and a matching desire for the self's utter abasement, even dissolution at the other."[23] Ephesians 5 allows us to see that the attenuation of devotional body and subjectivity is a necessary component of faith. Religious fidelity is a queer concept not only because it unfixes and dematerializes the positions of gender and agency on which its accommodatory logic relies. Fidelity is also queer because it is an imitation of something (someone?) beyond the human language and imagination that construct it. Indeed, to really believe that faith is an imitation rather than an invention is to occupy the depths of credulity or the heights of arrogance. We can never know for sure.

Augustine and the Failure of Conversion

Few writers explore the queerness of Pauline faith as assiduously as Saint Augustine. Augustine's prolific and unsystematic writings proved a formative influence not only on centuries of religious thought but also on the view of secular love that would enter the bloodstream of Western culture through the vernacular love lyrics of Francesco Petrarch, one of Augustine's great admirers. Long before Freud, Lacan, or Foucault provided us with a systematic assessment of the alienation and incoherence of desire, Augustine represented confession and conversion as fundamentally erotic aspirations. Professions of faith are equally prayers for it, one's own inconstant desire for God a source of frustration only erratically relieved by temporary moments of ecstatic certainty.

Augustine has been seen by many as the puritan *avant la lettre* who ruined sex for the Christian West at best and legitimated centuries of violence against women and sexual minorities at worst.[24] But to read Augustine's writings from a queer perspective is to recognize that they include insights that contradict the stern policing of sexuality to which they have often been put. This is not only because, as several scholars have noted, pleasure and desire are at the center of Augustine's theology.[25] It is also because Augustine knows that faith is another name for desire, and as such is characterized by the same intensities and opacities. Burras, Jordan, and MacKendrick summarize the Augustinian dilemma thus:

> In [Augustine's] short work *The Excellence of Widowhood* (ca. 413), he is even more explicit in connecting divine commandment to supplication: "let us beg Him to give us what He commands us to have. He commands us to have what we do not yet possess, in order to remind us of what we should ask" (17). God, that is, demands our supplication, makes us ask, by making impossible demands of us, commanding us to have what we do

not. Thus is fed not only humility, but desire, reaching, or burning, for the perpetually tantalizing not-quite-there. Thus, too, is desire sustained.[26]

Rather than forbid lust, Augustine struggles to redirect it toward God. But his desire to desire God, his prayer to learn to pray for the right thing, is founded on an awareness of infidelity: he does not want what he should. Throughout the *Confessions*, Augustine traces the disjunction between resolution and faith. Two books after his conversion in the garden, Augustine famously laments that "I myself cannot grasp the totality of what I am. . . . I have become a problem [*queastio*] to myself, and that is my sickness [*languor*]" (*Confessions* 10.8.15, 10.33.50).[27] Such spiritual *languor*—illness, weakness, indolence—appears in Augustine's infamously disingenuous youthful prayer: "Grant me chastity and continence, but not yet" (*Confessions* 8.7.17). Augustine recounts his attempt to pray according to the letter rather than the spirit: "I was afraid you might hear my prayer quickly, and that you might too rapidly heal me of the disease [*morbo*] of lust which I preferred to satisfy [*expleri*] rather than suppress [*exstingui*]" (*Confessions* 8.7.17). Hoping to explore his worldly desires before they are extinguished, Augustine seeks compromise between his will and God's through a tactic of delay.

Yet such recalcitrance is necessary for salvation. The difference between what we should want and what we do want makes possible the resistance that gives obedience meaning. In Geoffrey Galt Harpham's elegant formulation, "Resistance to temptation is both imperative and impossible," so asceticism "is always defined as a quest for a goal that cannot and must not be reached."[28] Confessing is *remembering* one's failure to achieve the true faith that would make loving, ungrudging submission possible. But even such seeming humility contains the seeds of its opposite. Describing one's past sins may take the form of boasting, as Augustine admits it once did for him: "I used to pretend that I had done things I had not done at all, so that my innocence should not lead my companions to scorn my lack of courage" (*Confessions* 2.3.7). Even more insidiously, self-deprecation can be indistinguishable from self-aggrandizement. As Augustine cautions, "Often the contempt of vainglory becomes a source of even more vainglory. For it is not being scorned when the contempt is something one is proud of" (*Confessions* 10.38.63). Because we can never be certain whether we are seeking humiliation or praise, absolution or adulation, penitence and the change it inspires remains aspirational. The conversion that Augustine depicts in the *Confessions* and *City of God* is not a decisive turn, but a cycle of resolution and backsliding, a periodic renewal of vows destined to be broken.

Augustine's insistence that infidelity is built into faith is inseparable from his rejection of the classical and patristic denigration of the body as the source of human weakness. As Peter Brown has influentially argued, "It was the entire momentum of [Augustine's] thought on the relation between body and soul that had led him, over the years, to place more weight upon the body than had any of his predecessors." Paul's letter to the Romans describes a conflict that Augustine would turn into what Brown calls a "fateful theological abbreviation" for the more general resistance of the human will to that of God.[29] Paul laments

> for we know that the law is spiritual [*spiritualis*]; but I am carnal [*carnalis*], sold under sin. For that which I work, I understand not. For I do not that good which I will; but the evil which I hate, that I do. . . . For I know that there dwelleth not in me, that is to say, in my flesh [*carne*] that which is good. For to will, is present with me; but to accomplish [*perficere*] that which is good, I find not. For the good which I will, I do not; but the evil which I will not, that I do. . . . For I am delighted with the law of God, according to the inward man [*interiorem hominem*]: But I see another law in my members [*membris*], fighting against the law of my mind [*mentis*], and captivating me in the law of sin, that is in my members. . . . Therefore, I myself, with the mind serve the law of God; but with the flesh, the law of sin. (V/DR, Rom. 7: 14–15, 18–19, 22–23, 25)

Tertullian, Jerome, Ambrose, Pelagius, and Origen took this passage literally and taught that the battle between flesh and spirit, members and mind, refers to the classical view in which the soul must either master the body or become its prisoner.[30] By contrast, Augustine treated flesh and spirit, respectively, as names for worldly appetite and ambition, on the one hand, and submission to God, on the other. Augustine's resistance to literalism and dualism, Brown argues, "made the self problematic as never before."[31] As I argue at greater length in chapter 5, the "hermeneutics of the self" that Foucault, drawing on the writing of Tertullian and Cassian, designates the unique characteristic of Christian morality, as distinct from a classical "morality of self-control," is for Augustine a process whose success resides in its failure: the more we confess, the more we learn that we do not know ourselves.[32] And insofar as a linear model of confession and conversion grounds modern ideals of sovereign subjectivity, the Augustinian position constitutes a usable resource on which queer challenges to modern ideals of faith and monogamy can draw.

For Augustine, the life of the spirit is one of monogamous worship of and obedience to deity; the life of the flesh is one of fragmentation and distraction. Not to be identified simply or exclusively with the body, the flesh is a figure for creaturely attachment not just to sex or food, but to a wide range of worldly powers and pleasures. Usually, Augustine's figural logic is understood as allegorical.[33] In this reading, the body is abstracted into a sign of the soul, and mastery of the flesh can lead to purity of the spirit—Augustine is associated with a doctrine of works that will be repudiated by the Protestant Reformers' cry of *sole fides, sole scriptura*. Yet Augustine himself specifies that the relationship between flesh and spirit is not allegorical but synecdochal. Understood thus, the body cannot be abstracted from the soul: they are indissolubly linked. *Both* are parts of the flesh that cannot be transcended through dutiful regulation of behavior. The word "flesh" *can* mean the body, Augustine acknowledges in *City of God*, but "Scripture does not confine the application of the term 'flesh' [*carnem*] to the body [*corpus*] of an earthly and mortal living being. . . . There are, in fact, many other ways in which it uses the noun, to describe different things; and among these different usages is its employment to denote man himself, that is, the essential nature of man [*id est naturam hominis, carnem nuncupat*], an example of the figure of speech known as 'part for whole' [*modo locutionis a parte totum*]" (*CG* 14.2).[34] Flesh is a synecdoche for human nature.[35] Augustine turns to Paul to demonstrate that bodily appetites do not so much corrupt the soul as manifest its otherwise invisible impurity:

Our present purpose is to track down the meaning of "living by the rule of the flesh" (which is clearly a bad thing, though the natural substance of flesh is not an evil in itself); and to enable us to achieve this purpose, let us carefully examine the passage in St. Paul's Epistle to the Galatians where he says,

> It is obvious what the works of the flesh are: such things as forni-
> cation, impurity, lust, idolatry, sorcery, enmity, quarrelsomeness,
> jealousy, animosity, dissension, party intrigue, envy, drunkenness,
> drunken orgies, and so on. I warned you before, and I warn you
> again, that those who behave in such ways will never have a place
> in God's kingdom. [Gal. 5:19–20]

> . . . Among the "works of the flesh" . . . we find not only those concerned
> with sensual pleasure, like fornication, impurity, lust, drunkenness and
> drunken orgies, but also those which show faults of the mind [animi vi-
> tia], which have nothing to do with sensual indulgence. For anyone can
> see that devotion to idols, sorcery, enmity, quarrelsomeness, jealousy, ani-
> mosity, party intrigue, envy—all these faults are of the mind, not of the
> body. (CG 14.2)

Merely to condemn the flesh is to miss the waywardness of the soul,
inverting cause and effect. Augustine bluntly proclaims that "those who
imagine that all the ills of the soul derive from the body are mistaken"
(CG 14.3). To the contrary, the soul is the original source of sin, for "it
was not the corruptible flesh that made the soul sinful; it was the sinful
soul that made the flesh corruptible" (CG 14.3). Satan's pride and envy
prove that one need not have a body at all in order to live by the rule of
the flesh. If we were to "attribute to the flesh all the faults of a wicked
life," we would make a causal error that would "absolve the Devil of all
those faults, since he has no flesh" in the literal sense (CG 14.3). Firmly
rejecting classical and Manichean dualism, Augustine maintains that
bodily renunciation may itself be a sign of carnal living, for "it may happen that a man refrains from sensual indulgence because of devotion to
an idol, or because of the erroneous teaching of some sect . . . and it is
the very fact of his abstention from fleshly indulgence that proves that
he is engaged in the 'works of the flesh'" (CG 14.2). Mistaking control
of the body for purity of the soul, asceticism shades into idolatry. This
definition of "flesh" as encompassing not just the body but the "the temporal life" more generally is a point that Martin Luther would make the
basis of his own refutation of a Catholic doctrine of works, observing
that "flesh . . . means . . . the entire self [den ganzen Menschen], body and
soul, including our reason [Vernuft] and all our senses."[36]

Augustine's pessimism about the salvific value of bodily renunciation rests on the conviction that in the pursuit of faith, the true struggle is between self-rule and obedience to God. Since the fall, the human creature "has become like the Devil . . . by living by the rule of the self" (*CG* 14.3). We choose to "promote our welfare" as we understand it, rather than obey divine commands, and thereby invert the proper hierarchy between creature and creator (*CG* 14.4). For Augustine, as John C. Cavadini reminds us, the prideful are the "self-pleasers" (*sibi placentes; CG* 14.13).[37] In the *Confessions*, Augustine's notorious theft of pears exemplifies this exaltation of self over deity. He was not driven by physical need or craving—he already had his own, tastier pears, and he threw the ones he stole to some pigs—but "solely with the motive of stealing" (2.6.12). Like flesh for the "whole man," this act of theft is a synecdoche for the multitude of sins that Augustine claims to have committed in which "confusion of [love and lust] boiled within me" (*Confessions* 2.2.2). He derived pleasure from "wickedness" as an assertion of will in which he endeavors to "viciously and perversely imitate my Lord" (*Confessions* 2.6.12, 2.6.14). Stealing the pears, Augustine recounts, was also a *social* pleasure, "excitement generated by sharing the guilt with others" (*Confessions* 2.8.16). He wants friends, not pears. Like the theft, the choice of human rather than divine love, which Augustine will make repeatedly throughout the *Confessions*, expresses his desire "to play God, to mimic divine freedom," as Burras, Jordan, and MacKendrick argue.[38] Being bad feels good because it is a way of telling God: you are not the boss of me.

As the bathetic Edenic parody of the pear theft illustrates, to live according to the flesh is compulsively to repeat the original sin of aspiration to deity. And in Augustine's view, we as humans are as helpless to withstand that compulsion as we are to prevent our own eventual deaths. Augustine describes the fall as a *poena reciproca* (*CG* 14.17)—a crime that punishes itself. As a result of his original disobedience to God, "man . . . *became carnal even in his mind* [*fieret etiam mente carnalis et*]; and he who in his pride had pleased himself was by God's justice handed over to himself. But the result of this was not that he was in every way under his own control, but that he was at odds with himself, and lived a life of harsh and pitiable slavery, instead of the freedom he so ardently desired" (*CG* 14.15; my emphasis). To become carnal in the mind is to "find oneself distracted and tossed about by violent and conflicting emotions," to lose the serenity of obedience in order to gain the thrill of transgression (*CG* 14.12). As Augustine neatly puts it, "The retribution for disobedience is simply disobedience itself. For man's wretchedness is nothing but his own disobedience to himself, so that because he would not do what he could, he now wills to do what he cannot. For in paradise, before his sin, man could not, it is true, do everything; but he could do whatever he wished, just because he did not want to do whatever he could not do" (*CG* 14.15). Now, "Who can list all the multitude of things that a man wishes to do and cannot, while he is disobedient to himself, that is, while his very mind and even his lower element, his flesh, do not submit to his will?" (*CG* 14.15). As Badiou explains it, "Sin is a subjective structure, and not an evil act." In this structure, the subject "presents himself as a disconnected correlation between an automatism of doing and a powerlessness of thought."[39]

For Augustine, sexual lust is the most pointed evidence of the incoherence of the fallen will. As I discuss at more length in chapter 3, unlike Ambrose and Jerome, for whom prelapsarian sex was unthinkable, Augustine imagines a paradisal eroticism that was a matter of volition: Adam and Eve could move their genitals as deliberately as they could wiggle their toes, and erection and ejaculation, like all bodily functions, were free of shame and excess. Now, however, the "the genital organs have become as it were the private property of lust, which has brought them so completely under its sway that they have no power of movement if this passion fails" (*CG* 14.19). Impotence, no less than arousal, attests to how little we know and control of ourselves and our desires. Augustine rejects Stoicism to insist that "if *apatheia* describes a condition in which there is no fear to terrify, no pain to torment, then it is a condition to be shunned in this life, if we wish to lead the right kind of life, the life that is according to God's will" (*CG* 14.9). Indeed, "If we felt none of those emotions at all, while we are subject to the weakness of this life, there would really be something wrong with our life." Quoting Cicero, Augustine assures us that such impassibility would exact "'the price of inhumanity of mind and insensitivity of body'" so "anyone who thinks that his life is without sin does not succeed in avoiding sin, but rather in forfeiting pardon" (*CG* 14.9).[40] Lust is salutary in that our awareness of its automatic operations can interrupt the illusion of self-sufficiency and self-possession and thereby restore a grateful and submissive relation to deity.

Augustine's own cofounded path to conversion exemplifies the "monstrous situation" of the divided self. The very act of resolution and prayer divulges self-division and self-deception in the distance between the ability to command (*imperare*) and to will (*voluntas*):

> Mind commands, I say, that it should will, and would not give the command if it did not will, yet does not perform what it commands. The willing is not wholehearted, so the command is not wholehearted. . . . So the will that commands is incomplete, and therefore what it commands does not happen. If it were complete, it would not need to command the will to exist, since it would exist already. . . . We are dealing with a morbid condition of the mind [*aegritudo animi est*] which, when it is lifted up by the truth, does not unreservedly rise to it but is weighed down by habit. (*Confessions* 8.9.21)

As the tortuous syntax and monotonous vocabulary of this passage indicate, the human experience of faith can never be identical with the practice of self-discipline, for the very reflexivity of that concept assumes the resistance that faith would overcome. Faith involves the struggle not to rule the self but to surrender to another. Strength of will requires absolute absorption by God. Failing this, the self becomes object of its own wrath:

> I was deeply disturbed in spirit, angry with indignation and distress that I was not entering into my pact and covenant with you, my God, when all my bones (Psalm 34:10) were crying out that I should enter into it and were exalting it to heaven with praises. . . . The one necessary condition, which meant not only going but at once arriving there, was to have the will to go—provided only that the will was strong and unqualified, not the turning and twisting first this way, then that, of a will half-wounded, struggling with one part rising up and the other part falling down. (*Confessions* 8.8.19)

Augustine illustrates the ephemerality of faith by describing his own struggle for conversion in terms of erotic stimulation and release. Like the carnal lust that both figures and manifests it, passion for God has a will of its own. "By inward goads [*stimulis*] you stirred [*agitabas*] me to make me find it unendurable until, through my inward perception, you were a certainty to me. My swelling [*tumor*] was reduced by your hidden healing hand," Augustine remembers (*Confessions* 7.8.12). Nonetheless, "I was not stable in the enjoyment of my God. I was caught up to you by your beauty and quickly torn away from you by my own weight. With a groan I crashed into inferior things" (*Confessions* 7.17.23). Understood as the rapturous surrender of passion, conversion is the temporary exhaustion of the will. Such release cannot be sustained.[41]

This struggle of will takes the form of self-accusation and delay up until the instant of conversion, a resistance of self to self also experienced as divine wrath: "I repeatedly said to you: 'How long, O Lord? How long, Lord, will you be angry to the uttermost? Do not be mindful of our old iniquities' (Ps. 6:4). For I felt my past to have a grip on me. It uttered wretched cries: 'How long, how long is it to be?' 'Tomorrow, tomorrow' 'Why not now? Why not an end to my impure life in this very hour?'" (*Confessions* 8.12.28). This rhetorical parallel between withholding God and truculent self displaces blame from human supplicant to divine object of desire. It thereby registers another paradox of prayer: the more deeply one craves what one prays for, the greater the risk that humble prostration will generate wounded entitlement. It is only in the willingness to interpret an ungendered child's chant ("Pick up and read, pick up and read") as divine command that Augustine reads, as if for the first time, Romans 13:13–14: "'Not in riots and drunken parties, not in eroticism and indecencies, not in strife and rivalry. But put on the Lord Jesus Christ and make no provision for the flesh in its lusts'" (*Confessions* 8.12.29). Struggle and frustration with the self give way to a radical openness: "At once, with the last words of this sentence, it was as if a light of relief [*luce securitatis*] from all anxiety flooded [*infusa*] into my heart. All the shadows of doubt [*dubitationis tenebrae*] were dispelled" (*Confessions* 8.12.29). As when the scales fall from Paul's eyes, the light of confidence replaces the darkness of uncertainty (Acts 9:18). To believe is to surrender.

Unfortunately, the shuddering moment of bliss does not last. Rather, the ongoing struggle within the self recounted in Paul's Epistles proves a more accurate model of faith than the triumphant rebirth described in the Acts.[42] Augustine's conversion signals a moment of rapt attention— forgetting self and world as exhorted by Paul's Letter to the Romans—

but soon enough he finds himself distracted. As Burras, Jordan, and MacKendrick point out, a full decade after the ostensibly "decisive moment" of his conversion in the garden, Augustine is still begging God for continence, now defined not just as sexual abstinence, which he has achieved, but as the single-minded devotion from which he never ceases to stray.[43] Throughout the final books of the *Confessions*, he continues to pray for a passion intense enough to fuse his will with God's and transform dutiful obedience into wholehearted desire. In Book 10, Augustine complains that

> for the present, because I am not full of you, I am a burden to myself. There is a struggle [*contendunt*] between joys over which I should be weeping and regrets at matters over which I ought to be rejoicing, and which side has the victory I do not know [*et ex qua parte stet victoria nescio*]. There is a struggle between my regrets at my evil past and my memories of good joys, and which side has the victory I do not know. (*Confessions* 10.28.39)

The oxymoron that will become one of the most hackneyed of Petrarchan tropes here expresses in chiasmic form the paradox of Christian affect, which responds to worldly pleasure and sorrow in exactly the opposite way one would expect. To rejoice in worldly pleasure or cry over worldly sorrow is to choose the flesh over the spirit, to learn through our emotions that we are "not full" of God, that we still want something else. Sorrow in the agonies delivered by the world, the sense that creation would be better without them, prevents wholehearted joy in God's ways. Here and elsewhere, formal repetition registers the suspenseful precarity of conversion: "There is a struggle"; "which side has the victory I do not know." Augustine's inability to respond to the world as he wishes gestures toward a conflict of flesh and spirit that physical continence does not resolve, for technical fidelity does not achieve the emptying of the self modeled by Christ.

Throughout Book 10, Augustine returns to ritual incantations that reveal the self-division that gives obedience value:

> Grant what you command, and command what you will. . . . O love, you ever burn and are never extinguished. O charity, my God, set me on fire.

You command continence; grant what you command, and command what you will. (*Confessions* 10.29.40)

Grant what you command, and command what you will. (*Confessions* 10.31.45)

Grant what you command, and command what you will. In this matter you know the "groaning" of my heart towards you (Ps. 37:9), and the rivers which flow from my eyes (Ps. 118:136). I cannot easily be sure how far I am cleansed from that plague (Ps. 18:13). I have great fear of my subconscious [*occulta*] impulses which your eyes know but mine do not (Eccles. 15:20). (*Confessions* 10.37.60)

The repetition of the prayer "Grant what you command, and command what you will [*da quod iubes et iube quod vis*]" manifests formally the paradox of prayer that we witnessed in Book 8: the more intense the desire, the more supplication shades into demand. This burning love is also given to the excesses of accusation and anger. Augustine's heart groans, his tears flow—and it may not have done any good.

The failure to stay converted dramatized in the *Confessions* is paradoxically the ground of faith, as Augustine explains in *City of God*: "And I venture to say that it is of service to the proud that they should fall into some open and obvious sin, which can make them dissatisfied with themselves, after they have already fallen through self-complacency. Peter's dissatisfaction with himself, when he wept, was healthier than his complacency when he was overconfident" (*CG* 14.13). Confession unites humanity with God because through it we endeavor to see ourselves as God sees us. Unlike the distraction and affirmation of human praise, the process of confession forces Augustine to "see how vile I was, how twisted and filthy, covered in sores and ulcers" (*Confessions* 8.7.16). Yet even as confession mimics divine perspective, disgust with the self also reminds us that we are *not* God—not sufficient in ourselves—and thereby renews our gratitude, love, and obedience. Indeed, attitudes of self-loathing and divine adoration are inseparable. As Brown observes, "*Confessio* meant, for Augustine, 'accusation of oneself; praise of God.'"[44] In relinquishing illusions of self-knowledge and self-reliance, one replaces grudging with gratitude. Because after the fall this predisposition is innate to the "whole man," it can only be constantly fought, never conclusively defeated. As Augustine himself wearily asks, "Is not human life on earth a trial [*temptatio*] in which there is no respite?" (*Confessions* 10.28.39). In Augustine's view, as in Paul's, however much we might want to want eternal faith, we only ever commit on a trial basis.

A Thousand Turns: Petrarch's Infidelities

The Pauline and Augustinian lesson that the experience of infidelity is inseparable from that of faith is central to secular romance in one of its most recognizable forms: the discourse of Petrarchan love. Although he had many predecessors from whom he freely borrowed—the troubadours, the Sicilian school, the *Roman de la Rose*, the *dolce stil nuovo* made famous by Dante—Petrarch is generally viewed as the founding figure of Western secular love poetry, the writer who popularized a model of eternal and unrequited passion that continues to shape many of the modern cultural scripts provided by film and music.[45] His blazons, oxymorons, slavish pining, aggressive demands for reparation, and, most uniquely, obsession with his own self-construction as poet, were so widely imitated on the Continent and in England that Petrarchism had become a cliché within a century of his death.[46] Indeed, because Petrarch's reputation precedes him, it has often prevented scholars from reading him closely enough to notice how perverse his model of love really is. Gordon Braden begins his study of Petrarchan love by confessing a dismissive attitude toward Petrarch that many scholars share: "I did not read Petrarch with any attentiveness until I in effect had to," Braden writes, because "my education had left me with a sheaf of not very interesting generalizations about Petrarchism and an impression that the topic was a much studied one."[47] Buried as they are under centuries of imitation and scholarship, Petrarch's lyrics can appear predictably, hopelessly constrained by heteronormative and patriarchal ideals. But the assumption that Petrarch offers nothing to queer scholars leaves in place a view that premodern writing has nothing to tell us about love and subjectivity. Read afresh through the framework of queer theology rather than a Christian humanist tradition, Petrarch offers a challenge to the normative view of monogamy he is usually understood to have helped found.

I examine a particularly queer aspect of Petrarch's genealogy: his lyr-ics' Augustinian emphasis on the necessarily promiscuous and unfaith-ful structure of both religious devotion and secular eroticism.[48] Like his favorite book, the *Confessions*, Petrarch's love poetry examines the expe-rience of not being able to want what one wants to want, to know what one really wants, or to stop wanting what one does not want to want. Both the title by which Petrarch named his sequence, *Rerum vulgarium fragmenta* ("Fragments of Common Things"; hereafter abbreviated as *RVF*), and those by which it has been known since the nineteenth cen-tury, the *Rime sparse* ("scattered rhymes") or, simply *Canzoniere* ("song book"), stress that each of the 366 poems offers a disjointed piece of a subject that never emerges as a coherent whole. Petrarch's *RVF* can be tiresome in its protracted self-involvement, repeated declarations of resolution and reform, and monotonous complaints of confusion and self-division. But the length, repetitiveness, and tedium of the sequence formally enact the impossibility of faithful love so consistently associ-ated with Petrarch's name.[49] Read from first to last, the *RVF* appears a strange source for any normative or idealized conception of love. Draw-ing on the Pauline turn from works to faith, Petrarchan love expands the definition of infidelity from the bodily to the affective realm. Focusing (as had Augustine and as would Calvin and Luther) on psychological rather than physical promiscuity, the *RVF* accentuates eroticism's con-stitutive faithlessness.

The Petrarch of the *RVF* is only in part the "eternally weeping lover" steeped in the narcissistic autopoesis so influentially described by John Freccero and memorialized in countless imitations.[50] He is, more expan-sively, an eternally ambivalent lover who is unable to extricate himself from the conflicting attachments and investments that call the self into being. Like Augustine, Petrarch is an unmarried father who identifies as a celibate rather than a patriarch. Both writers practice what Jack Halberstam has called "the queer art of failure": they dispute a norma-tive narrative of worldly success and maturity defined in large part by a progressive set of achievements (marriage, property, children, grand-children).[51] Augustine recounts not only his illicit trysts with mistresses and long-term relation with a concubine, but also the passions for male friends that pose even greater threats to his worship of God. Idolatry might be the truest form of earthly love—dramatically risking divine damnation—but in Augustine's *Confessions* even the most passionate idolatry is ultimately fickle. Even as Augustine recalls the misery of his "lacerated and bloody soul" at the death of a friend whom he loved in denial of "the human condition," "as if he would never die," he admits that amidst his mourning "I felt a greater attachment to my life of misery than to my dead friend" (*Confessions* 4.7.12, 4.6.11). His friend is not everything to him, Augustine confesses: his love, though deep and sincere, falls short of the attachment exemplified by the classical pair Orestes and Pylades, neither of whom was willing to live without the other. He gets over his friend's death, finding "repair and restoration" in "the solace of other friends, with whom I loved what I loved as a substitute for you; and this was a vast myth and a long lie" (*Confessions* 4.8.13). This "myth," or "lie" that we tell ourselves, is the belief that we can find true satisfaction in things of the world, which are always ultimately fungible and replaceable. Idolatry disturbs conventional definitions of proper affection because it is both misplaced devotion and inability to commit.

Petrarch is a similarly lapsed idolater. Beyond his rejection of a normative maturation defined by reproduction, Petrarch's very devotion to Laura is queer insofar as it is premised on the deferral not only of sexual relation but also of coherent gendered subjectivity. Although heterosexual in terms of the embodied gender of its object choice, Petrarch's love for Laura is an instance of what scholars have described as queer heterosexual desire.[52] The queerness of Petrarch's multiple models of love appear most spectacularly in *RVF* 23, where Petrarch famously metamorphoses into a spate of Ovidian characters. This poem, the longest in the *RVF*, contains the oft-discussed analogy whereby Petrarch plays Acteon to Laura's Diana.[53] Although Acteon's doomed voyeurism has received the lion's share of attention in critical discussions of *RVF* 23, it is in fact the only instance in the poem in which Petrarch depicts himself as a man desiring a woman, imagining his relation to Laura as cisgendered and heterosexual, as it were. The Acteon myth of masculine silencing and mutilation is but one moment in a series of gender-fluid identifications with women and men who desire men. Petrarch imagines himself as Cygnas immortalized for his devotion to Phaeton, the greedy Battas turned to stone for his betrayal of Mercury, Bylbis in love with her brother, Echo pining for Narcissus, and Semele consumed by her sight of Jupiter. Petrarch specifically disavows identification with Jupiter as the

masculine force that inseminates Danae, but he longs to be Jupiter rav-
ishing Ganymede. This homoeroticism inflects both secular and sacred
ties in the *RVF*. Petrarch's poems to his patron Cardinal Giovanni Colonna are characterized by professions of love and submission to equal
those to Laura. And, of course, when Petrarch prays to Christ in his
penitential poems, he reiterates the homoeroticism of *RVF* 23 by affirming desire for a male god known as such not by displays of Olympian
power but by submission to public mockery, mutilation, and death.

Because Petrarch's poetic language affirms absence, Nancy Vickers argues, "At the level of the fictive experience which he describes, successes
are ephemeral, and failures become a way of life."[54] Indeed, Cynthia Marshall points out, Petrarch does not depict a happy or redemptive ideal of
love as self-affirmation, but rather "a conception of love involving *loss* of
self, an emotional economy acknowledging, however painfully, an un-
dercurrent of *desire for suffering* in the erotic experience."[55] Petrarchan
love, in this view, anticipates Bersani's famous statement that sexuality is
a "tautology for masochism" in that it pursues a "radical disintegration
and humiliation of the self."[56] This (queer) view of desire as a salutary
challenge to the dangerous illusion of "the sacrosanct value of the self," I
have been arguing, has one of its earliest and most extensive statements in
Augustine's desacralization of human subjectivity and aching for dissolution into God. Augustine's awareness that the absolute absorption of faith
is impossible amidst the distraction (*distensio*) of human life helps explain
the promiscuous subjectivity of Petrarchan love. For Petrarch is not only
torn between God and Laura, or between eternal salvation and earthly
love and fame (binary tensions long noted by his readers). He is dispersed
among multiple attachments and concerns. The foremost of these, to be
sure, is Laura, but the *RVF* also passionately addresses Italian politics and
empire (*RVF* 53, 128); the corruption of the Avignon papacy (*RVF* 136–
138); his loyalty to friends and patrons, most notably Colonna, who with
Laura is one of the "chains [*le catene*]" that bind Petrarch to the world,
one half of the "double treasure [*doppio tesauro*]" of earthly love whose
loss ensures that he will have "eyes always wet [*umidi gli occhi sempre*]"
(*RVF* 266.10, 269.5, 11); and, possibly, the temptations of another female
love, "another fire [*un altro foco acceso*]" kindled with "new tinder [*di nova
esca*]" after Laura's death (*RVF* 271.7; see also *RVF* 270). Scattered across
so many commitments, Petrarch cannot focus exclusively on any of them.

The point of a theological reading of Petrarch is to suppose neither, on the one hand, that the *RVF* affirms that religious worship is the better course nor, on the other, that Petrarch's goal is the reconciliation of discordant impulses (spiritual and worldly commitment, Christian and classical thought).[57] I am arguing that the form, not the objects, of Petrarchan love is the most significant consequence of its Pauline and Augustinian genealogy. Attention to the theological model of love that Petrarch adopts allows us to see that distraction and infidelity are as structurally central to worldly attachments as to the spiritual longing on which they are modeled. "Distraction," James T. Chiampi writes, "is an essential predicate of attention."[58] It is the possibility of diversion and interruption—the lure of other desires, other possibilities—that gives attachment and concentration value. The *RVF* depicts a secular love that is promiscuous and divided not because it departs from a spiritual model of unwavering faith and devotion, but because it is *modeled on* an Augustinian theology that assumes the *impossibility* of unwavering faith and devotion.

By accentuating the queerness of the theological model of faith and grace on which the *RVF* is premised, I want to contest the moralizing tone taken by scholars who assume the virtue of monogamy—whether in the form of conversion to God or in the idealization of fidelity to Laura as evidence of the virtue of Petrarch's passion. The consistent attachment to Laura documented in the *RVF* would appear to be the epitome of monogamy, but it is also a monogamy that changes meaning as it is habitually relinquished and recuperated. The structure of the *RVF* as a whole dramatizes the recursive, repeatedly failed nature of faith and conversion. Rather than whole-hearted conviction, the sequence allows us to witness love as an aspiration that undoes itself, a nagging dissatisfaction with the nature of desire expressed in the wish to be someone who feels differently. A queered theological perspective would amend John Freccero's apt formulation to say that Petrarch can't stop weeping not because he loves Laura too much but because he loves her too little.

Poem 118, which commemorates the sixteenth anniversary of Petrarch's first sight of Laura, exemplifies the infidelity of the *RVF* as a whole. Written, at least within the fiction of the sequence, the same year Petrarch's daughter was born and his brother became a Carthusian monk, namely, 1343, this poem laments not so much the unrequitedness of his desire as its dispersal among multiple objects. Petrarchan love, like Petrarchan subjectivity, is never rigorously monogamous:

> Now remains behind the sixteenth year of my sighs, and I move forward toward the last; yet it seems to me that all this suffering began only recently.
>
> The bitter is sweet to me, and my losses useful, and living heavy; and I pray that my life may outlast my cruel fortune; and I fear that before then Death may close the lovely eyes that make me speak.
>
> Now here I am, alas, and wish I were elsewhere, and wish I wished more, but wish no more, and, by being unable to do more, do all I can;
>
> and new tears for old desires show me to be still what I used to be, nor for a thousand turnings about have I yet moved.
>
> [*Rimansi a dietro il sestodecimo anno*
> *de' miei sospiri, et io trapasso inanzi*
> *verso l'estremo; et parmi che pur dianzi*
> *fosse 'l principio di cotanto affanno.*
>
> *L'amar m'è dolce, et util il mio danno,*
> *e 'l viver grave; et prego che gli avanzi*
> *l'empia fortuna, et temo no chiuda anzi*
> *Morte i begli occhi che parlar mi fanno.*
>
> *Or qui son, lasso, et voglio esser altrove,*
> *et vorrei più volere, et più non voglio,*
> *et per più non poter fo quant' io posso;*
>
> *e d'antichi desir lagrime nove*
> *provan com' io son pur quel ch' i' mi soglio,*
> *né per mille rivolte anchor son mosso.*] (*RVF* 118.1–14)

Like so many lyrics in the *RVF*, 118 dwells on the "now," creating an illusion of present attention. Poised between what is behind and what is before, the poet imagines "the last" year of his sighs approaching even as he looks back on the past sixteen. In the present tense of the second quatrain, oxymoron abounds: what is bitter seems sweet, losses are useful, and the process of living *grave*—in Durling's translation "heavy" captures the sense that life is burdensome, but the Italian conveys something grimmer and more ominous, a grave or serious condition from which Petrarch may not recover. His prayer that he may outlive his *empia fortuna* describes his current state as not merely "cruel" or unfortunate, but more generally unholy, impious, and godless. Yet the final clause, set off by a second hard caesura, confesses the simultaneous fear not of God's abandonment but of Laura's death, thus retrospectively transforming the meaning of *empia* to refer to a world without Laura, rather than the poet's own conflicted impiety or God's imagined rejection.

The sestet of 118 translates into secular terms the Augustinian will which is unable fully to want what it wants to—or knows it should—want. Time and space, the here and now, converge in the statement, "Now here I am, alas, and I wish I were elsewhere." As Ullrich Langer points out, the "sighs" of the octave are made audible here in the disruptive "alas."[59] The difference between reality and desire appears in the shift of mood from the indicative (*voglio*) of "I wish I were elsewhere" to the conditional (*vorrei*) of line 10: "and I wish I wished more, but wish no more." The first wish, to be elsewhere, is itself reduced to aspiration, a second order wishing to "wish more." Being "here"—still in love with Laura, still shedding "new tears for old desires" now, after sixteen years—rather than "elsewhere" is a psychological state that is both wanted and unwanted. The wish to wish indirectly discloses a failure of conviction at the same time that it manifests precisely the fidelity imagined by Augustine, in which the remnants of willfulness authenticate submission as voluntary.

This sestet could be said to characterize the whole sequence, for by this point, about a third of the way through the 366-poem sequence, Petrarch has already vowed several times that he is ready to turn from Laura to God. Yet these resolutions—which will continue until the end of the *RVF*, depict conversion as not as a decisive turn, but "a thousand turnings about"—*mille rivolte*. As he will complain in *RVF* 264, "A thousand times I have asked God [*mille fiate ò chieste a Dio*]" for help (*RVF* 264.6). Petrarch's turns pose the same set of questions that Goldberg locates at the center of contemporary philosophical responses to Paul's conversion: "What is a conversion? Is it, as the etymology of the word suggests, a turn with? Or is it a turning around? Or back? Does it represent a break? An end? A beginning?"[60] In Petrarch's case as in Paul's (and Augustine's), the answer to all of these questions is: yes, but not exactly. For the Italian *rivolte* contains multiple puns that a literal translation, as in Durling's "turnings about," cannot capture. The physical gyrations that go nowhere ("nor . . . have I yet moved") are also, most obviously, repeated affective circles from one object and orientation (God, divine love) to another (Laura, earthly love). Petrarch's turns are also "re-volts" in the sense of the rebellion, defection, and apostasy that are inseparable from the experience of devotion.[61]

Along with these theological meanings, Petrarch's *rivolte* puns on the poetic sequence itself, evoking the multiple *volte*, or turns in rhyme and thought that are a mark of the Petrarchan sonnet. The recreation of the self through poesis both seeks and resists the self-abnegation of conversion.[62] The artful expression of dissatisfaction, the foregrounding of authorial skill, constitutes a tedious, protracted resistance against the soteriology of grace that grounds the *RVF*. No less than the rapturous, pliant saint, the captivated lover is grateful simply to serve. "True" love is known in that it effaces the "lie" of self-pleasure and demands nothing in return. By contrast, Petrarch's poetry, as the characters "Franciscus" and "Augustinius" agree in Petrarch's *Secretum* and as centuries of readers have recognized, expresses not self-effacing devotion but self-promoting ambition for worldly gratification in the forms of fame and sex. Remarking that Petrarch is in love at least as much with Laura's name as with her mind or her body, since the multiple puns it affords allow him to pursue the "illusory immortality" accorded the poet laureate, Petrarch's Augustinius charges that "you'd rather abandon yourself than your little books."[63] Self-effacement and self-aggrandizement converge in Petrarchan praise.

When the Petrarch of the *RVF* complains that he is "here" and wishes to be "elsewhere," it is a warning that he will turn again. But this dissatisfaction with his own desires is also a sign of hope. It demonstrates that his faith in the possibility of faith is still alive. The same striving that reveals failure also eschews complacency—the alluring *apatheia* that, as Augustine argues, makes one beyond recovery. For however much Augustinius of the *Secretum* argues for a Stoic self-direction, Augustine of the *Confessions*, as we have seen and as Petrarch well knew, understood the divided, unknowable, uncontrollable will to be the paradigmatic trait of human creatures forever wishing to wish more, wanting to want something other than what they want. And Petrarch's recognition of this paradoxical helplessness—that in "being unable to do more," one does all one can—is central to the Augustinian (and, later, Protestant) understanding of divine grace, rather than human will, effort, or action, as the source of faith and salvation.

Petrarch's ceaseless activity precludes rapt openness to undeserved divine grace or human love, and the result is just the disorientation one would expect after a thousand turns. Throughout the sequence, Petrarch remarks on his own uncertainty about who he really is and what he really wants so regularly as to border on the comic:

Alas, what am / I? What was I? [*Lasso, che son? che fui?*] (*RVF* 23.30);

My thoughts have become alien to me [*Da me son fatti I miei pensier diversi*] (*RVF* 29.36);

What am I saying? or where am I? and who deceives me but my- / self and my excessive desire? [*Che parlo, o dove sono, et chi m'inganna / altri ch' io stresso e 'l desiar soverchio?*] (*RVF* 70.31–32);

So powerful is the will that carries me away; and / Reason is dead [*sì possente è 'l voler che mi transporta, / et la ragione è morta*]" (*RVF* 73.24–25);

Thus often she has relit and extinguished my heart / . . . and often I am angered by it [*Così più volte a 'l cor racceso et spento, / . . . et spesso me n'adiro*] (*RVF* 135.74–75);

Love carries me off where I do not wish to go [*Amor mi transporta ov' ir non voglio*] (*RVF* 235.1);

What are you doing? What are you thinking? Why do you still / look back to a time that can never return anymore? [*Che fai? che pensi? ché pur dietro guardi / nel tempo che tornar non pote omai?*] (*RVF* 273.1–2);

And so my soul, overcome by sorrow, as, weeping it grows / angry with itself, shaken from sleep returns to itself [*onde l'anima mia dal dolor vinta, / mentre piangendo allor seco s'adira, / sciolta dal sonno a se stessa ritorna*] (*RVF* 356.12–14).

These struggles with the impure and fragmented self capture the Augustinian paradox of a faith that must assiduously seek out its own failures *and* own up to them. A literal translation of the final line of *RVF* 118—"nor through a thousand turnings are anchors moved"—captures this dilemma as well as anything. Like the anchor twisted helplessly about by the waters under which it is submerged, Petrarch remains helpless to lift himself from the depths of creaturely distraction. That emblem of steadfastness, the anchor—also, the *anchorite* who seeks to avoid temptation by retreating from the world—is equally a picture of insensibility and paralysis.[64]

The feature of the sequence that would seem most to affirm Petrarch's faithful devotion to Laura is the set of eighteen "anniversary" poems marking the passage of time over the twenty-one years of her life (detailed in what are usually called the *in vivo* poems, *RVF* 1–263) and the ten years that follow her death (the subject of the *in morte* poems, *RVF* 264–366).[65] Lest readers fail to keep track of how long he has suffered, Petrarch provides a recap two poems before the end of the *RVF* as a whole: "Love held me twenty-one years gladly burning in the fire and full / of hope amid sorrow; since my lady, and my heart with her, / rose to Heaven, ten more years of weeping [*Tennemi Amor anni ventuno ardendo / lieto nel foco et nel duol pien di speme; / poi che Madonna e 'l mio cor seco inseme / saliro al Ciel, dieci altri anni piangendo*]" (*RVF* 364.1-4). Petrarch dates his first sighting of Laura on April 6, 1347, the historical anniversary of the crucifixion as it was calculated in his time, "the day when the sun's rays turned pale with grief for his / Maker [*il giorno ch' al sol si scoloraro per la pietà del suo fattore i rai*]" (*RVF* 3.1–2).[66] Equating his personal "misfortunes [*guai*]" of unrequited love with the "universal woe [*commune dolor*]" greeting Christ's death, Petrarch conspicuously signals his idolatrous displacement of worship from creator to creature (*RVF* 3.7, 8). While her subject isn't idolatry per say, Vickers's account of Petrarchan poesis is helpful here: his project is one of "re-membering the lost body, of effecting an inverse incarnation—her flesh made word."[67] In taking Laura as a figure for divine goodness, Petrarch fails to grasp the crucifixion's lesson of humility and compassion. Laura's death occurs exactly twenty-one years later, on April 6, 1348, Easter Sunday, her ascent repeating that of Christ, Petrarch's sorrow at her death replacing joy at Christ's resurrection. In the *Secretum*, Augustinius and Franciscus concur that the moment Petrarch met Laura was the moment he went "off course," no longer "fearing God" as he had in his youth.[68] Petrarch's obsession with "the place and the time and the hour [*il loco e 'l tempo et l'ora*]" when he first saw Laura or, more elaborately, "the day and the month and the year and the season / and the time and the hour and the instant and the beautiful / countryside and the place where I was struck [*'l giorno e 'l mese et 'l anno / e la stagione e 'l tempo et l'ora e 'l punto / e 'l bel paese e 'l loco ov' io fui giunto*]" depicts this moment as the point of no return (*RVF* 13.5, 61.1–4). As Langer notes, the "*rivolta d'occhi*," the sight of and/or glance from Laura's eyes, that Petrarch reports in *RVF* 72 depicts the encounter as a break with static, continuous, progressive time (*RVF* 72.35).[69] Petrarch's ritualistic incantation of his anniversary asserts the sacred nature of his attachment, depicting the instant it began as a point of contact between time and eternity, the quotidian and the miraculous. Similar work is performed by two of the many puns on Laura's name on offer in the sequence: *l'aura* (the spirit, breath) and *l'ora* (the hour, the time), the latter itself closely related to the always fleeting present moment, the "now" (*or*; of which more below). Every anniversary that Petrarch celebrates, from this perspective, marks one more year of adoring creature over creator, and therefore one more year in which he proves his love for Laura by risking his very soul.

Yet the anniversary poems, often understood as affirmations of his turn from God to Laura, are more accurately described as some of the *mille rivolte* that occur throughout the *RVF*. These poems are interspersed with palinodes in which Petrarch recants his love. Indeed, many of the anniversaries themselves struggle to relinquish secular love in favor of divine grace, as in *RVF* 62, which marks the eleventh anniversary with prayers that God will "lead my wandering thoughts / back to a better place, remind them that today you were on the / Cross [*reduci i pensier vaghi a miglior luogo, / rammenta lor come oggi fusti in croce*]" (*RVF* 62.13–14). The structure of the *RVF*, which by all evidence Petrarch revised and rethought multiple times, marks the strange temporality of a faith that is never stable.[70] The anniversaries appear sporadically, with no clear correlation between the number of poems and the number of years that have passed. Along with the shifts in verb tense from poem to poem as well as within individual poems, the anniversary songs depict time not as linear or teleological, proceeding punctually and predictably from one moment to the next, but as recursive and irregular, accelerating and dragging. Rather than ground the sonnets in history, the anniversaries expose the disjunction between calendrical and experiential time, defying any attempt to advance from error to truth, Laura to God, flesh to spirit. In this light, the initial encounter with Laura is less a rupture or state of emergency than a predictable part of the ongoing crisis that is faith.[71]

"Now" (*or*) is one of the most common words in the *RVF*. It appears throughout the sequence to announce moments of insight and resolution, the sense of a new beginning, that accompanies conversion. Yet these conversions are as unstable as this word's referential status. Read in the context of the full sequence, "now" calls attention to itself as a deixis whose meaning is entirely contextual and therefore can always mean something else.[72] The first poem in the sequence, likely one of the last in order of composition, is retrospective, narrated by a Petrarch who describes himself as "now" "in part" (*in parte*) other than the author of the poems to follow:

> You who hear in scattered rhymes the sound of those sighs with
> which I nourished my heart during my first youthful error, when
> I was in part another man from what I am now:
>
> for the varied style in which I weep and speak between vain
> hopes and vain sorrow, where there is anyone who understands
> love through experience, I hope to find pity, not only pardon.
>
> But now [*or*] I see well how for a long time I was the talk of the
> crowd, for which often I am ashamed of myself within;

and of my raving, shame is the fruit, and repentance, and the clear knowledge that whatever pleases in the world is a brief dream.

[*Voi ch' ascoltate in rime sparse il suono*
di quei sospiri ond' io nudriva 'l core
in sul mio primo giovenile errore,
quand' era in parte altr' uom da quel ch' i' sono:

del vario stile in ch' io piango et ragiono
fra le vane speranze e 'l van dolore,
ove sia chi per prova intenda amore
spero trovar pietà, non che perdono.

Ma ben veggio or sì come al popol tutto
favola fui gran tempo, onde sovente
di me medesmo meco mi vergogno;

et del mio vaneggiar vergogna è 'l frutto,
e 'l pentersi, e 'l conoscer chiaramente
che quanto piace al mondo è breve sogno.] (*RVF* 1.1–14)

This poem opens the *RVF* with a retrospective account of conversion. Rather than begin at the beginning, the sequence purports to begin at the end, when Petrarch describes the *RVF* as a commemoration of his "first youthful error, when I was in part another man from what I am now." The "scattered rhymes" and "varied style" befit a man caught "between vain hope and vain sorrow." This is a subject unable to achieve coherent thought or selfhood—an Augustinian self, in other words, desperately conscious of the rebellion of his own will. Petrarch's error is at once a mistake and a circuitous route to the truth that he "now" thinks he sees, to the man that he "now" thinks he is. Ashamed of and contrite for the poetic "raving" (*vaneggiar*: raving, wandering, vanity, emptiness, illogic) that makes up the *RVF*, Petrarch nonetheless introduces the sequence as itself depicting a felix culpa in which the "fruit" of his "raving" is "shame," "repentance," and the "clear knowledge that whatever pleases in the world is a dream." Richard Strier has rightly argued that the poem's opening leaves uncertain just how much the sober and contrite Petrarch we confront "now," at the opening of sequence, has changed from the sighing, weeping, hopeful lover who has become "the talk of the crowd."[73] To be sure, the "clear knowledge" Petrarch claims to have achieved in this first sonnet is of little help, as he acknowledges a third of the way through the *RVF* as a whole in a scolding self-accusation ("'Brother, you keep showing / others the way, where you have often been astray and are now, / more than ever [*Frate, tu vai / mostrando altrui la via dove sovente / fosti smarrito et or se' più che mai*]'" [*RVF* 99.12–14]) then again after Laura's death ("I see the better but I lay hold on the worse [*veggio 'l meglio et al peggior m'appiglio*]" [*RVF* 264.136]). Because, as Strier puts it, Petrarch "conceives of ethical life in affective terms," the problem is as much how he feels as what he knows.[74]

But whereas Strier reads this partial penitence as a sign that Petrarch defends his earthly desires as moral and valuable, I argue that it dramatizes the need for a more hesitant ethics of promiscuity that resists the celebration of monogamy that Strier and others have seen in Petrarch's lyrics. *RVF* 1 foregrounds not a confidently ironized self, but one too mixed up to be fully deciphered, much less defended. This is why Petrarch throws himself on the mercy of readers ("you who hear") who know ourselves to be as compromised as he is. His poetic fragments are vulgar not only because they are written in the common language but because they describe a common, humbling experience. Virginia Burras's definition of shame, drawn from the work of Silvan Tompkins, Leon Wurmser, and Eve Sedgwick, is helpful here. Burras argues that shame raises the question of identity "not only in relation to others but also, and perhaps more crucially, in the relation of self to self," for it "reflects not only the acceptance of limits but also an aspiration to exceed one's own limits."[75] In seeing ourselves from the outside, we confront mortifying truths. By the same token, when we wince at the recognition of others' shame, we acknowledge our connection to them. In this challenge to the "very distinction between inside and outside," Burras writes, shame can be "saving" because it "marks the mutually constitutive and transforming meeting point of self and other at the limits of mutual exposure."[76] In *RVF* 1, the dynamic of prayer and forgiveness that recognizes mutual failure is as central to secular community as to religious salvation. Petrarch asks "you"—*us*, his unseen audience—for pity and pardon (*pietà, perdono*) before he asks God or Laura. "You"/we, unlike omnipotent deity or unavailable mistress, are part of the motley crowd that "understands love through experience" and therefore must forgive the poignant, public self-humiliation that is the *RVF*.

The confrontation with infidelity as a technique of the humility that permits the imagination of a purer faith emerges in the erraticism of the conversions that punctuate the *RVF*. For at least as frequently as the anniversary poems remark the endurance of Petrarch's passion for Laura, the palinodes declare that "now" he has definitively turned to God. These vertiginous *rivolte* occasionally appear in a single poem. For instance, whereas poem 1 of the *RVF* allows for partial, incomplete conversion, poem 62, which celebrates the eleventh anniversary of Petrarch's first sight of Laura, also begs his *Padre del Ciel* for grace:

> Father of Heaven, after the lost days, after the nights spent
> raving with that fierce desire that was lit in my heart when I
> looked on those gestures so lovely to my hurt,
>
> let it please you at last that with your light I may return to a
> different life and to more beautiful undertakings, so that, having
> spread his nets in vain, my harsh adversary may be disarmed.
>
> Now turns, my Lord, the eleventh year that I have been subject
> to the pitiless yoke that which is always most fierce to the most
> submissive:
>
> have mercy on my unworthy pain, lead my wandering thoughts
> back to a better place, remind them that today you were on the
> Cross.
>
> [*Padre del Ciel, dopo i perduti giorni,*
> *dopo le notti vaneggiando spese*
> *con quel fero desio ch' al cor s'accese,*
> *mirando gli atti per mio mal sì adorni,*
>
> *piacciati omai col tuo lume ch' io torni*
> *ad altra vita et a più belle imprese,*

sì ch' avendo le reti indarno tese
il mio duro avversario se ne scorni.

Or volge, Signor mio, l'undecimo anno
ch' i' fui sommesso al dispietato giogo
che sopra i più soggetti è più feroce:

miserere del mio non degno affanno,
reduci i pensier vaghi a miglior luogo,
ramenta lor come oggi fusti in croce.] (*RVF* 62.1–14)

The poem struggles to imagine a decisive pivot that will relegate the irrecoverable years, the *perduti giorni*, to a decisive past, a before that contrasts with an "after" (*dopo*) liberated from the nets of fame and desire set by the "harsh adversary" who may be either Satan or Laura. But in the discrepancy between the two "nows" of the poem—*omai* (at last, henceforth) in line 5 and "*or*" (now) in line 9—Petrarch acknowledges that before and after are themselves deixis whose meaning cannot be fixed. The momentary hope of the octave that he will "at last" return to the fold itself pivots with the poem's *volta* so that the sestet begins with the recognition that he is still waiting for the moment of rebirth registered in *omai*. Time, in the form of the almost imperceptible seconds required to speak or read four lines of poetry, has slipped by and Petrarch finds himself not at a new beginning, but facing the start of an eleventh year that "Now turns" (*or volge*). This struggle for faith occurs at the juncture of chronological time and what Agamben calls "operational" or "messianic" time: the time that we take to achieve the representation of time itself. This messianic time presses through punctual time, for "Inasmuch as the 'now' has already ceased to be once it has been uttered (or written), the attempt to grasp the 'now' always produces a past."[77] The pivot to eternal fate is replaced by the recursive revolutions of human prayer, but these revolutions themselves mark the distance between aspiration and actuality.

RVF 62 is not the last poem in which the "now" of redemption is joyously heralded only to recede into the lost days of the past. In *RVF* 142 Petrarch inverts the incantatory blessing of the "place and the time and the hour" when he first saw Laura to assert that

Now the shortness of life and the place and the season
show me another pathway to go to Heaven
and bear fruit, not merely flowers and leaves.

Another love, other leaves, and another light,
another climbing to Heaven by other hills
I seek (for it is indeed time), and other branches.

[*ora la vita breve e 'l loco e 'l tempo*
mostranmi altro sentier di gire al cielo
et di far frutto, non pur fior et frondi.

Altr'amor, altre frondi, et altro lume,
altro salir al ciel per altri poggi
cerco (che nè ben tempo), et altri rami.] (*RVF* 142.34–39)

Since *RVF* 142 is not an anniversary poem, and since the anniversary poems do not reliably appear in chronological order anyway, we cannot be sure which specific year to map it onto. But we can guess that this poem is set about four to six years after the more famous *RVF* 62, since the previous anniversary poem, *RVF* 122, commemorates the "seventeenth year [*Dicesette anni*]" of Petrarch's love (*RVF* 122.1) and the subsequent one, *RVF* 145, anticipates the continuation of his "trilustral sighing [*sospir trilustre*]" (*RVF* 145.14).[78] *RVF* 142 does not pray for future conversion but describes in the present tense a turn from the "lovely branches [*bei rami*]" (*RVF* 142.14) of the "laurel [*lauro*]" (142.13) to those "other branches" of the Cross. The concluding lines of this sestina insist that "Now" (*ora*: *this* hour, *this* time) he will take "another pathway," contemplating *the* Passion. Faith as humility and compassion promises to "bear fruit"—the fruit of shame and repentance announced in *RVF* 1. This produce is more substantial than the flimsy "flowers and leaves," poesie and pages, that have revealed worldly monogamy to be irreducibly acquisitive and self-promoting, the sovereign, integral self to which monogamy attests as ephemeral and virtual as pages of scattered rhymes. In promising to forget Laura and all her name stands for—temporal fame, success, wealth—Petrarch promises to give up on what Augustine called "the lie of self-pleasing." There is something else, something other (*altro*, another, appears six times in five lines) both in and beyond the self.

But, with over two hundred poems and at least twenty years to go until the end of the sequence, Petrarch is inevitably distracted, brought back to himself. Sixty-two poems and somewhere between one and five years later, he again resolves in *RVF* 204 that "*Now* with so clear a light and such signs, we must not lose our / way [*Or con sì chiara luce et con tai segni / errar non dèsi*]" (*RVF* 204.9; my emphasis).[79] Another sixty poems and about seven to twelve years later, Petrarch laments that "until *now* no prayer or sigh or weeping of mine has helped / me [*Ma infin a qui niente mi releva / prego o sospiro o lagrimar ch' io faccia*]" and exhorts himself to "Decide wisely, decide [*Prendi partito accortamente, prendi*]" to "*now* raise yourself to a more blessed hope by gazing / at the heavens [*or ti solleva a più beata spene / mirando 'l ciel*]" (*RVF* 264.9, 23, 48; my emphasis).[80] Ninety-one poems later he addresses "time [*tempo*]" and the "revolving heavens [*ciel volubil*]" themselves, swearing that "*Now* through experience I understand your frauds [*ora ab experto vostre frodi intendo*]" (*RVF* 355.1, 4; my emphasis).[81] The "now"—*ora*—both marks "this time" as different and sets this revelation in time itself, through the process of trial and experience that can happen only in the vulgar, common world that the unique use of Latin here (*ab experto*) conspicuously disavows.

The final poems of the *RVF* have been read as staging the true conversion that has been so long deferred. In poem 364, with only two poems to follow in the *RVF* as a whole, Petrarch declares that

> *Now* I am weary and I reproach my life for so much error, which had almost extinguished the seed of virtue; and I devoutly render my last parts, high God, to You,
>
> repentant and sorrowing for my years spent thus.
>
> [*Omai son stanco, et mia vita reprendo*
> *di tanto error che di vertute il seme*
> *à quasi spento; et le mie parti estreme,*
> *alto Dio, a te devotamente rendo*
>
> *pentito et tristo de' miei sì spesi anni*] (*RVF* 364.5–9;
>   my emphasis)

This poem comes at the end of the sequence, followed by two poems appealing first to the "invisible, / immortal King of Heaven [*Re del cielo, invisibile, immortale*]" to "help my strayed frail soul and fill out / with your grace all that she lacks [*soccorri a l'alma disviata et frale, / e 'l suo defetto di tua gratia adempi*]" (*RVF* 365.6–8) and then to the Virgin to "commend me to your Son [*raccomandami al tuo Figliuol*]" (*RVF* 366.135). For many readers, these poems enact a decisive, final conversion, one that exceeds the partial reform with which the sequence began and which it has enacted. By this optimistic logic, *RVF* 1 retrospectively opens the sequence *in media res*, promising an epic journey that may contain romance digressions but ultimately reaches its divinely ordained goal.[82]

To be sure, we have no way of proving otherwise, since *RVF* 366 is the last poem. But we have heard such professions of faith (or, as Chiampi puts it, "reawakening of shame") too many times throughout the *RVF* to be entirely certain.[83] Read in the context of the *mille rivolte* that we have witnessed, the palinodes with which the sequence concludes may be no more than our last record of Petrarch's struggle to feel right, for the historical fiction that sets *RVF* 364 ten years after Laura's death (in 1358) also sets the end of the sequence sixteen years before Petrarch's own death (in 1374)—years that "we," his audience past and present, know were taken up with continuous and careful revision to the "flowers and leaves" of the book we are "now" about to close.[84] We may be finished with the sequence, but Petrarch is not. Indeed, Petrarch begs the Virgin for the same pity he asked of us, and in the process returns to the erotic struggles that have been the obsessive topic of the *RVF*:

> Virgin, turn those beautiful eyes that sorrowing saw
> the pitiless wounds in your dear Son's sweet limbs, to my
> perilous state, who come dismayed to you for counsel.

> [*Vergine, que' belli occhi*
> *che vider tristi la spietata stampa*
> *ne' dolci membri del tuo caro figlio,*
> *volgi al mio dubio stato,*
> *che sconsigliato   a te vèn per consiglio*]. (*RVF* 366.22–26)

Praying for the Virgin's attention is also praying for *her* distraction. In a repetition of his desperate hope for a glance ("*rivolta d'occhi*") from Laura, Petrarch asks this Virgin to turn her eyes from Christ's "pitiless wounds" to his own "perilous state." Ecce homo becomes "look at *me!*"; the final address to the Virgin in *RVF* 366 is little different from the initial address to "you"/us in *RVF* 1. As Augustinius laments at the end of the *Secretum*, "We are back where we started."[85]

This final prayer for mercy and grace also registers their deferral. It thereby opens up the space of uncertainty that makes faith matter:

> Virgin, fill my weary heart with holy repentant tears,
> let at least my last weeping be devout and without earthly mud,
> as was my first vow, before my insanity.
>
> Kindly Virgin, enemy of pride, let love of our common origin
> move you, have mercy on a contrite and humble heart; for if I
> am wont to love with such marvelous faith a bit of deciduous
> mortal dust, how will I love you, a noble thing?
>
> If from my wretched and vile state I rise again at your hands,
> Virgin, I consecrate and cleanse in your name my thought and
> wit and style, my tongue and heart, my tears and my sighs. Lead
> me to the better crossing and accept my changed desires.
>
> The day draws near and cannot be far, time so runs and flies,
> single, sole Virgin; and now conscience, now death pierces my
> heart: commend me to your Son, true man and true God, that
> He may receive my last breath in peace.
>
> [*Vergine, tu di sante*
> *lagrime et pie adempi 'l meo cor lasso,*
> *ch' almen l'ultimo pianto sia devoto,*
> *senza terrestro limo,*
> *come fu 'l primo   non d'insania voto.*
>
> *Vergine umana et nemica d'orgoglio:*
> *del comune principio amor t'induca*

miserere d'un cor contrito umile;
ché se poca mortal terra caduca
amar con sì mirabil fede soglio,
che devrò far di te, cosa gentile?

Se dal mio stato assai misero et vile
per le tue man resurgo,
Vergine, i' sacro et purgo
al tuo nome et pensieri e 'ngegno et stile,
la lingua e 'l cor, le lagrime e i sospiri.
Scorgimi al miglior guado
et prendi in grado   i cangiati desiri.

Il dì s'appressa, et non pote esser lunge,
sì corre il tempo et vola,
Vergine unica et sola,
e 'l cor or coscienzia or morte punge:
raccomandami al tuo Figliuol, verace
omo et verace Dio,
ch' accolga 'l mio   spirto ultimo in pace.] (*RVF* 366.118–137)

Petrarch's prayer that the Virgin "let at least my last weeping be devout and without earthly mud, / as was my first vow, before my insanity" supposes a past moment of true faith, before the rupture of his love for Laura. Like so many of the poems of the *RVF*, as well as the narrative of the *Secretum*, this appeal casts Petrarch's struggle not as renewal but as a re-turn back to the past self recalled in the first poem of the sequence, before that fateful April day when he veered off course. But such a pure, devout former self is conspicuously fictional. For it was *that* self that was so easily distracted by "a bit of deciduous mortal dust" that his faith has remained in fragments for thirty-one years. At the same time, it is the failure of a self believed to be devout that makes possible the recognition of its insufficiency, its lack of sovereignty over itself. As Chiampi observes, the final recantation of *RVF* 366, even as it repeats that of *RVF* 1 and so many other poems, "also serves to transform the earlier poems into essential possibilities of that conversion: conversion is always away from sin—a nothingness."[86]

Accordingly, the closing argument undermines itself, for it reveals that the weeping described throughout the *RVF*, even in moments of sincere conversion, has been tainted with "earthly mud" and therefore not entirely "devout." This "earthly mud" may be Petrarch's own fleshly self or it may be the "deciduous mortal dust" that is Laura, that inappropriate object of "marvelous [*mirabil*] faith." Petrarch offers to correct his idolatry by redirecting his passion. Making love for the virgin Laura a fortiori evidence of the worship that he will accord an even worthier Virgin, the prayer underscores the promiscuity of faith as a concept. His "changed desires," or infidelity to Laura, evince his newfound faith as "*now* [*or*] conscience, *now* [*or*] death pierces my heart." And the proof, he swears, will be in the poetry, for "if" he can rise again, he will "consecrate and cleanse in your name my thought and / wit and style, my tongue and heart, my tears and sighs." Consecration to another (*sacro*, giving or sacrifice) and cleansing of one's self (*purgo*, purging or purification) are twinned, impossible goals. The reflexive action of self-sacrifice and purification requires precisely the division that a self-abnegating devotion would heal.

From this perspective, Petrarch's attacks on Laura, often understood as expressions of misogyny, may equally respond to his own resistance to the faith he claims to pursue.[87] Carla Freccero has argued that "what is articulated in the Petrarchan lyric exchange between an 'I' and a 'you' is a relation of both desire and identification . . . such that Laura comes to resemble, not so much an 'other' object of desire, but a kind of Petrarch in drag."[88] I would add to this astute reading that this drag betrays its performativity, and not only because of the inscription of heterosexual difference that Freccero observes. It is also because what Petrarch seeks in his identification with Laura is the lack of interest in the world that he both admires and censures in *her*. Drawing on the model of Dante's *Rime petrose*, Petrarch expresses frustration at Laura's imperviousness to human desire, complaining that "it does / not please you to gaze so low with your lofty mind [*m' a voi non piace / mirar sì basso colla mente altera*]" (*RVF* 21.3–4); characterizing Laura as "so cruel a beast [*sì aspra fera*]" (*RVF* 22.20) possessed of a "tiger's or she-bear's heart [*un cor di tigre o d'orsa*]" (152.1); charging that she is "concerned for naught but honor [*a cui di nulla cale / se non de'onor*]" (*RVF* 263.5–6); comparing her to Narcissus (*RVF* 23.141–146); calling her a "Medusa" who has turned him to "a stone dripping vain moisture [*un sasso / d'umor vano stillante*]" (*RVF* 366.111–112). Such accusations make legible not just petulance at being repulsed, but also resistance to the ideal of purity that Petrarch condenses into that imaginary, otherworldly creation that is "Laura."[89] If we return to *RVF* 118 for a moment, we might postulate that its final line—"nor through a thousand turnings are anchors moved"— refers not to Petrarch himself but to Laura, who, like an anchoress, really has left the world behind, attaching her entire being to God.

Anger at Laura responds not only to her lack of interest in Petrarch, but to her lack of interest in the secular world. Absent the conflicted will that makes faith stumble and thereby confirms the need for grace, the fiction of Laura's purity appears as a Stoic *apatheia* that, if we follow Augustine, forecloses the humility that makes possible not only the passionate abandon of prayer but also the compassionate service of *caritas*. The pursuit of purity that is dramatized in Petrarch's pursuit of Laura as earthly love (her proper name), poetic achievement (*lauro*), and the human soul (*l'aura*) carries its own dangers of misprision, idolatry, and violence. Awareness that purity and perfection may unleash such cruelty explains why human faith must be premised on the potential for failure, grounded on the thousand turnings—the infidelities—that Petrarch hyperbolically cites in *RVF* 118 and enacts throughout the sequence. Because love necessarily lapses, as Petrarch observes in *RVF* 56, "before the day of his / last departure no man is to be called happy [*'nanzi al dì de l'ultima partita / uom beato chiamar non si convene*]" (*RVF* 56.13–14).

Yet this precarity is also a form of hope. For an erotic ethos based on attention to our own promiscuous motives, desires, and convictions relinquishes the comforts of believing ourselves pure. Humility about our own opacities and failures inspires compassion for the limited, impure truth—in the sense of loyalty, reliability, and sincerity—that others can offer, as well as gratitude that we are loved despite our failures. In addressing itself to "you"/us, the *RVF* asks us to cultivate an awareness that we are not only promiscuous in ourselves but also porous in our relation to others. It enjoins not mere toleration of difference without the self but receptivity to strangeness within as fragments of the truth that we can heal as well as injure.

And this may be the truest form of faith in all its density. For if one's attachments are impermanent, so are one's failures. Michael Warner concludes an essay on queer and Christian hermeneutics by gesturing to the queer promise of conversion. The value of such a relinquishment of stable selfhood, Warner suggests, is not salvation but openness to a self that can always start over as if reborn. Promises of conversion, he writes, "offer you a new and perpetual personality, and they tell you your current one was a mistake you made. They tell you to be somebody else. I say: believe them."[90] Petrarch, like Augustine, and, more perversely, like Warner, believes in just such a self in flux—one based not on the progress or maturation of a normative personal history, but the renewal and surprise of messianic time. This is the subjectivity that grounds an ethics of promiscuity in a poetic archive we wouldn't expect: the English lyrics written at the same time as—and, I argue, as a theoretical challenge to—the "rise" of monogamous love and companionate marriage increasingly coded as white.

2

The Color of Monogamy

Queer Theory, Classical Philosophy, Christian Theology

I have been arguing that our perception of the secular love tradition
so influentially shaped by Petrarch changes significantly when we
recognize that he renders in secular terms a Pauline and Augustinian
conviction that faith is always aspirational, love always promiscuous.
Through the influence of Petrarch, a Pauline theology of the divided
will is translated into secular terms in some of the most canonical English Renaissance love poems. In this chapter, I ask: To what extent can
that insight inform our understanding of the historical racialization of
affect and sexuality embedded in modern norms and ideals? And how
does the originally Catholic tradition of celibate devotion within which
Petrarchan love originates relate to the beliefs of the Protestant Reformation that profoundly influenced the structure of Anglo-American
politics, secularity, intimacy, and eroticism? To begin to answer these
questions requires distinguishing theological discussions of faith from a
secular ideology of monogamy. Whereas both queer critics and modern
Christians tend to treat the two as cohesive and mutually supporting,
they develop according to different logics and values. This chapter
explores the complex and contradictory genealogy of monogamy as it
emerges in both classical Greek and Roman discourses of friendship
and Protestant ethnographies based on marital practices. Surprisingly,
modern and secular ideals of coupledom have a lot in common with
the classical philosophy of friendship that has been taken by many
queer critics to present an alternative to heteronormative romance;
they have less affinity with a Pauline theology of an impure and divided
human will. Attending to the logical and historical intricacies of both
classical friendship and Pauline soteriology, I propose that Christian
views of subjectivity are queerer than their classical counterparts in
some respects. I further argue that considering the racial dimensions

of the concepts of friendship and monogamy helps us rethink a standard genealogy of queer studies, which includes classical philosophies of friendship while marginalizing (or excluding) religious accounts of subjectivity and relationality.

I take as my example of the racialized aspects of monogamy and promiscuity in William Shakespeare's spectacularly promiscuous sonnets, which struggle to reconcile an aspiration to the virtue and fidelity of friendship with a reality of ambivalence and faithlessness. Shakespeare secularizes Petrarch's conflicting desires for God and Laura into a *ménage a trois* among a "fair" young man, a "woman colored ill," and a speaker whose self-introduction ("my name is Will" [Sonnet 136.14]) punningly collapses autobiographical persona with allegorical personification of the fallen will that so troubled Augustine.[1] All three of these poetic characters, the sequence hints at multiple points, may also be taking additional, unnamed lovers. Because the mistress in these poems is obsessively but ambiguously described as "black," her participation in the sequence's threesome draws attention to the racial identities that inform what Eve Sedgwick influentially diagnosed as the triangulation of desire.[2] When the mistress explicitly enters the sequence as the embodiment of "black" beauty in Sonnet 127, it is retrospectively revealed that the sequence has all along deployed a racialized vocabulary to grapple with the manifold impurities of faith it so assiduously documents. The sonnets' frequent references to the mistress's black hair, eyes, skin, and "deeds" (131.13) allow us to appreciate that the youth and speaker are also racialized—as *white*.

I begin by discussing the racial dimension of "monogamy," itself a concept that emerges in distinction to the polygamous practices attributed to non-Christians. As I argued in the introduction to this book, the disavowal of the conceptual hybridity of race implicit in charges that its application to premodern periods is anachronistic—and the resulting isolation of biology from culture, phenotype from faith—works in concert with the historical catachresis of institutionalized periodization. By contrast, the historical specificity of the term "monogamy" has received little scrutiny. Reading the histories of race and monogamy in conjunction with one another, I argue, reveals their cooperative formation. To be monogamous—whether in classical friendship, premodern sworn brotherhood, or modern coupledom—is to aspire to the privilege that comes with a distinctly racialized sexual respectability. The flip side of this privilege, of course, is its denial to those who choose not to commit.

In the following section, I approach classical friendship as part of a longer history of what David L. Eng describes as a "racialization of intimacy" that relies on "the forgetting of race."[3] As Eng and others have argued, an urgent task for queer theory is the study of how racial difference troubles categories of normativity and transgression.[4] A reconsideration of the resources that queer theory has found in the past is, I propose, an essential part of this project. According to classical theory, perfect and egalitarian friendship is available only to those who achieve the wisdom and virtue exhibited above all in self-mastery. Those "Asiatic barbarians" whom Aristotle deems "natural" slaves to their own fickle appetites are neither constant nor sincere enough to sustain friendship's bond. Given that the sovereign self of friendship is becoming racialized and Christianized amidst the emergence of slavery and colonization in the early modern period, as Ivy Schweitzer has shown, to historicize friendship is to reveal its potential to validate as well as to resist the nascent hierarchies of a liberal democracy premised on privatized ideals of individual integrity, autonomy, and responsibility.[5] This history reveals that the rationality and integrity that provide the grounds for friendship as a virtuous and egalitarian bond had been associated with racial whiteness well before the American context in which the emergence of "race" is often set. Shakespeare's sonnets are part of this history: read as a bond between specifically white men, the sonnets' unrealized ideal of male friendship also collaborates with the racial order that, as Kim F. Hall has observed, governs the sequence from the very first line of the very first poem: "From *fairest* creatures we desire increase" (1.1; my emphasis).[6] Monogamy and respectability are understood as "fair" (a word that, along with the emergence of slavery and colonization, increasingly merged aesthetic and racial hierarchies); promiscuity and ignominy as "dark."[7]

Having traced the affinities between classical friendship and monogamous coupledom, I propose in the subsequent section that the Christian theology so influentially disseminated by the Pauline Letters assumes a more conflicted and promiscuous subjectivity than that of classical thought. Particularly in its Protestant elaboration by the Augustinian monk Martin Luther, Christian theology paradoxically tempers the rigors of classical friendship with a more forgiving ethics of promiscuity—the *recognition* of impurity and self-deceit so central to the soteriology by which Protestant Reformers distinguished themselves from Catholic, Jewish, and Muslim others. Taking seriously a theological view of the opacity and intractability of the individual will may, I argue, disturb the same mutually sustaining sexual and racial categories that the unexamined deployment of its contrary, sincerity, helps to construct. However much the sonnets seek to idealize "fair" male friendship, they question the same racialized sexual distinctions they make.

As I argue in the final section of this chapter, "blackness," precisely because of its uncertain and unstable meaning, becomes in Shakespeare's sonnets the vehicle for recognition of shared promiscuity. As against monogamous union with a lover who is "fair, kind, and true," the poems to the mistress struggle to imagine a more compromised, and therefore more honest and humane, relational landscape (105.9, 10, 13). Resisting the lifelong dyads of classical friendship and companionate marriage, the sonnets attempt instead to imagine a communal, dispersed *caritas* that is asocial in the sense discussed by Daniel Juan Gil: disruptive both of early modern homosociality and of modern ideals of interpersonal intimacy and companionate marriage.[8] This encounter with difference grapples with a conflicted desire for what Michel Foucault calls "friendship as a way of life."[9] Yet Shakespeare does not merely celebrate hybridity or sexual liberation. Rather, the racist and misogynist invectives that erupt throughout these poems indicate that the speaker's aspiration to "fairness"—as beauty, as innocence, as whiteness—as an ideal makes a relational ethos of humility and forgiveness impossible to sustain.

The Invention of Monogamy

Tracing the racial politics of sexual respectability, a number of feminist and queer of color theorists have argued that the monogamy often treated as proof of both authentic love and personal integrity is ideologically attached to whiteness.[10] As any number of reactionary cultural documents, from the Moynihan Report to the Focus on the Family website, make clear, the white, monogamous, procreative couple is an American national ideal. More recently, in the mainstream secular sphere this ideal has been extended to monogamous same-sex couples.

The inclusion of LGBTQ couples in a narrative that equates mutual commitment with national belonging has in fact been treated as a sign of modern progressiveness in opposition to the presumed homophobia of American minorities or the perverse sexualities of Islamic terrorists.[11]

The racialization of sexual respectability has a long and intricate history, one that has been obscured by the view that "race" is a modern invention. Insofar as desire is considered to be private and spontaneous, Sharon Holland argues, "the erotic touches upon that aspect of racist practice that cannot be accounted for as racist practice but must be understood as something else altogether."[12] One form of racist practice that we understand as something else is the cultural privilege awarded to monogamous coupledom. Monogamy in its modern sense—commitment to a relationship with one other person—testifies to one's faithfulness in both the objective sense of constancy and the subjective sense of credibility: it is a guarantor of respectability and good citizenship. Historically, in the United States the view that monogamy is a sign of maturity, responsibility, and propriety has naturalized not only the material privileges that marriage brings but also a range of policies directed at destroying forms of kinship and relationality understood as antithetical to white Christian identity.[13]

Renaissance lyrics are often assumed to treat monogamous coupledom as the ideal end of desire, expressing a cultural ethos summarized by Adam Phillips: "Monogamy makes the larger abstractions real, as religion once did. Faith, hope, trust, morality; these are domestic matters now. Indeed, we contrast monogamy not with bigamy or polygamy but with infidelity, because it is our secular religion."[14] Yet it is no less anachronistic to speak of "monogamy" in this sense in the Renaissance than it is to speak of "race." While certainly the concept of erotic fidelity is an ancient one, the notion of mutual and exclusive commitment was not called "monogamy" until the twentieth century. In this way, "monogamy" is not unlike those other anachronistic terms, "homosexuality" and "heterosexuality," both of which were coined in the nineteenth century—as was "sex," an activity that, as Will Stockton and James M. Bromley have observed, surely happened before the modern era but was not designated by its modern term or limited to modern practices.[15] As Jeffrey Masten has shown, attention to the longer history of the words we habitually and unthinkingly use compels us also to attend to

the sedimented meanings that shape assumptions about what constitutes normative, perverse, or transgressive desire: "Etymology, then, in
its lingering tastes of the past in the present, forces us to develop ever-
expanding lexicons of erotic and affective terms and their relations."[16] In
subjecting "monogamy" to the kind of queer philological study analyzed
at length by Masten, I seek to bring attention to the concept's evolution
through anthropological, religious, and racialized studies that suggest
that the modern association of monogamy with whiteness is there from
the start, even if the connotations of both "monogamy" and "whiteness"
have shifted.

The terms "monogamy" and "monogamous" as names for a relational
category appeared in the English language only in 1612, originally designating "the practice or principle of marrying only once; i.e. of not re-
marrying after the death of a first spouse."[17] About one hundred years
later "monogamy" comes to mean having only one spouse at a time (the
OED dates this usage to 1708). Only in the late eighteenth century did
monogamy come to mean sex with a single partner; it was first used in
this way (apparently) as one category for the mating habits of animals
(the OED gives instances from 1770 and 1785). By the early nineteenth
century, we see "monogamy" used anthropologically, as one term in a
taxonomy of sexual or marital practices across different cultures. Only
in the late nineteenth century does "monogamy" come to mean fidelity
within marriage (the OED's first instance is 1865). If we believe that the
OED is accurate, or at least in the ballpark, "monogamy" seems not to
have been used to describe sexual fidelity in nonmarital relationships
until the twentieth century.[18]

Much as "heterosexuality" as a term and concept enters the English
language at roughly the same time as "homosexuality," with norms so-
lidifying only with the designation of behaviors understood as marginal
or deviant, monogamy is itself a back formation from bigamy, a much
older term (the OED gives first use as ca. 1325), which initially meant
either remarriage or marriage to two persons at once.[19] "Monogamy" is
also preceded by "polygamy," which (again) could mean either multiple
remarriages or a group marriage and which first appeared in English
in the sixteenth century in a specifically Protestant context. The OED
traces the first use to the writing of Richard Taverner, a sixteenth-
century Lutheran translator of the Bible into English and a propagan-

dist for Protestant reform of the English Church. In his 1538 translation of the Commonplaces of the Lutheran theologian Erasmus Sarcerius, next to the final section on Christian rules of marriage Taverner places a marginal gloss that reads "Poligamie, that is, the having of many wyves togyther is forbyden." Taverner's gloss is adjacent to the passage in which Sarcerius declares that

> Neither is there read any commandment in the old testament for the having of many wives, although examples do testify that it was there, by chance also suffered at those times for increase of yssue [issue] or for other causes. But the newe testament doth utterly forbid the having of many wives, and that by the authorite of Christ, who bringeth us back agayn to the true instinct of nature, and right ordinance of God.[20]

Around the same time, in 1547, one "I. B." (likely either John Bale or John Bradford) affirms, "So is it not to be founde in any apostels wrytynge, that any Chrysten man . . . hath bene Polygamous (that is to saye) hath had manye wyues."[21] The *OED*'s next recorded use appears in the full title of the Calvinist divine William Fulke's 1579 treatise, which attacks "*D. Heskins, D. Sanders, and M. Rastel, accounted (among their faction) three pillers and archpatriarches of the popish synagogue*" in a familiar Reformation conflation of Catholics and Jews as "*vtter enemies to the truth of Christes Gospell, and all that syncerely professe the same.*" Fulke cites "the incest of Juda & the Poligamie of the Patriarks" as dangerous examples to be avoided by true Christians.[22] A final early example occurs in Fynes Moryson's travelogue in a section on the climatic theory of ethnicity, which notes of "Jews, Asians, and persons from the southern climes" that "Poligamy be permitted among them (I meane the hauing of many wiues for one man)."[23] Polygamy in all of these early English instances is associated with the obscure Jewish past, the East, and the Southern Hemisphere, what in the eighteenth century would come to be called "monogamy" with the present of northwestern, Protestant Europe. This philological background supplements the connections that premodern scholars have observed between exotic tales of harems, orgies, sexual servitude, and sodomy in travelers' reports.[24] With the rise of European colonial aspiration, as Carmen Nocentelli argues, "polygamy became a symptom of an aberrant libido that could potentially operate as a principle of human classification," thereby fusing the institutionalization of monogamous heterosexual marriage with the socialization of racial difference.[25]

The conjoined histories of the concepts of race and monogamy suggest that relational categories were part of the early vocabulary of racial difference and vice versa. They remind us that race and sexuality in the past as well as the present both include and exceed embodied identity. Premodern categories make legible the longer genealogy of what Jasbir Puar calls "Orientalist queernesses (failed heteronormativity as signaled by polygamy, pathological homosociality)," which Western feminist and LGBTQ theory and politics sometimes continue, unwittingly, to ascribe to African and Middle Eastern bodies.[26] The privileging of Western modernity and secularism as the grounds of sexual rights, in Puar's analysis, shapes an unspoken, racialized "homonationalism" in which queer activism can converge in surprising ways with Western neoliberal and imperial projects.[27] Classical friendship is part of this associational complex.

Friendship, Homonormativity, and Whiteness

Secular, modern ideals of monogamy derive, to a surprising extent, from a classical ideal of dyadic friendship limited to virtuous male citizens "by nature free" and impossible for anyone who is "intended by nature to be a slave."[28] The late medieval and early modern concept of companionate marriage—one that today includes both gay and straight couples—was imagined as an equal and virtuous relationship free of lust or self-interest, one to which the sixteenth-century writer Edmund Tilney devoted a book entitled *The Flower of Friendshippe*.[29] As James Bromley has argued, insofar as it offers a culturally sanctioned pattern of love characterized by inwardness and constancy, friendship contributes to the eventual regulation of all sexuality by monogamous marriage.[30] The legacy of this history still lingers in the curriculum of the "Loving Couples, Loving Children" workshop funded by George W. Bush's $1.5 million Supporting Healthy Marriage Program, launched in 2003 and reauthorized by Congress in 2010, which is explicitly "organized around the concept that the underpinning of a healthy relationship is a strong friendship."[31] This view of friendship as the source of commitment is reflected in the history of the very term. The word "friend" is derived from the Old English *freond*, which equally signified love and freedom: the friend is one who is free to go but chooses to stay. Along with its modern meaning, "friend" in premodern English could designate a lover or kinsperson, affiliations that rested on ties other than political or economic compulsion. The companionate model of marriage, in which spouses are also friends, began to take shape at the same time that the states of freedom and slavery that classical and Christian writers had described in affective terms were becoming attached to racialized whiteness and blackness, respectively. Political conditions, in this view, were external expressions of inward states of rational self-mastery, on the one hand, or enslavement to brute appetite, on the other. Figurative deployments of slavery thus naturalized that institution's expansion and minimized its brutality.

Friendship "as a way of life," to again evoke Foucault's influential phrase, has been embraced by early modern queer scholars as evidence of a culturally central form of same-sex love, and it has often been celebrated as an egalitarian alternative to the domination and hierarchy central to heterosexual relations. Because of friendship's prominence in classical and Renaissance philosophy and political theory, it offers evidence of what Laurie Shannon calls "the powerfully homonormative bias in Renaissance thought [that] favors both self-likeness (constancy) and same-sex affects" and whose "rhetoric tendentiously aims at the highest degree of integrity and unsubordinated being as a kind of private sovereignty of the self, a rhetoric formulated against the gendered contingencies of life within authoritative hierarchies whether political, social, or marital."[32] Mindful that in "prevailing models of the liberal subject . . . the production of equals has entailed a concomitant disenfranchisement of others," Shannon cautions against "judging early modern likeness from a post-liberal perspective" and instead takes a historicist perspective that attunes us to "specific opportunities" that homonormative ideals "afforded sixteenth-century subjects and selves."[33]

I want to propose that it is not an either-or. We can appreciate that friendship makes visible a valuable historical alternative to modern compulsory heteronormativity while also scrutinizing the exclusionary implications of its idealization of likeness and self-sovereignty.[34] According to classical theory, the equal relationship that is perfect friendship is available only to those who achieve the wisdom and virtue exhibited above all in self-mastery. Those who are "natural" slaves to their own fickle appetites are neither constant nor sincere enough to sustain friendship's bond. As Puar maintains with regard to contemporary homonationalism, the contrast between a universalized queerness and an oppressive heteronormativity "operates as an alibi for complicity with all sorts of other identity norms, such as nation, race, class, and gender, unwittingly lured onto ascent toward whiteness."[35] To address the collaboration of racial, sexual, and gendered norms, Puar rightly argues, we as queer critics must be attuned to our own implication in their work, however "painful," even shaming, such awareness is. For, Puar continues, "allowing for complicities signals not the failure of the radical, resistant, or oppositional potential of queerness, but can be an enabling acknowledgment."[36] Offering an analysis of the politics of attraction to likeness more generally, Holland observes that racial distinction may lurk in the erotic yearnings often treated as presocial, even preconscious:

> We often only have eyes for the spectacularity of racist practice, not its everyday machinations that we in turn have some culpability in. This desire to see ourselves as exempt from racist violence, no matter how small, is part of the same logic that attempts to excise life choices, erotic choices, from these larger systems. . . . For example, to say that I am not hurting anyone when I say that I prefer to sleep with one racialized being over another, is to tell a different story about the erotic—one where the autonomous becomes clouded by the sticky film of prejudice morphed into quotidian racism.[37]

If, as Holland argues, "there is no 'raceless' course of desire," then homo- as well as heteronormative mutuality and egalitarianism premised on likeness cannot escape a consciousness of "race" in the multiple significances of color and culture, embodiment and belief, that early modern discourses help make legible.[38] Holland puts in conversation Kwame Anthony Appiah's contrast between aesthetic preference and moral treatment and Emmanuel Levinas's question "Is the Desire for the Other (*Autrui*) an appetite or a generosity?"[39] This conjunction, she proposes, allows us to "surmise that what we need to do is turn an appetite—an 'aesthetic preference'—into an antiracist stance; a 'generosity' that has great potential" to "unmake the (queer) autonomy of desire—the thing that is shaped, like many other emotions, and circumscribed by the racist culture that we live in."[40] It is from this perspective that I want to examine classical philosophies of friendship, the racial dimensions of which, I argue, come to the fore in Shakespeare's sonnets to his male beloved. These poems remind us that, as Roland Greene maintains, in the interchange between Petrarchan poetry and colonial discourse, "there is no love that does not take account of race, class, and politics."[41]

In the utopian discourse of Greek *philia* and Latin *amicitia*, friendship was both model and ground for an ideally virtuous polity of equals. The relationship that Aristotle deems "complete," or perfect, friendship (the Greek is *teleia*) is one between "good people similar in virtue."[42] As known and "*reciprocated* goodwill," friendship displaces formal law or justice as the greatest political good: "if people are friends, they have no need of justice" (*NE* 8.2.3–4, 8.1.4; original emphasis). In reality, however, perfect friendship, as opposed to friendship based on utility or pleasure, is extremely rare for two reasons. First, there are not enough men (for Aristotle, perfect friends are always *male*: women are just not smart or virtuous enough) who are "both good without qualification and advantageous for each other" (*NE* 8.3.6).[43] Second, much like erotic passion, complete friendship "is like an excess" and therefore "directed at a single individual," not distributed among many (*NE* 8.6.2).[44] Friendship demands "equality and similarity, and above all the similarity of those who are similar in being virtuous" (*NE* 8.8.4) to the extent that "the excellent person is related to his friend in the same way as he is related to himself, since a friend is another himself" (*NE* 9.9.10; see also *NE* 9.4.5–6). The dynamic of friendship is one of aspirational narcissism. In friendship, one loves the friend not merely because he is like the self but, more importantly, because he manifests the virtue that "the excellent person" cultivates. The greatest virtue of all is continence, or self-mastery. The "self-lover" of perfect friendship "gratifies the most controlling part of himself, obeying it in everything" and differs from "the self-lover who is reproached . . . as much as the life guided by reason differs from the life guided by feelings, and as much as the desire for what is fine differs from the desire for what seems advantageous" (*NE* 9.8.6).

Aristotelian confidence in the reality of such a union between rational equals, as Schweitzer argues, gives way to the elegiac tradition initiated by Cicero's *De amicitia*.[45] In this dialogue, Laelius takes the occasion of the death of his friend Scipio Aemilianus to reiterate in personal terms the abstract Aristotelian principles of identity and equality in virtue that prompt the "man who both loves himself and uses his reason to seek out another whose soul he may so mingle with his own as almost to make one out of two."[46] Because the friend is as close to "another self [*alter idem*]" as one can find, Laelius's eulogy for Scipio is also an encomium to his own ability to choose reason and duty over passion and desire (*On Friendship* 21.80). Laelius's "bereavement," he confirms in the closing passage, is a "trial" that will prove that "it was [Scipio's] virtue that caused my love and that is not dead" (*On Friendship* 27.103, 102).

Cicero here takes to its logical conclusion Aristotle's maxim that because "reciprocal loving requires decision, and decision comes from a state," one must distinguish between "the wish for friendship," which "comes quickly," and friendship itself, which does not (*NE* 8.5.5, 8.3.8). For Cicero, in order to discover whether "the characters of friends are blameless," both must restrain their attraction to the other: "It is the part of wisdom to check the headlong rush of goodwill as we would that of a chariot, and thereby so manage friendship that we may in some degree put the dispositions of friends, as we do those of horses, to a preliminary test" (*On Friendship* 17.61, 63). But, as Aristotle's long meditation on the dissolution of friendships admits, this test cannot be passed as long as friendship is spoken in the imperfect grammar of the living present. The friend can always change, revealing his seeming love of virtue to have been a cover for appetite or advantage all along. Cicero's choice of fictional elegy rather than abstract treatise makes formally explicit what Aristotle leaves unsaid: the perfect (*teleia*) friend is the dead friend. Accordingly, as Jacques Derrida observes, classical friendship inhabits the temporality of the "future anterior" in which death is the culmination of friendship insofar as it confirms purity of virtue on both the friend's behalf and one's own.[47]

Michel de Montaigne's account of friendship preserves the view that it is a dyad based on equality of virtue, but he replaces the cautious prudence of classical philosophy with the ecstatic certainty of Christian mysticism or Neoplatonic ecstasy. Montaigne's *parfaict amitié* is complete from the start, initiated by a love at first sight that annihilates individual boundaries. In his elegy for his friend Étienne de La Boétie, Montaigne situates feeling as itself a form of secular faith:

> If you press me to say why I loved him, I feel that it cannot be expressed except by replying: "Because it was him, because it was me." Mediating this union there was, beyond all my reasoning, beyond all that I can say specifically about it, some inexplicable force of destiny [*je ne sçay quelle force inexplicable et fatale*]. . . . At our first meeting . . . we discovered ourselves to be so seized by each other, so known to each other and so bound together that from then on none was so close as each was to the other. . . . There is no one particular consideration—nor two nor three nor four nor a thousand of them—but rather some inexplicable quintessence of them all mixed up together [*je ne sçay quelle quint essence de tout ce meslange*] which, having captured my will brought it to plunge into his and lose itself and which, having captured his will, brought it to plunge and lose itself in mine with an equal hunger and emulation [*concurrence pareille*]. I say "lose itself" in very truth; we kept nothing back for ourselves: nothing was his or mine.[48]

Montaigne's repeated use of the inexpressibility topos, along with his lexicon of penetration, engulfment, and seizure, dissolves the lines between subject and object, activity and passivity, that make rational assessment and argument possible. Friendship for Montaigne is a relationship of faith that "*must* belong," as Derrida puts it, "to what is incalculable in decision." As a "break with calculable reliability and with the assurance of certainty—in truth, with knowledge," faith in the friend cannot be justified.[49] To say anything more specific than "because it was him, because it was me" is to move from the realm of faith to that of empirical proof.

Precisely because Montaigne's friendship involves no calculation of quality or benefit, it can be immediately consummated, reaching its perfection in its inception. Whereas Aristotle and Cicero recommend wariness, Montaigne's love for La Boétie is evinced in instantaneous trust. His representation of friendship has the structure of Pauline faith that Giorgio Agamben ascribes to love more generally. It "has no reason" but rather is "an experience of being beyond existence and essence, as much beyond subject as beyond predicate." In fact, "the moment when I realize that my beloved has such-and-such a quality, or such-and-such a defect, then I have irrevocably stepped out of love."[50] But this faith, paradoxically, requires that identity and equality give way to difference and hierarchy. The friend is not just another self, but a better, more trustworthy, one: Me 2.0. Montaigne writes of La Boétie that "all the arguments in the world have no power to dislodge me from the certainty which I have of the intentions and decisions of my friend. . . . I would have entrusted myself to him with greater assurance than to myself" (*Essays* 213). When Montaigne places more faith in La Boétie than in himself, he also attributes to La Boétie greater foresight and benevolence than he himself has. This introduces the question of Montaigne's own trustworthiness. Should La Boétie believe in him?

Montaigne's apotheosis of La Boétie makes visible a new dimension of Derrida's insight that the enemy is the "phantom friend" who equally permits the ideal of perfect (*teleia*) friendship and impedes that very telos.[51] The enemy haunts friendship not only as the structural contrary against which the friend defines himself. More troublingly, the enemy concealed within the friend may ambush us at any time, as may the stranger concealed within ourselves. This undecidability appears in the derivation of *hospes* (the friendly host) from *hostis* (the stranger who may prove grateful guest or hostile enemy) and the parallel formation of the English "friend" and "fiend" (the latter originally meant not devil but enemy).[52] The friend's superiority, however benevolent, may also give rise to enmity. Aristotle's paradoxical statement, "O my friends, there is no friend," Derrida argues, registers this inconceivable because self-contradictory essence of friendship: "On the one hand, in effect, *one must* want the greatest good for the friend—hence one wants him to become a god. But *one cannot* want that, one cannot want what would then be wanted."[53] As a relation of mutuality and equality, perfect friendship demands human imperfection, and therefore the possibility of disappointment. If the friend is better than the self, he may be a mentor or benefactor, but he is not a true friend. If the friend is *no better* than the self, he may turn out to be an enemy.

Shakespeare's sonnets, it has been widely noted, draw on the same classical ideal of friendship as Montaigne. But what is striking about the sonnets is the extent to which the relationship they depict diverges in nearly every way from the rational and steady bond they evoke, drawing out instead the enmity that may lurk within amity. Whereas Montaigne makes himself vulnerable because he believes he will not be hurt, Shakespeare's speaker, Will, cultivates what Tim Dean calls an "ethical disposition of vulnerability to the other" that acknowledges risk and difference.[54] To be sure, the sonnets' speaker claims that he and the youth have achieved the "total interfusion of . . . wills" in which "each gives himself so entirely to his friend that he has nothing left to share with another" portrayed by Montaigne (*Essays* 214, 215). Speaking in the present indicative, the grammar of facts, the sonnets' Will confidently describes his relationship with the youth in terms of mutual identification and fidelity: "my friend and I are one" (42.12); "'Tis thee, myself, that for myself I praise" (62.13); "As easy might I from myself depart, / As from my soul, which in thy breast doth lie" (109.3–4). But these confident assertions are belied by the sequence's frequent expressions of suspicion and admissions of mutual betrayal—in fact, the declaration that "my friend and I are one" is itself an ostentatiously facetious consolation for the youth's affair with the mistress: although "Both find each other, and I lose both twain," if the friend is another self then "she loves but me alone" (42.11, 14). Sonnet 42 offers but one example of a consistent collapse of the idealized homoerotic friendship that Will strives for with the youth and the promiscuous heteroerotic appetite that makes both men "slave to slavery" in their desire for the mistress (133.4). Read all together, the poems to the young man depict neither the rational virtue of Aristotle or Cicero nor the Neoplatonic meeting of the minds of Montaigne. Will's feelings for the man he calls "the master mistress of my passion" (20.2) instead resemble the more debased categories that Montaigne calls the "fickle, fluctuating, and variable" love men feel for women or the "license of the Greeks" that "required a great disparity of age and divergence of favours between the lovers" (209, 210).

In other words, whereas the identity of classical friendship acts as a prophylactic against disappointment and betrayal, the sonnets depict a series of entanglements in which all of the parties get hurt—and inflict wounds of their own. The sonnets, as Stephen Guy-Bray bluntly puts it, provide ample evidence that the young man, no less than the mistress, has done "bad things" with "bad people."[55] Will asserts that the young man does "most common grow" (69.14), but urges him to "No more be grieved at that which thou hast done" (35.1) and promises that if he at least appears repentant, the "tears of pearl that thy love sheds" will "ransom all ill deeds" (34.14). Likewise, Will himself confesses that "I have frequent been with unknown minds" and "I have hoisted sail to all the winds" (117.5, 7) and laments "What potions have I drunk of siren tears" and "What wretched errors hath my heart committed" (119.1, 5). He excuses his infidelity on the grounds that it serves "to prove / The constancy and virtue of your love" (117.13–14) by inflicting pain: "if you were by my unkindness shaken, / As I by yours, y'have passed a hell of time" (120.5–6). Such reciprocal betrayal, paradoxically, restores equality and mutual possession through an economy of forgiveness in which "your trespass now becomes a fee; / Mine ransoms yours, and yours must ransom me" (120.13–14).

If in classical friendship the enemy is the phantom of the other, in Shakespeare's sonnets the slave is the phantom of the self. Sonnets 57 and 58 explore the impurity of devotion through the ambiguously racialized metaphor of slavery. Certainly, the trope of erotic enslavement was well-worn by Shakespeare's time, and it appears not only here but in subsequent depictions of Will's male beloved as "slave to slavery" in his relation to the mistress and himself as the mistress's "proud heart's slave and vassal wretch" (133.4, 141.12). But to emphasize the metaphoricity, and therefore the political neutrality, of this convention at the expense of its literal referent is itself a racialized argument. It assumes that Shakespeare's own whiteness removes him from the reality of the history of slavery, thereby perpetuating what David Nirenberg has described as the "remarkable consensus that the earlier vocabularies of difference are innocent of race."[56] But, as I have been arguing, the ambiguity of race should not be conflated with its absence. In early modernity, the naturalization of forced servitude as black, one initiated by the Portuguese slave trade and gradually adopted by Spain and England, intersected with a long record of white and Asiatic slavery from both classical antiquity and the medieval and early modern Ottoman practice of using conquered persons as forced servants and concubines.[57] John M. Archer compellingly argues that while they do not explicitly mention "race" in the sense of skin color, Shakespeare's Sonnets 57 and 58 cannot be separated from a long history of bondage whose racial referent was rapidly constricting in his time.[58] The sixteenth-century Valladolid debates over the natural slavery, indeed humanity, of Indigenous Americans and the increase in the European trade of West Africans as forced labor were known in Shakespeare's England, where slaves were increasingly depicted as "black"—that catch-all term for dark skin—in visual and literary representation.[59]

Precisely because the racial meaning of slavery was unstable, as was its distinction from other forms of servitude, it provides Shakespeare a complex and troubling vehicle for contemplating the limits of friendship as a relation based on identification and self-mastery. Sonnets 57 and 58 rigorously contest an ideal of homonormative friendship as a uniquely virtuous and respectable relation between a male pair "by nature free" of irrational and self-destructive appetite. Instead, these poems depict monogamous devotion as a struggle of wills vying for domination:

57.
Being your slave, what should I do but tend
Upon the hours and times of your desire?
I have no precious time at all to spend,
Nor services to do till you require.
Nor dare I chide the world without end hour
Whilst I, my sovereign, watch the clock for you,
Nor think the bitterness of absence sour,
When you have bid your servant once adieu.
Nor dare I question with my jealous thought
Where you may be, or your affairs suppose,
But like a sad slave stay and think of nought
Save where you are how happy you make those.
   So true a fool is love, that in your will,
   Though you do anything, he thinks no ill. (1–14)

58.
That god forbid, that made me first your slave,
I should in thought control your times of pleasure,
Or at your hand th'account of hours to crave,
Being your vassal bound to stay your leisure.
O let me suffer, being at your beck,
Th'imprisoned absence of your liberty—

> And patience tame to suff'rance bide each check,
> Without accusing you of injury.
> Be where you list, your charter is so strong,
> That you yourself may privilege your time
> To what you will; to you it doth belong
> Yourself to pardon of self-doing crime.
>> I am to wait, though waiting be so hell,
>> Not blame your pleasure, be it ill or well. (1–14)

Both sonnets begin with Will's self-identification as "slave," only to probe the meaning of that term. Itself derived from the Middle Latin *sclavus*— "identical," the *OED* tells us, "with the racial name *Sclavus*," or Slav—the modern slave differs from the classical *servus* (either servant or slave) in having been unequivocally stripped of any right to free will. Early justifications for the destruction and enslavement of West Africans and Indigenous Americans, as I have noted, often cited the Aristotelian concept that literal enslavement was the proper condition of those bound to irrational appetites. Will's shifting identifications across the two poems as "slave," "servant," "slave," "fool," "slave," and "vassal" strains synonymy. Different forms and degrees of servitude—the involuntary bondage and compulsory labor of the slave, the contractual and remunerated work of the servant, the feudal allegiance of the vassal—are not interchangeable as metaphors. This failed substitution formally probes the meaning and limits of a conventional idiom that compares commitment to bondage. What can or should one expect in return for devotion? At what point does generous love become humiliating enslavement? Is the distinction a matter of fact or faith? Does pleasure in the thought of enslavement not depend on an actual position of freedom? Does the fantasy of such pleasure not minimize the violence and dehumanization of slavery?

These two sonnets' dissection of Will's thoughts registers the resistance that inevitably accompanies devotion and without which submission cannot be felt as voluntary. The struggle to be possessed by heartfelt love appears in Sonnet 57's final couplet: "So true a fool is love, that in your will, / Though you do anything, he thinks no ill." The 1609 Quarto prints "in your Will," making typographically explicit the lines' interpretive crux. Are "your will" and "your Will" synonymous? Is this allegory or autobiography? We cannot tell, and neither can the speaker. This poem, as well as the one that follows, dramatizes the struggle to "think no ill" through its emphasis on the prohibition of instinctual response to the beloved's absence: "Nor dare I chide," "Nor think," "Nor dare I question with my jealous thought," "think of nought," "That god forbid, . . . / I should in thought control your times of pleasure," "without accusing you of injury," "I am to wait . . . / Not blame your pleasure." This series of negations registers just the discrepancy between the friend and Will that Sonnet 57's final couplet obscures. Whereas Masten treats "the idea of friendship as material ingestion and incorporation" as a laudable "attempt to imagine mutual and unhierarchized same-sex intercourse," Derrida, Michel de Certeau, and Carla Freccero have argued that friendship's ideal of fusion as the ultimate expression of likeness and equality rests on a logic of sacrificial anthropophagy.[60] The spiritual metabolism that perfects Montaigne's friendship with La Boétie manifests itself in Shakespeare's sonnets as the wish to abolish difference through assimilation, a wish thwarted by the recalcitrant and opaque will of self as well as other.

The divergence of wills in these poems is manifested in the quotidian activity of waiting in the senses of both anticipation and service. Waiting *for* the youth to affirm desire by coming back shades into waiting *on* him (a resonance retained in the modern vernacular interchangeability of "waiter" and "server"). Waiting prioritizes the other's time over one's own, affirming through suspension of activity that one has nothing better to do, "no precious time at all to spend." In Roland Barthes's account, such patience is the ultimate evidence of love:

> "Am I in love?—Yes, since I'm waiting." The other never waits. Sometimes I want to play the part of the one who doesn't wait; I try to busy myself elsewhere, to arrive late; but I always lose at this game: whatever I do, I find myself there, with nothing to do, punctual, even ahead of time. The lover's fatal identity is precisely: *I am the one who waits.*[61]

The discrepancy between the eager, (im)patient lover and the dilatory beloved—the roles of waiting and being waited on—exposes a difference in affection. To love is also to choose the "hours and times" of the "sovereign" beloved's desire or pleasure over one's own. This choice concedes hierarchy: "*To make someone wait*: the constant prerogative of power."[62]

The banal experience of waiting for someone, as we all know, can become an excruciating exercise in the tolerance of vulnerability and unpredictability. Because it arouses anxiety and resentment, waiting may threaten the very love it should demonstrate, a risk that Phillips neatly summarizes in the observation that "if somebody you are longing to see makes you wait too long for them, it is extremely difficult to appreciate them when they finally arrive; and to recuperate your desire for them."[63] In order to preserve the spell of love, one must not only wait but must also learn not to mind waiting. This preserves the belief that both parties want each other at the same time and in the same way, that both offer "free" love and not grudging servitude. To "control" the beloved's "times of pleasure" or "crave" an "account" of just what took so long is to distrust the other's sincere interest in one's own happiness. To "think of nought / Save where you are and how happy you make those" (that is, those *other people whom you are with instead of me*) is to struggle to accept that the beloved enjoys the absence that torments the lover. At the same time, to offer absolute freedom is as much a threat as a gift, and it (again) requires precisely the actual freedom denied by the metaphor of enslavement. The concession that the beloved may "Be where you list" and "you yourself may privilege your time / To what you will"—in other words, *do what you want*—has as its unspoken counterpart *and so will I*.

Imagining himself as having lost self-determination and been "made your slave" by a "god"—erotic subjection, as I discuss in the next section, could be equally attributed to Cupid or Christ—Will can only obey his own demonic attachment: "I am to wait, though waiting be so hell / Not blame your pleasure, be it ill or well." When waiting becomes "hell," it also becomes an *act* in the Pauline sense of compelled service and therefore, as Luther would stress, the fearful performance of a hypocrite that replaces rather than reflects sincere devotion. This involuntary servitude, which, as I discussed in this book's introduction, Luther likened to "Babylonian Captivity," is at odds with the "Freedom of the Christian" who waits with wholehearted joy. The homonormativity of friendship falls short of the identity and equality ideally attributed to it. Insofar as "the marriage of true minds" continues to signify a racialized integrity and respectability that justify political and social privilege, to challenge this ideal is to make way for the imagination of forms of relationality premised on disproportionate and changing desires rather than mutual vows—friendship as a way of life beyond the racially pure dyad of the homonormative as well as the heteronormative couple.

Sweet Little Lies

As I have been arguing, the ethics of promiscuity that finds expression in secular love lyrics may be traced to a Pauline theology in which the delusion of sovereign subjectivity must be relinquished. Whereas the Aristotelian theory of friendship derives from the conviction that those who "are by nature free" have achieved the "rule of the soul over the body," the Pauline tradition, as I discussed in chapter 1, insists that the mind and soul are no less subject to fleshly corruption than the body. Shakespeare's sonnets accentuate such failure of self-mastery in the speaker's tongue-in-cheek self-appellation as "Will." As many critics have noticed, "will" in early modern English could signify intention, purpose, wish, drive, lust, and both male and female sexual organs, an overdetermination announced most flamboyantly in Sonnets 135 and 136, between which the word appears a total of twenty-one times.[64] Lisa Freinkel points out that the relentless capitalization of "Will" in the only edition of the full sequence from Shakespeare's lifetime, the 1609 Quarto, underscores a Lutheran conviction that any analogy or similitude between divine and human love is actually a catachrestic expression that registered all that humanity is *not*.[65] The poetic and typographical assertions that the speaker's "name is Will" (136.14) locate the sequence's threesome within a Christian tradition of fellowship patterned on God's love for human creatures who can never deserve it.[66] Humility and forgiveness in this structure replace virtue and integrity as the foundation of love. But, as the sonnets demonstrate, these Christian qualities are difficult to cultivate, requiring no less self-control than the classical rationality they replace. In the sonnets' presecular view, Will as human creature can neither love with the freedom and generosity of God nor discern whether he is motivated by humble love, emulous pride, or grudging compliance.

The theological structure of love, as I argued in chapter 1, helps us to understand the contradictions and perversities of secular experience, particularly insofar as Pauline and Augustinian theology assumes the ideal model of love, God's, to be impossible for human creatures.

Faith must waver, in this view, in order to rescue humanity from its own soul-killing delusions of innocence and autonomy. This conviction only intensifies in Protestant theology. When Luther and Calvin seek to explain why election is a cause for gratitude rather than resentment, they emphasize that we are not loved because of what we do or who we are. The whole point of Pauline Christianity—and this is true of Augustinian Catholicism as well as the Protestantism of Luther and Calvin—is that we do not *deserve* to be loved by anyone, including and especially God. Moments in which obedience is experienced as imposition rather than pleasure function to remind the human creature that love is a gift rather than an entitlement. The love we feel and the love we attract, whether spiritual or secular, is inexplicable, and to that extent it is an object of prayer and seduction as well as a cause of both gratitude and anger. In the secularized and racialized politics of eroticism that I have been tracing, the ability to love in the right way—that is, monogamously—is a sign of election understood as sincere and unfeigned goodness. Such sincerity, as Ann Pellegrini has argued, is an indication of authentic political and cultural belonging because it cannot be externally compelled.[67] Understood as a secular version of grace, true love reconfigures meanings of freedom and bondage so that the sincere aspiration to affective monogamy, rather than mere technical fidelity, becomes a racialized sign of integrity and credibility. At the same time, the self-assured righteousness that characterizes much modern white evangelical affect is, for Luther and Calvin, a sign of reprobation.

Luther's "Preface to the Epistle of St. Paul to the Romans," which seeks to explain why election is a cause for joy rather than resentment, emphasizes the inexplicability not only of God's love for us, but also of ours for him. Here as elsewhere, Luther is at pains to define obedience in affective terms. In his treatment of the human failure of autonomy, Luther's insight that "we act heteronomously rather than as self-willed, autonomous creatures" is, as Freinkel puts it, "at once a psychological and a philosophical one."[68] Luther deems the Letter to the Romans "the most important document [*das rechte Haupstück,* "the true centerpiece"] in the New Testament, the gospel in its purest expression," for it condenses Pauline teachings on faith, sin, grace, and election into a single book.[69] Because each encounter offers a fresh appreciation of the miracle of divine love, this tract "can never be read too often, or studied too much"

("Preface" 19/3). It is a commonplace to understand Protestant theology as opposing faith to works. But Luther, and Calvin after him, in fact makes the two inseparable by locating righteousness not in what we do but in how we *feel* about what we do. What Romans teaches, according to Luther, is that sin includes not just doing bad things but also doing good things for the wrong reason. According to Luther, the

> law must be fulfilled in your very heart [*Herzens Grund*], and cannot be obeyed if you merely perform certain acts. Its penalties do indeed apply to certain acts done apart from our inmost convictions [*Herzens Grund*], such as hypocrisy and lying. Psalm [116] declares that all men are liars, because no one keeps God's law from his heart [*Herzens Grund*]; nor can he do so; for to be averse to goodness and prone to evil are traits found in all men [*jedermann findet bei sich selbst Unlust zum Guten and Lust zum Bösen*]. If we do not choose goodness freely, we do not keep God's law from the heart [*Herzens Grund*]. ("Preface" 20/3–4)

Citing Psalm 116 ("I said in my fear, All men are liars"), which Paul also alludes to in Romans 3 ("let God be true, and every man a liar, as it is written"), Luther explores an insight that, as we have seen, is developed at length in Augustine's *Confessions* and, in secular terms, in Petrarch's love lyrics: we are helpless to tell the truth about our own motives and feelings because we may ourselves mistake or misinterpret them (GB Ps. 116:11; Rom. 3:4). Luther takes this insight to its logical conclusion, insisting that in our innermost hearts we are all potentially and intermittently insincere and therefore sinful. (The repetition of *Herzens Grund* in the German makes this insistence more prominent than the variable phrasing of the English.) As Luther explains,

> Sin, in this light, means something more than the external works done by our bodily action [*äusserliche Werk des Leibes*]. It means all the circumstances that act together and excite or incite us to what is done; in particular, the impulses operating in the depths of our hearts [*des Herzens Grund mit allen Kräften*]. . . . Even where nothing is done outwardly, a man may still fall into complete destruction of body and soul. In particular, the Bible penetrates into our hearts, and looks at the root and the very source of all sin, i.e., unbelief in the depth of our heart. ("Preface" 22/6)

Whenever we obey the law "unwillingly and under compulsion [*mit Unlust und Zwang*]" rather than "from free choice and out of love for the law [*freie Lust und Liebe zum Gesetz*]," the law shows our actions to be only lies, hypocritical performances that substitute external compliance for internal desire ("Preface" 20/4). God can penetrate to psychic depths that we cannot; he knows us better than we know ourselves. We can fool ourselves and others, but not him.

The law requires something impossible: our love for what it makes us do. It is directed, in other words, at hearts and minds, not just bodies. As Calvin explains, when God commands particular behavior, "he requires you to apply the same rule in regulating your mind. It were ridiculous, that he, who sees the thoughts of the heart, and has special regard to them, should train the body only to rectitude."[70] True obedience stems from heartfelt desire, not external compulsion. And because the law exacts a feeling over which we have no control, it makes us aware through affective rather than rational means of our sinfulness. Paul explains the dynamic thus: "What shall we say then? Is the Law sin? God forbid. Nay, I knew not sin, but by the Law, for I had not known lust, except the Law had said, Thou shalt not lust" (GB, Rom. 7:7). "Lust" here is not just sexual desire, but willfulness more generally. The Vulgate's "Sed peccatum non cognovi, nisi per legem: nam concupiscentiam nesciebam, nisi lex dicerte: Non concupisces" gives both the nominal and verbal forms of concupiscence as a more general longing or striving. The law shows us to be liars not only when we bear false witness to others, but, more profoundly, because we lie to *ourselves* when we imagine we are free from desire for things of the flesh, whether sex, wealth, power, or praise.

Because they address feeling rather than action, the final two commandments (against lying and coveting) are for the Protestant Reformers essential to producing the awareness of failure that makes possible those precious moments of sincere love and gratitude in which the human will is briefly aligned with God's. As Luther puts it in *The Freedom of a Christian*:

> The commandments show us what we ought to do but do not give us the power to do it. They are intended to teach man to know himself, that through them he may recognize his inability to do good and may despair of his own ability. . . . For example, the commandment, "you shall not

covet" [Exod. 20:17] is a command which proves us all to be sinners, for no one can avoid coveting no matter how much he may struggle against it. Therefore, in order not to covet and to fulfill the commandment, a man is compelled to despair of himself, to seek the help which he does not find in himself elsewhere and from someone else.[71]

We are all proven sinners, Calvin explains, because desire for that which we do not already possess may exist without "deliberation and assent, when the mind is only stimulated and tickled [titillatur] by vain and perverse objects" (Institutes 2.8.49). It is only in being told that we are not allowed to feel this way that we come to see our feelings as violations of the law that "no thought be permitted to insinuate itself into our minds, and inflame them with a noxious concupiscence tending to our neighbor's loss" (Institutes 2.8.49). The command that we love our neighbor is in essence a demand that we love like God, without regard to others' desert or our own reward. This heartfelt generosity and altruism are at odds with coveting or concupiscence. The commandments against lying and covetousness make us aware of our inability to love that which is unlovable or that which can offer us nothing in return.[72]

Lutheran and Calvinist soteriology can be summed up in the maxim that God requires us to love as he does, and the law reveals that we can't. The ninth and tenth commandments (against lying and coveting), in particular, reveal human love to be self-serving rather than altruistic, and to that degree suffused with aggression. This theological insight, as Jacques Lacan demonstrates, also helps us understand the structure of secular desire. For Lacan, as for Luther and Calvin, the Pauline maxim that "I knew not sin, but by the Law" designates the unspeakable hostility at the center of jouissance, the Thing that gestures toward "whatever is open, lacking, or gaping at the center of our desire" (84).[73] Lacan is quite explicit: "With one small change, namely, 'Thing' for 'sin,' [Chose à la place de péché] this is the speech of Saint Paul on the subject of the relations between the law and sin in the Epistle to the Romans, Chapter 7, paragraph 7."[74] Humanity defends itself against this unbearable dimension of its will by denying the bad feelings that permeate love, or, as Lacan puts it, "lying about evil [la mal]."[75] The biblical prohibition against lying, Lacan maintains, "is related to what presented itself to us as that essential relationship of man to the Thing, insofar as it is commanded by the pleasure principle, namely, the lie that we have to deal with every day in our unconscious."[76] This command "included the possibility of the lie as the most fundamental desire," which is to say that we desire misrecognition of our own erotic impulses and motives. The lie we tell ourselves is that we want what is good for us and for others.[77]

As Lacan interprets it, the invaluable insight of Pauline theology is that our desire is not good or redemptive. If this reading resonates strikingly with Leo Bersani's critique of the *"redemptive reinvention of sex"* that is because, as I have been arguing, Christian theology has profoundly shaped Western secular descriptions of love and sexuality.[78] Religious writing is valuable to psychoanalysis, Lacan argues, because it takes seriously impulses unavailable to objective observation:

> Whether from personal conviction or in the name of a methodological point of view, the so-called scientific point of view . . . there is a paradox involved in practically excluding from the debate and from analysis things, terms, and doctrines that have been articulated in the field of faith, on the pretext that they belong [*appartiennent*] to a domain that is reserved for believers. . . . We analysts, who claim to go beyond certain conceptions of prepsychology relative to the phenomena of our own field or who approach human realities without prejudice, do not have to believe in these religious truths in any way [*Pour nous analystes . . . il n'y a nul besoin de donner à ces vérités religieuses une adhésion*], given that such belief may extend as far as what is called faith, in order to be interested in what is articulated in its own terms in religious experience—in the terms of the conflict between freedom and grace, for example.[79]

One can believe in the structure of religious devotion without having faith that its objects are real or its content true. To address "human realities" is to admit the ambivalence and irrationality that theology assiduously locates at the core of desire, the amoral core, as it were, of Christianity. "Under these conditions," Lacan comments, "it is hardly surprising that everyone is sick [*malade*], that civilization has its discontents [*qu'il y ait malaise dans la civilization*]."[80]

The command that Freud found so repellant, to love one's neighbor as oneself, as the "fulfilling of the law" (GB, Rom. 13.10), sums up the perversity of a rule that is designed not to be followed but to be broken.[81] What Freud calls the "cultural" (or civilizational) super-ego [*Kultur-Über-Ich*] gets Pauline theology exactly wrong when it "issues a command and does not ask whether it is possible for people to obey it. On the contrary, it assumes that a man's ego is psychologically capable of anything that is required of it, that his ego has unlimited mastery over his id."[82] In Luther's and Calvin's reading (as in Lacan's), the biblical command presents not an obstacle but an incitement to aggression. Assuming its own violation, the command produces knowledge of the hostility it prohibits, a hostility that, as Freud also recognized, is the other side of covetousness: judging others by ourselves, we learn that the stranger "has more claim to my hostility [*Feindseligkeit*] and even my hatred," for "if it will do him any good [*Nutzen bringt*] he has no hesitation in injuring me, nor does he ask himself whether the amount of advantage [*Nutzen*] he gains bears any proportion to the extent of the harm he does to me."[83] In this light, the command to love the neighbor "at bottom . . . is the same thing" as that to love the enemy.[84] To love our neighbors as ourselves is to love similarly unworthy creatures in full awareness of a mutual determination to seek advantage, a disposition directly at odds with the humility that Paul enjoins. The intolerable commandment to love "can cause as much unhappiness as aggressiveness itself" because it punctures the fiction that love is entirely, to again evoke Bersani, pastoral, innocent, or redemptive.[85]

As these Protestant and psychoanalytic readings of Romans demonstrate, Paul's account of subjectivity is at odds with the definition of faith as something that one can confidently or conclusively achieve. It is also distinct from the Marxist view of faith as pure ideology, neatly captured in Althusser's summary of Pascal: "Kneel down, move your lips in prayer, and you will believe."[86] For Paul and Augustine, as for Luther, Calvin, and Lacan, we never know for certain *what* we really believe or why we really pray. Luther observes that the command to love without aggression, resentment, or entitlement effectively arouses the very hatred it appears to prohibit: "A man only hates the law [*feinden wird*] the more, the more it demands what he cannot perform" ("Preface" 21/4). This hatred, however, is salutary because, as Calvin puts it, "we cannot aspire to [God] in earnest until we have begun to be displeased with ourselves. For what man is not disposed to rest in himself [*in se requiescat*]? Who, in fact, does not thus rest, so long as he is unknown to himself; that is, so long as he is contented with his own endowments, and unconscious and unmindful of his misery?" (*Institutes* 1.1.1). Ugly feelings of hatred and misery offer warning signs that love, and therefore faith, has failed. They thereby compel the distraught believer, to recall Luther, "to seek the help which he does not find in himself elsewhere and from someone else." It is only after confronting our own imperfection that we are prepared to be grateful for the unmerited election that otherwise would seem random and unfair.

The good news is that God shows mercy to those who love him, but there is a catch: loving God is not something anyone can choose or will. Since the law is spiritual, Luther explains,

> No one keeps it, unless everything you do springs from your inmost heart. Such a heart is given us only by God's spirit, and this spirit makes us equal to the demands of the law. Thus we gain a genuine desire for the law, and then everything is done with willing hearts [*freiem Herzen*], and not in fear, or under compulsion. . . . But this joy, this unconstrained love [*Solche Lust freier Leib*], is put into our hearts by the Holy Spirit. ("Preface" 21/5)

In other words, God gives us the ability to love him because he loves us. Election is not just about God's inscrutable preferences, which, Luther and Calvin remind us, have nothing to do with merit of our own and therefore seem arbitrary, unjust, even abusive. Election is also the name for the source of our own unfathomable feelings. Faith is inseparable from the pangs of love that can come out of nowhere and disappear just as inexplicably. "No one," Luther assures us, "can give faith to himself, nor free himself from unbelief" ("Preface" 25). The Christian God, in this light, sounds a lot like the pagan Cupid, an affinity registered in Renaissance art and allegory, which often treated the love between Cupid and Psyche as an allegory for that between Christ and the human soul.[87] Once given the divine gift of love, we gain "freedom from sin and the law" (29) and no longer hate the God who imposes it. We want what God wants. Obedience and freedom, law and desire, are indistinguishable. Freedom means "taking pleasure simply in doing good [*Gut zu tun mit Lust*]"—obeying and liking it ("Preface" 30/14). As Luther explains in *The Freedom of a Christian*, "Love by its very nature is ready to serve and be subject to him who is loved."[88]

As Luther and Calvin are well aware, this freedom is also described as a form of ethnic belonging in Paul's Letter to the Galatians. Paul's assurance that "there is neither Jew nor Grecian, there is neither bond nor free, there is neither male nor female; for ye are all one in Christ Jesus" is followed by a qualifier that ties this transcendence of the flesh *to* the flesh: "And if *ye be* Christ's, then are ye Abraham's seed, and heirs by promise" (GB, Gal. 3:28–29; emphasis in original). In clinging to the bondage of the law rather than the freedom of love, the observant Jew places himself outside what Paul will call the "household of faith" a few chapters later (GB, Gal. 6:10)—a metaphor teased out in Paul's long discussion contrasting the descendants of Hagar with those of Sarah: "He which was of the servant, was born after the flesh, and he which was of the free woman, *was born* by promise" (GB, Gal. 4:23; emphasis in original). To choose the law over grace, action over faith, is to reject this heritage and thereby to remove oneself from the household, the ethnos, of Abraham's freeborn son Isaac. As I noted in this book's introduction, numerous scholars have examined how this seeming inclusiveness positions the Jew as the recalcitrant subject who does not want to be included. As Freud puts it, "When once the Apostle Paul had posited universal love between men as the foundation of his Christian community, extreme intolerance on the part of Christendom toward those who remained outside [*die drausen Verbliebenen*] it became the inevitable consequence."[89] As Medovoi and Balibar have noted, such intolerance has expanded to include all who refuse assimilation into a secular version of Christian culture summed up in an ideal of whiteness. In the Crusades as in modern Islamophobic discourse, Derrida observes, the Muslim shares the role of the self-excluding other who is a danger not as a political enemy but as "an enemy of *the* political—more precisely, a being radically alien to the political as such."[90]

The Pauline Letters thus depict bondage and freedom as heritable biopolitical attributes—Jerome's Vulgate describes Hagar as an *ancilla*, which, like *servus* could mean either slave or servant, an ambiguity registered in the tensions between the Geneva Bible's translation as "servant" and the Douay-Reims's and King James's translations as "bondwoman."

This is consistent with the Septuagint Greek text of Genesis—the version likely read by New Testament authors—where Hagar is called a *paidiskê*, a diminutive of *pais*, meaning both "young girl, maiden, damsel" and "a young female slave, a courtesan."[91] For Luther, faith as an ethnic attribute becomes literalized in the figure of the Jew who does not so much do the wrong thing as feel the wrong way, obeying involuntarily: "Such were the Jews, and such too are all hypocrites, for they live without joy and love. In their hearts they hate the divine law and, as is the way with all hypocrites, they habitually condemn others. They regard themselves as spotless, although they are full of envy, hatred, pride, and all kinds of impurity [*Unflats*, "filth," but also "vituperation"]" ("Preface" 26). The Jews are like everyone in that they hate the divine law and fail to obey it wholeheartedly, but they are distinct from true believers in that they "regard themselves as spotless." They are hypocrites—the Greek word ὑποκριτής originally meant "actor"—because when they "appear to be godly" even as they "commit secret sins," they perform devotion they do not feel. As Ania Loomba, Kim Hall, Sujata Iyengar, Dennis Britton, and Imtiaz Habib (among others) have shown, such suspicion was directed not only at Jews, but also at Muslims and, in Protestant writing, at Catholics. In England, adherents of these three religions were frequently conflated as irredeemably black on the inside as well as the outside. Like the category of "Moor," the designation of "black" could include persons of Middle Eastern, South Asian, North African, sub-Saharan African, Indigenous American, and sometimes Iberian and Irish origin or descent.[92] This collapse of racialized and religious others to Christianity, and especially Protestantism, made blackness a property of the soul that manifested itself on the skin, whether through its color, cosmetics, or texture (in premodern writing, soft skin, along with dark skin, is sometimes treated as a racialized characteristic).[93] Religious and racial distinction, dogma- and color-line racism, culture and biology, were intertwined in shifting and unpredictable ways that continue to shape erotic aspirations and sexual hierarchies.

Yet by Luther's own logic, the distinction between humble and sincere Christians and proud and hypocritical religious and racial others can easily break down, for one can never be secure in one's own faith. As Claire McEachern deftly explains, "The hallmark of a sincere faith is the fear that one might not be sincere."[94] The line of dogma in early modern thought is as uncertain as that of color. Luther's warning not to be like observant Jews—not to be confident of one's own rectitude—needs to be given only because Christians *are already* like this. The hypocrisy and slavishness that Luther attributes to Jews must, by his own logic, be recognized as the truth of the Christian self as well. What distinguishes the elect (and Luther excludes Catholics, along with Jews, Muslims, and pagans from this category) is awareness and confession of infidelity and unworthiness. The difference between the redeemable and unredeemable sinner is the *desire*, so assiduously traced in Augustine's *Confessions*, not to be loved but to love, a second order desire to desire that is perpetuated through its own failure. What Luther called the freedom of a Christian is the opposite of the sovereign self of classical *askesis*. The freedom of a Christian is freedom from (or loss of) the self that Paul announces when he introduces himself as *Paulus, servus Jesus Christi*, "servant/slave of Christ" (Rom. 1:1). To love properly is to aspire to the selfless and monogamous desire for God enjoined in the first commandment prohibiting idolatry, which insists that we have no competing affections. But to aspire to the love of God (in both the objective and subjective senses of that double genitive) is also to recognize that we will never love him enough or in the right way, for we will never wholeheartedly want what God commands, nor will we experience duty as choice.

Lascivious Grace

It is customary to read Shakespeare's sonnets as striving for exactly the distinction between faithful self and treacherous other that Luther's treatment of Paul at once invokes and undercuts. The conventional division of the Sonnets into 126 sonnets to the youth followed by 28 to the mistress formally registers a narrative that, in Joel Fineman's influential formulation, constitutes nothing less than the invention of a new poetic subjectivity—"the poetics of heterosexuality" in the sense of difference—whereby the speaker's own ambivalence, duplicity, and opacity to himself appears in a shift in object of address.[95] The sonnets, Fineman argues, feature a speaking subject who wants what he does not admire, as rational and assured praise for a beautiful and virtuous object (the "fair" youth) is replaced by expressions of compulsive yearning for one who is debauched and repulsive (the "foul" mistress). This view has not gone uncontested, either as poetic history or as a reading of the sequence. Noting that many of the poems have no gendered pronouns or other information to identify the addressee, and that the order of the sonnets may not have been authorized by Shakespeare, several scholars have argued that, as Heather Dubrow puts it, the sonnets not only explore rather than depart from the subjective dilemmas of Petrarchism but also "repeatedly problematize the narrative impulse that the conventional wisdom so unproblematically assigns to them."[96] Accordingly, poems usually read in reference to the youth may be to the mistress and vice-versa, with the result that praise and blame, admiration and disgust, may be more evenly distributed—and the sequence may be neither as homoerotic nor as misogynist as it is often deemed. By contrast, Valerie Traub argues that "the formal operation of the sequence" is "relevant to the ongoing manufacture of gender and desire" insofar as most readers first encounter the sonnets as a sequence that, read from start to finish, begins with an ideal of purity that is gradually degraded.[97] Distinctions persist due to the temporal nature of reading itself, even if they cannot be verified by objective formal, material, or historical evidence.

Rather than stake my claim on a certainty about the order or addressees of the sonnets, I propose along with a number of previous critics that even if we focus only on those poems in which the addressee is specified, we have ample evidence that the speaker's relationship with the youth is as compromised and faithless as that with the mistress.[98] But compromise is not necessarily a bad thing; an acceptance of impurity may lead to a more ethical relation with others than a demand for love that is "fair, kind, and true" (105.9, 10, 13). In relinquishing the classical ideal of self-sameness and mastery in favor of the Pauline division and distraction that equally influenced Petrarch, Augustine, Luther, and Calvin, Shakespeare also struggles against the assumption that desire finds its *telos*, or perfection, in monogamous coupledom, whether in the form of classical friendship or companionate marriage. In what is often regarded as the first subsequence of the sonnets, focused on the youth, the effort to renounce the desire for progress appears explicitly in the speaker's promise to "forgive" and "excuse," rather than deny or prohibit, the affair between youth and mistress (40.9, 42.5). In the second part, conventionally understood as addressing the mistress, Will concedes the similarity of his two loves: "thou art covetous, and he is kind" (134.6). Once we read the sequence—in whatever order—through a framework that cultivates not monogamous purity but a secular approximation of what Will calls "Lascivious grace," the gendered, sexual, and racial distinctions it maps appear as conspicuously artificial as they are fragile (40.13).

The black mistress's oft-discussed promiscuity takes on new significance when set within the theological tradition that, I have been arguing, in fact structures the secular love given voice in Petrarchan lyric, in which it is impossible to tell what is going on in one's own heart, much less beneath the surface of another's skin. Grace, as both divine forgiveness and secular love, is in this tradition *always* "lascivious"— wanton, gratuitous, injudicious, promiscuous—precisely because it is undeserved and indiscriminate. It is in Sonnets 127–154, when the mistress's conjoined blackness and promiscuity become a consistent topic of the sequence, that we witness both the promise and the difficulty of a secular attempt to replicate "lascivious grace." In Kathryn Schwarz's elegant phrase, these last twenty-eight poems "disclose the improbable, unworkable qualities of taxonomic segregation."[99] Understood in terms of modern evangelical family values—and, frankly, in terms of the social structures that Luther and Calvin would have endorsed—this shift would appear to be the farthest thing from Christianity. But my focus is on the logical end, rather than the historical use, of a theology in which the recognition of human impurity makes necessary the promiscuous structure of Christian fellowship and treats the classical dyad as a distracting worldly lure. As Will Stockton has meticulously demonstrated, the ultimate ideal of Christianity may well be group marriage, a fellowship of all believers incorporated into the body of Christ. This plural union, Stockton argues, appears in the slippage between the command to love one's neighbor as oneself and that to love one's wife as one's own flesh, so that communal and private bonds become interchangeable.[100] Calvin sets forth a vision of communal confession that is also one of communal fellowship, arguing that "we are to deposit our infirmities into the breasts of each other, with the view of receiving mutual counsel, sympathy, and comfort; and secondly, That mutually conscious of the infirmities of our brethren we are to pray to the Lord for them" (*Institutes* 3.4.6). This relationship of shared shame, as Huston Diehl has argued, fosters a sense of community premised not on judgment but on forgive-

ness for the inevitable failings and injuries of others, the same forgiveness we would wish for ourselves.[101]

Shakespeare's sonnets strive in the final twenty-eight poems for such
mutual compassion, expressed in the form of unmerited love—the only
form that human love can take. This position is voiced in the closing
couplet of Sonnet 150, in which merit and grace dissolve into one another: "If thy unworthiness raised love in me, / More worthy I to be
belov'd of thee" (150.13–14). However, the sonnets also accentuate the
elusiveness of the humility on which fellowship in deficiency is based.
Forgiveness remains as imperfect as the rationality and self-control celebrated by classical philosophy. The threat to the mistress that "if I should
despair, I should go mad, / And in my madness might speak ill of thee"
(140.9–10) is repeatedly carried out in racialized and misogynistic assertions such as "I have sworn thee fair, and thought thee bright, / Who
art as black as hell, as dark as night" (147.13–14) and "I love what others do abhor" (150.11), as well as in the two Anacreontics that close the
sequence, in which the mistress is deemed the source of "strange mala-
dies" (sexually transmitted diseases) that incurably plague the speaker
(153.8). Race becomes the vehicle for distinguishing between faithful self
and promiscuous other, even as the traditional moral semiotics of color
provides the veneer of racial neutrality.

Changes in Shakespeare criticism crystalize a larger cultural habit
of suppressing the racial dimensions of ideals of sexual purity. Until
the mid-1990s, editors and critics habitually assured us that "black"
just meant that the mistress was a brown-eyed brunette, in contrast
to Petrarch's blonde and blue-eyed Laura, denying that Shakespeare's
sequence has anything like modern "race" in mind when it describes
the mistress as "black" and dwells on her "dun" (brown, swarthy, dark)
"breasts" and her "black" "face" and "complexion" (127, 130.3, 131.10–12,
132.13–14).[102] Such uneasiness with racialized sexuality, as several scholars have pointed out, appears in the mistress's conventional appellation
as "the dark lady," despite the fact that this name appears nowhere in the
sequence.[103] This occlusion of race, more problematically, permits the
persistence of the same semiotics of color, in which sexual immorality
is envisioned as internal blackness, that Medovoi describes as "dogma-
line racism." The mistress is, in Fineman's analysis, "black on the inside,
as any orthodox Petrarchan would have known at first abhorrent sight,"

both "corrupt and corrupting" or, in John Kerrigan's estimation, "decidedly dark in the conduct of her love-life" to the extent that "morally she inhabits, as she sexually enshrines, a 'hell.'"[104]

Such dogma-line racism works in concert with the ideals of sexual innocence whose prejudicial and violent effects queer theory has allowed us to appreciate. Most critics take the speaker's sexual slurs as a matter of misogynistic course, while those who have explicitly championed the dark lady have proceeded as though the best line of defense is to question the charge that she has—and likes having—multiple sex partners. Yet in accepting the terms in which misogynist culture evaluates promiscuity, scholars have allowed to stand the more general assumption that such behavior, if true, would really be blameworthy; many have also accepted the Petrarchan equation of "fairness" with virtue and dignity.[105] As Jonathan Goldberg has argued, Shakespeare's mistress complicates modern definitions of normativity according to gender of object choice by making visible a Renaissance sexual taxonomy focused on respectability: "The threatening sexuality that the dark lady represents—outside marriage and promiscuous and dangerous to homosocial order—is closer to sodomy than almost anything suggested in the poems to the young man."[106] Traub has observed that both male and female readers who align themselves with feminism tend to disavow any identification with the mistress, while both male and female readers who align themselves with gay, lesbian, and queer studies tend to identify with the young man or the speaker's more idealized and respectable attachment to him.[107] Accordingly, Traub maintains, rather than merely celebrate the sonnets' explicit depiction of male homoerotic love, we must recognize that the "displacement of sodomy onto the dark lady is strategic and structural," making visible the "historical interarticulation of male-male desire and misogyny" that produces hierarchies of gender and sexual practice.[108] The acceptance of the assessment of female promiscuity as particularly degrading affirms a general critical pattern that Traub resists and that is explained in more general terms by Goldberg. In Goldberg's account, because early modern writers described female desire in the most stigmatized of ways as an excuse for exerting legal and institutional forms of control, feminist scholarship has generally responded by constructing a "legend of good women" that denies imputations of excessive sexual appetite and, in the process, accords normative femininity only to women who are morally pure, suffering subjects.[109] Such purity, as Jennifer Brody has insisted, has historically been racialized: "White women who are sexually deviant are blackened; black women who are sexually virtuous are never really pure."[110] We see an early instance of this dynamic in Will's charge to the mistress that "In nothing art thou black save in thy deeds," which summarizes a cultural logic in which bodily attributes are conflated with spiritual states (131.13).

The absence of an affirmative theory of female promiscuity bespeaks the limitations of queer as well as feminist theory. Given the psychological and physical attacks to which women are uniquely vulnerable in a society premised on male supremacy, the always feminized, heteroerotic slut is a sad figure, neither as edgy as the gay male cruiser nor as empowered as the straight male playboy or philanderer. Although Dean provocatively and persuasively endorses promiscuity as "an ethical philosophy of living that is available to anyone, irrespective of gender or sexuality," his examples of this practice are all male.[111] Many feminists, by contrast, have tended to endorse as the healthiest form of female relationship a same-sex union of mutual love, trust, and nurture, a fantasy that Amber Hollibaugh has called "lesbian Cinderella-ism."[112] Indeed, as I have argued elsewhere, the more women deviate from a pastoralizing ideal of love (whether for men or for women), the more they are treated as ideological victims of male sexual needs.[113] With regard to representations of female promiscuity and sadomasochism, I have proposed that we take a page from queer theory focused on men. In the case of Shakespeare's black sonnet mistress, rather than deny that she is promiscuous, I suggest that we explore the possibilities that open up when we accept and revalue female promiscuity.[114]

Focusing here on the conjunction of racial impurity and sexual promiscuity as alternatives to the sameness and self-sovereignty of classical friendship, I draw on the arguments of José Esteban Muñoz, Roderick Ferguson, and Sharon Holland that queer studies must expand its citational repertoire to include feminist and queer of color critique.[115] This body of writing affords a nuanced conceptual framework and vocabulary for discussing female sexuality, which otherwise falls outside the bounds of a culturally conservative respectability often endorsed in the name of feminism. One canonical text of this alternate archive is Gloria Anzaldúa's *Borderlands/La Frontera*, which refuses to honor racial, historical, or sexual boundaries. Anticipating recent work on queer temporality, Anzaldùa identifies as an icon of *mestiza* consciousness the sixteenth-century figure of Doña María, or La Malinche, the translator and mistress to Cortés who remains a figure of racial and national betrayal. La Malinche is also known as La Chingada ("the fucked one"), a term that for Anzaldùa registers the predicament of the Chicana who can practice neither feminist nor racial solidarity without sacrificing desire and autonomy.[116] Repurposing the heritage of *malinchismo* as a sign of racial shame and betrayal into the resistance of the *malinchista*, Anzaldùa argues for sexual promiscuity both as a literal repudiation of patriarchal constraints and as a figure for an impure politics that goes beyond identity, loyalty, and opposition. As La Malinche's queer Chicana descendent, the *mestiza* "has discovered that she can't hold concepts or ideas in rigid boundaries. . . . The new *mestiza* copes by developing a tolerance for contradictions, a tolerance for ambiguity. . . . Not only does she sustain contradictions, she turns the ambivalence into something else."[117] While Anzaldùa is most typically understood as a lesbian Chicana feminist, her work is also queer—her own self-description years before that term became institutionalized as the name of a theoretical movement—in the sense that it resists sexual or identitarian monogamy, stressing instead both racial and sexual indeterminability.[118]

In refusing to accept the abjection of female promiscuity, Anzaldùa (along with pathbreaking feminists of color like Audre Lorde and Angela Davis) offers an early instance of a reading method that Jennifer Nash has more recently described as "racial iconography." Focusing in particular on racialized pornography, Nash seeks to uncover "the possibilities of female pleasures within a phallic economy" and "the possibilities of black female pleasures within a white-dominated representational economy."[119] Insofar as pornographic depictions of black women represent an extreme of white, masculine sexual ideology more generally, Nash proposes that we can use this archive "as a tool for shifting the black feminist theoretical archive away from the production and enforcement of a 'protectionist' reading of representation, and toward an interpretative framework centered on complex and sometimes unnerving pleasures."[120] Similarly, Amber Jamilla Musser addresses the historically and materially embedded racial and gendered experiences of masochism. She reads masochism "as a relational, contingent term that describes a plethora of relationships" and thereby illuminates the "contradictions, various imaginaries, multiple forms of power, and diverse responses to that power" that escape evaluations of S/M as either stabilizing or subverting regimes of domination.[121] Nash's and Musser's work, like that of Mireille Miller-Young, Nicole Fleetwood, and Ariane Cruz, seeks to illuminate the feminist and queer potential of an "illicit eroticism" usually viewed through the lens of stigma or injury.[122] Read collectively, this work builds on the pro-sex feminist insight that the feminist effort to protect women from imputations of indecent behavior may end up replicating conservative sexual mores. Many white feminist writings of the sex wars either ignored the difference that race makes to perceptions of female sexuality or, in Hortense Spillers's words, replaced the racist caricature of the "supersexed black female" with that of the "unsexed black female"—both of which denied the nuances of time and history.[123] Working to correct this distortion, black feminist critics have discussed in detail two effects on feminism of the intertwined ideals of racial and sexual purity in Atlantic chattel slavery. In the first wave of US feminism, as modesty, sexual innocence, silence, and self-effacement became the qualities associated with the cult of true womanhood, African American women sought to emulate "ladylike" behavior to attain social respect and parity with white women. In the second wave, black female eroticism was suppressed in favor of a focus on the traumatic legacy of slavery's sexual violence.[124] Most recently, a newer body of queer feminist of color theory that includes the work of Nash, Musser, Miller-Young, Fleetwood, and Cruz confronts the historical legacy of racial violence but resists the silencing effects that legacy has had on discussions of racialized sexuality.

Given the pornographic perspective of so many of Shakespeare's sonnets, these poems also provide an overlooked archive for retheorizing racialized female promiscuity across a longer time span. When Will makes the rhetorical intent of his uses of stigma so explicit—"if I should despair I should grow mad, / And in my madness might speak ill of thee" (140.9–10)—he also reveals his own moral condemnation to be instrumental rather than sincere, thereby undercutting his repeated assertion of sincerity and authenticity as racialized properties. Elsewhere, he attempts to persuade the mistress to indulge him because she can measure the extremity of his desire for her by that of her own desire for other men. In other words, the differentiation that he attempts to draw between "fair" male infidelity and "black" female promiscuity gives way to an argument for erotic identification across racial and gendered lines. To be clear, I do not propose that this argument reveals a proto-queer-feminist consciousness on Shakespeare's part. Rather, by taking seriously an erotics of the divided will, Shakespeare's sonnets read as a whole symptomatically confess the fragility of the racial and sexual taxonomies that underpin the modern Western ideal of sincere, monogamous love.

In its very transparent rhetoricity, Will's identification with the black mistress concedes the Pauline insight that one can never quite separate sincerity from insincerity, proper from improper habits of desire. Sonnet 142, to take one striking instance, accentuates the promiscuity of Christian *caritas*. Here, Will asserts the similarity between his and the mistress's erotic aims despite their different objects:

> Love is my sin, and thy dear virtue hate,
> Hate of my sin, grounded on sinful loving.
> O but with mine compare thou thine own state,
> And thou shalt find it merits not reproving,
> Or if it do, not from those lips of thine,
> That have profaned their scarlet ornaments,
> And sealed false bonds of love as oft as mine,
> Robbed others' beds' revénues of their rents.
> Be it lawful I love thee as thou lov'st those
> Whom thine eyes woo as mine impórtune thee.
> Root pity in thy heart, that when it grows,
> Thy pity may deserve to pitied be.
>   If thou dost seek to have what thou dost hide,
>   By self-example mayst thou be denied. (142.1–14)

As Stephen Booth notes, these lines together enact the doubling of Will and the mistress through chiasmus (inverted repetition: love/hate/Hate/loving) and anadiplosis (repetition of the last word of one grammatical and formal unit as the first word of the next: hate/Hate).[125] In asking her to do what he just has—"with mine compare thou thine own state"— Will introduces the third repetition in as many lines, formally enacting the poem's larger argument that they are comparable in their unstable and multiple desires. Much as the sonnets to the young man insisted that mutual betrayal must be met by mutual forgiveness, this sonnet asserts that an affinity of desire must yield affinity of pity.

The second quatrain initially appears to continue the "slander" threatened in Sonnet 140 by charging that the mistress's lips have "profaned their scarlet ornaments / And sealed false bonds of love." But that intervening "as oft as mine" implicates Will in exploiting the ambiguous significance of the kiss. When is a kiss just a kiss? When does it "seal" a more lasting "bond"? Similarly, the charge that the black mistress has "Robbed others' beds' revenues of their rents" is impossible grammatically to distinguish from a confession that Will is equally guilty of seduction. Grammar, syntax, and metaphor, in other words, resist the poem's thematic distinctions between "fair" male monogamy and "black" female promiscuity. Immoderate desire here is a source of identification and legitimation, bringing subject and object into a chiasmic relationship in which they are fungible rather than singular. "Be it lawful I love thee as thou lov'st those / Whom thine eyes woo as mine importune thee": the two lines fold in on themselves, so that the mistress's love and wooing are mirrored in Will's own love and importunity. The mistress's promiscuous past, like Will's own, is rendered "lawful" by her recognition that he desires her as much as she desires others. Her pursuit of future trysts provides the ground for Will's appeal: do unto me as you would have others do unto you. Moral censure is not the end of seduction but its logical premise.

Sonnet 142 begins with what we might read as a glib paraphrase of the Sermon on the Mount ("Judge not, that ye be not judged. For with what judgment ye judge, ye shall be judged, and with what measure ye mete, it shall be measured to you again" [GB, Matt. 7:1–2]). It ends by transforming the golden rule (usually summed up as "do unto others as you would have them do unto you") into an appeal for erotic *caritas* (a formulation I will discuss at length in chapter 5).[126] Unlike what in the vernacular would be called a "pity fuck," the compassion for which Will pleads rests not on a hierarchical relationship of pity but on kindness: identification of another's weakness as one's own. In Calvin's assessment, the golden rule of *caritas* reappearing from Leviticus, Matthew, Luke, and Paul's Epistles "transfers to others the love which we naturally feel for ourselves" (*Institutes* 2.8.54). What is significant in Will's adaptation of this rule in Sonnet 142 is that it takes seriously the black mistress's interest in other men as active and legitimate, defining "love" in an explicitly sexual sense and grounding responsiveness to others' desires on awareness of one's own. Reciprocity exceeds a contract among two, becoming a larger principle of community. This placement of lover and beloved in a circuit of universal good will is, to be sure, a rhetorical device. But such persuasion can only succeed if it treats as legitimate the mistress's desire to have her will in the future as she has in the past—that is, if it replaces the singular and eternal commitment of monogamy with an open-ended set of encounters and strategic affiliations. At the same time, in imagining relations that are noncommittal but intimate and ongoing, the sonnets repudiate the binary that Elizabeth Freeman has observed whereby "the magical sign" for queer relationality "has been the flip side of the cohesive couple, the purely physical and often anonymous sexual encounter—and not the tangled network of ex-lovers, concomitant relationships, unconsummated erotics, and so forth that structure so many queer lives, and that often get homogenized as 'just friends.'"[127] Such queer networks are not at odds with the secular love tradition. They are at the core of one of its most canonical texts.

What I am arguing is that the same set of poems that have been understood to attack the black mistress's promiscuity look very different when we set aside the assumption that such behavior, particularly in women, is destructive of both self and society. Insofar as we as feminist and queer scholars *use* poetry as a site to retheorize gendered, racial, and sexual possibilities, a critical framework that sees promiscuity as not only inevitable but also salutary, one paradoxically provided by the logic of Pauline theology, can help us to read against the grain of an ideology of monogamous coupledom and the racial and gendered hierarchies it sustains. The religious vocabulary in Sonnet 144, for instance, contests the purity and predictability upon which classical friendship no less than modern marriage rests:

> Two loves I have of comfort and despair,
> Which like two spirits do suggest me still;
> The better angel is a man right fair,
> The worser spirit a woman coloured ill.
> To win me soon to hell, my female evil

> Tempteth my better angel from my side,
> And would corrupt my saint to be a devil,
> Wooing his purity with her foul pride.
> And whether that my angel be turn'd fiend,
> Suspect I may, yet not directly tell,
> But being both from me both to each friend,
> I guess one angel in another's hell.
>> Yet this shall I ne'er know, but live in doubt,
>> Till my bad angel fire my good one out. (144.1–14)

The first quatrain, several critics have observed, asserts a strict dichotomy between the two loves. Will associates comfort with the "man right fair" described as a "better angel" and a "saint" and credited with "purity"; he associates despair with the "woman colored ill" described as a "worser spirit" and "female evil" and accused of that original sin of "foul pride." However, as we have seen, Pauline and Reform thought admit no such soothing binaries. Saints, as the poem itself admits, may become devils, and there is no neat epistemological relation between salvation and comfort, damnation and despair. Getting too comfortable about one's own salvation is just as bad as giving up on it altogether.

When the second and third quatrains detail the behavior of these loves who "suggest me still," the insufficiency of the initial ontological and epistemological taxonomy becomes even more apparent. Although the neat parallelism of the first quatrain leads us to expect that the youth is "suggest[ing]"—wooing or urging—Will as constantly ("still") as the mistress, the mistress is the subject of all of the verbs of the second quatrain. Will claims that her motive is "to win me soon to hell," to lead him to despair of the man's love and thereby lure him to sex with her, if we accept Booth's gloss of "hell" as slang for vagina. The medieval tableau with Will at its center is here reconfigured as a struggle between Will and the woman for the male "better angel," who, as Sedgwick long ago noted, is markedly passive in the octave, belying the speaker's initial claim that the two loves exhaustively vie for his soul.[128] The woman colored ill may endeavor to "win" both Will and the youth, but the man right fair does not seem to care either way.

Continuing in the present tense, Will admits in the third quatrain that the youth may *already* "be turned" from "angel" to "fiend." This conversion (or perversion) has been a feature of the sequence all along, even if Will cannot "directly tell," or empirically verify it. Like the youth's "purity," the contest to "win" Will may never have been a contest in the first place, since one of the poem's jokes is that neither love seems terribly concerned about the speaker. Instead, as Will complains, "being both from me both to each friend." This rare use of "to . . . friend" as a verb meaning "to offer friendship, aid, or support" evokes the common medieval and early modern use of "friend" to mean "lover" in a sexual sense and thereby recalls the sexual *caritas* for which Will pleaded in Sonnet 142. The sight rhyme of "friend" with "fiend" retrospectively supplements the obvious theological meaning of "fiend" in line 9 as a synonym for devil with its original meaning of "enemy." The first quatrain's crisp convictions quickly give way to the subjunctive mood of doubt and conjecture: friends and enemies, identity and difference, comfort and despair, fair and foul mingle promiscuously with one another. If, in the couplet the woman structurally remains the "bad angel," *she* will be the one to comfort the poet by ending or revealing a friendship that the "good" male angel would have continued secretly to enjoy. In the poem's secular soteriology, living in doubt is a necessary condition of achieving what salvation one can find in intimacy and love—a condition that appears repeatedly throughout the sequence. Keeping the faith is something one tries to do while awaiting an ever-deferred revelation of truth. It requires ongoing wariness of comfort *and* despair, both of which avoid the exhaustive work of patience.

This is not to lose sight of the fact that Will's rhetoric of identification is instrumental, nor that subsequent poems return to the racialized and misogynistic attacks against the mistress's inconstant and deceptive behavior. As Schwarz observes, "By reading for unity, we may find what we presuppose a coherent misogynist approach that fulfills its disciplinary functions. By suspending presumption, we can recover a fragmentary, porous, and in all senses partial account of the relations among social subjects."[129] Schwarz focuses on gendered difference, but the fragmentation, porosity, and partiality she recommends may equally describe the complex of mutually formative racial and sexual taxonomies that I have been tracing. The very fact that Will approaches the mistress's promiscuity in so many different ways, from sympathetic identification to wounded condemnation, enables us to see his evaluations of her racial and sexual identity in provisional and circumstantial, rather than pure or absolute, terms. Shakespeare's sequence depicts neither linear regression from a paradise of white male friendship to the hell of racial and sexual promiscuity, nor a more conciliatory progress from prideful condemnation to humble forgiveness. Rather, these poems enact the same recursive dynamic that we have seen in Augustinian conversion and Petrarchan love. Any given poem, indeed any given line, represents but a fragment of a larger, irresolvable maelstrom of human will.

Amidst such flux, the "marriage of true minds" idealized by homonormative (white) friendship is no more possible—or ethically desirable—than the mystical conjugal transformation of two bodies into one flesh. When, in the final twenty-eight poems, the speaker of the sonnets turns attention away from the whiteness and monogamy so insistently conflated in the first 126 poems addressed to the young man and toward the blackness and promiscuity of the mistress, he also relinquishes a fantasy that two minds can become one. The promiscuous entanglements across modern categories of race and sexuality depicted in the sonnets struggle toward a disposition of vulnerability to the strange and unbidden, even as these poems reveal just how difficult it is to let go of the illusion of innocent and autonomous selfhood and the gratifying aggressions this ideal legitimates.

3

The Shame of Conjugal Sex

Saint Paul versus the US Supreme Court

So far, I have been tracing the conceptual intricacies of Christian faith as it theorizes race, gender, desire, and subjectivity. In this chapter, I discuss how a theological conviction of human infidelity and self-opacity challenges mainstream modern valuations of matrimony as a sanctified union deserving of the myriad legal, social, and economic benefits that come with a marriage certificate. As numerous queer scholars have pointed out, the view that conjugal sex is uniquely innocent includes the concomitant view that sex outside of marriage poses a danger both to individual health and happiness and to social order. The "hierarchical valuation of sex acts," long ago censured by Gayle Rubin, legitimates the sexually and racially discriminatory effects of a distribution of resources based on marital status: the economically independent two-parent family was at the center of the white, neoliberal fantasy of the Clinton administration's welfare reform and the Bush administration's marriage program.[1]

Responding to the overwhelming privileges afforded those who wed, and the corollary discrimination and material loss faced by those who do not, LGBTQ activism over the past two decades has, as Michael Warner puts it, endeavored to "overcome stigma" by conforming to dominant culture rather than "chang[ing] the self-understanding of that culture."[2] Beginning in 2001, when the Netherlands became the first country to sanction same-sex marriage, this strategy of beating discrimination by legally joining those it benefited saw widespread success. In 2015, with the Supreme Court's ruling in *Obergefell v. Hodges*, the United States joined Canada, South Africa, parts of Mexico, and most of Western Europe in legalizing same-sex marriage; since then, more countries have implemented marriage equality, with Taiwan becoming the first Asian country to allow same-sex couples to marry in May 2017. This expansion of marriage rights, as Gayatri Chakravorty Spivak and Wendy Brown have observed of liberalism and legal rights more generally, is something we "cannot not want" insofar as it ends discrimination based on a couple's gender and opens the way to claims for legal and political redress of injustice.[3] In the United States, for instance, the right to marry was originally tied to the legal category of personhood and thereby denied to African American slaves.[4] Yet making marriage more inclusive does little for sexual minorities and may further legitimate cultural and legal discrimination against those who willfully remain outside the "charmed circle" of conjugal coupledom now that they can legally join it.[5] It is as urgent as ever to change how the dominant culture understands itself.

A central claim of this book is that one way to create such change is to look more closely at some of the foundational writings of the dominant culture: Christian theology and canonical love poetry. As I discuss in the remainder of this first section, both the majority and the dissent in *Obergefell* appeal to history and tradition. But this appeal obscures the ambivalence about the purpose and value of marriage expressed in two profoundly influential cultural documents, the Anglian Book of Common Prayer and the Pauline Letters. In the section that follows, I trace the challenge posed to modern sexual hierarchies by the sixteenth-century Protestant conviction that, in Luther's words, "the sin of lust . . . flows beneath the surface" of matrimony.[6] In the third section, I argue that in the Renaissance both medical discussions of orgasm and Shakespeare's sonnets on procreation attest to the cultural influence of the view that even married, reproductive sex cannot be wholly sanctified. In the final section of this chapter, I examine how the desire for sexual innocence itself gives license to pornographic and violent fantasies in a pair of lyric sequences usually understood as translating Petrarchan poetics from a testimony of unrequited love into propaganda for Christian companionate marriage, Edmund Spenser's *Amoretti* and *Epithalamion*.

Because US secular norms tend to be shaped by modern Protestantism, an excavation of these biblical, theological, medical, and poetic attempts to grapple with the experience of arousal can prove as useful to queer and feminist thought as the secular and modern frameworks more usually invoked. Paul, Augustine, Luther, and Calvin have no interest in combatting stigma—they agree that it would be best not to want sex at all, and next best to enjoy it as little as possible. But, in its grim assurance of universal depravity, Pauline soteriology resonates remarkably with such queer insights as Warner's observation that "perhaps because sex is an occasion for losing control, for merging one's consciousness with the lower orders of animal desire and sensation, for raw confrontations of power and demand, it fills people with aversion and shame."[7] For Warner, queer ethics must be based on the recognition that sex *cannot* be elevated. "In those circles where queerness has been most cultivated," Warner writes, "the ground rule is that one doesn't pretend to be *above* the indignity of sex. . . . A relation to others, in these contexts, begins in an acknowledgment of all that is most abject and least reputable in oneself. . . . If sex is a kind of indignity, then we're all in it together."[8] In its recommendation that this indignity be confined to marriage, the theological tradition I have been tracing differs from queer theory. But it also complicates the moralization of married and procreative intercourse now taken for granted by modern evangelicals, popular culture, and US law. Any serious reading of this material reminds us that the "Judeo-Christian" history from which modern marriage is usually derived is a pretty recent invention. Precisely because it accentuates what Leo Bersani deems the "ineradicable aspects" of sex that are "anticommunal, antiegalitarian, antinurturing, antiloving," the body of writing I examine can be a vital conceptual tool for challenging the "*romantic reinvention of sex*," along with the hierarchies it authorizes.[9]

A brief look at the arguments both for and against marriage equality in *Obergefell v. Hodges* indicates that queer apprehension of the coercive normativity of the redemptive reinvention of sex has proved prescient. The majority and dissent in *Obergefell* disagree on the proper legal definition of marriage, but they find common ground on one principle: sex has no value in itself, without the trappings of love or family. The expansion of marriage rights, in fact, grows out of the romanticization of sex in the majority opinion in *Lawrence v. Texas*, the 2003 ruling decriminalizing sodomy. Here, Justice Anthony Kennedy overturns the Court's previous defense of antisodomy statutes in *Bowers v. Hardwick* by affirming that "to say that the issue in *Bowers* was simply the right to engage in certain sexual conduct *demeans* the claim the individual put forward, *just as it would demean a married couple* were it to be said that marriage is simply about the right to have sexual intercourse."[10] In other words, to simply want the right to have consensual sex when, how, and with whomever one wants would indeed be demeaning. When he writes for the majority in *Obergefell*, Kennedy reiterates throughout this conflation of dignity, love, and committed coupledom. Reasoning that prohibiting same-sex marriage violates the Fourteenth Amendment, Kennedy argues that the liberties that cannot be denied without due process of law "extend to certain personal choices central to individual dignity and autonomy, including intimate choices that define personal identity and beliefs."[11] In an appeal to what Janet Jakobsen has shown is a structurally Protestant association of freedom with self-regulation, Kennedy proclaims that the choice to marry "is inherent in the concept of individual autonomy" because "through its enduring bond, two persons together can find other freedoms, such as expression, intimacy, and spirituality" otherwise unavailable (*Obergefell* 3, 10).[12] Marriage "responds to the universal fear that a lonely person might call out only to find no one there," Kennedy avers, and "embodies the highest ideals of love, fidelity, devotion, sacrifice, and family" (*Obergefell* 11, 17). Accordingly, to deny same-sex couples the right to "aspire to the transcendent purposes of marriage and seek fulfillment in its highest meaning" is to "impose stigma and injury of the kind prohibited by our basic charter" (*Obergefell* 14, 12).

The dissent in *Obergefell* was having none of this talk of love. All four of the dissenting justices—Roberts, Scalia, Thomas, and Alito—wrote opinions whose primary argument was that the definition of marriage should be decided by voters and legislators, not a "judicial Putsch" (*Obergefell* 34). But, as Roberts's and Alito's opinions make clear, a robust investment in what Lee Edelman calls "reproductive futurism" and in protecting a particular ideal of the Western, nuclear family lies beneath the indignant claim that marriage rights cannot properly be expanded by the Court.[13] Roberts avers that the heterosexual norm of marriage "is no historical coincidence" but arises to meet the "vital need" of conceiving and raising children (*Obergefell* 21). In undermining this definition, Roberts warns, the Court threatens the very existence of the human race, which "must procreate to survive" (*Obergefell* 21). Doggedly ignoring the existence of both birth control and reproductive technology, Roberts writes that "sexual relations that can lead to procreation" between a couple that plans to "stay together rather than going their separate ways" is the only hope of a future (*Obergefell* 21). Alito similarly insists that "for millennia, marriage was inextricably linked to the one thing that only an opposite-sex couple can do: procreate" (*Obergefell* 43). He goes on to lament that "the tie between marriage and procreation has frayed. Today, for instance, more than 40% of all children in this country are born to unmarried women. This development undoubtedly is both a cause and a result of changes in our society's understanding of marriage" (*Obergefell* 43). Same-sex marriage, by Roberts's and Alito's logic, will only hasten this vicious cycle whereby the more marriage is conceptually distinguished from procreation, the more procreation will happen outside of marriage.[14] The specter of the promiscuous queer merges with that of the undeserving welfare queen—a figure at once queer and black in relation to white norms, as Cathy Cohen and Dorothy Roberts argue—as a threat to decent and hardworking "real" Americans.[15] The conjoined religious, racial, and national identifications at play here are further accentuated by Roberts's warning that same-sex marriage will usher in alternative kinship practices such as polygamy, which has "deep roots in some cultures around the world" (*Obergefell* 28).

While many who support marriage equality rightly cringe at these hysterical defenses of white family values, it is important to note that *all* of the Justices concur that monogamous marriage is the bedrock of "our" society and as such must be rewarded with unique dignity and promoted with tangible benefits. In *Obergefell*, the majority as well as the dissent is quite candid about the coercive dimension of marriage. These arguments confirm the queer critique expressed succinctly by Warner: marriage confers "selective legitimacy" that is "designed both to reward those inside it and to discipline those outside it: adulterers, prostitutes, divorcees, the promiscuous, single people, unwed parents, those below the age of consent—in short, all those who become, for the purposes of marriage law, queer."[16] Because marriage is a "building block of our national community," Kennedy writes, it is also a union between the couple and the state: "Just as a couple vows to support each other, so does society pledge to support the couple, offering symbolic recognition and material benefits to protect and nourish the union" (*Obergefell* 12). The dissenting Justices agree. Roberts notes that "by bestowing a respected status and material benefits on married couples, society encourages men and women to conduct sexual relations within marriage rather than without," and Alito adds that "states formalize and promote marriage . . . in order to encourage potentially procreative conduct to take place within a lasting unit" (*Obergefell* 21, 43). In all of these opinions, the uneasy fusion of coercion and choice that Elizabeth Freeman and Janet Jakobsen have seen in marriage comes to the fore.[17]

What Teemu Ruskola has observed of Kennedy's majority opinion in *Lawrence* is equally true of the pernicious logic of the majority in *Obergefell*: once the legal question is the right to "intimacy" rather than "sodomy," there is "little or no justification for protecting less-than-transcendental sex that is not part of an ongoing relationship."[18] The decriminalization of sodomy is certainly welcome news, Ruskola concedes. But its logic participates in a compulsory normativity in which "we will know whose sex is good and whose is bad" based on the legal status of the relationship in which it takes place.[19] Perhaps most problematically, in *Lawrence* the Court promotes "'compulsory heterosexuality' in its new, second-generation form, Adrienne Rich updated for the millennium."[20] Likewise, what Lisa Duggan calls "the new homonormativity" aligns gay marriage rights with an embrace of neoliberal privatization by "promising the possibility of a demobilized gay constituency and a privatized, depoliticized gay culture anchored in domesticity and privacy," which will "shrink gay public spheres and redefine gay equality against the 'civil rights agenda' and 'liberationism.'"[21] To the extent that they posit a disembodied queerness and value individual choice over social justice, proponents of the new homonormativity, like those of the old heteronormativity before it, take white men as the universal and paradigmatic political and sexual subject. They accordingly treat queer movements that address race- or gender-based discrimination as distracting at best and divisive at worst.

As I argued in chapter 2, attention to the conflicted and uneven histories of modern racial and sexual categories can remind us of their ongoing mutual constitution. Katherine Franke demonstrates that the tacit framing of same-sex marriage as an expansion of white respectability as against "dysfunctional, 'broken' families" reveals that "a conception of marriage as the pinnacle of mature personhood and mutual responsibility is so saturated with racial and gender stereotypes that some things do not even have to be said to convey the feeling of truth and obviousness."[22] *Obergefell* offers an example of how historical amnesia props up the white queer neoliberal identity politics critiqued in Duggan's analysis of homonormativity as well as in Jasbir Puar's analysis of homonationalism.[23] Although both the majority and the dissent in *Obergefell* appeal to numerous touchstones of history—between them, they mention the Carthaginians, the Aztecs, the Kalahari Bushmen, and the Han Chinese; and they cite Confucius, Cicero, Edward Coke, John Locke, William Blackstone, and Alexis de Tocqueville—both sides' opinions are based on a strikingly presentist and American perspective on marriage.

Ironically, given its Christian basis, the *Obergefell* opinions repress the more anxious account of marriage offered by Reformation theology. We see this ambivalence in the Book of Common Prayer, whose "Solemnization of Matrimony" remains central to Anglo-American secular marriage culture ("Dearly beloved, we are gathered here today . . ."). First published in 1549 and disseminated most influentially through the 1662 edition, this liturgy remained substantively unchanged until 1928. Comparing the 1662 and 1928 ceremonies in the Book of Common Prayer, we can appreciate that the former's explicit anxiety about the sex that takes place *within* marriage is conspicuously effaced in the latter's reluctance to mention conjugal sex at all. The nuptial state, the 1662 ceremony warns,

> is not by any to be enterprized, nor taken in hand unadvisedly, lightely, or wantonly, *to satisfie mens carnal lusts and appetites, like brute beasts that have no understanding*: but reverently, discretely, advisedly, soberly, and in the fear of God, duly considering the causes for which matrimony was ordained.
>
> First, it was ordained for *the procreation of children*, to be brought up in the fear and nurture of the Lord. . . .
>
> Secondly, it was ordained *for a remedy against sin, and to avoid fornication, that such persons as have not the gift of continency, might marry, and keep themselves undefiled members of Christs body.*
>
> Thirdly, it was ordained for the mutual society, help and comfort, that the one ought to have of the other.[24]

In the version used for nearly four hundred years, wedlock may offer a remedy against sin and fornication, but it does not magically transform any conjugal sex to a chaste expression of love, as the couple at the alter is warned against marrying only to satisfy "carnal lusts and appetites."

It is only when the ceremony is revised in 1928 that the Book of Common Prayer endows matrimony with the ability to sanitize the sex that takes place within it. This twentieth-century version explains that marriage

> is not to bee enterprised, nor taken in hand unadvisedly, lightly, or wantonly, but reverently, discreetly, advisedly, soberly, and in the fear of God, duly considering the causes for which matrimony was ordained. First, It was ordained for *the increase of mankind according to the will of God*, and that children might be brought up in the fear and nurture of the Lord . . . Second, It was ordained *in order that the natural instincts and affections, implanted by God, should be hallowed and directed aright; that those who are called of God to this holy estate, should continue therein in pureness of living*. Thirdly, It was ordained for the mutual society, help, and comfort, that the one ought to have of thither, both in prosperity and adversity.[25]

Here, the carnal lusts, brute beasts, fornication, and defilement of the 1662 service are carefully bowdlerized as "natural instincts and affections, implanted by God" to be "hallowed and directed aright" to foster "pureness of living." The most recent revision to the Book of Common Prayer, in 1979, removes discussion of sex altogether. Here, the opening line suppresses the possibility that marriage might be contracted "wantonly," admonishing only that it should not "be entered into unadvisedly or lightly, but reverently, deliberately, and in accordance with the purposes of which it was instituted by God."[26] The 1979 "Solemnization" also departs from the four-hundred-year tradition of naming the causes of marriage as procreation, fellowship, and avoidance of fornication—a tradition inscribed, as Roberts writes in *Obergefell*, in the early American definition of marriage: "In his first American dictionary, Noah Webster defined marriage as 'the legal union of a man and woman for life,' which served the purposes of 'preventing the promiscuous intercourse of the sexes, . . . promoting domestic felicity, and . . . securing the maintenance and education of children'" (*Obergefell* 22). In fact, the modern ceremony folds sex into companionship, even to the point of making procreation optional: stressing the discourse of friendship that I discussed in chapter 2, the 1979 ceremony lists the three purposes of conjugal union as "for their mutual joy; for the help and comfort given one another in prosperity and adversity; and, when it is God's will, for the procreation of children and their nurture."[27] In the wake of the so-called sexual revolution, the originally uneasy description of marriage as a remedy against sin and defilement (the lengthiest reason given before 1928) is whittled down to the brief, resolutely G-rated "mutual joy."

The modern erasure of sex from the Anglican marriage ceremony exemplifies a larger principle of family values discourse that makes conjugal sex uniquely, even magically, innocent. This Disney version of marriage, frequently assumed by evangelical and queer thought alike, has little basis in the New Testament, which does not directly justify marriage on the grounds of either fellowship or procreation. Indeed, as Richard Rambuss has pointed out, "Christianity, at least in its early scriptural incarnations, is not an especially hospitable faith around which to build a heteronormative family values cultural project. In fact, the Christian scriptures are rich in figures and narratives that point the way toward, and even sacralize, other forms of kinship, other ways of spiritual belonging."[28] God's command in Genesis to "be fruitful, and multiply" and his pronouncement that "it is not good that the man should be himself alone, I will make a help meet for him," are not explicitly connected to marriage as contract or institution at all (KJB, Gen. 1:28, 2:18). The Old Testament indirectly questions the unique status of straight, monogamous marriage by depicting a range of divinely sanctioned forms of kinship: polygamy, incest, group marriage, and same-sex commitment (practices, we saw in chapter 2, that English Reformers emphasized to distinguish Protestantism from other religions), which bear little resemblance to the heterosexual couple for which the Supreme Court claims such a venerable and invariable history. The New Testament directly questions whether monogamous marriage has positive spiritual value at all. Jesus repeatedly urges his followers to give up everything and follow him, and Paul cites this celibate and communal lifestyle as the spiritual ideal.[29]

Paul begins his discussion of marriage in 1 Corinthians 7 by declaring that "it *were* good for a man not to touch a woman. Nevertheless, to avoid fornication, let every man have his wife, and let every woman have her own husband" (GB, 1 Cor. 7:1–2).[30] People are permitted to marry if, as the note to this verse in the Geneva Bible puts it, they "have not the gift of continency, and this gift is by a peculiar grace of God." But, as Paul makes clear, no one is *required* to marry: the dispensation is "by permission, not by commandment" (GB, 1 Cor. 7:6). In fact, it would be better if everyone could remain single, like Paul himself: "For I would that all men were even as I myself *am*. But every man hath his proper gift of God, one after this manner, and another after that. Therefore I say unto the unmarried, and unto the widows, It is good for them if they abide even as I *do*. But if they cannot abstain, let them marry; for it is better to marry than to burn" (GB, 1 Cor. 7:7–9; emphasis in original). Marriage provides an outlet for excessive desire, preventing both the act of fornication and the distracting fantasies and yearnings that disrupt the spiritual relation with God. As the Geneva gloss explains, "It is better to marry than to burn" means "So to burn with lust, that either the will yieldeth to the temptation, or else we cannot call upon God with a quiet conscience." Sex in 1 Corinthians is matrimony's chief motivating force. Paul never mentions the other two reasons that the Book of Common Prayer gives for marriage (procreation and companionship) as compelling arguments to wed.

Later in 1 Corinthians, Paul emphasizes that celibacy is preferable to marriage not because of the bodily act of sex but because of the distracting affective dimension of worldly attachments:

> And I would have you without care. The unmarried careth for the things of the Lord, how he may please the Lord. But he that is married careth for the things of the world, how he may please *his* wife. There is difference also between a virgin and a wife. The unmarried woman careth for the things of the Lord, that she may be holy, both in body and in spirit, but she that is married, careth for the things of the world, how she may please her husband. (GB, 1 Cor. 7:32–34; emphasis in original)

The Geneva glosses this as: "They that are married, have their wits drawn hither and thither, and therefore if any man have the gift of continency, it is more commodious for him to live alone"; even though "they that are married may care for the things of the Lord also," they are "divided, meaning into divers cares." The union of marriage formally recognizes the division of both parties between flesh and spirit, this world and the next. Marriage, in the Pauline tradition, is a concession to promiscuous attachments.

To marry, in Paul's account, is not so much an alternative to burning as an admission that one *does* burn, that one does not love God from the bottom of one's heart. Not only are spouses and children a distraction from "the things of the Lord," but from the point of view that looks forward to the second coming, there is no need to perpetuate the human species. "And I say this, brethren, because the time is short," Paul explains, "hereafter that both they which have wives, be as though they had none. . . . And they that use this world, as though they used it not; for the fashion of the world goeth away" (GB, 1 Cor. 7:29, 31). This shortened, or constricted, time that remains between the resurrection and the apocalypse, Giorgio Agamben explains, describes the human experience of the messianic event as one of "paradoxical tension between an *already* and a *not yet* that defines the Pauline conception of salvation."[31] The Pauline subsumption of history in eschatology, chronological into messianic time, deems human action meaningful only insofar as it is directed to its own end. Believing that the extension of human life is the deferral of the full presence of the Messiah, the religious celibate shares what Edelman designates the queer's "willingness to insist intransitively—to insist that the future stop here."[32]

But what of an equally well-known Pauline discussion of marriage, the final verses of Ephesians 5 urging human spouses to emulate the union of Christ and Church? Included in the "Solemnization of Matrimony" in the Book of Common Prayer and favored by modern evangelicals, Ephesians 5 would seem to contradict the ideal of virginity in 1 Corinthians 7. It is certainly taken this way by John Calvin, who marshals it as evidence against the Catholic requirement of lifelong virginity for clergy: "Christ deigns so to honor marriage as to make it an image of his sacred union with the church. What greater eulogy could be pronounced on the dignity of marriage? How, then, dare they have the effrontery to give the name of unclean and polluted to that which furnishes a bright representation of the spiritual grace of Christ?"[33] Yet, as I observed in chapter 1, numerous queer implications are imbedded in the figural logic of Ephesians 5 whereby first, a human institution preceding Christianity is taken as the model of a faith that is unrepresentable except through catachrestic accommodation, and then second, this catachresis comes proleptically to justify the holiness of the institution itself. Here, I want briefly to recall that even the most heteronormative reading of this analogy requires us to repress the sexual dimension of wedlock. Paul's single reason for marriage in 1 Corinthians 7—to extinguish lust—is explicitly excluded in Ephesians' warning not to read literally the analogy between marriage to a spouse and marriage to Christ. In repeating Ephesians' elision of sex in favor of a view of marriage as delibidinized companionship or procreation, the *Obergefell* Justices avoid a Christian tradition in which marriage does not so much sanctify creaturely appetite as confess that it cannot be rendered fully innocent.

A Hospital for Incurables

Of course, the *Obergefell* opinions are right that marriage, defined as a public declaration of love or a means of ordering reproduction, has existed in many cultures throughout history. This includes the Western European cultures with which the Court is most concerned, and particularly that of the sixteenth- and seventeenth-century English Protestantism whose views so profoundly shaped the establishment of the United States as a nation and which remain, in secular form, central to American law and culture. One of the most tenacious narratives about early modern sexuality is that the Protestant Reformation ushered in a new idea of companionate marriage that displaced both the Catholic idealization of celibacy and the medieval romance of adultery.[34] In this view, Catholics, following the example of Christ and his apostles, had distrusted marriage as a sign of attachment to the world, the flesh, and the devil and seen virginity as an expression of pure, uncompromised faith that set the clergy apart from the laity. By contrast, this story goes, Protestants deemed marriage the highest spiritual state for clergy and laity alike. Such readings suppose a sharp break between a Catholic idealization of celibacy and a Protestant celebration of marriage. To be sure, Protestant theologians departed from Catholic doctrine in their support for clerical marriage, and secular rulers in Protestant states justified the suppression of religious orders and seizure of monastic property by condemning these communal institutions as sites of sodomy and fornication. In Protestant states, including early America, marriage became the only legitimate adult way of life.[35] But it is important to separate the historical effects of the Protestant repudiation of clerical celibacy from the conceptual model of sex and subjectivity that grounded the view that most people, including clergy, were better off married. Sixteenth-century views of companionate marriage were neither as new nor as optimistic as they are often assumed to have been. Insofar as Reform theology does not deny the indignity of conjugal sex but, true to its Augustinian roots, "renders shame productive," it also queerer than it is usually thought to be.[36]

From at least the twelfth century, the Catholic Church upheld celibacy as a superior state, a view based on the writings of the early Church Fathers, who saw asceticism as the condition most conducive to a holy lifestyle. Tertullian, though himself married, deemed conjugal relations inherently sinful, arguing that insofar as marital sex involves the "commixture of the flesh," it "consists of that which is the essence of fornication."[37] And against Jovinian's argument that marriage was as holy an estate as virginity, Ambrose, Origen, and Jerome all insisted on the superiority of the ascetic life, with Jerome notoriously insisting that "nothing is filthier than to have sex with your wife as you might do with another woman. . . . Every too ardent lover of his own wife is an adulterer."[38] While marriage might mitigate the sin associated with sex, it nonetheless indulged sensual desires that were a reminder of humanity's fall. As Coppélia Kahn points out, once "sexual pleasure . . . enters explicitly and legitimately into marriage, whoredom becomes an internal threat rather than an external one."[39] Even the holiest of conjugal sexual relations could not achieve the spiritual purity of lifelong virginity.

Differences in sexual behavior reinforced the distinction between a worldly, sexually active laity and a celibate clergy whose sacred status was manifested in the ability to effect the miracle of transubstantiation.[40] This unique holiness justified privileges like exemption from taxation even as the prohibition of clerical marriage allowed the Church to amass wealth and property by denying priests legal heirs.[41] Precisely because clerical celibacy was so instrumental to the consolidation of Church power, the Church actively *encouraged* lay marriage, which was officially listed as one of the seven sacraments by the Fourth Lateran Council in 1215. As Dyan Elliott demonstrates, beginning in the twelfth and thirteenth centuries the Church increasingly questioned the legitimacy of "spiritual marriage," a legal union in which both parties consent to maintain sexual abstinence (either temporarily or permanently) in an effort to reconcile a worldly institution with celibate devotional practice. So just when the Church was more rigorously demanding clerical celibacy and rejecting priests who married or had children, it was also teaching that sexual intercourse was central to Christian marriage.[42]

Scholastic theologians in the twelfth through fourteenth centuries, most famously Thomas Aquinas, explored what Pierre J. Payer describes as "the legitimate choices open to people in regard to sex" and accordingly offered a positive account of sexual pleasure within the confines of marriage.[43] In fourteenth- and fifteenth-century European literate culture as well as theological writing, we witness the prominence of a model of marriage that is hard to distinguish from the companionate marriage often said to have been invented by Protestants, in which husband and wife equally consent to a union based on chaste love and mutual support. Italian humanists had promoted the joys of matrimony, and in later medieval English romance, depictions of adulterous and excessive passion decreased in favor of a focus on chaste, respectable, moderate love that led to the altar.[44] These cultural ideals were officially upheld by the Catholic doctrine that the single and essential requirement for a binding marriage was the mutual and voluntary consent of both parties. A priest's blessing, like that of parents, was desirable but not required for a union to be valid in the eyes of the Church and the law.

The widely accepted narrative of the rise of companionate marriage not only suppresses the complex reality of medieval law, religion, and culture. It also ignores what influential reformers like Luther and Calvin actually wrote about marriage, as well as the views expressed in a good deal of sixteenth- and seventeenth-century Protestant writing. Certainly, during the institution of Protestantism in England there were many popular pamphlets supporting clerical marriage and singing the praises of domesticity more generally. But religious historians have noted that these works' pervasiveness may indicate that the populace needed to be convinced that sex could be reconciled with sanctity, rather than widespread agreement about the innate value of matrimony.[45] Many English Protestants, like their Catholic forbears, suspected that carnal desire, even that satisfied within marriage, was innately perverse and sinful—a qualm manifested in the refusal of some Protestants, including Elizabeth I, to accept communion from married bishops.[46]

Nor was this doubt about the spiritual status of sex limited to laypersons. It also appears in the writings of Luther and Calvin, a theological affinity that can be attributed in part to the shared Augustinian heritage of Catholicism and Protestantism.[47] As I discussed in chapter 1, Augustine departed from previous Church Fathers in his rejection of a classical dualism in which bodily appetites could be mastered through ascetic discipline. In a formulation followed by Luther and Calvin, the works of the flesh for Augustine signified all attachments to the world, including feelings of pride, desire, and aggression that one might not act upon, or even be conscious of. In the *Confessions*, for instance, Augustine's nocturnal emissions provide a reminder of the opacity and intractability of the will. Even after he has become celibate, Augustine confesses, images of lust still "attack" him in his sleep, revealing "how great a difference [there is] between myself at the time when I am asleep and myself when I return to the waking state."[48] In this gulf between self and self, will and agency, Augustine experiences the elusiveness of the continence he seeks. As Foucault notes, nocturnal emissions posed a similar problem for Cassian, for whom "carnal conjunction" had more to do with mind than body.[49] Nocturnal emissions provided data on the soul, Peter Brown writes, to "inform of the movement of forces that lay beyond immediate consciousness."[50] Yet whereas Cassian believed that "the very depths of a person could shift in a collaboration of the will with the grace of God," Augustine was certain that "deliverance never would occur in this life."[51] The disobedient will with which we are born follows us to the grave (and perhaps beyond).

This conception of innate human depravity helps shape Augustine's view of conjugal relations. Rather than deny that there was sex in paradise, as did previous patristic writers, Augustine insisted that rational and innocent sex could have taken place, even if we cannot imagine such a thing now. Before the fall, he explains in *City of God*, "the marriage in paradise would not have known this opposition, this resistance, this tussle between lust and will," since "the will would have received the obedience of all the members, including the organs of sex."[52] In Eden, "those parts of the body were not activated by the turbulent heat of passion but brought into service by deliberate use of power when the need arose" (*CG* 14.26). The fall introduced the *poena reciproca* in which, as we have seen, "the retribution for disobedience is simply disobedience itself," and man is at perpetual "odds with himself . . . his very mind and even his lower element, his flesh, do not submit to his will" (*CG* 14.15). Prelapsarian genitals were as much under the will's control as hands or feet; postlapsarian sex is inspired by arousal beyond the will's control. Accordingly, Virginia Burras explains, Augustine defends the institution of marriage on the grounds that the conjugal bond allows for the "mutual entrustment of shame" when partners expose to one another helpless and humiliating desires.[53]

The Protestant defense of marriage as a divine concession to creaturely need retained the Augustinian view of postlapsarian sex as a shameful badge of the divided will. Luther and Calvin did insist on the holiness of clerical as well as lay marriage, but their reasoning was more complex and less celebratory than has often been supposed. In fact, the claim that marriage may be more conducive to holiness than virginity rests on the belief that although celibacy remained the spiritual ideal, it was possible only for the chosen few who, singled out for God's special grace, were "eunuchs for heaven" (GB, Matt. 19:12), free from the desire for sex. For the vast majority of humanity, attempts to remain celibate result only in painful yearning, masturbation, and secret fornication; hypocritical pride before humanity is accompanied by resentment toward God. Conjugal sex, in this view, differs from fornication not because it is more rational or innocent, nor because it produces legitimate offspring. Marriage is a sign of holiness because it constitutes personal and public acknowledgment of one's innate human depravity and consequent dependence on God's grace, not one's own merit, for salvation.

Given the centrality of celibacy to clerical privilege, it should be no surprise that a redefinition of the relation between sex and holiness was integral to the Protestant Reformation.[54] The Protestant ideal of companionate marriage grew out of the association between celibacy, idolatry, and institutional corruption. Far from a model of otherworldly sanctity, monastic life, Protestant Reformers charged, was rife with sexual license that would make most laypersons blush. The problem with priests, monks, and nuns is not virginity itself, but avowed celibates' refusal to admit their creaturely drives, as Calvin explains: "Our only reason for disapproving of the vow of celibacy is, because it is improperly regarded as an act of worship, and is rashly undertaken by persons who have not the power of keeping it" (*Institutes* 4.13.18). Disgusted that "the people continue to admire as if the monastic life alone were angelic, perfect and purified from every vice," when in fact "you will scarcely find one in ten [monasteries] which is not rather a brothel than a sacred abode of chastity," Calvin describes the vow of lifelong chastity as an act of "insane audacity," an arrogant denial of human nature that is all the more galling in that celibates "aspire to the praise of humility" (*Institutes* 4.13. 11, 15, 3). "Priests, monks, and nuns," Calvin writes, "forgetful of their infirmity, are confident of their fitness for celibacy. . . . How can they presume to shake off the common feelings of their nature for a whole lifetime, seeing the gift of continence is often granted for a certain time as occasion requires?" (*Institutes* 4.13.3). Celibates make a promise that is not theirs to keep because true chastity—like true faith—is a gift of God. Then, in their "contumacious obstinacy," they eschew the physic of marriage, allowing the "disease of incontinence" to fester (*Institutes* 4.13.21).

However much they attack the hypocrisy of vowed celibates, Luther and Calvin still concede that God may give the gift of bodily and spiritual purity to a chosen few. What Dale B. Martin has remarked of Jesus's sexuality is here a general principle of the response to virginity: "Not to experience desire at all renders someone, in our world, so abnormal as to be practically nonhuman."[55] Luther describes those who "have made themselves eunuchs for the sake of heaven" as "spiritually rich and exalted persons," but insists that "such persons are rare, not one in a thousand, for they are a special miracle of God."[56] Calvin, similarly, acknowledges that "virginity . . . is a virtue not to be despised" and that those who have this gift should remain celibate so that "they may be less encumbered in [God's] service" (*Institutes* 2.8.42, 43).[57] Yet he immediately warns that "since there are many on whom this blessing is conferred only for a time, let everyone, in abstaining from marriage, do it so long as he is fit to endure celibacy. If he has not the power of subduing his passion, let him understand that the Lord has made it obligatory on him to marry," for "even if he abstains from the outward act . . . his mind may in the meantime be inwardly inflamed with lust" (*Institutes* 2.8.43). Like Augustine, Calvin stresses that virginity is not just a physical state. Rather, "by continence I mean not merely that by which the body is kept pure from fornication, but that by which the mind keeps its chastity untainted. For Paul enjoins caution not only against external lasciviousness, but also burning of mind" (*Institutes* 4.13.17). True virgins do not need to refrain from sex because they do not want it in the first place. These elect burn only for God.

Protestant Reformers, in short, did not dispute the Pauline view of sex as a pathological compulsion derived from the fall. Instead, they made it the basis of their defense of clerical marriage: since lay marriage had always been encouraged, even elevated to a holy sacrament, it was its expansion to clergy and theological redefinition that was Protestantism's real break with the Catholic Church. Luther maintains that the drive to copulate "is not a matter of free choice or decision but a natural and necessary thing" (*Estate* 148). Those who attempt to withstand an urge "more necessary than sleeping and waking, eating and drinking, and emptying the bowels and bladder" ensure that the libido will "[go] its way through fornication, adultery, and secret sins, for this is a matter of nature and not of choice" (*Estate* 148). Luther follows Augustine in affirming that "since the fall marriage has been adulterated with wicked lust"—it is much better to marry than to burn, but marriage still "may be likened to a hospital for incurables which prevents inmates from falling into graver sin" (*Sermon* 413, 414). The medicine of conjugal sex must be taken in modestly calibrated doses, Luther cautions: "A man has to control himself and not make a filthy sow's sty of his marriage" (*Sermon* 415).

Calvin is even more expansive about the dangers that lurk in the nuptial bed. Even as those without the gift of continence "cure their infirmity" by engaging in conjugal sex, they must take care that the treatment not exacerbate the disease:

> When spouses are made aware that their union is blessed by the Lord, they are thereby reminded that they must not give way to intemperate and unrestrained indulgence. For though honorable wedlock veils the turpitude of incontinence, it does not follow that it ought forthwith to become a stimulus [*irritamentum*] to it. Wherefore, let spouses consider that all things are not lawful for them. Let there be sobriety in the behavior of the husband toward the wife, and of the wife in her turn toward the husband; each so acting as not to do anything unbecoming the dignity and temperance of married life. Marriage contracted in the Lord ought to exhibit measure and modesty [*modum et modestiam*]— not run to the extreme of wantonness [*lasciviam*]. This excess Ambrose censured gravely, but not undeservedly, when he described the man who shows no modesty or comeliness [*nullam erecundiae vel honestatis*] in conjugal intercourse, as committing adultery with his wife. (*Institutes* 2.8.44)

In light of the Reformers' acceptance of the Augustinian principle that postlapsarian humans lack the capacity to control not just body but mind, such calls for "sobriety," "dignity," "temperance," "measure," "modesty," and "comeliness" in "conjugal intercourse" are both comic and futile. If arousal defies the conscious will, one must wonder how conjugal sex acts can avoid "anything unbecoming the dignity and temperance of married life." What would modest and comely sex look like? Are there rules? Wouldn't such rules themselves push the bounds of modesty in that their formulation requires thinking about what *could* render human sex more like what goes on in a "sow's sty"? If there are no rules, how can a couple know at what point their perfunctory due benevolence begins to "run to the extreme of wantonness"? And even if conjugal intercourse never becomes "intemperate and unrestrained" in reality, what of fantasy? Might not the same be said of the spouse as Calvin says of the virgin: "Even if he abstains from the outward act . . . his mind may in the meantime be inwardly inflamed with lust" (*Institutes* 2.8.43)?

As a "hospital for incurables," marriage is not a sign of innocence but an admission of sinful desire. Marriage is holier than celibacy because it replaces "contumacious obstinacy" with a humble, public acknowledgment that "the sin of unchastity urges and lurks within" (*Institutes* 4.13.21). In Luther's and Calvin's theology, the differentiation of good and bad sex, disease and cure, that so profoundly shapes modern law, culture, and government policy had yet to take place. As the delibidinized, companionate, procreative view of marriage we currently take for granted emerged slowly and unevenly, some of the period's major cultural forms questioned whether it was attainable, or even appealing. Below, I examine Shakespeare's and Spenser's lyrics as two important examples of this ambivalence.

Procreation and the Dilemma of Orgasm

The focus on procreation by the dissent in *Obergefell*, as in white evangelical and right-wing political discourse more generally, works to desexualize marriage. In a particularly pithy formulation of this view, Edelman aligns reproduction, Christianity, and heteronormativity in describing "the envy-, contempt-, and anxiety-inducing fixation on [queers'] freedom from the necessity of translating the corrupt, unregenerate vulgate of fucking into the infinitely tonier, indeed sacramental, Latin of procreation."[58] The privileging of procreative sex, Edelman observes, requires that

> all sensory experience, all pleasure of the flesh, must be borne away from this fantasy of futurity secured, eternity's plan fulfilled. . . . Paradoxically, the child of the two-parent family thus proves that its parents *don't* fuck and on its tiny shoulders it carries the burden of maintaining the fantasy of a time to come in which meaning, at last made present to itself, no longer depends on the fantasy of its *attainment* in time to come.[59]

Reproductive futurism subordinates the present act of sex ("fucking") to its future potential ("procreation"), mimicking a triumph of spirit over flesh. This "comic book version of heterosexuality" is at once teleological and typological, with the final part, the Child, retroactively revealing love, marriage, and sex to have been directed at obeying the divine command to "be fruitful, and multiply" all along.[60]

The first seventeen sonnets in Shakespeare's sequence, conventionally called the "procreation sonnets," are perhaps the best-known cultural monument to a fantasy of delibidinized procreation that suppresses the details of the male erection and ejaculation upon which conception depends. In considering this absence of sex in the context of religious and medical representations of orgasm, as well as that of Shakespeare's own Sonnet 129, I consider the implications for a longer history of sexual discourse of Annamarie Jagose's argument that orgasm is not just a bodily reflex; it is "a complexly contradictory formation, potentially disruptive of many of the sedimenting critical frameworks by which we have grown accustomed to apprehending sexuality."[61] Among these, I argue, are the gendered and racial hierarchies that inform the segregation of sex from propagation that Edelman describes.

Shakespeare's procreation sonnets are replete with images of husbandry and planting (1, 3, 13, 15, 16); thrift, traffic, moneylending, and usury (4, 6, 9, 13); distillation (5, 6); printing (11); and breeding (12). Urging the fair youth to marry and beget an heir (or ten, as Sonnet 6 suggests), the poetic speaker, Will, lays bare the economic dimension of marriage as a means of regulating sexuality and privatizing wealth.[62] He says nothing about passion or companionship: reproduction in the procreation sonnets is *work*. These poems treat sex as an activity about "as exciting as putting up preserves," as Richard Halpern puts it, and this is part of the sonnets' strategic separation of a poetics of the sublime, focused on the disruptiveness of *jouissance*, from a poetics of the beautiful, focused on the monotony of procreation.[63] These poems convey a grim Christian view of reproduction in which, as Martin summarizes, "marriage . . . was completely implicated in the dreaded cycle of sex, birth, death, and decay, followed by more sex, birth, death and decay."[64] This cycle appears in the opening poem of Shakespeare's sequence:

> From fairest creatures we desire increase,
> That thereby beauty's rose might never die,
> But as the riper should by time decease
> His tender heir might bear his memory:
> But thou, contracted to thine own bright eyes,
> Feed'st thy light's flame with self-substantial fuel,
> Making a famine where abundance lies—
> Thyself thy foe, to thy sweet self too cruel.
> Thou that art now the world's fresh ornament
> And only herald to the gaudy spring
> Within thine own bud buriest thy content,
> And tender churl mak'st waste in niggarding.
>   Pity the world, or else this glutton be—
>   To eat the world's due, by the grave and thee. (1.1–14)

The "we" of line 1 assumes that the desire to reproduce beauty naturally follows from an appreciation of "fairest creatures." Who does *not* want more fair creatures in the world? What kind of person would allow "beauty's rose" to die? We get an answer in the second quatrain: "But thou." In the procreation sonnets, as Aaron Kunin observes, the youth is not part of the "we" for whom Will speaks.[65] He is at odds with this natural and theological imperative to perpetuate God's creation. In response, Will warns (in an apocalyptic vision, as we have seen, shared by Justice Roberts), "If all were minded so, the times should cease, / And three-score year would make the world away" (11.7–8). Setting himself athwart the "we," at odds with the consensus of "all," the youth is designated as queer insofar as he, to borrow another of Edelman's phrases, is "*not*

'fighting for the children,'" but is stubbornly standing "outside the consensus by which all politics confirms the absolute value of reproductive
futurism" to insist, like the Pauline apostle and the modern sinthomo-
sexual, that "the future stop[s] here."[66] The procreation sonnets urge the
youth to conform his desires to the commonsense assertion that, faced
with the choice to "increase" or "die," "we" will always choose the former.

As readers at least since Oscar Wilde have noticed, however, the sonnets will go on to replace the labors of reproductive sex with the pleasures of *poetic* generation. Initially, the sonnets treat poetry as a fallback
option, arguing that "a mightier way" of defeating time and death would
be to till those "many maiden gardens yet unset," who "With virtuous
wish would bear your living flowers" (16.1, 6–7). But the speaker gradually leaves off begging the youth to take action and "Make thee another
self for love of me" in favor of assuring him that poetry will itself take
care of the future: "As he takes from you, I engraft you new" (10.13, 15.14).
The imperative to reproduce, so seemingly urgent in the early sonnets, is
never mentioned again after Sonnet 17, which makes a final, if feeble, attempt to convince the youth to supplement poetry with progeny in order
to defeat mortality. The "yellowed" pages of Will's verse may one day be
"scorned" as poetic hyperbole if they are not supplemented by flesh-and-
blood offspring who will provide living testimony to the youth's erst-
while beauty: "But were some child of yours alive that time, / You should
live twice in it and in my rhyme" (17.9, 10, 13–14). From this point on,
the sequence confidently advertises its own independent preservative
power, which, as Kunin points out, requires neither the youth's participation nor his consent: "So long as men can breathe or eyes can see, /
So long lives *this*, and *this* gives life to thee" (18.13–14; my emphasis).[67] A
turn from biological procreation, as scholars have long noticed, is also a
turn away from women and toward a fantasy, at least as ancient as Plato's
Symposium, of male intellectual creation. The poet's love replaces dutiful
generation with something both more pleasurable and more dignified.
The asexual reproduction of poetry preserves *spiritual* beauty through
what Freud would call sublimation, the redirection of libidinal impulses
to culturally sanctioned projects.[68]

This sidelining of compulsory heterosexual reproduction in favor
of voluntary same-sex love and poetic creation might seem to be unproblematically queer, offering a challenge to modern heteronormative

family values. But, as I discussed in chapter 2, Shakespeare's homoerotic poetics themselves incorporate gendered and racial exclusions inimical to queer universalism. Insofar as the reproductive imperative on which "we" all agree is limited to increasing "*fair* creatures," we must notice with Sharon Holland that "jettisoning the biological as the province of women in order to open up the space for queer (re)production does not facilitate the dismantling of racism's foundational logics."[69] The fair youth of the sonnets is being scolded for what Holland summarizes as "the failure to (re)produce the Anglo-Saxon."[70] Moreover, Holland writes, "If we were to take reproduction here as part of the matrix of racialized desire, we can then see how this turn away from reproduction is racially marked, not because it reveals a loss of Anglo-Saxon sanguinity per se, but because it also produces reproduction as a function of white racial belonging rather than as a function of all racial belonging."[71] The sonnets' biopolitical project assumes that "we" do not desire the increase of *less* fair creatures, through childbirth or through poetry; "we" do not mind if their genes *or* their memories die. Sonnet 11 is quite explicit about the sequence's ruthless logic of selective preservation: "Let those whom nature hath not made for store, / Harsh, featureless, and rude, barrenly perish" (11.9–10).

I build here on Kim F. Hall's argument that by attending to the racialized import of the word "fair," we can appreciate that the delibidinized or sublimated generation that the sonnets recommend also bespeaks a nascent white supremacist ideology.[72] The poetic preservation of fair creatures, no less than their physical increase, is based on racial selection that shrugs at the possibility that creatures who are not fair—not beautiful, not white—will "barrenly perish." A celebration of "legitimate" procreation, no less in Shakespeare's sonnets than in modern attacks on "welfare queens," cannot fully dissever itself from eugenics. Indeed, as a reproductive technology, poetry is not entirely separate conceptually from modern forms of asexual human generation. In-utero and in-vitro fertilization, egg donation, and surrogacy all involve deciding who will donate sperm, ovum, or womb. Would-be parents receive detailed information to help in donor selection: medical history, education level, height, hair and eye color, hobbies, and—often first and foremost—racial and ethnic background. Assuming the desire for racialized selection, modern reproductive assistance makes medically explicit the erotic life of racism that Shakespeare's poetic reproduction romanticizes and naturalizes.

Rather than treat the sonnets' male homopoesis as a wholly laudable alternative to the ideal of reproductive futurism, we might notice that its willful division of passion from procreation itself undermines a modern view that married, reproductive sex is uniquely innocent. The problem with sexual generation—and this is a problem, I want to stress, that Shakespeare's procreation sonnets conspicuously obscure—is that it requires orgasm, which is a particularly poignant expression of the feebleness of postlapsarian will. As Augustine recognized, lust

> disturbs the whole man, when the mental emotion combines and mingles with the physical craving, resulting in a pleasure surpassing all physical delights. So intense is the pleasure that when it reaches its climax there is an almost total extinction of mental alertness; the intellectual sentries, as it were, are overwhelmed. (CG 14.16)

Nor do marriage or procreation mitigate this loss of control. For while "any friend of wisdom and holy joys who lives a married life . . . would prefer, if possible, to beget children without lust of this kind," Augustine insists,

> not even the lovers of this kind of pleasure [voluptatis] are moved either to conjugal intercourse or to the impure indulgences of vice [inmunditias faglitiorum: "filthy outrage" or "disgrace"], just when they have so willed. Sometimes the impulse is an unwanted intruder, sometimes it abandons the eager lover, and desire cools off in the body while it is at boiling heat in the mind. (CG 14.16)

The Renaissance translation of City of God is more explicit, stressing "the shame that accompanies copulation, as well in harlotry as in marriage."[73] It is because sex betrays spiritual impotence that even though conjugal and procreative intercourse is "lawful and respectable," it nonetheless "blushes to be seen" to the extent that "a man would be less put out by a crowd of spectators watching him visiting his anger unjustly upon another man than by one person observing him when he is having lawful intercourse with his wife" (CG 14.18, 19).

Augustine's account of Edenic affection anticipates modern idealizations of marriage: "Between man and wife there was a faithful partnership based on love and mutual respect" (*CG* 14.26). Imagining in-utero fertilization *avant la lettre*, Augustine describes prelapsarian reproduction in which male semen can enter the womb as easily as female semen—long believed to be the content of menstruation—can leave it, all without penetration:

> Although we cannot prove this in experience, it therefore does not follow that we should not believe that when those parts of the body were not activated by the turbulent heat of passion but brought into service by deliberate use of power when the need arose, the male seed could have been dispatched into the womb [*ita tunc potuisse utero coniugis salva integritate feminei genitalis virile semen inmitti*], with no loss of the wife's integrity, just as the menstrual flux can now be produced from the womb of a virgin without loss of maidenhead. For the seed could be injected through the same passage by which the flux is ejected. Now just as the female womb might have been opened for parturition by a natural impulse when the time was ripe, instead of by the groans of travail, so the two sexes might have been united for impregnation and conception by an act of will, instead of by a lustful craving. (*CG* 14.26)

Unfortunately, Augustine tells us, this immaculate conception "was not in fact experienced by those for whom it was available, because their sin happened first, and they incurred the penalty of exile from paradise before they could unite in the task of propagation as a deliberate act undisturbed by passion" (*CG* 14.26). The prelapsarian love theoretically possible for Adam and Eve is emphatically not within our postlapsarian capacity. As a result, Augustine admits, even his own clinical discussion of emission, menstruation, conception, and parturition is "bound to induce a feeling of shame, under present conditions," for after the fall the very attempt to imagine virtuous sex "now suggests to the mind only the turbulent lust which we experience, not the calm act of will imagined in my speculation" (*CG* 14.26).

The conviction that irrational lust was the motor of generation was not limited to religious writing. In fact, this view was essential to early modern anatomical tracts and marital advice books ostensibly focused on explaining conception, pregnancy, and childbirth to a lay audience. Throughout the sixteenth and seventeenth centuries, works such as Thomas Vicary's 1586 *The English-Mans Treasure*, Helkiah Crooke's 1615 *Mikrokosmographia*, Nicolas Culpepper's *Directory for Midwives* (published in two parts in 1651 and 1676), the anonymous 1684 *Aristotle's Masterpiece*, and Nicholas Venette's 1703 *The Mysteries of Conjugal Love Reveal'd* offered to reveal the secrets of great sex on the grounds that both male and female orgasm were necessary to procreation.[74] These manuals advertised the medical credentials of their authors, perhaps because they were often hard to distinguish from pornography in their explicit rendering of male and female genitalia, erection, penetration, and ejaculation. Crooke seeks to avoid this generic confusion when he prefaces his *Mikrokosmographia* with a denial that his "figures are as obscoene as Aretines."[75] The fact that Crooke takes the time to distinguish this medical textbook from Pietro Aretino's notorious *I Modi* (often regarded the first modern printed pornography) indicates that he is aware that his explicit descriptions have the potential to titillate readers. Indeed, his disavowal of this potential may also have served to advertise it.

In general, early modern medicine tended to eschew the Aristotelian view of women as contributing to generation only passive matter to be shaped and quickened by male form. Vicary, for instance, follows the Hippocratic and Galenic principle that conception is a collaborative effort requiring the ejaculation of both male and female seed, in which "eche of them worketh in the other, and suffereth in the other, [to] engender Embreon," while Culpepper elaborates that "conception is an action of the womb, after fruitful seed both male and female is received, mixed and nourished, & its strength is stirred up to do its office."[76] Because female as well as male orgasm in the early modern period was deemed essential to conception, anatomical tracts and conjugal advice books were as interested in female arousal as male arousal. According to *Aristotle's Masterpiece*, not only conception but also penetration requires female arousal, for the vaginal passage plays nearly as active a role in intercourse as the penis. As this popular medical text has it, "Whilst the passage is replete with Spirit and Vital Blood, it becomes more strait for embracing the *Penis*."[77] With the sixteenth-century "discovery" of the clitoris as an external "female penis," anatomies also encouraged clitoral stimulation as necessary to reproductive sexuality. Culpepper, for instance, notes that "the part at the top [of the pudenda] is hard and nervous, and swells like a Yard [penis] in Venery."[78] More expansively, Venette explained that "there is a part above the *Nymphae* longer more or less than half a finger, called by Anatomists *Clitoris*, which I may justly term the Fury and Rage of Love. There Nature has plac'd the seat of Pleasure and Lust, as it has on the other hand in the *Glans* of Man. There it has plac'd those excessive Ticklings, and there is Leachery and Lasciviousness establish'd."[79] Venette's comment betrays a more general ambivalence shared by many anatomies: they deemed female arousal and orgasm necessary to conception even as they expressed anxiety about its propriety and deemed clitoral hypertrophy a foreign affliction peculiar to the Indies, Turkey, and North Africa.[80]

Early modern anatomies share the view that conception requires mutual orgasm, and orgasm requires a loss of reason and self-possession—an equally ecstatic and shaming surrender of the self and its interests. Crooke describes sexual arousal as "a sting or rage of pleasure, as whereby we are transported for a time as it were out of our selues," and he follows Augustine in denying that such arousal is exclusively physical, for "this part or member is not erected without the help of the imagination."[81] Extolling the connection between arousal, orgasm, and procreation, Crooke portrays loss of dignity as necessary to the perpetuation of the species:

> The wonderfull prouidence of Nature hath giuen to all Creatures certayne goades and prouocations of lust, and an impotent desire of copulation for the preseruation of the seuerall kindes of Creatures. . . . This sting of pleasure was very necessary, without which man especially the one sexe in scorne and detestation of so brutish and base a work, the other for fear of payne and trouble, would have abhorred this worke of Nature.[82]

Nearly a century later, Venette adds that "as soon as the Fancy is touched, and the small Fibres of the Brain shaken by the Thoughts of Love, there is an internal Sweat in our Privy Parts, and the Spirits which rush thither with Precipitation."[83] Whereas handbooks detailing the mechanics of sex would seem quite distinct from Protestant admonishments to avoid excessive arousal, these manuals remained uneasy about the act of generation, recognizing its relation to fornication and sodomy—"brutish and base" work for men that, if successful, will bring women "payne and trouble." The sacrificial schema Edelman describes is, in the early modern view, one that *begins* with vulgar fucking and is only retroactively recategorized as tasteful procreation.

Shakespeare's Sonnet 129 indicates that the belief that orgasm necessarily overcomes reason and self-interest might help account for the procreation sonnets' avoidance of sex. Here, the speaker regrets succumbing to what Crooke calls the "goades and prouocations of lust":

> Th'expense of spirit in a waste of shame
> Is lust in action, and till action lust
> Is perjured, murd'rous, bloody, full of blame,
> Savage, extreme, rude, cruel, not to trust,
> Enjoyed no sooner but despisèd straight,
> Past reason hunted, and no sooner had,
> Past reason hated as a swallowed bait,
> On purpose laid to make the taker mad;
> Mad in pursuit, and in possession so,
> Had, having, and in quest to have, extreme,
> A bliss in proof, and proved, a very woe,
> Before, a joy proposed, behind, a dream.
>> All this the world well knows, yet none knows well
>> To shun the heav'n that leads men to this hell. (129.1–14)

The first sentence of the poem—stretching from lines 1 to 12—is primarily devoted to adjectives and adjectival phrases describing what lust is like *before* action, or consummation. The regular iambs and multisyllabic words of the first twelve lines combine with the breathless accumulation of adjectives to propel the reader quickly through the poem, mimicking what Christian doctrine and anatomical science agreed are the "goads and provocations of lust." The effect is intensified by the formal repetitions in the long first sentence. Participial phrases translate action into descriptive quality: "Enjoyed no sooner," "despisèd straight," "Past reason hunted," "Past reason hated," "On purpose laid." Anadiplosis, the repetition of the last word of one line as the first word of the next, structurally registers the speaker's enclosure within the "mad"—enraged, insane—force of lust, which "make[s] the taker mad; / Mad in pursuit, and in possession so." The repeated oscillation between past, present, and future in verb tense as well as specific temporal markers forges a sense of helpless, inevitable compulsion to repeat: "is lust . . . till action"; "Had, having, and in quest to have"; "in proof, and proved"; "Before . . . behind." The grammar and rhetoric of lines 1–12 override line breaks and distinctions between quatrains so that we are mired in the speaker's own experience of loss of logical thought and purposive agency. There is no sense of development or teleology, simply an outburst in which bliss and woe, self-gratification and self-loss, are indistinguishable.

The grammatical and lexical loss of control enacted by the first twelve lines is summarized in the couplet as "All this." This belated assertion that the "hell" of postcoital shame is common knowledge casts Will's agitation as fury at the human condition, the loss of self and agency that Bersani influentially described as the "self-shattering" of *jouissance*. The speaker's inability to withstand the lure of self-dissolution is registered in the word "heav'n," a disyllabic word that must be compressed for the line to scan. Set amidst the calm, determined monosyllables of the final iambic couplet, "heav'n" names the thwarted will to transcend the "hell" of creaturely self-division. As early modern slang for the genitals, "hell" offers an Augustinian synecdoche for our more pervasive inability to know or direct our own actions and motives.

While the self-loathing of Sonnet 129 would appear to be worlds away from the reproductive propaganda of the first seventeen sonnets, 129 may retrospectively illuminate the procreation sonnets' clinical, sexless depiction of biological reproduction, which allows speaker, addressee, and readers to avoid thinking about what is required for the propagation these poems urge. Reading Sonnet 129, orgasm sounds like something one wouldn't wish on an enemy, much less a "fair" beloved. But in the accounts of writers as different as Augustine and Crooke the indignity detailed in 129 is indispensable to human reproduction. Moreover, one cannot know whether a given "expense of spirit" has been a performance of procreative duty or a "waste of shame" until well after the fact. Given that sodomy was defined as a "waste" of semen on sex that fails to serve a reproductive purpose, the absence of information as to the gender of Will's partner in 129 is telling—this could equally be the "fair" youth or the "black" mistress.[84] Because after the fall the human will became divided and inscrutable, the divine command of Genesis to "be fruitful, and multiply" cannot be purposively obeyed, even by married hetero-sexual couples.

In other words, when it comes to procreation, obedience to divine command is rendered impossible not only by the inscrutable and di-vided will but also by simple biological facts. Any given instance of het-erosexual intercourse is known to be procreative only retrospectively, and the precise operations of human pregnancy are as immune to agency and decision as those of digestion and planting. This is true now, when pregnancy cannot be tested until at least a couple of weeks after concep-tion; in the early modern period the timespan between a given sex act and certain knowledge of pregnancy was several months.[85] In the heat of the moment, procreation and sodomy cannot be conclusively distin-guished, for *post*lapsarian couples can never be sure whether they are having sex in compliance with God's *pre*lapsarian command to multiply or their own lustful impulses. To put it another way, the mutual orgasm deemed necessary to procreation also makes the dutiful sex of Christian matrimony hard to distinguish from the "Saracen enjoyment" that, Jef-frey Cohen has shown, made *jouissance* a mark of racial difference.[86]

Due Benevolence

To reverse Edelman's formulation, in Renaissance medical tracts the tony Latin of procreation—along with the racial and cultural hierar-chies of the humanist education that Latin exemplifies—is inevitably translated into the vernacular of fucking. But what of that other jus-tification of marriage, companionship based on spiritualized love and friendship? Is Shakespeare typical in his disgust at sexual climax? Or is it possible to imagine modest and comely copulation? For many lit-erary critics, Edmund Spenser's *Amoretti* and *Epithalamion* respond to this last question with a strong "yes," asserting the dignity and mutual respect of conjugal desire. Written to commemorate Spenser's mar-riage to his second wife, Elizabeth Boyle, the *Amoretti* and *Epithalamion* were published in a single volume as companion poems in 1595. Read-ing this pair of lyric sequences according to theories of the "Puritan art of love" deemed to accompany the rise of companionate marriage, scholars have widely agreed that they offer a firmly Protestant alterna-tive to Petrarchan convention.[87] In this view, previous sonnet sequences anatomize the pain of desires that are at once illicit and unrequited. These earlier Petrarchan lyrics reveal the psychic cost of the division of passionate love from legitimate marriage, and they are a product, in part, of a Catholic idealization of virginity as the highest spiritual state. Spenser's love lyrics tell a different story, this argument goes, one in which lawful desires are pursued through sincere courtship and satisfied in loving Protestant marriage.[88] Their commemoration of "such loue not lyke to lusts of baser kind" and declaration that marriage is an institution in which "spotlesse pleasure builds her sacred bowre" reassures us that, yes, there is innocent sex.[89]

Resisting this optimistic reading, a number of critics have rightly noted the tensions inherent in Spenser's Reformed views of human love.[90] I build on this work to focus in this last section on the profound anxiety expressed by the *Amoretti* and *Epithalamion* about both the speaker's own desires and his beloved's responses. The poems are deeply conscious of what Warner calls the "indignity" of sex, the human vulnerability and aggression that erotic desire uniquely manifests. Together, the *Amoretti* and *Epithalamion* demonstrate that Protestant ideals of sexual innocence and married chastity may themselves encourage the failure of mutuality and recognition that foment psychic and physical violence. The *Amoretti* and *Ephithalamion* offer a Pauline portrait of marriage, with the speaker, at least, following the principle that it is better to marry than to burn (in "boyling sweat," no less [*Amoretti* 30.7]). Paul, as I discussed above, quite explicitly prefers celibacy, declaring that "It *were* good for a man not to touch a woman" (GB, 1 Cor. 7:1). "Nevertheless," he concedes, once married,

> let the husband give unto the wife due benevolence, and likewise also the wife unto the husband. The wife hath not the power of her own body, but the husband; and likewise also the husband hath not the power of his own body, but the wife. Defraud not one another, except *it be* with consent for a time, that ye may give yourselves to fasting and prayer, and again come together, that Satan tempt you not for your incontinency. (GB, 1 Cor. 7:2–5; emphasis in original)

Paul's accommodation presumes equal desire between husband and wife, each entitled to use the other's body to quench the burning that could lead to "incontinency." One spouse's desire becomes the other's debt. This scenario may help explain how a married couple has modest and comely sex: if one partner is just doing a favor or paying a debt, then copulation may achieve something like "sobriety" rather than "run to the extreme of wantonness." Moreover, as Kahn points out, Protestant writers' emphasis on marital chastity "lodges the problem of desire in women."[91] Spenser's *Amoretti* and *Epithalamion* are symptomatic of the gendered asymmetry Kahn examines, for in these poems the beloved is never burning and has no interest in claiming any benevolence that the poet might offer her. Spenser's poetic speaker idealizes his beloved as a paradigm of chastity so absolute as to border on apathy and cruelty. (I'll call these personae "Edmund" and "Elizabeth," respectively, although such autobiographical designations, however traditionally assumed, are Spenser's own fictionalizations.) Like Petrarch's virginal Laura, Spenser's Elizabeth "seems to scorne / base thing, and think how she to heauen may climb" (13.10). She wants out of her body, that clod of "earth" that is "loathsome and forlorne" and "hinders heauenly thoughts with drossy slime" (13.11, 12). By contrast, "My loue is lyke to yse, and I to fyre," Edmund complains, wondering how his "exceeding heat / is not delayd by her hart frosen cold"; instead, "I burne much more in boyling sweat" (30.1, 5–6, 7). In what was by the 1590s well-established Petrarchan convention, the *Amoretti* depicts Edmund and Elizabeth's courtship as an allegory of the struggle between the pure spirit (hers) and the corrupt flesh (his). The difference is that in Spenser's story, Elizabeth "halfe trembling" allows herself to be "fyrmely tyde" "with her owne goodwill" three-quarters of the way through the *Amoretti* (67.11–12). The *Epithalamion* celebrates their nuptials, equally characterized by Edmund's impatient passion and Elizabeth's bashful reluctance. Rejecting a Pauline principle of mutual incontinence, in other words, Spenser makes marriage respectable at the cost of female sexual arousal. If her mind is only on heaven, Elizabeth's consent to worldly marriage is consent to undesired sex.

For a number of critics, the preoccupation with Elizabeth's lack of sexual appetite is the highest form of praise. She is "above tempests and passions"; as "female creator-nurturer," she fosters a marriage in which "materiality is incorporated into spirituality, chastity is redefined"; she redeems Edmund, showing "how a woman may tame a man to love her

so that his simplicity may be truly naked, his grace spotless."[92] Chival-
rous praise of female purity accords with the cultural feminist claim that
men's sexual rapaciousness appears in a general will to dominance, but
women are instinctively cooperative and nurturing.[93] In this ubiquitous
cultural narrative, men want sex ("materiality") and women want love
("spirituality"). Already domesticated themselves, women can "tame"
feral men, teaching them to enjoy backrubs and bubble baths instead
of porn and promiscuous sex. A good woman can save even the most
inveterate playboy from his own base instincts, gently compelling him
to grow up and settle down.

Because what Henry Abelove dubs "sexual intercourse so-called"
("cross-sex genital intercourse [penis in vagina, vagina around penis,
with seminal emission uninterrupted])" can be accomplished without
female arousal but not without male erection, female innocence protects
an ideal of marriage as somehow above the sex it legally sanctions.[94]
But the idealization of female chastity, whether in service of normative heterosexuality or feminist separatism, also tends to naturalize
male sexual rapacity and violence. As Rubin has argued, the tendency
of some second-wave feminists to treat heterosexual sex as "dangerous
and violent" is "predicated on a Victorian model of distribution of libido
in terms of male and female. There was the good woman who was not
sexual. There is the man who is sexual. So whenever sex happens between a good woman and a man, it's a kind of violation of her."[95] In this
view, male aggression becomes normalized, creating what Carol Vance
describes as "a culturally dictated chain of reasoning" through which
"women become the moral custodians of male behavior. . . . Self-control
and watchfulness become major and necessary female virtues."[96]

It is in the conviction that female consent is not a sufficient measure
of the difference between wanted and unwanted sex that the two sides
of the feminist sex wars unexpectedly converge. For while they disagree
on the extent to which women's enjoyment of promiscuity, BDSM, and
pornography is a sign of sexual self-determination or patriarchal false
consciousness, both pro- and antisex feminists agree that within a culture that assumes male initiative and female passivity, bare "consent" is
on a continuum with coercion. Following Rubin's and Vance's logic, we
can see that for women's "no" to be understood as inviolable, "yes" must
go beyond mere, or even affirmative, consent—rather, women must be

permitted to desire and initiate sex. This challenge to traditional ideas of courtship must be understood in the context of a cultural romanticization of male persistence. The need for women to play hard-to-get lest they devalue themselves by seeming too "easy" was already a cliché by the sixteenth century. Once refusal is rescripted as coyness, bare consent—or even the absence or abatement of physical resistance—counts as the difference between seduction and rape, legitimating a whole range of coercive behaviors. If women can *only* properly say "no" (or "wait"), then refusal is hard to distinguish from deferral. In a culture that measures a woman's value in inverse relation to her availability, withholding sex becomes the means of achieving love and marriage. Concomitantly, the aggression uniquely lauded in the white male—not taking no for an answer—is recategorized as romance. As Catharine A. MacKinnon puts it, given the cultural valorization of (white) male pursuit, one in which even initially resistant women are assumed to be susceptible to courtship and seduction, "That consent rather than nonmutuality is the line between rape and intercourse further exposes the inequality in normal social expectations. . . . If sex is ordinarily accepted as something men do *to* women, the better question would be whether consent is a meaningful concept."[97] In other words, for both pro- and antisex feminists, unwanted sex will be distinguishable from wanted sex only when women can do the asking without appearing pathetic or pathological. Until then, there is all too fine a line between being swept off one's feet and being badgered into submission.

Spenser's *Amoretti*, obsessed as it is with female sexual purity, brings this problem to the fore in courting his "stubborne damzell" (29.1) and "hop[ing] her stubborne hart to bend" (51.11). Edmund wants Elizabeth's consent but not her *desire*. He repeatedly distinguishes spiritual love from physical lust, insisting that he does *not* want Elizabeth's "*base* affections" (8.6; my emphasis). He wants "such loue not lyke to lusts of baser kynd," "*chast* affects," "*chast* desires" (6.3, 6.12, 8.8; my emphasis). This dynamic, in which female chastity checks male appetite in service of Christian marriage, is also racialized throughout the *Amoretti*. Elizabeth's attractive combination of desirability and lack of desire earns her the epitaph "proud fayre," two qualities that reinforce one another. In the Petrarchan iconography that shapes the *Amoretti*, Elizabeth is "proud" in the sense of prideful because she is beautiful, and she is beautiful because she is white. But she is also "proud" in the sense that she is not subject to shameful "lusts of baser kind," and this pride sustains her fairness as a valuable property.

Another of Spenser's works, *The Faerie Queene*, offers a specific racialization of lust that sets that of the *Amoretti* and *Ephithalamion* in relief. As I have discussed elsewhere, in one episode, the maiden bride Amoret—whose name allegorizes the nuptial love celebrated in the *Amoretti*—enacts the danger of female desire, even within marriage.[98] Having been kidnapped on her wedding day before the marriage could be consummated, Amoret actively yearns to be reunited with her husband. Her desire, however, is expressed as ravishment by her own passions: Amoret is "snatched vp" "vnawares" by the monster Lust.[99] Spenser's detailed description of this monster brings to the fore the racialization of lust that I discussed in chapter 2. "All ouergrowne with haire," with his "neather lip" resembling "a wide deepe poke," his "huge great nose" "empurpled all with bloud," and his "wide long eares," Lust is an assemblage of male and female genitalia (*The Faerie Queene* 4.7.5, 6). Spenser's precise description of Lust's obscene features derives from racial and protocolonial discourses that understand lust, and the *crimen contra natura* it provokes, as the specific attribute of Irish, Indigenous American, Eastern, and African peoples. Lust, a seminaked "wilde and saluage man," is also an insatiable sodomite and cannibal who "liu'd all on rauin and on rape / Of men and beasts; and fed on fleshly gore," and the size of his labia-like ears exceeds those "of Elephants by *Indus* flood" (*The Faerie Queene* 4.7.5, 6).[100] The multiple anatomical, racial, colonial, and moral contexts that come together in the figure of Lust suggest that white femininity cannot be reconciled with sexual appetite, even within the confines of marriage. Even after she is rescued, Amoret, "sorely bruz'd," remains "neare vnto decay" (*The Faerie Queene* 4.7.35) until King Arthur, the poem's representative of divine magnanimity, treats her with drops of "pretious liquor" (*The Faerie Queene* 4.8.20)—the blood of Christ that, the Gospel of John tells us, "cleanseth us from all sin" (GB, 1 John 1:7). The lesson of the allegory is that even the most seemingly virginal among us may be swept away by lust, a vulnerability that no human act, including marriage, can remedy. The best we can do is face up to this shame and hope for grace.

The episode of Amoret and Lust in *The Faerie Queene* allows us to see that the sexual purity celebrated in the *Amoretti* and *Epithalamion* at once naturalizes male violence and racializes female innocence—no coincidence, given Spenser's own colonial activities in Ireland.[101] Yet insofar as *The Faerie Queene* is an allegory, Lust and Amoret represent not only a colonial encounter *between* virginal self and debauched other but also a battle *within* the divided soul. In this psychomachia, the threat figured by the racialized other is revealed to reside, ineradicably, within the deepest recesses of the self. The episode of Lust and Amoret illuminates *Amoretti* 58, the sequence's strongest statement of the Augustinian conviction of innate human corruption on which Reformed arguments for clerical marriage were grounded. Here, it is the lady's fallen condition, rather than the poet's, that is the focus. This sonnet stands out amidst the multiple assertions of Elizabeth's sexual purity, for it suggests that poet and mistress may be equally frail and fleshly creatures:

> *By her that is most assured to her selfe.*
> Weake is th'assurance that weake flesh reposeth
>   In her owne powre and scorneth others ayde:
>   that soonest fals when as she most supposeth
>   her selfe assurd, and is of nought affrayd.
> All flesh is frayle, and all her strength vnstayd,
>   like a vaine bubble blowen up with ayre:
>   deuouring tyme and changeful chance haue prayd
>   her glories pride that none may it repayre.
> Ne none so rich or wise, so strong or fayre,
>   but fayleth trusting on his owne assurance:
>   and he that standeth on the hyghest stayre
>   fals lowest: for on earth nought hath enduraunce.
> Why then doe ye proud fayre, misdeeme so farre,
>   that to your selfe ye most assured arre? (58.1–14; Spenser's
>   emphasis)

The meaning of this sonnet depends in large part on how one reads the line that prefaces it: "By her that is most assured to her selfe." If one reads "by her" as meaning "concerning her," as Richard McCabe has suggested, one can paraphrase it as "concerning the woman who is most certain of and attached to herself."[102] The sonnet would be, like those that precede and follow it, in the poet's own voice, and it would similarly combine accusations of the lady's pride with exhortations to recognize her human vulnerability. In the larger context of the *Amoretti*, the deeply held Protestant belief that human fallibility makes marriage necessary sounds here like a cynical ploy of seduction at best. The reminder to Elizabeth that she, too, is only human resonates with *Amoretti* 10's prayer to Cupid that "her proud hart doe thou a little shake" and "al her faults in thy black booke enroll" so "That I may laugh at her in equal sort" as she laughs at his courtship (10.9, 12, 13). The warning that pride goes before a fall (in *Amoretti* 58 literalized as a tumble from the "hyghest stayre") is less an exhortation to the "mutual society, help, and comfort" endorsed by the Book of Common Prayer than a wish to even the score.

We can also, however, read "by" in its more conventional sense of signifying creative property or origin. In this case, a paraphrase of the line would be "written by the woman who is most self-assured, addressed to herself."[103] As self-address, the sonnet admits Elizabeth's susceptibility to the fleshly desire that the poet has previously denied her, a lack of continence formally registered in the irregular meter, feminine and apocopated rhymes (reposeth/supposeth; ayde/unstayd), and headlong enjambments of the first quatrain. The pulls of carnal desire and the temptation to believe that "weake flesh reposeth / In her owne powre" are equally symptomatic of the fallen human will. And the only defense against such temptations, in Augustinian as well as Reform theology, is to recognize that one *cannot* consistently defend against them. Such humility allows the always-fallen creature, as Luther puts it, "to seek the help which he does not find in himself elsewhere and from someone else."[104] In relations to humanity as well as deity, it is recognition of shared vulnerability that offers the possibility of a true *imitatio Christi*. The indignity of lust is, in this view, central to salvation.

Through to the end of the sequence, the speaker of the *Amoretti* continues to reject the possibility that his marriage will include any such shame. In *Amoretti* 84, the poet prays for the "measure and modesty" that Calvin enjoined in conjugal relations:

> Let not one sparke of filthy lustfull fyre
>   breake out, that may her sacred peace molest:
> ne one light glance of sensuall desyre
>   Attempt to work her gentle mindes vnrest.

But pure affections bred in spotlesse brest,
   and modest thoughts breathd from wel tempred sprites,
   goe visit her in her chast bowre of rest,
   accompanyde with angelick delights.
There fill your selfe with those most ioyous sights,
   the which my selfe could never yet attayne:
   but speake no word to her of these sad plights,
   which her too constant stiffenesse doth constrayne.
Onely behold her rare perfection,
   and blesse your fortunes fayre election. (84.1–14)

As in the allegorical attack of Lust on Amoret in *The Faerie Queene*, the poet's own "filthy lustfull fyre" and "sensuall desyre" are dangerous not because they threaten physical assault, but because they may arouse kindred passion. If the poet "molests" Elizabeth's "sacred peace" with indecent proposals or untoward advances, he will "work her gentle mindes unrest" by inciting either lust or horror—only the latter of which is reconcilable with an ideal of female innocence. Yet Edmund's hope that his mistress will be an exception to the rule that "All flesh is frayle" obviates the need for marriage. Read in the context of Reform theology, the *Amoretti*'s prayer that Elizabeth will be immune to all traces of desire and its commotions is equally a hope that she will escape the economy of sin and solace that compels human beings to marry. If the beloved is herself given the grace easily to endure both inward and outward celibacy, then marriage and conjugal intercourse would constitute a defilement of one of God's chosen few.

In this account, the relation between poet and lady is defined by male sensuality and female innocence, not mutual need and companionship. And if the beloved's chastity can be reimagined as "too constant stiffenesse"—excessive rigidity and haughtiness—then courtship and marriage are characterized not by reciprocity, but by a contest between desire and frigidity. Critics have often applauded this view of courtship as a dynamic of conquest and surrender, understanding the mistress's ultimate acceptance of the poet's appeals in the *Amoretti* as a salutary relinquishment of her inappropriate pride and autonomy. In persuading Elizabeth to trade (bad, Catholic) virginity for (good, Protestant) marriage, Edmund has done her a favor.[105] I would argue, to the contrary, that denial of female appetite and choice desexualizes legitimate Protestant copulation, on the one hand, and makes it sound rather like rape, on the other. The wish that Elizabeth's "sacred peace" remain undisturbed by lust is equally a wish for sex with a woman who tolerates penetration but doesn't *want* it, even as the condemnation of her "too constant stiffenesse" as unholy pride justifies unwanted advances and sexual force.

The wish for sexual control, in other words, may help orchestrate the same erotic fantasy it appears to resist. Even as he marvels that "her cold so great / is not dissolu'd through my so hot desyre" (30.2–3), Edmund reveals that this encounter between male passion and female purity can be even kinkier than the mutual burning cited by Paul as the reason for marriage. For the contest between concupiscence and chastity in the *Amoretti* both defers the vanilla sex Edmund claims to want and provides material for sadomasochistic fantasy. In *Amoretti* 24, for instance, Edmund invites Elizabeth to spank him for his naughty desires: "since ye are my scourge I will intreat, / that for my faults ye will me gently beat" (24.13–14). Elsewhere, he inverts their roles, complaining that whereas "The paynefull smith with force of feruent heat / the hardest yron soone doth mollify," he cannot "beat" into submission "her hart more harde than yron" (32.1–2, 6). These reciprocal images of punishment (for lust, for pride) exploit the etymology of chastity, which derives from the Latin *castus* and retains the sense of castigation.[106] (A number of Christians, most famously Origen and Abelard, took this to the extreme of self-castration, an operation whose name is derived from the same root.)[107] Chastity itself may foster perversity. But in noting that Edmund's flogging fantasies are at odds with the "sobriety," "dignity," "modesty," and "comeliness" that Calvin required of "conjugal intercourse," we must keep in mind Amber Jamilla Musser's observation that BDSM is not inevitably disruptive of the norms of sexuality, agency, and subjectivity that it appears to transgress. Rather, sadomasochism's "meaning is always mobile and contingent, dependent on the speaker and his or her philosophy or worldview."[108] In the case of the *Amoretti*, "Edmund's" worldview is one in which the burden of keeping lust at bay falls on women, with the result that when he imagines sex games that he hopes Elizabeth won't *want* to play, the interchangeability of positions operates as a thin screen for a fantasy of sexual violence.

Perhaps precisely because it concludes with Elizabeth's acceptance of a marriage proposal, the *Amoretti* provides critical ground for asking MacKinnon's question in the context of a long history of companionate marriage: Has consent *ever* been a "meaningful concept"? For when Elizabeth, the woman that Edmund has habitually characterized as a "beast so wyld," submits to the domestication of marriage (67.13), this is consent in the sense of acquiescence but not desire. Although Elizabeth, now "feareless," "sought not to fly," her passive waiting is a far cry from mutually active desire (67.10). Along with burning in his own "boyling sweat," Edmund greedily inhales her "dainty" and "sweet" "odours" (64.3, 14), stares at "her nipples lyke yong blossomd Iessemynes" (64.12), notes that his "frayle thoughts" were "too rashly led astray" by settling "twixt her paps" (76.6, 9), and compares her body to a "goodly table of pure yvory" serving up "sweet fruit of pleasure" (77.2, 11). Such earthy sensuality is exactly what Edmund does *not* want Elizabeth to feel. Were she to break out in "filthy lustful fire" (inhaling Edmund's odor, gaping at his nipples, or fantasizing about devouring his flesh), that would make her less proud, more human. But it would also make her less *fair*—less white, less desirable—staining her jasmine nipples and ivory flesh from within.

The *Ephithalamion* confirms the *Amoretti*'s association between female innocence, whiteness, and proper sexuality. It also suggests that female consent without desire—enduring rather than enjoying sex—is a key feature of the whiteness of vanilla sex. "Few women," MacKinnon notes, "are in a position to refuse unwanted sexual initiatives" given their legal and economic subordination. This included, at the time MacKinnon was writing, the absence of laws defining forced sex within marriage as "rape," a legal omission that, as I also discuss in chapter 4, sheds significant light on the sexual violence that may be sanctioned under a seemingly gender-neutral principle of "due benevolence."[109] In the *Amoretti* Elizabeth's distaste for the bodily being that "hinders heauenly thoughts with drossy slime" (13.12) suggests a disinclination for sex that, as Benjamin Kahan's work on celibacy has shown us, must be distinguished from repressed desire.[110]

The possibility that deflowering a reluctant bride may be tantamount to raping her in fact shapes the genre of the wedding song in the sixteenth century. Unlike its classical antecedents, the early modern epithalamion implicitly denies the mutuality of due benevolence. In Catullus's wedding songs, and especially Poem 61, bride and groom are equally excited about the wedding night. The bride here is so "eager to be with her husband" that she will "fasten her heart with affection / as trailing ivy will fasten / around the base of a tree."[111] By contrast, in his *Poetics* Julius Caesar Scalinger's description of the epithalamion repeatedly refers to the rape of the Sabines as the origin of Roman marriage, thereby stressing the continuity between marriage, rape, and imperial conquest.[112] A fantasy of forceful male passion overcoming fearful female purity is, in George Puttenham's description, central to the epithalamion tradition as such. Puttenham explains that the first part of the epithalamion was "very loude and shrill, to the intent there might be no noise be heard out of the bed chamber by the skreeking & outcry of the young damosell felling the first forces of her stiffe & rigourous young man."[113] The joke (ha ha) is that we cannot tell whether the bride is screaming in pleasure or pain, whether she desires sex or suffers it.

Spenser's *Epithalamion*, by contrast, risks no such jests about Elizabeth's agony *or* her arousal—far from shrieking, she keeps almost preternaturally quiet. The enjoyment that Edmund anticipates for himself depends on the bride's continuing sexual purity and passivity, not an awakening of mutual appetite. And female chastity is cast as a white property even more insistently in the *Epithalamion* than it was in the *Amoretti*. Elizabeth is not only "clad all in white, that seems a virgin best" (150). A blue-eyed blonde, she is white nearly all over:

> Her goodly eyes lyke Saphyres shinging bright,
> Her forehead yuory white,
> Her cheeks lyke apples which the sun hath rudded,
> Her lips lyke cherryes charming men to byte,
> Her breast like to a bowle of creame vncrudded,
> Her paps lyke lyllies budded,
> Her snowie neck lyke to a marble towre. (171–177)

Straining to express his bride's overwhelming fairness, Edmund deploys similes of ivory, lilies, marble, and fresh, "uncrudded," cream. The expanse of white contrasts with Elizabeth's red cheeks and lips, a poetic convention that, Sujata Iyengar has demonstrated, yoked pale skin to chastity through the blush.[114] Because a blush is less visible on dark skin, the absence of somatic evidence of shame or embarrassment was in the early modern period a trope for *lack* of modesty. In the *Epithalamion*, Elizabeth blushes throughout the wedding. Staring at the "lowly ground" as the guests gaze upon her, she will not "dare lift vp her countenance too bold / But blush to hear her prayses sung so loud" (161, 162–163). As the vows are solemnized, the poet comments, "How the red roses flush vp in her cheekes, / And the pure snow with goodly vermill stayne, / Like crimsin dyde in grayne" (226–228). He praises the "goodly modesty" of his bride's downcast gaze "That suffers not one looke to glaunce awry, / Which may let in a little thought unsownd," even as he asks, "Why blush ye loue to give to me your hand, / The pledge of all our band?" (235–239). The bride's blush, of course, betrays "unsound" knowledge of the imminent consummation that in early modern England, more than any hand-fasting (the ceremonial binding of hands) or exchange of rings, supplied the final and inviolable "pledge of all our band."

Whereas the bride blushes to complete the ceremony that will make her benevolence her husband's due, the groom cannot wait to get the formalities over with: "Ah when will this long weary day have end," he asks, "and lende me leave to come unto my love?" (278–279). The images of Olympian adultery and amorous abandon that shape his fantasies of the wedding night acknowledge that marriage may well liberate rather than banish his lust. Edmund imagines his new wife passively waiting in the nuptial bed, "Like vnto Maia, when as Ioue her tooke, / In Tempe, lying on the flowry gras, / Twixt sleepe and wake" (307–309). In comparing his bride to the famously bashful Pleiade, whom Jove "took" while she was half asleep, the poet here collapses marital consummation, pagan adultery, and rape. This fantasy of himself as Jove and his bride as the semiconscious Maia recalls the description of the Sun's ravishment of the sleeping Chrysogone in *The Faerie Queene*, where female passivity renders sex sinless. Chrysogone, the narrator informs us, bore the offspring of this encounter "withouten paine, that she conceiu'd / Withouten pleasure"—a return to a prelapsarian state of sexual innocence that comes at the expense of female agency (*The Faerie Queene* 3.6.27.2–3). Edmund's identification with Jove's unrestrained indulgence persists in the following stanza, when he prays that this night with Elizabeth will match Jupiter's trysts with Alcema and Night (328–331), revealing that this fantasy of sexual prerogative it is not a momentary flight of fancy but a structuring principle of the conjugal union that the *Epithalamion* celebrates.

As bridegroom no less than as suitor, Edmund's images of amorous excess and entitlement conflict with his pleas for a divine "calme and quieteness," or, as he puts it a bit later in the *Epithalamion*, "sacred peace" (354). Until it is "tyme to sleepe," he hopes that

> The whiles an hundred little winged loues,
> Like diuers fethered doues,
> Shall fly and flutter round about your bed,
> And in the secret darke, that none reproues,
> Their prety stealthes shal worke, and snares shal spread
> To filch away sweet snatches of delight,
> Conceald through couert night.
> Ye sonnes of Venus, play your sports at will,
> For greedy pleasure, carelesse of your toyes,
> Thinks more upon her paradise of ioyes,
> Then what ye do, albe it good or ill. (357–367)

The shift here from the first person "us" and "we" of previous stanzas to the second person "you" and "your" obscures both agency and subjectivity. Similarly, an allegorical sleight of hand separates the bridegroom from the activities he imagines, attributing them instead to the "little loves"—the Italian would be *amoretti*, reminding us that this "greedy pleasure" was the object of his courtship, the purpose of marriage, all along. In fantasy, the bridegroom eschews both traditional morality and the illusion of love and self-control. Enjoying the license to act as "good or ill" in the bedroom as he wishes, with none—including, perhaps, his bride—to "hinder" him, he indulges in what Augustine characterized as the dream of divine omnipotence.

Yet this fantasy is not without the shame that attends sexual desire, as the *Epithalamion* reveals in the confession that love's "stealthes" and "snares" can "filch away sweet snatches of delight" only in "the secret dark, that none reproues." Even the poem's later references to the procreative potential of this union do not divest it entirely of shame or sin—nor should they, according to the Augustinian view of sexuality on which Reform theology was grounded. Edmund's plea that Cynthia "inform" Elizabeth's "chast wombe . . . with timely seed" (386) is prefaced by a reminder of Cynthia's own dalliance with Endymion, who, in this account, seduced her with "a fleece of woll" (379). Likewise, the poem's praise of Juno as she who "with awful might / The lawes of wedlock still dost patronize" (390–391) is ironic in light of the preceding stanzas' celebration of Jove's affairs with Maia, Alcema, and Night. Just for good measure, Edmund also appeals to the unnamed "Genius" of procreation to "Send vs the timely fruit of this same night" and to "fayre Hebe" and "Hymen free" (the gods of youth and nuptial ceremonies, respectively) to "Grant that it may be so" (398, 404, 405, 406). This multiplication of pagan deities allegorizes the recognition that forces beyond conscious control determine whether the night's "sports" will retroactively be revealed as "good" or "ill." In the present tense of the wedding night, "greedy pleasure" is the objective, its procreative outcome a belated alibi.

Detailing the ultimate failure of Protestant restraint, I would argue, is the point of Spenser's poetic meditations on courtship and marriage— like all of the commandments, that against sexual excess is made to be broken so that humanity might perpetually confront its humiliating imperfection. As the feminist sex wars remind us, matters of sexuality, no less than politics, can make strange bedfellows. In this case, a shared conviction of the indignity of sex, as well as the ethical urgency of recognizing that indignity, surprisingly brings together contemporary queer and early Christian analyses of marriage. As Bersani cogently puts it, "*the value of sexuality itself is to demean the seriousness of efforts to redeem it.*"[115] Unlike modern evangelicals, politicians, and Supreme Court Justices, early modern thinkers, from theologians to anatomists to poets, were aware of and explicit about this counterintuitive value. More attention to this early writing can helpfully disrupt modern discourses that assume the universal and transhistorical sanctity of conjugal sex— along with the legal and extra-legal exclusion and violence that such an assumption justifies.

4

The Optimism of Infidelity

Divorce and Adultery

Free Love

Concluding with an accepted proposal and paired with a wedding song, Spenser's *Amoretti* has often been considered the only major English sonnet sequence that features the marriage of the principle figures. This description is accurate, but only if we specify that it is the only major sequence that features the marriage of speaker and addressee *to one another*. In fact, the first and last secular sonnet sequences in England, Philip Sidney's *Astrophil and Stella* and Mary Wroth's *Pamphilia to Amphilanthus*, feature title characters who are married—to other people. By explicitly declaring their sequences adulterous, Sidney and Wroth situate marriage itself within a Petrarchan tradition that enacts what Jack Halberstam describes as "the perverse turn away from the narrative coherence of adolescence-early adulthood-marriage-reproduction-childbearing-retirement-death."[1] Sidney and Wroth continue this tradition by depicting not unrequited love, but adulterous desire that cannot by definition achieve the formal *telos* of legal marriage and therefore is innately incoherent, irresponsible, and promiscuous—all concepts etymologically embedded in adultery as a term for the contamination of matrimony by illicit sex—in its aims and loyalties.[2]

Sidney's and Wroth's sequences are no more amenable to an idealization of companionate marriage than Petrarch's conflicted addresses to the celibate Laura, for they feature lovers who will never be headed to the altar for the simple reason that both have already been there. The couples depicted in these poems are trapped in marriages to other people and therefore unavailable for unions founded on love (until it became a civil matter in 1857, divorce required a special dispensation from the Anglican Church and so was exceedingly difficult, expensive, and rare; remarriage after divorce was forbidden in nearly all cases). These sequences portray what C. S. Lewis called the "romance of adultery," which he relegated to a medieval Catholic past that, in his view, had been superseded by a Protestant culture of marriage.[3] Sidney and Wroth reveal the insufficiency of this historical narrative and the cultural norms that have been mapped onto it. Rather than pine for marriage, their sonnet sequences represent open adultery as an alternative to institutionalized monogamy. Like many modern critiques of lifelong coupledom, their sonnet sequences question whether legally binding commitment as such is a good thing. But unlike most modern critics, Sidney and Wroth make this critique by drawing on the Protestant elevation of faith over works—the disposition, I have been emphasizing, that Luther had called the freedom of a Christian. When, a few decades later, John Milton champions at-will divorce by appealing to the Christian doctrine of charity, he makes explicit the secular theology of free love that shapes Sidney's and Wroth's lyrics. Adultery and its conceptual shadow, divorce, are surprisingly central to this theology.

In this first section, I discuss the complex interplay of love, adultery, divorce, and remarriage in New Testament and Reform theology. I then examine Milton's divorce pamphlets (the topic of the second section of this chapter), along with Sidney and Wroth's adulterous sonnet sequences (the topic of the third and fourth sections), as they contemplate alternative relational models premised on the view that any given commitment may turn out to be a mistake. Rather than lifelong monogamy, these writers depict mobile and overlapping affinities. For Laura Kipnis, adultery is "more of a critical practice than a critical theory": the adulterer acts out knowledge and desire that cannot be otherwise articulated.[4] For the early modern writers I discuss here, desire outside of marriage is explicitly and publicly theorized as questioning the very premises of that institution as an end in itself. And whereas in modern thought secularism appears the only route to challenging the inviolability of the marriage contract, Milton, Sidney, and Wroth base their endorsements of divorce and adultery on the Pauline distinction between duty and love, letter and spirit, that infuses faith itself with a salutary faithlessness. In their emphasis on interiority, these writers participate in a cultural project of privatizing love, which scholars have rightly seen as an ideological foundation of heteronormativity, capitalism, and neoliberalism.[5] Yet by taking this privatization to its logical extreme, they also provide grounds for removing intimacy from institutional regulation and reward altogether, making, in Milton's words, each individual "a Law in this matter unto himself."[6] As I argue in this chapter's final section, however, the alternatives that these writings offer to relational ideals of public signification and futurity are useful to modern queer thought not just as positive models, but also because they alert us to the exclusions upon which freedom may be premised: to formulate a theory of "free love," they draw on racial and colonial hierarchies that make sincerity and freedom white, Christian properties. Sidney, Wroth, and Milton are part of the longer history that precedes and conditions present queer associations of secularism with Western reason and modernity, religion with superstitious and oppressive non-Western cultures. The ideal of sexual autonomy, no less than those of monogamy and marriage, has its own racialized genealogy.

The complexity of adultery in Christian thought is belied by the unequivocal prohibition of the Seventh Commandment, "Thou shalt not commit adultery" (GB, Exod. 20:14). Even if we assume that cheating covers only physical acts, it is hard to pinpoint just which acts cross the line. And in the New Testament, at least, infidelity does not require physical contact at all. Like the commandments against lying and coveting that I discussed in chapter 2, that against adultery addresses thoughts as well as actions. The Geneva Bible's gloss on the Seventh Commandment indicates that adultery includes *any* desire for a person other than one's spouse: "But be pure in heart, word, and deed" (GB, Exod. 20:14n). Similarly, the Gospel of Matthew decrees that "whosoever looketh on a woman to lust after her, hath committed adultery with her already in his heart" (GB, Matt. 5:28), to which the Geneva gloss adds, "Chastity is required in both body and mind." The Seventh Commandment, in other words, is destined to be broken. Even if purity of word, deed, and body is possible, purity of heart and mind is not. As we have seen, Luther and Calvin believed that the inscrutable desires of the heart could render even the most punctilious outward obedience hypocritical and therefore blameworthy. Calvin affirms that "Paul's definition of chastity is purity of mind, combined with purity of body. . . . He not only says that it is better to marry than to live in fornication, but that it is better to marry than to burn."[7] In Christian thought, adultery, like coveting and lying, is not something done just by those who are uniquely weak or unethical. It is a universal psychic condition.

To confuse matters further, in the New Testament adultery is often conceptually conflated with divorce and remarriage. In that sense, it resembles not only what we now call serial monogamy, but also the bigamy or polygamy associated with non-Christian peoples and non-European locales. As I discussed in chapter 2, "monogamy" originally meant marrying only one person in a lifetime; "bigamy" and "polygamy" could signify remarriage after death or divorce. This strict allotment of one marriage per person—at least during the lifetime of the original spouse—appears throughout the Gospels and the Pauline Epistles. Matthew, Mark, and Luke all record Jesus equating divorce and remarriage with adultery:

> I say therefore unto you, that whosoever shall put away his wife, except it be for whoredom, and marry another, committeth adultery; and whosoever marrieth her which is divorced, doeth committeth adultery (GB, Matt. 5:28; see also 19:9);

> Whosoever shall put away his wife and marry another, committeth adultery against her (GB, Mark 10:11; the Geneva Bible's gloss on this verse helpfully explains, "For the second is not his wife, but his harlot");

> Whosoever putteth away his wife, and marrieth another, committeth adultery, and whosoever marrieth her that is put away from her husband, committeth adultery. (GB, Luke 16:18)

And in his First Letter to the Corinthians, immediately after conceding that "it is better to marry than to burn," Paul designates marriage a final decision: "And unto the married I command, not I, but the Lord, Let not the wife depart from her husband. But if she depart, let her remain unmarried, or be reconciled unto her husband, and let not the husband put away *his* wife" (GB, 1 Cor. 7:10–11). English law took this admonishment to heart. Until 1857, those few couples granted legal "separation from bed and board" were not allowed to remarry during the lifetime of the original spouse; if marriage was indissoluble, any marriage after the first was bigamous. In practice, early modern persons found ways of getting around these restrictions: wealthy and aristocratic couples could obtain parliamentary approval to remarry, and those of the poor and middling sort, for whom dynastic control over title and property were not at issue, frequently took it upon themselves to separate and remarry without explicit legal sanction.[8] Proscriptions against divorce and remarriage have faded in modern law and culture. But they linger in state authority over separation and right to remarry and in the cultural adulation accorded lifelong marriage. First marriages are treated as entirely joyous occasions; second (not to mention third, fourth, fifth) marriages are haunted by the memory of vows that have been broken.

The modern romanticization of wedded love is itself a departure from Christian scripture. Insofar as worldly marriage is a concession to the life of the flesh—not just carnal desire, but also questions of property, procreation, respectability, citizenship, healthcare, and inheritance—it is also a compromise of sorts. Paul, as I discussed in chapter 3, presents marriage to an earthly spouse as inferior to a single-minded, unadulterated devotion to the bridegroom Christ. Indeed, Dale Martin has argued that Jesus's prohibitions against divorce and remarriage may function to discourage matrimony altogether: people will think twice before forming a bond that they cannot get out of. The New Testament may therefore challenge the institution itself in favor of the communal and celibate life practiced by Jesus and the men and women who followed him.[9]

The difficulty of achieving an apostolic turn from the world helps explain why love for Christ is often figured as a *second* love. For Paul, Luther, Donne, and a number of other Christian thinkers, the romance of conversion can be imagined only in relation to repudiation of previous loyalties (to Judaism, to Catholicism, to worldly concerns). Conversion is equally a turn away from past mistakes and toward love for Christ; getting into a new relationship entails getting out of the previous one. Being born again from the ashes of an originally sinful self is the most recognizable figure for conversion, but getting married again is another. We see this conceit in John Donne's Holy Sonnet "Batter my heart," in which the speaker complains that he is "betrothed" to the worldly lures of Satan and pleads with God to "Divorce me, untie or break that knot again" (10–11). This poem itself derives from the Pauline comparison of the Christian believer to a woman freed from a distasteful marriage:

> So then, if while the man liveth, she taketh another man, she shall be
> called an adulteress; but if the man be dead, she is free from the Law, so
> that she is not an adulteress, though she take another man. So ye, my
> brethren, are dead also to the Law by the body of Christ, that ye should
> be unto another, *even* unto him that is raised up from the dead, that we
> should bring forth fruit unto God (GB, Rom. 1:3–4).

Christ's bodily death liberates humanity from the way of the flesh. Luther
argued that whereas the Old Testament order of law inspires feelings of
helplessness and hatred, the New Testament order of grace fills believers
with hope and gratitude. Commenting on the above-quoted passage,
Luther explains that "the woman is not obliged, nor even merely permitted to take another husband; rather, the point is that she is now quite
at liberty for the first time to please herself about taking another husband."[10] Likewise, once our "old sinful self" is "put to death by the spirit,
our conscience is set at liberty, and each [law and conscience] is released
from the other. . . . Now for the first time, [conscience] can really cling to
Christ as a second husband, and bring forth the fruit of life."[11] This new-
found sexual abandon figures the replacement of sober and deliberate
duty with irrepressible devotion. To "cling" to a new beloved with frank
appetite is to exceed the fleshly work of due benevolence. The overwhelming love that Luther equates with true, spiritual faith is defined
by freedom from all compulsion beyond one's own passions—including
the compulsions of law, custom, and comfort captured by that figure
of a first, unsatisfying marriage. Commitment for commitment's sake
is not necessarily a good thing. In this view, liberty is the property of a
Christian.

Understood in secular terms, the structural logic of Christian conversion can productively complicate the political significance of what
Theodor Adorno describes as the bourgeois view that "love is supposed
to be involuntary, pure immediacy of feeling."[12] For many scholars,
the association of love with autonomy and privacy helps to perpetuate
both capitalist and neoliberal interests by displacing, as Lauren Berlant
puts it, "historical forms of reciprocity onto emotional registers, especially when they dramatize experiences of freedom to come that have
no social world for them yet."[13] The equation of desire with freedom
serves capitalism, Adorno argues, whether one stays, leaves, or cheats.

Monogamy performs its ideological sleight of hand by substituting "abstract temporal sequence" for a "hierarchy of feelings."[14] The "accidental element" of love's inauguration defies individual choice, and so would seem "in flat contradiction to the claims of freedom," but it also eludes external administration.[15] "Even, and precisely, in a society cured of the anarchy of commodity production, there could scarcely be rules governing the order in which one met people," Adorno continues, so "the irreversibility of time constitutes an objective moral criterion."[16] Voluntary commitment, for better or for worse, to a relationship that began with a fortuitous encounter confirms that love is immune to social or financial calculation:

> Even though social advantage, sublimated, preforms the sexual impulse, using a thousand nuances sanctioned by the order to make now this, now that person seem spontaneously attractive, an attachment once formed opposes this by persisting where the force of social pressure . . . does not want it. He alone loves who has the strength to hold fast to love. It is the test of feeling whether it goes beyond feeling through permanence.[17]

But infidelity—whether in the form of covert adultery or open abandonment—equally sustains a capitalist ideology in which private self-determination obscures the determining force of the larger socioeconomic structure (which, as I have argued in chapters 2 and 3, is also a racialized structure). In repudiating prior commitments, the individual responds to shifting costs and benefits that are the antithesis of pure and eternal love:

> The love, however, which in the guise of unreflecting spontaneity and proud of its alleged integrity, relies exclusively on what it takes to be the voice of the heart, and runs away as soon as it no longer thinks it can hear that voice, is in this supreme independence precisely the tool of society. Passive without knowing it, it registers whatever numbers come out in the roulette of interests. In betraying the loved one it betrays itself.[18]

The fantasy of individual affective liberty places the capitalist subject in a double bind whereby "the fidelity exacted by society is a means to unfreedom, but only through fidelity can freedom achieve insubordination to society's command."[19] If love is the ultimate example of false consciousness, it only makes sense, as Kipnis polemically suggests, to be against it.

Chasing after true love, we practice what Berlant calls "cruel optimism," which she defines as "a binding to fantasies that block the satisfactions they offer, and a binding to the promise of optimism as such that the fantasies have come to represent."[20] Put in psychoanalytic terms, as a form of misrecognition (*meconnaissance*), "the psychic process by which fantasy recalibrates what we encounter so that we can imagine that something or someone can fulfill our desire," love is practically synonymous with cruel optimism.[21] Nonetheless, Berlant writes, insofar as "fantasy parses ambivalence in such a way that the subject is not defeated by it," we must "take seriously the magical thinking, or formalism, involved in seeing selves and worlds as continuous."[22] Reflecting on Eve Sedgwick's critique of a paranoid style of thought, in which "dreams are seen as easy optimism, while failures seem complex" and skepticism is the only ethical or serious response to "ordinary attachments," Berlant notes that the "queer tendency" of the reparative mode "is to put one's attachments back into play and into pleasure, into knowledge, into worlds. It is to admit that they matter."[23] Such an approach is not without its risks. For the critic invested in the power of ideas, "overvaluation of reparative thought is both an occupational hazard and part of a larger overvaluation of a certain mode of virtuously intentional, self-reflective personhood."[24] Those who believe in the possibility of political change must be wary that "the exhausting repetition of the politically depressed position that seeks repair of what may be constitutively broken can eventually split the activity of optimism from expectation and demand."[25] This is the cruel—or "stupid," or "toxic"—optimism of acceptance and adjustment, in which hoping that the future will be better substitutes for actual material and structural change.[26] Still, optimism may also provide "the bare minimum evidence of not having given up on social change as such" because "the energy that generates this sustaining commitment to the work of undoing a world while making one *requires* fantasy to motor programs of action, to distort the present on behalf of what the present can become."[27] Demystification reveals the limits, even the futility, of protest; optimism fosters protest by distorting reality into something that can change.

Adultery is optimistic (in all of the senses traced by Berlant) in its repudiation of the pieties of monogamous coupledom in favor of attachments and affinities that are more contingent and open ended. Given that sex is, in Janet Jakobsen's words, "a social relation constituted by and constitutive of the various social relations that have made this historical moment possible," to reject the dominant ideal of lifelong monogamy is also to reimagine the socioeconomic structures that monogamy naturalizes.[28] The relation between love and money, cultural and economic order, that capitalist and neoliberal ideology obscures becomes unavoidable when we contemplate the *end* of a marriage.[29] Adultery, in its pursuit of such an end, is in Kipnis's concise formulation, "the current secret code for wanting something *more*," a grasp at a utopian ideal of love that is not compulsory.[30] As Kipnis also observes, such optimism is, in contemporary culture, widely discredited as not only personally naïve but also historically outmoded: "So exiled have even basic questions of freedom become from the political vocabulary that they sound musty and ridiculous, and vulnerable to the ultimate badge of shame—'That's so 60s!'—the entire decade having been mocked so effectively that social protest seems outlandish and 'so last-century,' just another style excess like love beads and Nehru jackets."[31] Those who seek free love (intimacy unconstrained by practical, material considerations and therefore free to end anytime) are seen as backward, left behind in a juvenile cultural stage that we as a society have long since grown out of. Justice Antonin Scalia voices just this view in his dissent in *Obergefell v. Hodges*. Even as Scalia dismisses the majority's argument that marriage is an expression of personal liberty, he also smirks at those who resist the regulation that marriage effects: "One would think Freedom of Intimacy is abridged rather than expanded by marriage. Ask the nearest hippie. Expression, sure enough, is a freedom, but anyone in a long-lasting marriage will attest that that happy state constricts, rather than expands, what one can prudently say."[32] Those who see the right to marry as a matter of personal liberty, no less than those who insist that legal privileges and state benefits should not be reserved for married persons, fail to recognize that marriage is about constriction, not freedom. To say "I do" is to agree to limit expression to "what one can prudently say" (and do); to choose such internment is a mark of maturity. Arguments for redefining or ending marriage can be taken no more seriously than the stoned ramblings of flower children.

As the embodiment of failed optimism, the hippie is a figure of what Elizabeth Freeman calls "temporal drag," the "countergenealogical practice of archiving culture's throwaway objects, including the outmoded masculinities and femininities from which usable pasts may be extracted."[33] Yet past experiences of uncommitted desire as a dimension of optimistic, even revolutionary, politics predate the advent of the hippie by many centuries. From the tradition of the troubadours, through medieval romance, at least up to the Renaissance lyric, the view that love does not necessarily lead to marriage, and may in truth be hindered by the socioeconomic considerations that shape legal matrimony, was at the center rather than the margins of literary culture. To read the Petrarchan love lyric against its usual genealogy as part of modern ideals of monogamy is to contest, with Freeman, what Dana Luciano has termed "chronobiopolitics," or "the sexual arrangement of the time of life" according to "teleological schemes of events or strategies for living such as marriage, accumulation of health and wealth for the future, reproduction, childrearing, and death and its attendant rituals."[34] I would add that the narrative of the rise of companionate marriage maps this progressive chronology of individual lives onto a linear model of history that, as I discuss in this book's coda, queer theory's confinement to modernity has left in place despite numerous critiques by scholars working on materials that precede the invention of "homosexuality" as an identity.

Building on Freeman's argument for the power of anachronism, I drag theological and Petrarchan defenses of free love into the present and into dialogue with current queer challenges to monogamy as *the* socially, financially, and politically sanctioned relational form. While more distant than the twentieth-century political movements Freeman discusses, the polemical and poetic writings of the English Renaissance also constitute "usable pasts." They "manifest the power of anachronism to unsituate viewers from the present tense they think they know and to illuminate or even prophetically ignite possible futures in light of powerful historical moments."[35] Such rejection of a punctual model of history upends received definitions of tradition and revolution, religious and secular culture. Along with asking the nearest hippie to hold forth on the squareness of marriage, we must consult documents of the more distant past that critique the psychic violence inherent in the legal enforcement of lifelong fidelity, even as the racial exclusions and aggressions they enact in the name of freedom must give us pause about any liberatory project, then or now.

The Divine Touch of Divorce

Whereas modern critics tend to align marriage with Christianity, and especially with Protestantism, Milton's prolific writings on divorce demonstrate that Reform theology could also be marshaled to radically redefine marriage to the extent that it is no longer central to social or economic order. Milton was a Puritan's Puritan if there ever was one. But we need to understand the term "Puritan" apart from the connotations of thin-lipped prudery it has in American culture, sardonically summed up in H. L. Mencken's famous definition of Puritanism as "the haunting fear that someone, somewhere might be happy."[36] If we look beyond the Hawthornian figure of the New England Puritan, we can see that Protestant theology may allow for a radical revision of modern ideals of long-term commitment as a good in itself. In doctrinal and historical terms, Milton's Puritanism referred to the conviction that religion must be purged of the Catholic dogma that Luther and Calvin had diagnosed as shackling humanity to wretched and hypocritical habits of mind and conduct. For Milton, the purgation of Roman doctrine from Christianity was critical to the pursuit of happiness. And the ability to leave intimate relationships was, Milton recognized, as vital to happiness as the ability to enter them.

Like many radical reformers, Milton believed that the freedom of a Christian consisted in sincere love rather than grudging obedience. Assiduously distinguishing the formal, legal bonds of marriage from the joyful love that he viewed as its true essence, Milton argued that unrestricted divorce was fundamental not only to worldly contentment but also to spiritual salvation. By denying divorce except in legally verifiable cases of adultery, impotence, or desertion, he argued, English law commanded spouses to public obedience to law and provoked private hatred. It thereby endangered the very souls of those who were unhappily married. Milton's claim that a marriage not based on "fit conversation" is no marriage at all questions whether the institution should be sanctioned by state or church, with all of the privileges, benefits, and restrictions that they manage. Instead, he maintains, marriage is best viewed as a private compact that individuals create and dissolve at will, no more subject to legal regulation than friendship. At the same time, we must remember that Milton is poised, as Gordon Teskey puts it, "on the threshold of a posttheological world," and therefore writes from a perspective (Teskey calls it "delirium") of excruciating self-consciousness about his own acts of poesis—including self-narration.[37] Accordingly, his appeals to divine charity can be read as entangled with a larger creation of himself as theorist of secular egalitarianism, with all of that role's obfuscations and illusions.

Milton's views on marriage and divorce usefully demonstrate how Christian theology may serve the queer ends of challenging modern evangelical family values, even as his idealization of friendship encapsulates many of the gendered and racialized hierarchies that I traced in chapter 2.[38] As Lee Morrissey points out, Milton is "anachronistic and decontextualizing," and Milton's use of biblical and classical source material provides a model for how we might in turn use his work to think through current problems, in this case the administration of private relations by public law.[39] When Milton's first and best-known argument for at-will divorce was published in 1643, it bore the full title *The Doctrine and Discipline of Divorce Restor'd to the good of both Sexes, From the bondage of Canon Law, and other mistakes, to Christian freedom, guided by the rule of Charity*. This opposition between the "bondage of Canon law" and "Christian freedom" is the central theme of all four of Milton's divorce pamphlets, *The Doctrine and Discipline of Divorce* (1643; revised edition 1644); *The Judgment of Martin Bucer* (1644); *Tetrachordon* (1645); and *Colasterion* (1645).[40] For well over a century before Milton addressed the topic, Protestant reformers invoked the Pauline distinction between faith and works to deny the sacramental status of marriage—that is, to refute the Catholic doctrine that the act of getting married could affect salvation one way or the other. As I argued in chapter 3, Luther and Calvin deemed marriage spiritually valuable insofar as it constituted both private admission and public confession that one was subject to the pulls of the world and the flesh and therefore unable to achieve the celibate, undistracted devotion of Paul and the original apostles. Doctrinally, this meant that in most Protestant states marriage became a civil matter, no longer a rite (like baptism or extreme unction) by which the Catholic

Church channeled grace to its members. Divorce likewise became easier to obtain in most Protestant states, for it was now seen as the dissolution of a worldly contract rather than the rupture of a mysterious consolidation of two persons into one flesh.

This was not so in England. Henry VIII famously broke from the Catholic Church to legally divorce Catherine of Aragon, but divorce remained under the jurisdiction of canon, not civil, courts.[41] During the reign of Henry's son, Edward IV, there were efforts to reform divorce law, but these ended when the Catholic Mary I came to the throne in 1553. Elizabeth I's accession in 1558 saw little change, and in 1604, under James I, the *Constitutions of the Canons Ecclesiastical* reasserted the pre-Reformation ruling whereby annulment or divorce could be granted only in exceptional circumstances and at great expense; divorced persons were generally not allowed to remarry while the former spouse lived.[42] In *The Judgment of Martin Bucer*, Milton deemed such prohibition the invention of "*a canonicall tyranny of stupid and malicious Monks*" (2:431; Milton's emphasis). Under a reformed Church, he insisted, "though mariage be most agreeable to holines, to purity and justice, yet is it not a naturall, but a civill and ordain'd relation" (*Tetrachordon* 2:601). Like Augustine, Luther, and Calvin, Milton denied that matrimony magically sanctified sex. How little difference the institution makes appears in *Paradise Lost*. Before the Fall, Adam and Eve innocently practice "the Rites / Mysterious of connubial Love," which "God declares / Pure"; after the fall "inflame[ed]" with "Carnal desire," "they thir fill of Love and Love's disport / Took largely, of thir mutual guilt the Seal."[43] The difference is not conjugal status—they are still married after the fall—but the postlapsarian *poena reciproca* of self-division. To believe that human ceremony can make the difference is to engage in idolatry. By contrast, Victoria Silver explains, for Milton "the person, idiom, teachings, and life of Jesus are the human, historical contingency that defies legal and logical absolutes."[44]

Counterintuitively, Milton bases his secularization of marriage law on scriptural exegesis. In his view, truly Christian marriage can be saved only by making divorce easy to obtain. In the context of his extensive analysis of the logic of marriage and divorce, monks and priests may be malicious, but perhaps they are not so stupid after all. Repeatedly, Milton accuses them of knowing exactly what they are doing: no less than the promotion of celibacy, the denial of divorce *discourages* marriage. By defining marriage as something that no one can get out of, and "making the yoke of mariage unjust and intolerable," canon law "causes men to abhorr it" (*Tetrachordon* 2:595). And by perpetuating the "lingring vainglory" of such "Antichristian canons," English law has placed its subjects "under the thickest arrows of temptation, where we need not stand" (*Tetrachordon* 2:601). Catholic clergy obscure their own sins by creating a situation that exposes everyone to the lures of fornication, adultery, and spiritual despair. Divorce frees love from "canonical tyranny" and thereby makes possible Christian sincerity, the congruity of inner and outer selves that is the opposite of hypocritical obedience.

Milton maintains that the "obstinate *literality*" and "alphabetical *servility*" of canon law must give way to the New Testament rule of charity (*DDD* 2:279, 280; Milton's emphasis). He cites Romans 13:10, "*Love onely is the fulfilling of every Commandment*," adding to the source text "only" for good measure, and throughout his pamphlets he quotes scripture to insist that "the christian arbitrement of charity is supreme decider of all controversie" (*DDD* 2:258; *Tetrachordon* 2:637; Milton's emphasis). Whereas opponents of divorce would argue that people should think carefully before getting married, Milton stresses the barbarity of forcing anyone to remain in an unhappy marriage, "to hunt an error so to the death with a revenge beyond all measure and proportion" (*Tetrachordon* 2:590). We can love our neighbors because we do not have to live with them; in forcing people to cohabitate, marriage constitutes a punishment, "committing two ensnared souls inevitably to kindle one another, not with the fire of love, but with a hatred *inconcileable*, who were they disseverd would be straight friends in any other relation" (*DDD* 2:280; Milton's emphasis). By contrast, divorce "like a divine touch in one moment heals all," releasing an incompatible couple from the forced proximity that makes them "live as they were deadly enemies in a cage together" (*DDD* 2:333; *Tetrachordon* 2:599).

Milton anticipates by several centuries Adam Phillips's observation that "it is no more possible to work at a relationship than it is to will an erection, or arrange to have a dream. In fact when you are working at it you know it has gone wrong, that something is already missing. In our erotic lives, in other words, trying is always trying too hard."[45] Citing Phillips, Kipnis satirizes the incorporation of what Max Weber so influentially described as the Protestant ethic of work into modern love. But Milton's writing reveals that American Puritanism is only one outcome of Reformation theology. In terms of secular eroticism, the view that "the freedom of a Christian" turned on heartfelt faith rather than grudging work also lends itself to arguments against working too hard. What makes a union a true marriage rather than the "*Idolatrous match*" suited to the superstitious rituals of Jews, Muslims, or Catholics, according to Milton, is sincere love (*DDD* 2:259; Milton's emphasis). The burning that Paul deems the cause of marriage is for Milton "not the meer goad of a sensitive desire"; it is the longing for "cheerfull society" that cannot be remedied by having sex with just anyone (*DDD* 2:251). If people don't like each other, when they obey the command to offer due benevolence, they can only "grind in the mill of an undelighted and servil copulation" (*DDD* 2:258). Conjugal sex becomes a transaction in which "the body prostitute[s] it selfe to whom the mind affords no other love or peace" (*Tetrachordon* 2:708). Legalistic views of marriage that allow divorce in cases of adultery, impotence, or frigidity but not incompatibility get things exactly backward by valuing works above love, flesh above spirit. Milton's depiction of an unsatisfying marriage as a relation of imprisonment, enslavement, and prostitution strikes at the very definition of matrimony as a good for its own sake. At the same time, these arguments also translate conditions of freedom and servitude into natural conditions—no accident, given that Milton also takes companionate marriage as a model of political society that can tolerate differences among equals (that is to say, true Christians).

Once we understand the purpose of marriage as happiness, Milton maintains, we can see that an unsatisfying union is no marriage at all: "Where love cannot be, there can be left of wedlock nothing, but the empty husk of an outside matrimony; as undelightfull and unpleasing to God, as any other kind of hyposcrisie" (*DDD* 2:256). As David Orvis elegantly puts it, "Sometimes divorce is the *only* way to keep God's commandments."[46] Were English divorce law in conformity with divine purpose, marriages would be as easy to dissolve as any other agreement that did not turn out as planned. "So when it shall be found by their apparent unfitnes," Milton avers, "that their continuing to be man and wife is against the glory of God and their mutuall happiness, it may assure them that God never joyn'd them" (*DDD* 2:277). True belief not only requires but also ensures freedom. Moreover, "if he joynd them not, then there is no power above their own consent to hinder them from unjoining. . . . Neither can it be said properly that such twain were ever divorc't, but onely parted from each other, as two persons unconjunctive, and unmariable together" (*DDD* 2:328). Since such a pair was never really married, "both are free, and without fault rather by a nullity then by a divorce may betake them to a second choys" (*Tetrachordon* 2:613). And while Milton cautions that divorce should not be undertaken "rashly" or "for casuall & temporary causes," he allows for no external judge of which causes are merely temporary and which irremediable (*Tetrachordon* 2:647). "If mariage may bee dissolv'd by so many exterior powers, not superior, as wee think," he asks, "why may not the power of mariage its self for its own peace and honour *dissolv it self*, where the persons wedded be free persons, why may not a greater and more natural power complaining dissolv mariage?" (*Tetrachordon* 2:628; my emphasis).

Thomas Luxon, Gregory Chaplin, and David Orvis have noted the centrality of classical and humanist discourses of friendship to Milton's view of marriage, and keeping this affinity in mind helps us to appreciate both how profoundly Milton redefines the conjugal relation and how inextricable this definition is from class, racial, and gendered distinctions between those who are capable of friendship and those who are not.[47] By Milton's logic it is as absurd to compel two people to stay married as it would be to make it illegal to end a friendship. And insofar as the dissolution of marriage requires the authorization of the state, even the most freely chosen contract contains a latent threat of future compulsion. In this sense, arranged marriage may be the prototype, not the opposite, of romantic marriage. Whereas Luther and Calvin emphasize the hypocrisy of the celibate life for those who have not been called, Milton emphasizes the hypocrisy of matrimony for those who are spiritual rather than bodily eunuchs:

> It is most sure that some ev'n of those who are not plainly defective in body, are yet destitute of all other mariageable gifts; and consequently have not the calling to marry; unlesse nothing be requisite thereto but a meer instrumentall body . . . it is as sure that many such not of their own desire, but by the perswasion of friends, or not knowing themselves do often enter into wedlock; where finding the difference at length between

the duties of a maried life, and the gifts of a single life; what unfitnes of mind, what wearisomnes, what scruples and doubts to an incredible offence and displeasure are like to follow between, may be soon imagin'd: whom thus to shut up and immure together, the one with a mischosen mate, the other in a mistak'n calling, is not a course that Christian wisdome and tendernes ought to use. As for the custom that some parents and guardians have of forcing mariages, it will be better to say nothing of such a savage inhumanitie, but only this, that the Law which gives not all freedome of divorce to any creature endu'd with reason so assassinated, is next in crueltie. (*DDD* 2:274–275)

The passage proceeds from defining marriage as a vocation to noting that it is hard to tell who really has been called, given how easy it is to confuse one's "own desire" with the "perswasion of friends." Along with its modern meaning, "friends" in the Renaissance could designate kin or guardians, so that private "perswasion" is difficult to separate from social, legal, and material coercion. For Calvin, one risks one's soul by taking monastic vows "because it is improperly regarded as an act of worship, and is rashly undertaken by persons who have not the power of keeping it."[48] For Milton, to assume the "mistak'n calling" of marriage is equally dangerous. The confines of law, no less than the walls of the monastery or convent, "shut up and immure" those within. An honest mistake may have the same effects as the "savage inhumanitie" of arranged marriages. What matters is not just how a marriage begins, but whether it can end at will. The "freedome of divorce" makes all the difference between voluntary and forced marriage.

No less than the "nearest hippie," Milton believes that true marriage is a radically interior bond, one to which not everyone is suited. In fact, the ability to divorce is a mark of Christian freedom. Milton's rejection of the law finds secular expression in his commendation of love that exists outside of, even actively defies, the formal ties of matrimony. Legal license or recognition is no more than a piece of paper to be discarded if and when spouses discover themselves to have been mistaken in their choice or calling. Milton's divorce pamphlets attest that both early modern and modern conservative thinkers are right. The "soulmate model of marriage"—the expectation that marriage will bring personal growth and fulfillment—endangers the traditional model of marriage as an institution whose purpose is securing property and rearing children.[49] Far from being good for society, or even for the children a union has produced, the compulsive preservation of an unsatisfying marriage encourages the hatred and hypocrisy that undermine ethical relations and stable public order.[50] And, as Milton's explicit analogy between a bad marriage and a bad government attests, the repudiation of ideals and attachments that have proven harmful has significant implications for questions of political compliance as well.[51]

Beyond merely allowing divorce, Milton calls for a restructuring of legal and social definitions of marriage so comprehensive as to take government out of marriage altogether. Because "error is not properly consent" and "there is no true mariage between them, who agree not in true consent of mind," "godly Magistrates" must "procure that no matrimony be among thir Subjects, but what is knit with love and consent" (*Tetrachordon* 2:612; *Martin Bucer* 2:445). Love is premised on hopeful distortion rather than exhaustive demystification. Always subject to error, the associations love optimistically forges become cruel if externally compelled. The true nature of marriage is a self-dissolving affective bond, improperly subject to legal regulation, and therefore too unstable to be the basis of society—a queer argument *avant la lettre*.

Public (In)Fidelity

I began with Milton's divorce tracts because they offer an extensive and systematic theological defense of the principle that ethical love need not be sanctioned by, and actually may be opposed to, the institution of marriage; they also defend single life on Protestant grounds. But Milton was hardly the first Protestant to deny that marriage is innately good. Equally profound challenges were raised by the two secular sonnet sequences that serve as bookends for what literary historians have described as the high point in the English Petrarchan lyric, Sidney's *Astrophil and Stella* and Wroth's *Pamphilia to Amphilanthus*. When Sidney wrote the first English Petrarchan sonnet sequence, *Astrophil and Stella*, he explicitly addressed it not to his wife, Frances Walsingham, but to a married woman, Penelope Devereux Rich.[52] Likewise, Wroth provides ample textual and paratextual indications that her own sequence, one of the last sequences of Petrarchan lyrics to be printed in England, is addressed not to her husband, Robert Wroth, but to a married man, her cousin William Herbert, Third Earl of Pembroke.[53] Rather than supporting the common view that companionate marriage superseded adulterous romance, these secular sonnet sequences depict love as a practice of (in) fidelity—the concurrent faith and betrayal, turning toward and turning away, necessary to conversion. In Sidney's and Wroth's writing, (in)fidelity's privileged relationship is adultery.

Even more than those of Petrarch, Spenser, or Shakespeare, these sequences encode semiautobiographical elements that blur the line between authentic personal experience and manufactured poetic fiction. "I am not I, pity the tale of me," Sidney writes in the voice of Astrophil; "dayle I will wright / This tale of haples mee," promises a shepherdess whose lament is overheard and recorded by Pamphilia.[54] The lyric "I's" of Astrophil and Pamphilia spin "tales" whose truth value is explicitly compromised by their rhetorical purpose of evoking pity for the predicament of the adulterer—both the poetic speaker and the author who has created this persona. To be sure, it would be silly to read these poems as factual documents or private letters. Indeed, as Robert Stillman has argued, we would do better to see impersonation as an escape from the confines of a single, biographical self, revelation itself a form of disguise.[55] But neither should we require that truth have empirically verifiable referents. Much as Sidney's and Wroth's lyrics may express a truth that is not reducible to empirical facts, their play with referents defies socially or legally enforced monogamy. Fidelity must be sincere to count as such, and enacting sincerity may require betrayal of previous vows. These sequences recognize, as did Paul, Petrarch, and Luther, that fidelity and infidelity are conceptually and practically implicated in one another. The (in)fidelity that Sidney and Wroth perform in the personae of Astrophil and Pamphilia expresses the imperfect fit between intention and desire. Adultery was fundamental to the English Petrarchan sonnet sequence that was and remains a profoundly influential sexual script, which Bruce Smith defines as a point at which individual experience intersects with social coordinates.[56] Sidney's and Wroth's public confessions of extramarital desire act out private dissatisfaction, *pace* Kipnis. But they also advance a theoretical critique of the imperative to lifelong, legally sanctioned commitment. The critical practice of deemphasizing topicality in order to posit a universal, disembodied lyric speaker has allowed these sequences to be too easily coopted by what Smith has called the "Myth of Companionate Marriage" and the legal and economic structures sustained by this myth.[57] Accordingly, I trace the biographical elements of these sequences not to uncover factual information about the authors' feelings or circumstances, but to consider how they themselves deployed biography to theoretical and rhetorical ends.

The precise nature of Sidney's relationship to Penelope Rich is unknown, but the fact that she is the model for his fictional Stella has been recognized since *Astrophil and Stella* first circulated in manuscript in the 1580s. In his manuscript copy, Sir John Harington, godson of Elizabeth I and a well-connected courtier, lawyer, and author, entitles the sequence "Sonnettes of Sr Phillip Sydneys ~~vppon~~ to ye Lady Ritch."[58] Harington's heading suggests that, whether or not Sidney and Rich actually had an affair, the first English sonnet sequence was received as celebrating specifically adulterous mutual desire. Harington's initial title describes the verses as "upon," or about, Rich and thereby allows for a reader who is *not* Rich. Crossing this out, Harington in his revised title casts Rich herself as the sole intended reader, situating the reader of the manuscript as a voyeur perusing an initially private correspondence between two prominent members of the Elizabethan court. Harington's interpretation is no accident: Sidney ostentatiously encodes the identification of himself as speaker and his beloved as Penelope Rich in several sonnets. He links himself to the sequence's speaker both in the name Astro*phil* and in autobiographical references to "my father" as the Lord Deputy of Ireland who had made "Ulster" "half tame" and to a tournament in honor of an embassy from "that sweet enemy, France" in which Sidney had famously participated (*AS* 30.9–10, 41.4). More strikingly, Sidney emphasizes Penelope Rich's marital status numerous times by mocking her husband, Robert Rich, by name. "Rich fools there be, whose base and filthy heart / Lies hatching still the goods wherein they flow," he complains,

> But that rich fool, who by blind fortune's lot
> The richest gem of love and life enjoys,
> And can with foul abuse such beauties blot,
> Let him, deprived of sweet but unfelt joys,

Exiled for aye from those high treasures which
He knows not, grow only in folly rich. (*AS* 24.1–2, 9–14)

Here, marriage, and particularly the conjugal sex that Robert Rich "enjoys," is a form of "foul abuse."[59] The final prayer, that Robert Rich will "grow only in folly rich" because he cannot appreciate the "high treasures" of his wife's love, imagines Penelope Rich already unfaithful. Later, Astrophil comments that "long needy fame / Doth even grow rich, naming my Stella's name" (*AS* 35.10–11). Sonnet 37, which was omitted from the 1591 pirated print edition but restored to the 1598 authorized version, is even franker in its identification of the model for Stella:

My mouth doth water, and my breast doth swell,
    My tongue doth itch, my thoughts in labour be;
    Listen then, lordings, with good ear to me,
For of my life I must a riddle tell.
Towards Aurora's court a nymph doth dwell,
    Rich in all beauties which man's eye can see;
    Beauties so far from reach of words, that we
Abase her praise, saying she doth excel;
    Rich in the treasure of deserved renown;
Rich in the riches of a royal heart;
Rich in those gifts which give the eternal crown;
    Who though most rich in these, and every part
    Which make the patents of true worldly bliss,
    Hath no misfortune, but that Rich she is. (*AS* 37.1–14)

By the end of the first quatrain, the somatic expressions of arousal with which the poem begins (watering mouth, heavy breathing, itchy tongue, labored thoughts) are revealed equally to be symptoms of confessional desire. But the "riddle" that Astrophil goes on to tell could have been solved by a fairly dim contemporary manuscript reader. The "nymph" who lives near "Aurora's court" (Penelope Rich was a lady-in-waiting to Elizabeth I) is "Rich" not just metaphorically but literally. Adjective *is* name. Capitalizing "Rich," Sidney emphasizes the contrast between the worldly wealth gained by marriage and the misery of forced union with the "rich fool" whose "enjoyment" of her constitutes "foul abuse."

The material and social benefits that this forced marriage brought to Penelope Rich's guardians requires, to borrow Milton's words, that her "body prostitute it selfe to whom the mind affords no other love or peace" (*Tetrachordon* 2:708).

Even for the wider audience of the print edition (including modern readers) who may not have heard of Penelope Rich, the "riddle," or narrative of the full sequence, makes clear that Stella is a married woman. In the Eighth Song the speaker tells us that Stella's "fair neck a foul yoke bare"—the bonds of matrimony, in this representation, are far more polluting than the embraces of adultery. The Eleventh Song, likewise, is a dialogue that stages a recognizable tableau of illicit desire as Astrophil appears at Stella's window.[60] Warning Astrophil to "be gone, be gone, I say, / Lest that Argus' eyes perceive you," Stella summarizes the sequence's more general play with public and private, biography and fiction (*AS* Eleventh Song, 41–42). Argus, the hundred-eyed monster who is sent by Juno to prevent Jupiter's adulterous liaison, figures household servants and a larger public of gossips who obstruct the lovers' satisfaction. Dramatizing this fear of perception itself confesses the illicit nature of the relationship and imagines its consummation despite external impediments: Argus was slain by Mercury, leaving Jupiter free to enjoy Io. (In *Pamphilia to Amphilanthus*, Wroth would similarly evoke Argus to signal adulterous desire that succeeds despite invasive surveillance.)[61]

If *Astrophil and Stella* conforms to the model of "Poor Petrarch's long-deceased woes" in its representation of thwarted love, it departs from its Petrarchan model in its emphasis on the addressee's reciprocal desire (*AS* 15.7). As I have argued elsewhere, piety about marriage among some modern critics has led to the denial of Stella's own erotic longings for Astrophil.[62] If we are to believe the scholarly consensus, Astrophil fails as miserably in his wooing as Petrarch—and that failure is precisely the point of the sequence in that it similarly compels him eventually to renounce his earthly desires.[63] Feminist readings of the sequence built on earlier avowals of Stella's sexual purity, arguing that Astrophil was not only immoral but also misogynistic. This critical agreement that sex with Astrophil would harm or humiliate Stella ends up supporting the view that women, at once guardians of morality and potential victims of male lust, cannot safely express desire outside of the confines of marriage. However much Astrophil, in Alan Sinfield's words, "quibbles on meanings of love to evade incompatibility between his wishes and Stella's," Stella must steadfastly maintain the distinction between debased, sensual lust and wholesome, spiritual love.[64] Stella, unlike Astrophil, demonstrates that even if she "suffers the conflict between emotions and honor," she "accepts her social responsibility," in Nona Feinberg's reading.[65] This conformity to expectations of female chastity, Thomas Roche comments, makes Stella an "exemplum of the proper discipline of passion by reason."[66] Given that Penelope Rich herself carried on a very public affair with Charles Blount for at least a decade, bearing several illegitimate children whom her husband, Robert Rich, was content to support until the couple was granted a divorce in 1605, her relation to a Stella who only, properly says "no" can be nothing short of ironic.[67] In effect, the resistance to biographical referents in favor of universal, anonymous speaker and beloved upholds the view that *Astrophil and Stella* endorses a transhistorical equation of marriage with morally acceptable desire.

The scholarly idealization of Stella's virtue must disregard prominent evidence internal to the sequence that her libidinal impulses are as intense and conflicted as Astrophil's. She professes love for a man not her husband (*AS* 69); attends clandestine trysts (*AS* Fourth Song, *AS* Eighth Song); becomes jealous of Astrophil's liaisons with other women (*AS* Eleventh Song); insists that she suffers as much as Astrophil (*AS* Eighth Song, *AS* 87); and, at the very least, kisses Astrophil several times (*AS* 80–82; as James J. Scanlon observes with distaste, these are not chaste pecks but passionate "tongue kisses"[68]). Disturbingly, the critical celebration of Stella's adherence to "social responsibility" and "proper discipline" glosses over the "foul abuse" that due benevolence to a loathed spouse would constitute. For some critics, Astrophil's adulterous desire is part of a larger "rape scenario."[69] Meanwhile, the fact that Stella is depicted as submitting to conjugal embraces that she does not desire— encounters that feminists have rightly named spousal rape—receives no comment.[70]

Until recently, Wroth's *Pamphilia to Amphilanthus* had been, if anything, even more subject to critical protectionism on the topics of women's desire and sexual autonomy. For a long time, the standard take on Wroth was that her poems responded to her worries about her reputation as both a "fallen" woman and a published woman writer.[71]

In this version of her biography, Wroth was seduced and discarded by her cousin, William Herbert, Third Earl of Pembroke; forced to marry a man she didn't love, then left in poverty after his death; and exiled from court after the combined scandal of publishing as a woman and bearing two illegitimate children. More recent work has shown this melodramatic narrative, and the critical truisms it produced, to be oversimplified. This scholarship has allowed us to understand Wroth as one of our best-documented examples of women who conducted surprisingly public extramarital affairs.[72] It also compels us to rethink the sociopolitical structure in which Wroth wrote. What Phyllis Rackin has observed of the Shakespearean canon can be extended to Renaissance England more generally: "Reminders that women were to be chaste, silent, and obedient probably occur more frequently in recent scholarship than they did in the literature of Shakespeare's time."[73]

We do not know when Wroth's affair with Pembroke, who was the model for Amphilanthus in her sonnet sequence, began. Scholars have variously proposed that it may have started before Wroth's marriage to Robert Wroth in 1604 (as the parallel fiction in *Urania* suggests), sometime early in her marriage (Ben Jonson commented that Mary Wroth was "unworthily married to a jealous husband"), or after her husband's death in 1614.[74] But we do know that it produced illegitimate twins around the spring of 1624, at which point Pembroke had been married to Mary Talbot for nearly two decades; that Pembroke's paternity was common knowledge; and that neither Wroth nor the twins, who were known by the Herbert surname, suffered any serious social consequences.[75] We also know that the prose romance with which *Pamphilia to Amphilanthus* was first printed, *The Countess of Montgomeries Urania*, was widely recognized as a roman à clef offering titillating gossip about the English nobility in the guise of fiction. The *Urania* includes numerous topical references to events involving Wroth, Pembroke, and their families, and a poem known to be Herbert's is attributed to Amphilanthus.[76] As Mary Ellen Lamb has noted, Wroth published a romance and sonnet sequence that "was not only flagrantly sexual in itself but which even implicated her own personal history in its sexuality."[77]

Far from depicting the relationship as one of chaste because unrequited Petrarchan desire, Wroth depicts Pamphilia's illicit love as both earthly and consummated. In the published version of *Pamphilia to Am-*

philanthus, Pamphilia describes her "flaming" heart (*PA* F1/P1.9) and promises that although "like a fire doth love increase in mee / . . . Yett love I will till I but ashes prove" (*PA* F55/P55.1, 14). Her likely pun on her lover's name here ("love I will") is supplemented by puns throughout the sequence on "worth"/Wroth and "will"/Will.[78] She frankly offers reciprocation to "Love": "Shine in those eyes which conquer'd have my hart; / And see if mine bee slack to answere thee" (*PA* F3/P3.3–4). She emphasizes "how many nights," "How many howrs," and "all these years" her desire has endured (*PA* F70/P67.1, 5, 8). She suggests that the affair has waxed and waned: "my joys now budd again / Lately growne dead" (*PA* P4/4). The unpublished manuscript version of the sequence includes an aubade—a poem set in the morning after lovers have spent a forbidden night together—and a song that reminds the addressee, "you did ask, I freely gave" (F117.16).

Of course, we cannot read either Wroth's romance or her sonnet sequence as a transparently factual description of any events. But we can read it as evidence that, whatever really happened, Wroth *wanted* her adulterous attachment to Pembroke to be public knowledge, at least among the political and literary circles of her kin, friends, and advocates.[79] Wroth circulated at least some of her poems in manuscript, almost certainly before 1611, when Ben Jonson appears to have written a poem praising Wroth on the grounds that "Since I exscribe your sonnets, am become / A better lover, and much better poet."[80] Given that she was married at age seventeen, it is likely that these poems were written after Wroth's 1604 marriage. And even if read as purely fictional, they express a fictional woman's erotic desire for a man not her husband. Rather than shock early readers, Wroth's adulterous lyrics appear to have won generally positive attention.[81] Contrary to assertions of her first modern critics, after the publication of her romance and sonnet sequence and throughout her life, Wroth retained her connections to powerful members of the courts of James I and Charles I and remained a prominent part of her country community.[82]

Wroth's identification with Pamphilia was certainly clear to her most notorious reader, Sir Edward Denny. Enraged by an episode in Wroth's romance based on his attempt to murder his own daughter when she was accused of adultery, Denny wrote a poem entitled "To Pamphilia from the Father-in-Law of Seralius," in which he attacks Wroth as a

"Hermophradite," "monster," and "common oyster" who "take[s] in pearles or worse at every tide." Wroth responded with a parody in which she throws these charges back at him and adds that his "Dirty doubt" constitutes an admission that he has indeed behaved just like the character depicted in her romance: "How easily now do you receave your own."[83] One contemporary, John Chamberlain, describes Denny's verses as a response to the fact that in the *Urania* Wroth "takes great liberty or rather license to traduce whom she please."[84] Wendy Wall articulates the most common early reading of Chamberlain's comment when she argues that it "expresses irritation that Wroth believed herself free to speak her mind publicly and escape repercussions."[85] In this view, the reaction to the *Urania* had everything to do with Wroth's transgression of the taboo against women's publication.[86] As Elizabeth Hanson has persuasively argued, however, although Wroth operated in a social world in which, then as now, "her gender could be made to signify in discrediting ways," the uproar over the *Urania* "seems to have had much more to do with who she hit than with the writer's gender or what she reveals about herself, despite the fact that her apparent surrogate, Pamphilia, is made both the subject of desire and an adulterous lover."[87] Wroth engaged in an act of aggression in writing the *Urania*, for it made available for public consumption a number of incidents in the lives of courtiers that, like her own affair with Pembroke, flew in the face of public prescriptions for moral behavior that continue to shape norms of respectability.[88]

By dedicating themselves to persons they will never marry, Sidney's Astrophil and Wroth's Pamphilia profoundly complicate the constancy that they profess. Fidelity and infidelity are not opposites, for fidelity to the true love requires infidelity to the legal spouse and vice versa. These sequences thus raise numerous questions about the historical emergence of monogamous coupledom. How do we understand the "heroics of constancy" in the context of a relationship in which due benevolence is legally owed to someone other than the beloved?[89] What are we to make of Astrophil's insistence that he had been faithful despite temptations from other women at court, or of Pamphilia's frequent outbursts of jealousy at Amphilanthus's new loves, when any such betrayal would be against adulterous vows that themselves violate the law?[90] Does the declaration of adulterous desire in sequences that were widely circulated in manuscript before they saw print publication suggest that something like "open marriages" were tolerated in Renaissance England? Was the propagation of illegitimate children as taboo as many scholars have assumed? And were women therefore as disproportionately sexually repressed as modern double standards suggest? Finally, a question I discuss at length in this chapter's last section: How did overdetermined distinctions of race and religion mediate secular notions of romance, adultery, and sincerity?

To ask these empirical questions is also to redefine early modern England as, to again cite Freeman's apt description, a "usable past" that can help "to unsituate viewers from the present tense they think they know and to illuminate or even prophetically ignite possible futures in light of powerful historical moments." In the past we think we know, adultery is illegal and deviation from disciplined monogamy is subject to an array of punishments from social ostracization to public shaming to imprisonment to (briefly, in the 1650s) execution. But looking more closely at how people actually lived their lives suggests, paradoxically, both that we don't know the past that well at all and that it may be more like the present than we think. A detailed history of adultery law and records of extramarital sex is outside the scope of this book. But I do want to propose that scholarship that has relied purely on the letter of the law and the instructions of conduct books has too easily conflated prescription with description. Joanna Rickman's study of illicit affairs indicates that what Alan Bray and Jonathan Goldberg have argued of sodomy could also be said of adultery: though draconian laws prohibiting it were on the books, unless it coincided with political rivalries or socioeconomic disruption, it was not uniformly prosecuted.[91] In this, adultery in Renaissance England was not unlike adultery in the twenty-first century United States, where it remains a crime in twenty-one states (a felony in five), punishable by fines ranging from $10 to $10,000 and jail time ranging from thirty days to five years.[92] And while we know that sodomy laws were only declared unconstitutional in 2003, it is less common knowledge that fornication remained criminal in some states as recently as 2014 and cohabitation is still illegal in Michigan and Mississippi as of the writing of this book (and was illegal in Florida from 1858 until 2016).[93] Because official records may obscure cultural norms, what Jack Halberstam calls "perverse presentism" ("application of what we do not know in the present to what we cannot know about the past") must be supplemented by a perverse historicism, in which the past may provide critique of and alternative to present practices and assumptions.[94] Sidney's and Wroth's poetry, straddling as it does the real and the aspirational, is a valuable resource for such perverse historicism.

Love Hurts

Astrophil and Stella and *Pamphilia to Amphilanthus* indicate that the "medieval romance of adultery" was alive and well in both practice and theory into and beyond the seventeenth century. For the most famous of romance protagonists, from Lancelot and Guinevere and Tristan and Isolde to Anna Karenina or Emma Bovary, extramarital love comes to signal the transcendence of everyday compromises and limitations. What makes adultery a figure for true love in so many romances, however, is not only its flouting of law and convention, but also the willingness of lovers to put up with the pain of separation, the fear of discovery, and the torments of punishment if they are found out. Adultery is therefore a continuation rather than a contrary of the Petrarchan desire that, as William Kerrigan and Gordon Braden have observed, cultivates its own obstacles in an unconscious effort to draw out the unpleasure of desire.[95] Adulterous love, rebelling against law and custom, creates a secular hagiography. Much as the religious martyr chooses spiritual salvation over bodily comfort, the erotic martyr gladly chooses agonizing passion over profit or respectability. Those who refuse to confine their love within marriage are martyrs for desire, embodying a secular form of the freedom of a Christian in which internal compulsion is evinced through the futility of any external pressure to betray the faith—even as its discourse of erotic enslavement relies on the same privileging of whiteness that we observed in some of Shakespeare's sonnets.

In Petrarchan tradition, the true lover is helplessly compelled by internal forces that allow him to withstand any level or variety of external pressure to abandon faith. The conceptual fusion of compulsion and choice, as Adorno argued, helps to sustain the damaging regime of capitalism by offering an imaginative refuge of freedom. But the sadomasochistic dimension of romance strains this ideological work by foregrounding love's losses as well as its gains. *Astrophil and Stella* describes such wounding attachment with equal parts disbelief, resentment, and surrender:

What, have I thus betrayed my liberty?
>Can those black beams such burning marks engrave
>In my free side? or am I borne a slave,
Whose neck becomes such yoke of tyranny?
Or want I sense to feel my misery?
>Or sprite, disdain of such disdain to have,
>Who for long faith, though daily help I crave,
May get no alms, but scorn of beggary?
>Virtue, awake: beauty but beauty is;
I may, I must, I can, I will, I do
Leave following that, which it is gain to miss.
Let her go. Soft, but here she comes. Go to,
>Unkind, I love you not—: O me, that eye
>Doth make my heart to give to my tongue the lie. (*AS* 47.1–14)

Formally, the poem makes audible the loss of sovereign subjectivity that is the mark of love. Beginning with an emphatic trochee—*what!*—the ragged meter of the poem conveys the disbelief and disorientation of intense love, even as the strong enjambments, feminine rhyme, and falling meter that open and close the octave (liberty, tyranny, misery beggary) express failure of resolution. This failure becomes explicit in the third quatrain and couplet, where the initially neat iambs reach a crescendo in the emphatic rhythm of "Let her go." But resolution falters with the dramatic entrance of Stella ("Soft, but here she comes."). The continuation of "Go to, / Unkind, I love you not" from quatrain to couplet refuses resolution and instead brings Astrophil back where he started. All of the "I's" in line 7, as well as that of line 13, fail to sustain intentionality in the presence of Stella's "eye." A single glance transforms "I" to "me," subject to object. The self-persuading lie of the tongue gives way to the truth of the heart.

Sidney here, as Roland Greene observes, also evokes "the more contemporaneous and concrete fact of slavery as a charged, unpredictable conceit for amatory experience" in which desire for mastery is itself a form of self-enslavement with the potential to render equivocal the proposition that "slavery is natural to anyone."[96] The loss of liberty described in sonnet 47 is also the height of freedom, for it is a testament to Astrophil's freedom to follow his heart, which reminds us that this is only metaphorical enslavement after all. In such a state, pleasure and pain are indistinguishable through normal criteria. As we saw in Augustine's *Confessions* and Shakespeare's sonnets, what the lover wants most is to *want* to give up the self entirely, to make another's will and desires one's own. To love another person is to relinquish the claims of autonomy and dignity attached to the post-Enlightenment ideal of a sovereign self, even as it assumes the privilege of having such a choice. *Astrophil and Stella* (and *Pamphilia to Amphilanthus*) follows a tradition, outlined in detail in Plato's *Symposium*, in which eros is characterized by a distinctly unpleasurable awareness of lack and need.[97] This longing was translated into Christian terms by one of Plato's most attentive readers, Augustine, who deems frustrated desire the mark of faith. Plato's secular definition of love as "desire for perpetual possession of the good" becomes for Augustine, and the Christian Neoplatonists after him, an insatiable longing that God gives us for himself, a longing that can only be captured in the most sensual of terms: "You called and cried out loud and shattered my deafness . . . You were fragrant, and I drew in my breath and now pant after you. I tasted you, and I feel but hunger and thirst for you. You touched me, and I am set on fire to attain the peace which is yours."[98]

In its reciprocity, the self-denying love of *Astrophil and Stella* departs from the Augustinian and Petrarchan tradition.[99] Sidney's Eighth Song stresses the mutuality of agonizing desire and contrasts it with the corrosive due benevolence of marriage. The song's setting is a pastoral landscape in which adultery is harmonious with nature:

> In a grove most rich of shade,
> Where birds wanton music made,
> May then young his pied weeds showing,
> New perfumed with flowers fresh growing,
>
> Astrophil with Stella sweet
> Did for mutual comfort meet;
> Both within themselves oppressed,
> But each in the other blessed.
>
> Him great harms had taught much care,
> Her faire neck a foul yoke bare,

But her sight his cares did banish,
In his sight her yoke did vanish. (*AS* Eighth Song 1–12)

In setting the meeting in a "grove most rich of shade," the narrator both conveys the secret, hidden nature of the scene we are about to witness and situates the married Stella as a willing, equal participant. However fresh and youthful the season, this is not the meeting of two blushing virgins, but a secret tryst between a married, sexually experienced woman and her would-be partner in adultery. Drawing on a Virgilian definition of pastoral in which bucolic scenes both contrast natural innocence with social hypocrisy and provide a cover of deniability for political critique, the Eighth Song is central to the sequence's representation of (in)fidelity as innately masochistic. The pastoral fantasy of desire beyond social pressure is explicitly contrasted to the actual situation in which Stella's "yoke" of marriage makes impossible the public legitimation of this relationship. At the same time, the pastoral contrast between nature and custom makes the fact of adultery a structural good insofar as it cordons Astrophil and Stella's love off from the compromises and coercions of the social institution of marriage, thereby ensuring its authenticity.

But the Eighth Song ultimately rejects the pleasures of the pastoral as a refuge from law. Stella does not succumb to Astrophil's bucolic appeal to "Time and place": "These birds sing, 'Now use the season'" (*AS* Eighth Song 52, 56). Instead, "her hands, his hands repelling, / Gave repulse, all grace excelling" (*AS* Eighth Song 67–68). A textual crux in line 68 allows us to appreciate how refusing even the fantasy of pastoral satisfaction does not deny desire but rather extends it. The pirated 1591 edition reads "all grace *expelling*," which would seem, on the face of it, to make more sense: in refusing to have sex, Stella banishes the generosity and freedom of pastoral *otium*, returning Astrophil to the *negotium*, or compromise, of the real world. But the 1598 "all grace excelling," which would seem at first glance a mere bowdlerization, is in fact far more perverse. Stella excels, or surpasses, the gracious gift of mere "mutuall comfort"—the extinguishment of painful arousal—and instead perpetuates it. She rejects a pastoral fantasy of escape from the reality of their respective "yoke" and "care" in favor of the heightened yearning that these prohibitions ensure. The prohibition against adultery may be what sustains the pair's

desire for one another. The psychoanalytic principle that deferred satisfaction is what keeps a love story going has long been embedded in the
formal explanation for romantic comedies that end in marriage.[100] In a
romance of adultery, which cannot strive toward such closure, desire has
no such formal teleology. This is adultery's attraction.

When Stella rejects Astrophil's exhortation that they "use the season"
in the second half of the poem, she insists that she does it not to hurt
him, but because it hurts *her*. Vowing that "'All my bliss in thee I lay,'" she
designates Astrophil the source of an earthly joy that is also inseparable
from beatitude, the "blessedness" whose religious meaning had merged
with the originally secular "bliss" by the tenth century. Yet she defers
the transcendent pleasure he offers: "'Trust me, while I thee deny, / In
my self the smart I try" (*AS* Eighth Song 93–94). Stella "tries"—tests,
explores, proves—her tolerance for pain. Denying release to herself and
Astrophil, Stella turns what started as pursuit of "mutual comfort" into
infinite delay of satisfaction or detumescence.

Sadomasochism as such, as Freeman observes, is a temporal phenomenon characterized by the rhythms of excruciating suspense and unnerving shock, withholding and release, "impulse and action," in which
pleasure and trauma coalesce.[101] This dynamic has more akin with lyric
than with narrative, a formal affiliation that helps explain the abrupt end
of the Eighth Song. With Stella's refusal of consummation, the pastoral
fiction breaks down, and with it the narrative frame that divides Sidney
from Astrophil, adulterous from innocent passion:

> Therewithal away she went,
> Leaving *him* so passion-rent
> With what she had done and spoken,
> That therewith *my* song is broken. (*AS* Eighth Song 101–104; my
>   emphasis)

Recalling the statement that "I am not I," this final quatrain again
draws our attention to the uncertain referent beyond the fiction of the
sequence. Astrophil is "passion-rent"; the third-person narrator confesses that "my song is broken." The situation is repeated in the Tenth
Song, where Astrophil enjoys an onanistic fantasy of himself and the
absent Stella "Joying, till joy make us languish," and the song itself breaks

off in orgasmic climax: "O my thought my thoughts surcease, / Thy delights my woes increase, / My life melts with too much thinking" (*AS* Tenth Song 42, 43–45).[102] In conspicuously staging these breakdowns of author and speaker, fiction and reality, *Astrophil and Stella* situates adultery as the prototype of fidelity precisely because of the painful delay and dissatisfaction that it requires. This is a formal delay as well, one in which narrative progress may always shatter into lyric fragmentation, allowing for the potentially endless dilation that Patricia Parker and Jonathan Goldberg have seen as a generic marker of romance itself. Such formal play is essential to the theoretical work of *Astrophil and Stella*. As Goldberg writes, in romance the "narrative principles that induce frustration, that deny closure," also make visible conceptual, relational, and social alternatives to the comforts of linearity and resolution.[103]

Sidney's vocabulary of grace and bliss makes adulterous desire that cannot be extinguished into a figure for love that demonstrates sincerity by patiently submitting to the unknown plans and timeline of another. If true love waits—and we might here recall Shakespeare's equation of love, service, patience, and *freedom*—it is because waiting draws out arousal, the end of which is at once threat and promise. Wroth's *Pamphilia to Amphilanthus* is even more explicit about the theological predicament on which erotic deferral is patterned. Like Sidney, she conspicuously combines sacred and profane language to express desire whose masochism confirms its truth. "None but martyrs happy burn," Pamphilia asserts: the burning that marriage should extinguish is beyond worldly structures of legitimation (*PA* F101/P94.35). Like Petrarch, Pamphilia urges herself to "Leave the discourse of Venus, and her son," and to turn to higher things. But, true to the Petrarchan tradition, she is unable to abandon the deities she describes as "Goddess of desire," "only Queene of lust," and "God of love" (*PA* F59/P58.5, F40/P95.13). Instead, her "soul endures" unceasing "paines," "flames," "stormes," "restless nights," "sighs unfaind," "griefe," and "torments" inflicted by Venus and Cupid's "sacred power" (*PA* F59/P58.4–12).

As in their response to Stella, critics have been reluctant to take seriously the possibility that Pamphilia represents a willfully, consciously masochistic desire. As a result, they have read poems that appear to put Cupid in his proper place in isolation from the full sequence and described them as signs of female virtue and wisdom. I propose, to the contrary, that two such poems, the songs "Love a child is ever crying" and "Beeing past the paines of love," dramatize the limits of rational responses to pleasure and pain. In the first of these, Pamphilia likens passion's insatiability to an allegorical child who is "never satisfi'd with having," whose "desires have no measure," who "vowes nothing butt faulce matter," and who "will triumph in your walying." Concluding that "Feathers ar as firme in staying / Woulves noe fiercer in theyr praying," Pamphilia deems Cupid worthy of contemptuous dismissal: "As a child then leave him crying / Nor seek him so giv'n to flying" (PA F78/P74.4, 5, 9, 13, 19–20).

The following song is more lighthearted, characterizing love not as a demonic child but as a pesky trifle. The speaker is a personified "Freedome" who, now "past the paines of love," urges others to extricate themselves: "Says loves delights were pretty / Butt to dwell in them 'twere pitty" (PA F79/P75.1–4). Each stanza concludes with a slight variation of this couplet, a repetition that until the last stanza appears formally to enact the reform of values that Freedom counsels. The final stanza, however, presents masochism as beyond such sound reasoning:

> Those that like the smart of love
> In them let itt freely move
> Els though his delights are pretty
> Doe not dwell in them for pitty. (PA F79/P75.17–20)

Some people, this stanza concedes, may actually "*like* the smart of love." In this case, freedom *from* the "paines of love" is the last thing they want, and they should "let [desire] freely move" in them. In retrospect, previous stanzas have been provisional. They are qualified by that "Els" that transforms the final refrain into a statement that can be roughly paraphrased as "if you don't like the smart of love, then even if his delights seem attractive, don't give in to them simply because of pity/sympathy." But there is, this stanza concedes, one good reason to "dwell in" love's "delights": because one enjoys them. What would appear to be pitiable submission is equally an assertion of "Freedom"—not the rational pursuit of self-interest that liberal secularism ascribes to that term, but a hagiographic attachment that confounds secular economies of cost and benefit and exceeds material limits and practices.

The fourteen poems grouped under the heading "A Crown of Sonnets Dedicated to Love" explicitly equate erotic fixation with religious faith. Elaine Beilin has rightly argued that "an exalted tone, flow of luminous imagery, and specifically religious diction distinguish the Crown" from the early poems in the sequence. Beilin, like several other critics, sees "the transformation of the old language of love sonnets to a new language of divine adoration" as affirming "the place of moral virtue in earthly love."[104] In such readings, the true "monster" in Wroth's labyrinth is the female sexuality that Pamphilia must learn to contain. I argue instead that the equation of religious language, sexual restraint, and "moral virtue" overlooks the ways in which spiritual devotion may resist conventional morality. Read in the context of Richard Rambuss's attention to "devotion's intensities and expressive perversities," Wroth's religious vocabulary explores the breakdown of the boundary between pleasure and pain, the ecstatic dissolution of the self in the other.[105] In the Crown's fusion of secular and spiritual worship, religion is not an alternative to adulterous passion, but the vehicle by which it is expressed.

Pamphilia begins Sonnet 1 of the Crown by asking, "In this strange labourinth how shall I turn?" (*PA* F82/P77.1); at the end of this sonnet, she concedes that amidst the "suspiton" and "shame" described in the first poem her only choice "Is to leave all, and take the thread of love" (*PA* F82/P77.5, 6, 14). The next sonnet in the Crown affirms that this thread "straite leads unto the soules content" (*PA* F83/P78.1–2). Yet the "soules content" is not a state of peaceful relaxation, but one of excess and subjugation: "His flames ar joyes, his bands true lovers might" (*PA* F83/P78.14). In subsequent poems in the Crown, Pamphilia exhorts herself and her reader to "Please him, and serve him, glory in his might" (*PA* F84/P79.9) and

> To taste this pleasing sting seek with all care
> For hapy smarting is itt with smale paine
> Such as although, itt pierce your tender hart
> And burne, yett burning you will love the smart. (*PA* F85/P80.11–14)

Her celebration of love's "pleasing sting" and "happy smarting" and her insistence that "burning you will love the smart" treat the enjoyment of pain as proof of free—unconstrained, sincere—love. When Pamphilia imagines the possibility of a love that "sin abolisheth," she reforms the definition of sin rather than the lust itself (*PA* F86/P81.6). Echoing the view that matrimony transforms husband and wife into "one flesh" Wroth, like Milton after her, attributes that office to sincere love, "In whom alone wee doe this power finde, / To joine two harts as in one frame to move; / Two bodies, butt one soule to rule the minde" (*PA* F87/ P82.2–4). Cupid's invisible bands render wedding bands at best irrelevant and at worst immoral.

What makes the Crown a crown is its formal circularity, with each poem beginning with the last line of the previous one and the final poem ending with the first line of the first poem. This circularity rejects linear development from the carnal to the spiritual, immaturity to adulthood, initial attraction to respectable marriage. Instead, it depicts the compulsion to repeat, formally registering the all-encompassing nature of erotic passion. Dubrow has rightly seen such repetition and circularity as characteristic of both Petrarchism in general and Wroth's sequence in particular.[106] Given that the Crown formally enacts—indeed is defined by—such circularity, it provides a fitting representation of *Pamphilia to Amphilanthus* as a series of returns rather than a linear narrative of transcendence. F89/P84, for instance, attempts to claim that the "briers / Of jelousie shall heere miss wellcomnes" (*PA* F89/P84.7–8). But the final poem of the Crown admits that, "Curst jealousie doth all her forces bend / To my undoing; thus my harmes I see" (*PA* F95/P90.11–12). The Crown ends where it began ("Soe though in Love I fervently doe burne, / In this strange labourinth how shall I turne?" [*PA* F95/P90.14]). It thereby recalls, in form as well as imagery, the Petrarchan lesson that desire's temporality is more circular than punctual. As Petrarch writes, "One thousand three hundred twenty-seven, exactly at the first / hour of the sixth day of April, I / entered the labyrinth, nor do I see where I may get out of it."[107]

Race and the Romance of Adultery

But we should pause before we celebrate the queer potential of Renaissance depictions of free love, whether in the form of Milton's reasonable pursuit of self-fulfillment or Sidney's and Wroth's masochistic self-abnegation. The writing I have been examining points to a past that is "usable" not only in the sense of positive example, but also for what it can tell us about the exclusionary, dystopian aspects of the optimism of divorce and adultery. The affective liberty championed in Sidney's and Wroth's poetry and in Milton's divorce pamphlets attests to the specifically Christian roots of the association of white, Western culture with freedom, sincerity, and virtue. Writing that seems to depict a radically privatized understanding of desire in fact relies on a publicly understood semantics of racialized religion and so perpetuates nascent religious, racial, colonial, and imperial hierarchies. What scholars working at the intersection of studies of race, colonialism, gender, and sexuality studies have cautioned about modern feminist or queer challenges to normativity is equally true of early modern alternatives: they may themselves endorse white and Western hierarchies.

In *The Doctrine and Discipline of Divorce* and *Tetrachordon*, the "infidel" repeatedly appears as a figure for the cruelty, self-destruction, hypocrisy, and superstition that Milton associates with the bondage and spiritual danger of unhappy marriage. Commenting on the verse from Paul's Second Letter to the Corinthians that he translates as "*Mis-yoke not together with Infidels*," Milton explains that this instruction derives from a twofold fear of uncleanness and seduction (*DDD* 2:262; Milton's emphasis).[108] The first stricture, Milton counsels in keeping with his larger dismissal of external appearance and custom, is pure superstition, for "the body of an Infidell is not polluted, neither to benevolence, nor to procreation" (*DDD* 2:267). But the fear of seduction is real. Merging one's life with that of an infidel can undermine "Christian liberty and conscience" (*DDD* 2:267). As the Geneva Bible's gloss to this verse explains, Christians, like the Jews in Deuteronomy, risk becoming "fellows with infidels in outward idolatry, as if it were a thing indifferent." Bondage and freedom, sincerity and hypocrisy, truth and delusion cannot coexist. One or the other spouse will eventually have to convert, and if the infidel refuses to take this role, the Christian spouse "may give over washing an Ethiope" (*DDD* 2:267).[109] Conjoined religious and racial difference for Milton encapsulates the "household persecutions" that characterize unhappy marriage: "that man or wife who hates in wedlock, is perpetually unsociable, unpeacefull, or unduteous . . . therefore is worse then an infidel. . . . The blamelesse person therefore hath as good a plea to sue out his delivery from this bondage, as from the desertion of an infidel" (*Tetrachordon* 2:687, 691).

Those English Protestants who "invest [marriage] with such an awfull sanctity, and give it such adamantine chains to bind with, as if it were to be worshipt like some *Indian* deity" are also worse than infidels, for they have made their erroneous beliefs into law (*DDD* 2:277; Milton's emphasis). Like Indians—and here Milton may mean either Indigenous Americans or East Indians, both of whom were frequently seen as pagan idolaters—they adore a god of their own invention. This is the same literalism against which Paul preaches when he says that "he is not a Jew, which is one outward, neither is that circumcision, which is outward in the flesh; But he is a Jew which is one within; and the circumcision *is* of the heart, in the spirit, not in the letter; whose praise is not of men, but of God" (GB, Rom. 2:28-29). Commenting on this dispensation, Milton writes, "How vain then and how preposterous must it needs be to exact a circumcision of the Flesh from an infant unto an outward signe of purity, and to dispence an uncircumcision in the soul of a grown man to an inward and reall impurity" (*DDD* 2:302). Having apotheosized marriage, the English turn the miseries it can visit into divine punishments that must be passively suffered: "We must let them all lye upon us like the vermin of an Indian *Catharist*, which his fond religion forbids him to molest" (*Tetrachordon* 2:590; Milton's emphasis). Milton here polemically conflates the asceticism of the Cathars, a Gnostic sect, with a derisive cartoon of Hindu reluctance to harm any life form. For the purposes of his argument, what these two non-Christian faiths share is the pursuit of purity that leads to an excessive and self-punishing literalism.[110] The problem is not getting circumcised, but believing that it makes a difference to salvation. Unable to unshackle themselves from soul-killing superstitions, Protestant idolaters, no less than racialized "infidels," impose an outward conformity to rites that are alien to sincere faith. True Christians, by contrast, understand that they are never pure, but rather born adulterated by a divided will that no mortification of the flesh can remedy. Milton, of course, does not invent a habit of mind that racializes erotic dispositions and relational forms. But the racial divisions he exploits in the divorce tracts reveal how theories of sexual liberty can perpetuate a tradition that collapses religious and racial others as irrational hypocrites in contrast to the charity and freedom of the sincere Christian. In this light, his definition of loving marriage as a model for good public government is revealed as resting on precisely the religious and racial exclusions deemed antithetical to the modern secular rationality with which Milton is often associated.

The understanding of secular love, like religious faith, as a feeling at once properly interiorized and racially visible finds precise statement in *Pamphilia to Amphilanthus*. Written and published decades before Milton's divorce tracts, Wroth's sequence suggests not direct influence, but evidence of the prevalence of the custom of conceptualizing embodied expressions of faith—whether religious or secular—in terms of racial difference. Comparing her secret love to pagan worship of the sun, Wroth depicts the difference between married and adulterous desire in terms of the Pauline distinction between the circumcision of the flesh and that of the heart:

> Like to the Indians, scorched with the sunne,
>> The sunn which they doe as theyr God adore
>> Soe ame I us'd by love, for ever more
>> I worship him, less favors have I wunn,
> Better are they who thus to blacknes runn,
>> And soe can only whitenes want deplore
>> Then I who pale, and white ame with griefs store,
>> Nor can have hope, butt to see hopes undunn;
> Beesides theyr sacrifies receavd's in sight
>> Of theyr chose sainte; Mine hid as worthles rite;
>> Grant mee to see wher I my offrings give,
> Then lett mee weare the marke of Cupids might
>> In hart as they in skin of Phoebus light
>> Nott ceasing offrings to love while I Live. (*PA* F19/P25.1–14)

Wroth's characteristically difficult syntax and dense enjambments beg for paraphrase. The abbaabba rhyme of the octave folds in on itself, formally manifesting the privacy of which it complains: "Like Indians who have gotten burnt by the sun they worship, I have also been cruelly used by love. But in fact I am worse off than they are. Even though they have black skin, they lack only external whiteness; I am pale with suffering and have no hope of getting better." The sestet resolves the apparent injustice described in the octave by recategorizing the Indians' performance of public ritual into evidence of the inferiority of their love:

"They can worship openly and communally; I have to hide my love. But my love is heartfelt, theirs only skin deep." The formal and conceptual voltas in this poem are misaligned, with the latter appearing only at line 11, rather than at the start of the sestet as we might expect. This divergence from Petrarchan alignment of form and matter itself situates rejection of convention as a sign of authenticity. Here, as Pamphilia prays that her love will persist ("Grant mee to see wher I my offrings give"), the internal rhyme of "mee" and "see" turns the line in on itself. She had feared that her offering of love was "hid *as* worthles rite" insofar as it cannot be publicized; this offering acquires value because it has no reward other than itself. "Cupid's might"—the divine economy of faith and grace in which "rites" are indeed worthless—is not subject to the rational calculation of "Phoebus's light."

Although in the octave the Indians' only complaint is "whitenes want," in the sestet this lack of whiteness signifies the substitution of externally performed ritual for internally felt devotion. The speaker's "pale" and "white" skin, by contrast, may, as James Bromley argues, "signify her status as a grieving lover." But insofar as Pamphilia's love takes place within an adulterous entanglement of many rather than a monogamous dyad, that grief is also a response to the erasure of intimacies to which Protestant England hypocritically denied institutional sanction or reward.[111] Assessed in terms of a Pauline theology that values spirit over flesh, faith over works, the Indians' ostentatious adoration of the sun is not only a distraction from worship of the Son in religious terms, but also a secular trope for their intellectual, ethical, and aesthetic inferiority. The speaker's whiteness makes visible her ability to love correctly. And this superior affective aptitude is part of a more general cultural superiority that by Wroth's day was already a familiar justification for expanded European trade and colonialism in the Mediterranean and Atlantic worlds alike, economic projects to which Wroth herself was financially and personally connected.[112]

The ambiguity of the term "Indian" in Wroth's sonnet accentuates the complex interplay of erotic, theological, racial, and imperial projects. Most scholars have assumed that "Indians" designates Indigenous Americans.[113] If we accept this reading of "Indians," Wroth's treatment of their idolatry is part of the English rationale for the colonization of the Americas and conversion of its Indigenous peoples on the grounds that this would save them from both Catholic tyranny and their own "lack" of true religion—an ideological rescue narrative continuous with that of Enlightenment colonialism.[114] But Wroth's own writings, court performances, and financial investments suggest that she may just as likely have had in mind East "Indians." Her description of these sun-worshippers as "black" supports an Eastern reading, for in 1604 Wroth, along with a number of other female courtiers, appeared in blackface in Ben Jonson's *Masque of Blackness*, a court performance depicting the desire of a troop of Niger's daughters to be turned white by James I. In Jonson's masque, the women's blackness comes from the sun, who "in their firm hues draws / Signs of his fervent'st love" and who has "shone / On their scorched cheeks with such intemperate fires" that he has made it impossible for them to achieve the Petrarchan ideal of fairness.[115] Like Jonson, Wroth would have viewed dark skin and sun-worship as both an Old and a New World phenomenon. Given that Wroth was an investor in the East India Company and that her prose romance shows her to be knowledgeable of and fascinated by relations between Europe, Africa, and Asia, it is more likely that the "Indians" of this poem evoke European views of *both* East and West Indians.[116] Along with Native American innocence, Wroth's "Indians" may equally signify the limits of English imperial ambitions for early modern readers who, as Shankar Raman has shown, were familiar with depictions of India as both the ultimate goal to which desire is directed and a site beyond the proper bounds of desire.[117] Whereas English writers saw themselves as financially and militarily superior to America's "noble savages," England was very much at the mercy of the Mughal and Ottoman Empires when it came to global trade.[118] Superior affective capacity in Wroth's poem may compensate for powerlessness in trade and diplomacy.

Wroth also would have been aware of her uncle Philip Sidney's fabulous racialization and nationalization of Eros as an English resident in *Astrophil and Stella*:

> Love, born in Greece, of late fled from his native place,
> Forced by a tedious proof, that Turkish hardened heart
> Is no fit mark to pierce with his fine pointed dart;
> And pleased with our soft peace, stayed here his flying race.
> But finding these North climes too coldly him embrace,

> Not used to frozen clips, he strave to find some part,
>   Where with most ease and warmth he might employ his art.
> At length he perched himself in Stella's joyful face,
>   Whose fair skin, beamy eyes, like morning sun on snow,
> Deceived the quaking boy, who thought from so pure light
> Effects of lively heat must needs in nature grow.
> But she, most fair, most cold, made him thence take his flight
>   To my close heart, where, while some firebrands he did lay,
>   He burnt unwares his winges, and cannot fly away. (AS 8.1–14)

Here, Turkish rule of Greece exiles the classical figure of love (the Ottoman Empire had captured Cyprus, mythologically the "native place" of Venus and Cupid, in 1573). The "hardened heart[s]" of Greece's Muslim rulers are as impenetrable to Cupid's "fine pointed dart" as they were to the swords of the medieval Crusaders who attempted to convert them. Yet while the first quatrain appears to celebrate England's "soft peace" as more hospitable to love than "Turkish hardened hearts," the remainder of the sonnet breaks down this distinction. It turns out that first the "North climes" then Stella's "fair" face proved too "cold" for love. Only Astrophil's "close" (secret, private, both confined and confining) heart provides refuge. As in Milton's warning against "Indian" idolatry and superstition, Sidney's just-so story relies on the instability of religious as well as racial identity. However "fair"—beautiful and white, beautiful because white—Stella is, to be too "cold" and unreceptive to love is to risk turning more Turk than Christian. While Sidney and Milton would doubtlessly have stopped short of this logical extreme, susceptibility to desire outside the law is evidence that one no longer lives under it. The racial and imperial dimensions of romance, whether Milton's "amatorious novel" or the more obvious political chivalric quest, are inseparable from its erotic ethics.[119]

The ever-present possibility of conversion and its inverse, perversion, also means that fidelity to the ideal of love may ultimately require infidelity to any particular object. This was Milton's insight in the divorce pamphlets, and it subtends Sidney's and Wroth's lyrics as unspoken possibility and threat. As we have seen, the sequences dramatize Astrophil's and Pamphilia's fruitless attempts to extricate themselves from their desires. But because they are trapped by internal rather than external bonds, there is nothing to hold them if they ever lose interest. Both sequences end by raising just this possibility. The penultimate poem in *Astrophil and Stella* has Astrophil asking Stella to "dismiss from thee my wit" so that he can do something other than write love poems (107.10). Formally, the sequence indicates that Stella grants this request, for there is only one more sonnet, and this final one ends the sequence on a curiously flat version of Petrarchan oxymoron: "in my woes for thee thou art my joy, / And in my joys for thee my only annoy" (108.13–14). The sequence's last word, "annoy" replaces the ecstatic "woes" of love with irritating discomfort or, perhaps, the listlessness and enervation of the French *ennui*, to which "annoy" is etymologically related. The Folger manuscript of *Pamphilia to Amphilanthus* offers a similarly ambiguous ending, with Pamphilia threatening Amphilanthus that "you one day may confess / You wrong'd my care, when I care less" (*PA* F117.33–34).

"When I care less." The most optimistic possibility of the romances of divorce and adultery may be that *this* love, too, shall pass. In locating that freedom internally and connecting it to the freedom of "true"—Christian—faith, Milton, Sidney, and Wroth may also depend on the nascent, intertwined identifications of religion with race and ethnicity that continue to undergird ideals of secular modernity and its discourses of rights and liberty. The writing of Milton, Sidney, and Wroth underscores freedom's costs and contradictions, and thereby reminds us of the exclusions inherent in ideals of autonomous desire, even as they expand its parameters.

5

On Erotic Accountability

Unforgivable Debts

In this final chapter, I consider the problem of erotic accountability: What do we owe those who love us? I focus on John Donne's religious and libertine lyrics, which speak not from the familiar position of the unrequited lover, but from that of the beloved who views love, with its attendant demand of commitment, as an imposition rather than a gift. Critics have tended to categorize these lyrics as Ovidian in their gleeful, materialistic sexuality, cordoning them off from the Petrarchan tradition of unrequited adulation, on the one hand, and from the tortured prayers of Donne's devotional poetry, on the other. Situating Donne's libertine poems within the Pauline tradition that I have been tracing, I argue to the contrary that Donne is at his most Petrarchan, and his most religious, when he confesses to a future of promiscuity.[1]

In this opening section, I discuss the theological concepts of charity and forgiveness as they inform secular discussions of ethical responsibility. In the second section, I situate Donne's confessions of spiritual and sexual promiscuity within an Augustinian and Protestant view that confession necessarily fails to convey the truth of the self. Rather than aspire to the expression of the truth of the self that Foucault saw as the goal of confessional practice, this tradition presupposes that the only thing one can confess is the obscurity of the self and its motives, an admission of guilt *in potentia* that enjoins an ethics of forgiveness for future infidelities and that renders confession an exercise in imagination and empathy. In the third section, I bring together queer and early modern materialist studies to examine the challenge posed to a Cartesian humanism by the Pauline conviction that the self is continually coopted by foreign forces within and without. Donne's theological attention to the entanglement of matter and spirit resists the ideals of romance and rationality that have often been deemed the signal characteristics of "human" sexuality. Focusing on what is perhaps Donne's best-known poem, "The Flea," as well as a recent adaptation by Alan Jenkins, I here argue that the perspective of the insect, like that of the god, renders human creatures disconcertingly interchangeable. The chapter's final section traces the positive valence of indifference as a secular approximation of divine *caritas*, the generous love for imperfect creatures regardless of merit. Donne's devotional, romantic, and libertine lyrics converge, I argue, in their awareness that the most ethical erotic disposition might be one that accepts the impersonal and promiscuous dimension of desire. Accordingly, they struggle with the implications of Pauline universalism as understood by Alain Badiou and Madhavi Menon. Like Badiou's Paul, Donne's poetic speakers recognize that "in the situation (call it: the world), there are differences. One can even maintain that there is nothing else."[2] Donne thereby explores the promise as well as the limitations of what Menon calls a "queer universalism" that resists stable racial, gendered, national, and sexual identity on the grounds that this is a "demand made by power," obedience to which is persistently interrupted by the mobility and unpredictability of desire and subjectivity that refuse to settle and cohere.[3]

Over the course of this book, I have been tracing the lessons for queer theory in the Pauline dictum that "all the Law is fulfilled in one word, which is this, Thou shalt love thy neighbor as thyself [*Omnis enim lex in uno sermone impletur: Diliges proximum tuum sicut teipsum*]" or, more simply, "love is the fulfilling of the law [*Plenitudo ergo legis est dilectio*]" (GB/V, Gal. 5:14; Rom. 13:10). On the face of it, this would appear to be a very good deal. Grace emancipates the Christian from the multiple prohibitions and injunctions of the Law, setting in their places the single requirement of love. As we have seen, this liberation from the law and the flesh has also historically been used to justify racial and sexual hierarchies and violences by projecting hypocrisy and hatred onto those who insist on difference and particularity. In this chapter, I continue to probe the affective, conceptual, and ethical impasses inherent in the injunction to love everyone. This command, as we have repeatedly witnessed, is rife with ambiguity and contradiction—*eros* and *agape, cupiditas* and *caritas*, are not experientially discrete.[4] In Galatians and Romans, the Vulgate respectively gives the imperative verb *dileges* (you will love, cherish, value) and the noun *dilectio* (delight, pleasure, goodwill), emphasizing not simply a passive or polite kindliness but rather an active and gratifying embrace.

The command to love one's neighbor as oneself is a command to deprioritize the self and its desires. To love is to perform an *imitatio Christi*. This imitation strives to approximate the divine self-abandonment of the crucifixion, which was itself an extraordinary exhibition of love for unloveable creatures. The substitution of grace for merit defines *caritas* as love that descends without regard to the object's response or requital.

It can be as burdensome to receive such love as it is difficult to feel it. Grace may be gratuitous, but it is not quite free. It exacts what Milton's Satan aptly describes as a "debt immense of endless gratitude, / So burdensome, still paying, still to owe."[5] We pay our affective debts by recognizing that they cannot be quit. And we come to understand how much we owe those who love us by experiencing our own incapacity to love our neighbors as—*sicut*, just like—ourselves. Just to be sure we know the various ways we miss the mark, Paul spells out what this love entails in the First Letter to the Corinthians. Here, the Vulgate gives the word *caritas* for Paul's *agape*. Feeling is a practice more consequential than anything else we do. Even self-sacrifice falls short of the divine model it imitates: "And though I feed the poor with all my goods, and though I give up my body, that I be burned, and have not love [*caritas*] it profiteth me nothing" (GB/V, 1 Cor. 13:3). Paul goes on to explain that to have the love that *could* bring profit, soteriologically speaking, we must not only *be* generous but also *feel* generously. The Geneva Bible's translation of *caritas* as "love," in contrast to the Douay-Rheims's (the early modern Catholic version) and the King James's (the authorized Anglican version) more literal choice of "charity," renders love as such indistinct from philanthropy:

> Love suffereth long, it is bountiful; love envieth not; love doth not boast itself, it is not puffed up, It doth no uncomely thing, it seeketh not her own things, it is not provoked to anger, it thinketh no evil; It rejoiceth not in iniquity, but rejoiceth in the truth; It suffereth all things, it believeth all things, it hopeth all things, it endureth all things. Love doeth never fall away. (GB, 1 Cor. 13:4–8)

Or, as the more familiar English Standard Version has it:

> Love is patient and kind; love does not envy or boast; it is not arrogant or rude. It does not insist on its own way; it is not irritable or resentful; it

does not rejoice at wrongdoing, but rejoices with the truth. Love bears all things, believes all things, hopes all things, endures all things. Love never ends. (ESV, 1 Cor. 13:4–8)

These verses remain among the most common readings at weddings of all Christian denominations. Significantly, they also are popular in non-religious ceremonies, where the scriptural origins can be easily ignored and the optimistic message appropriated as the secular common sense that, as I discussed in the introduction to this book, privileges interiority and sincerity in its definitions of freedom, virtue, and intimacy. As I noted above, the adaptation of the communal concept of charity to the private bond of love is aided by the Geneva Bible's translation of *caritas* as "love," one unevenly followed in the early modern period but fairly standard in modern editions.[6] If love is really love, it will be free of the self-regard that prompts envy, pride, and boasting; it puts up with everything without anger or so much as thinking a bad thought (*no cogitat malum*, in the Vulgate's rendering). "Love never ends"; it achieves infinity and eternity, because it has nothing to do with the merit of the beloved or the benefit of the lover. This definition is secularized in another popular wedding reading, Shakespeare's Sonnet 116, which pronounces that "Love is not love, / Which alters when it alteration finds, / Or bends with the remover to remove" but rather "bears it out even to the edge of doom" (116.2–4, 12). Unconditional love, to state the obvious, does not require that any conditions be met, including those of reciprocity, fidelity, or even desirability. This definition of love as selfless and long-suffering, persisting even when it is neither returned nor wanted, structures the more general view that lifelong romantic commitment is both expression and foundation of an ethical and happy life.

However, as Paul recognizes (and with him, a long line of his readers), we can no more voluntarily obey an order to love than an order to be happy, especially when the two are assumed to be one and the same. A guiding thesis of this book has been that theology is useful to think with because, like psychoanalysis, it denies the liberation that it promises. The ineradicable presence of all that *caritas* is *not*—what Paul calls "sin" and what Freud and Lacan call "the Thing"—ensures that love will never be the only motive or feeling that occupies our innermost hearts. It is from within this nonredemptive framework that we can forge what

I have been calling an ethics of promiscuity, in which cultivating the humility and compassion of self-forgetting replaces the claims of innocence that justify self-preservation. An ethics of promiscuity admits the contingency and opacity of our desires. It recognizes the limits not only of innocence but also of forgiveness and understanding. The ideals of love, forgiveness, grace, and charity dangle before us a freedom—a purity—we cannot achieve. To declare love or desire is to make a demand, if not for reciprocation at least for a response. Insofar as we may not get the response we want, feeling love brings with it the anxiety and bitterness in which so many lyrics wallow. But *being* loved can also evoke resentment and cruelty. To be loved is to become indebted, accountable for how we treat those who love us, even if the love is not something we sought or want. Precisely because of our entanglement with others, our inability fully to extricate ourselves from their needs and demands, on the one hand, and what we need from them, on the other, we cannot offer unconditional love. This also means that we cannot forgive— etymologically, relinquish our claims on—others, nor can we presume that we will be forgiven.

Attentiveness to promiscuity as it emerges in theological and poetic writing recognizes the imbrication of two ethical dispositions that Judith Butler understands as mutually exclusive alternatives: an ethics of "conviction" and an ethics of "responsibility." An ethics of conviction, Butler writes, "takes the self to be the ground and measure of moral judgment."[7] Resting on belief in a sovereign self that has accurately evaluated its own virtue—a self that believes itself to be more sinned against than sinning—this ethics of conviction operates according to principles of self-defense, judgment, and persecution. By contrast, an ethics of responsibility requires us to "avow the limits of any self-understanding, and to establish these limits not only as a condition for the subject but as the predicament of the human community."[8] In this "ethics based on our shared, invariable, and partial blindness about ourselves," Butler writes,

> The recognition that one is, at every turn, not quite the same as how one presents oneself in the available discourse might imply a certain patience with others that would suspend the demand that they be self-same at every moment. Suspending the demand for self-identity or, more particularly, for complete coherence seems to me to counter a certain ethical violence,

which demands that we manifest and maintain self-identity at all times and require that others do the same. For subjects who invariably live within a temporal horizon, this is a difficult, if not impossible, norm to satisfy.[9]

Cultivating an ethics of responsibility is not merely a matter of rehearsing clichés like "people change" or "nobody's perfect." Rather, it is taking seriously the logical end of those clichés, which is an acknowledgement of our own radical foreignness and unpredictability, and therefore the unstable ground of any promise of love or benevolence. To acknowledge our own and others' nonsovereignty is therefore to "acknowledge the limits of acknowledgement" in anticipation of "inevitable ethical failure."[10] Someone will get hurt. Someone will have to be forgiven:

> To know the limits of acknowledgment is to know even this fact in a limited way; as a result, it is to experience the very limits of knowing. This can, by the way, constitute a disposition of humility and generosity alike: I will need to be forgiven for what I cannot have fully known, and I will be under a similar obligation to offer forgiveness to others, who are also constituted in partial opacity to themselves.[11]

Invoking the concept of forgiveness, Butler also introduces those of expectation and judgment, on the one hand, and betrayal and injury, on the other. Butler builds on Emmanuel Levinas's meditations on the responsibility of the victim to examine the "moral predicament that emerges as a consequence of being injured."[12] The desire to punish persecutors and thereby assert the right to have been treated otherwise puts us on the treacherous ethical ground of taking self-preservation as the highest good. But to turn the other cheek is to give up our right to protect ourselves. In an "ethic from the region of the unwilled," we recognize that when we love, we put ourselves at the mercy of an other whom we cannot compel to do our bidding.[13] When we experience injury, as we inevitably will, we must decide how to *respond*, and we will be *responsible* for this decision, implicated in a narrative that we have not chosen.[14]

Love is, for Butler, a paradigmatic example of the relational ethic of responsibility. Love cannot be coerced and therefore compels us to respond to the experience of vulnerability, to answer to encounters and feelings that we can neither select nor regulate. That is its pleasure as well as its horror. Butler here draws on Theodor Adorno's argument that unrequited love affords ethical insight. The "offended or slighted" lover, Adorno writes,

> becomes aware that in the innermost blindness of love, that must remain oblivious, lives a demand not to be blinded. He was wronged; from this he deduces a claim to right and must at the same time reject it, for what he desires can only be given in freedom. In such distress he who is rebuffed becomes human. . . . With his plea, founded on no titles or claims, he appeals to an unknown court, which accords to him as grace what is his own and yet not his own. The secret of justice in love is the annulment of all rights, to which love mutely points.[15]

Adorno's description of love in terms of freedom and grace offers a secular account of a Pauline soteriology in which appreciation of lack of desert, here "the annulment of all rights," allows the believer to understand election as merciful rather than unjust. We must cede the right to be loved, Butler explains, because "if we were to respond to injury by claiming we had a 'right' not to be so treated, we would be treating the other's love as an entitlement rather than a gift; being a gift, it carries the insuperable quality of gratuitousness."[16] Love is valuable only insofar as it "does not belong to contract"—it is experienced not as a decision, but as a foreign, inexplicable, even invasive force. To give or receive love is confront our own opacity, for "that we are compelled in love means that we are, in part, unknowing about why we love as we do and why we invariably exercise bad judgment."[17] This is why Cupid's arrows remain such an apt symbol for the instigation of desire, as well as the accompanying sense of victimization that Petrarch made so central to the secular love tradition.

The ethics of responsibility Butler endorses begins with acknowledgement of one's own opacity to oneself, and this humbling admission compels compassion for other's failures. Yet Butler, like Adorno and Levinas, nonetheless writes primarily from the perspective of the injured. To the degree that the ethics of responsibility entails an obligation of mutual forgiveness, I would argue, it remains in the realm of what Jacques Derrida terms "conditional" forgiveness, which is premised on innocence rather than guilt. As Derrida explains it, conditional forgiveness is "proportionate to the recognition of the fault, to repentance, to the transformation of the sinner who then explicitly asks forgiveness."[18] Confession, repentance, and reform would seem intuitively linked to forgiveness—how could we forgive someone who is not sorry, who has not changed, who would not hesitate to harm us again? But, as Derrida points out, forgiveness premised on conversion can only be directed at a person "who from that point is no longer guilty through and through, but already another, and better than the guilty one. To this extent, and on this condition, it is no longer the *guilty as such* who is forgiven."[19] The logic of conditional forgiveness requires not only that we separate sin from sinner, treating the crime as "an act or a moment which does not exhaust the person incriminated, and at the limit does not become confused with the guilty, who thus remains irreducible to it."[20] It also requires that we separate past sinner from present penitent. In this conversion narrative, the person who committed the crime is unforgivable in two senses. First, we could not forgive someone who did not repent and ask to be forgiven. Second, with penitence, the person who harmed us ceases to exist, is re-formed (in evangelical parlance, reborn) as a new person who will eschew the sins of the past self. Understood thus, conditional forgiveness is not forgiveness as the term is usually understood, a dispensation that pardons rather than punishes. Conditional forgiveness is itself a form of punishment. Latent within it is the violence that Slavoj Žižek has deciphered in conversion as "erasing the traces of one's past ('everything old has passed away') and beginning afresh from a zero-point: consequently, there is also a terrifying *violence* at work in this 'uncoupling', that of the *death drive*, of the radical 'wiping the slate clean' as the condition of the New Beginning."[21]

Absolute forgiveness, by contrast, is in Derrida's account "*unconditional*, gracious, infinite, aneconomic forgiveness granted *to the guilty as guilty*, without counterpart, even to those who do not repent or ask forgiveness."[22] This irrational, even mad, dispensation of grace is, for Derrida, the only true forgiveness: "an act of forgiveness worthy of its name, if there is such a thing, must forgive the unforgivable, and without condition."[23] Forgiveness requires that we "forgive both the fault and the guilty *as such*, where the one and the other remain as irreversible as the evil, as evil itself, and being capable of repeating itself, unforgivably, without transformation, without amelioration, without repentance or promise."[24] To assimilate this radical definition of forgiveness to Butler's ethics of responsibility, to situate the unforgivable within such an ethical system, we must extend the opacity and blindness that Butler puts at the heart of ethical relationality to require a disavowal of the stance of moral superiority and dominance that forgiveness itself implies. As an exception to the law through which sovereignty expresses itself, Derrida explains, forgiveness does not oppose the juridico-political order but founds it. Forgiveness is implicated in relations of power; humility and compassion are themselves limited because mixed up with their contraries. The ethics of reciprocal forgiveness not only requires a mutual relinquishment of claims, but also implies continued debt. When we owe an apology, we also owe sincerity and subjection. And throwing ourselves on the mercy of the person whom we have wronged can be sincere only insofar as we recognize that we may be unforgivable after all.

Love again provides a case in point. We are not only or always, as in Adorno's and Butler's examples, in the position of the rebuffed or betrayed lover. *That*, after all, is a position in which vulnerability and injury gives us moral authority. In forgiving unrequitedness, we show ourselves charitable and virtuous. We relinquish our claim to dominance and acknowledge the ethical violence of what Roland Barthes sums up as "the lover's constant thought: *the other owes me what I need*."[25] But this is the easier role to take. We also, as often as not, play the part of the unresponsive, unfaithful, or betraying beloved. As anyone who has ever been sent an unwanted drink, turned down an invitation to coffee or to sex, or ended a relationship knows, to be desire's object makes us responsible for the hurt that ensues when we lose interest, or never have it in the first place. If to desire is to become vulnerable, it is also an act of faith that forges a relationship of debt and accountability. As Giorgio Agamben explains Pauline faith, *pistis* (*fides* in Latin) is originally a juridico-politico concept: submission to another's power to reject us is an act of trust, an offer of credit to a receiver who then becomes obligated, indebted, accountable.[26] The assumption of vulnerability that for Adorno and Butler inaugurates humanity tests other as well as self.

Situations of nonreciprocity thus require absolute, unconditional forgiveness. The singular or serial betrayal of a promise of monogamy—cheating on someone we love—may be subject to confession, penitence, and conversion: I was wrong, I am sorry, I regret it, I will never do it again. But when we cause an injury because we do not want another as much as he or she wants us to, or when we have lost a formerly intense desire, have we done something *wrong*? However much hurt indifference or unresponsiveness causes, we cannot not reform or repent unless we can feel otherwise. The same opacity of feeling that makes love a gift also makes us innocent of the pain we inflict, even as the subject of such pain experiences our indifference as persecution. We must be forgiven for something that we will not change; we remain the same person who has brought pain, and we perpetuate the injury of rejection by withholding the gift of our love. Oriented from the perspective of the unresponsive beloved rather than the unrequited lover, we can expand Butler's inquiry into the ethics of giving an account of oneself in the dual sense of telling a story and taking responsibility for what we do *not* feel. How can we give an account of lost or absent desires? Can we be held accountable for the obligations and injuries that ensue when others commit themselves to us? Perhaps we must not only forgive those who do not return our feelings. More perversely, we must ask forgiveness for *loving* and thereby placing a demand, making a claim—even one we are ready in advance to forgive—on someone who may not have asked for such responsibility.

What I have described is, again, a secular version of a dilemma central to Christian theology. In Pauline theology, human creatures have been offered absolute, infinite, gratuitous love that they are ontologically incapable of returning. The problem is not being loved too little, but being loved too much—more than we can possibly reciprocate. When Christ pays humanity's debts, the gift of grace forgives in advance the sins we will commit, all of which can be summed up in the failure of *caritas*, of putting self before others, individualized flesh before self-dissolving spirit. At the same time, this absolute forgiveness is conditional. We *must* ask forgiveness while knowing that asking does not make a difference, that we will not change. To be conscious of this predicament is to recognize that our confession, penitence, and conversion are always, from the point of view of the future selves we will become, incomplete, unreliable, insincere. In "acknowledging the limits of acknowledgment," in Derrida's words, we acknowledge that we are recidivists and therefore unforgivable except in the absolute sense that is inhuman ("mad," in Derrida's assessment) insofar as it defies rationality.[27]

It is unsurprising that Adorno and Butler write from the perspective of the afflicted lover rather than that of the indifferent beloved. This is the stance of the innocent. It is also, and equally unremarkably, the perspective of most love poetry, even that which recognizes the cyclical infidelities and distractions that love entails. All of the lyrics that I have discussed thus far have featured speakers who may be unfaithful, ambivalent, self-deceiving, or married to other people, but who still want to want to love and be loved in return. Below, I consider the counterexample of Donne's libertine lyrics, which engage with an Augustinian theory of confession and conversion to examine the problem of accounting for the lack of attachment to the idea of true love.

Failed Confession

I begin with a Holy Sonnet that eschews the conventional trajectory of confession, repentance, and reform on which conditional forgiveness is premised. Donne is at his most Petrarchan in the Holy Sonnets not because his love is spurned or delayed to the afterlife, but because it is immanent in the present.[28] Whereas it is common—in early modern imitation as in modern scholarship—to define Petrarchism according to its most recognizable expression of pleading to be loved, Donne's adaptations recognize that the *Rerum vulgarium fragmenta* is equally occupied with the speaker's own inability to love the right things in the right way. *The* question for Donne's speakers is the first line of one of his less frequently discussed Holy Sonnets: "Wilt thou love God as he thee?" Evoking the inscrutable Augustinian will and the unknowable future in that first word, "Wilt," the speaker's self-address (the second line specifies the "thou" as "My soul") might as well be a sermon to others whose desires he has no way of predicting. Like so many of Petrarch's lyrics, Donne's Holy Sonnets trace the limitations and infidelities of the speaker, his struggle to love God more than "the world, flesh, yea, Devil."[29] Donne's speakers, in both religious and secular verse, are in the structural position of the Christian creature who can never love God enough—and who does not know whether he will be damned or forgiven for this ineptitude. In addressing a God whose overwhelming love he cannot consistently or wholeheartedly return, Donne explores his own unregenerate infidelity. The prospect of grace should inspire gratitude. But it just as often breeds resentment. At the same time, as critics have often noticed, Donne's struggles with submission also flout essentialized views of gender and sexual normativity—hence competing descriptions of the Holy Sonnets' speaker as "erotic, abandoned, and female"; indeterminately gendered; insecurely and anxiously masculine; and homodevotional.[30] In terms of both sexuality and subjectivity, the Holy Sonnets are confessions, but not in the Foucauldian sense of putting the truth of the self into discourse. Rather, these are failed expressions of penitence that anticipate a future in which the contrition they express will fade and resolution will prove insincere.

The Holy Sonnet "Oh, to vex me" is one such case. Spoken entirely in the present tense, the poem expects a future in which the speaker will be just as *bad* as he is now:

> Oh, to vex me contraries meet in one:
> Inconstancy unnaturally hath begot
> A constant habit, that when I would not
> I change in vows and in devotion.
> As humorous is my contrition
> As my profane love, and as soon forgot;
> As riddlingly distempered, cold and hot;
> As pray'ng, as mute; as infinite, as none.
> I durst not view Heav'n yesterday, and today
> In prayers and flattering speeches I court God.
> Tomorrow I quake with true fear of his rod.
> So my devout fits come and go away
> Like a fantastic ague, save that here
> Those are my best days when I shake with fear. (1–14)

Petrarchan oxymoron—contraries met in one—is the poetic formula for a psychomachia that has melded into stasis. "Inconstancy" begets "a constant habit"; the poet is "cold and hot," "praying" and "mute," "infinite" and "none." In equating "contrition" with "profane love" and describing both as equally "humourous"—subject to changing moods, brought on by imbalances of bodily fluids, or humors—and "soon forgot," the speaker makes "vows and devotion" fundamentally insincere, a matter of momentary caprice that leaves no lasting impression. The figure of simile itself anticipates the fungibility of affects and attachments. The habitual mutability, the speaker confesses, has not been consigned to "yesterday," rendered past by conversion or prayer "today," however confident. Nor will the "true fear" that grips him "Tomorrow" last any longer than a fever.

Formally, the poem enacts the same lack of control that troubles the poet. The "contraries" that in the first line are grammatically the subject intentionally "vex" their object, the poet. The meter is conspicuously irregular, alternating between excess and insufficiency: lines 2 and 9 are a foot too long, lines 4, 5, and 13 a foot too short; lines 4 and 5 have feminine ends, the falling meter of devotion and contrition making audible the will's impotence. Throughout, the alternation between slow, deliberate monosyllables and more hurried polysyllabic phrases dramatizes that between conscious decisions and impetuous desires. Meanwhile, the repeated enjambments enact a self that, despite moments of genuine resolution, is compulsively unfaithful, propelled into an inevitable future of change: "Inconstancy unnaturally hath begot / a constant habit," "when I would not / I change," "As humorous is my contrition / As my profane love."

The poet's inability to stop himself is perhaps most manifest in the sonnet's conclusion, where sentence structure and stanzaic units are at odds. The poem's final sentence begins at the end of the quatrain and continues into the couplet: "So my devout fits come and go away / Like a fantastic ague, save that here / Those are my best days when I shake with fear." Devotion is no more than a fit or a fever—the ague here is not just a figure, as Kimberly Anne Coles observes, but a physical manifestation of the soul's always fluctuating state.[31] This final oxymoron—which can be paraphrased as "my best days are the days I am most miserable"— gestures at the paradoxical consolation imagined by such English Protestant divines as William Perkins and Richard Hooker, whereby anxiety and self-loathing were actually good things because they manifested belief in the possibility of reprobation.[32] True devotion takes the form of fear because it recognizes the profound helplessness of the individual creature to atone, answering in the affirmative that devastating question that Donne asks in another Holy Sonnet: "And can that tongue adjudge thee unto hell / Which prayed forgiveness for his foes fierce spight?" ("What if this present," 7–8). This soteriological uncertainty is matched by the assurance that without divine intervention, the speaker has in store a future of courting God and profane mistresses alike with "prayers and flattering speeches" that may, in retrospect, turn out to have been insincere rather than heartfelt. Any present sonnet will be consigned to just such a past.

"Oh to vex me" can be read as a reflection not only on a spiritual past, but also on Donne's secular oeuvre, which encompasses both intense vows of devotion and nonchalant defenses of libertinism. The inconsistency and obscurity of Donne's arguments has attracted charges that Donne and his writing are, to cite just a few of the adjectives used by twentieth-century critics, "sad," "uncomfortable," "disgusting," "sick," "repellant," "twisted," "debased," and "bordering on the freakish."[33] In this view, confession and conversion must be final, straightforward acts, not the ongoing, even incomprehensible, process that Donne depicts in "Oh to vex me." But if we take seriously the Pauline sentiments of "Oh to vex me," we can understand the diversity of attitudes expressed in Donne's writing as a performance of an opaque and multifaceted self, more typical of the self-doubt, defensiveness, and indirection that Brooke Conti has shown characterized early modern confessional writing more generally.[34]

The earliest surviving portrait of Donne, painted in 1591 when he was eighteen and still a Catholic, bears the motto *Antes muerto que mudado*, "Sooner dead than changed." Amidst the virulent anti-Catholicism of the 1590s, this was quite a statement, its bravado accentuated by the fact that it is written in Spanish, the language of England's hated rival. In light of his subsequent conversion a few years later, this oath is also an irony that Donne's scholars have never tired of remarking. In John Carey's blunt assessment, "The first thing to remember about Donne is that he was a Catholic; the second, that he betrayed his Faith."[35] In Carey's reading, Donne's conversion is an act of apostasy, a failure of loyalty to his family (several of whom had been exiled or executed for their beliefs) and the faith of his youth. Worse, it proceeds not from genuine conviction, but cynical self-interest manifested in the instability of his lyrics, which flitter between Petrarchan earnestness, Ovidian insouciance, and Christian prayer.[36] The contradictions of Donne's verse are symptomatic of a lack of integrity, a "mode of self-creation through self abandonment," in Jonathan Goldberg's words.[37] So understood, Donne's writing is incapable of confessing any authentic truth or experience. Whatever its genre, Donne's poetry compulsively stages what Stanley Fish describes as "the continual reproduction of a self that can never be the same, that can never be 'its own.'"[38]

Since the seventeenth century this charge that Donne cannot be trusted has been connected to the charge that he is hard to understand. Donne says many different things—often in a single, compressed utterance, as Samuel Johnson notoriously observed in his complaint that "the most heterogeneous ideas are yoked by violence together" in metaphysical poetry.[39] It can be daunting to try to decipher Donne's meaning even on the most literal level, much less to see how his various utterances cohere into an identifiable ethics, philosophy, or subjectivity. This indeterminacy and instability, critics have frequently observed, appears formally in Donne's frequent recourse to a vocabulary of fluidity, vapors, dissolution; his images of transitional and marginal states; uses of the passive voice with its indeterminate agency and the subjunctive mood with its emphasis on the doubtful or counterfactual; gerunds in place of proper nouns; distorted syntax; irregular meter; slant, sight, and feminine rhymes.[40] Such lack of cohesion has been central to the evaluation of Donne's disturbing effects on his readers. Conflating Donne with his poetry, Ben Jonson predicted that "Donne himself, for not being understood, would perish," while John Dryden complained that Donne "perplexes the minds of the fair sex with nice speculations of philosophy, when he should engage their hearts, and entertain them with the softness of love."[41] And he cannot be up to any good in so confusing his readers, especially the women who are his frequent addressees. Hence the charges of misogyny that his verse has attracted.[42]

For those scholars who defend Donne, one solution has been to offer conditional forgiveness based on a narrative of his writing as well as his biography in terms of conversion and maturation, with his satires and libertine lyrics deemed the products of the callow Jack Donne, that louche Catholic known to contemporaries as a "great visitor of Ladies," and the Holy Sonnets and poems of eternal love seen as the output of Dr. Donne, the Anglican divine and loyal husband.[43] Donne's first biographer, Izaac Walton, described Donne as a "second *St. Austine*" (that is, Augustine) and claimed that Donne's "golden age" was not his youth but "thy later yeares, so much refind, / From Youths Drosse, Mirth, &

Wit," an assessment printed along with Donne's portrait in the frontis-piece to the 1635 edition of his poems.[44] Whereas the first collection of Donne's poetry, in 1633, printed the poems with no regard to genre, the 1635 edition grouped the poems generically and thereby sanctioned Walton's developmental narrative, and modern editions tend to retain the 1635 divisions in some form.[45] What one commendatory verse in the 1633 edition called "the *Promiscuous* printing of his poems, the Looser sort, with the Religious," depicts conversion as provisional and recursive; the generic organization from 1635 on understands it as a linear progress from one spiritual state (wanton youth) to another (disciplined adulthood).[46]

The longstanding critical desire for coherence and consistency in Donne reveals the persistence of the disciplinary mechanism of confession as Foucault summarizes it in his later work on the Christian structure of modern government and subjectivity. Yet Donne's writing bespeaks another view of confession, one that does not lend itself to the overarching dialectic of truth and power that Foucault locates in Catholic practices. In Foucault's account, the history of confession is central to a shift in his emphasis from "techniques of domination" or "coercion-technologies" administered though clinics, prisons, and schools, to "techniques of the self" or "self-technologies" that can be traced to a Christian pastoralism.[47] The best-known discussion of confession as a technology of the self appears in *The History of Sexuality, Volume One*, where Foucault describes the translation of Counter-Reformation religious practice into a secular incitement to discourse.[48] In contrast to classical *askesis*, which pursues autonomous constitution and administration of the self, Christian pastoralism aims at self-renunciation. Confession, as both professing faith in God and telling the truth of the self, is essential to this renunciation.

In his 1980 lectures on "The Hermeneutics of the Self," Foucault traces the logical convergence of two forms of confession. *Exomologesis*, the publication of oneself as a sinner described by Jerome and Tertullian, requires theatrical self-mortification—sackcloth, ashes, self-flagellation, clawing at one's skin—as a means of witnessing the repudiation of one's past, sinful self and new choice of spirit over flesh, divine over human will. *Exagoreusis*, the exhaustive verbalization of one's thoughts and desires outlined by Cassian, allows sinners to recognize themselves as such and to give themselves over to the direction of God as mediated through the care of the ecclesiastical superior. Although the public penance of *exomologesis* and the private confession of *exagoreusis* would seem to operate according to different logics, Foucault writes, the "obligation to macerate the body and the obligation of verbalising the thoughts . . . are deeply and closely related." This is because "the revelation of the truth about oneself cannot be dissociated from the obligation to renounce ourselves. We have to sacrifice the self in order to discover the truth about ourselves, and we have to discover the truth about ourselves in order to sacrifice ourselves."[49] The sinner becomes a martyr (the Greek word for "witness") and thereby a saint. As Mark Jordan elegantly explains this dynamic, "The endless revelation is for the sake of becoming someone else. . . . I tell the truth of myself in order no longer to be myself; I speak myself to become something other than myself."[50] Confession is never for God, who already knows all about us. Confession is for our own good: as the old Alcoholics Anonymous formula has it, we cannot change until we admit we have a problem. The technologies of the self that Foucault sees at the root of modern biopolitical regimes directed at worldly salvation in the forms of health and security require self-sovereignty not in the sense of mastery but of sincerity. What we want tells us who we are in a moral as well as an identitarian sense.[51]

The view that sincerity is the greatest moral value is both shared and significantly complicated by the Augustinian-Protestant tradition that I have been tracing. Augustine and his Protestant heirs offer a version of confession that diverges in consequential ways from the "acts of truth" that Foucault sees as the decisive contribution of Western Christianity to modern disciplinarity.[52] In Augustine's writing, confession, whether as profession of faith or admission of sins, is successful only when expected to fail. Failed confession, by design, paves the way for failed conversion, at least if we understand success as a full and final renunciation of one's old, sinful self and assumption of a new, better identity. Christian self-study, in this Augustinian view, is not a will to knowledge or power but a struggle to accept their elusiveness. As Augustine's *Confessions* makes clear, a blind and diseased will is the essence of human nature. The failure sincerely to want what we think we should is essential to salvation. In this view, confession cannot achieve the truth of the self that Tertullian, Jerome, and Cassian recommend. Instead, the more one confesses, the more one is confronted with the reality that Augustine so incisively formulates: "*Mihi quaestio factus sum* [I have become a question (or puzzle) to myself]."[53]

The process of confession serves to persuade the penitent that the most concerted efforts to know or master the self are destined to fail. Even the most virtuous of humans, Augustine proclaims, "are no longer to place confidence in themselves, but rather to become weak. They see at their feet divinity become weak by his sharing in our 'coat of skin' (Gen. 3:21)," for "if anyone lists his true merits to you, what is he enumerating before you but your gifts [*munera*]? If only human beings would acknowledge themselves to be but human [*si cognoscant se homines homines*]."[54] To assume one's humanity is to become weak, to empty oneself of any pretension to strength or merit. So far, this is not unlike the self-renunciation at which both *exomologesis* and *exagoreusis* aim. But Augustine's point is that these processes of acting or speaking one's sin always leave something out. To assume humanity—to acknowledge oneself to be human—is also to confess ignorance of the self: "There is something of the human person which is unknown even to the 'spirit of man which is in him.' But you, Lord, know everything about the human person. . . . For what I know of myself [*me sciam*] I know because you grant me light, and what I do not know of myself, I do not know until such time as my darkness becomes 'like noonday' before your face (Isa. 58:10)."[55] As Virginia Burras, Mark Jordan, and Karmen MacKendrick argue, "Because it remains unverifiable to the extent that the soul's intentions are never fully knowable, the truth of confession is also haunted by the possibility of the lie. . . . The very attempt to achieve self-transparency augments the sense of opacity, hiddenness, elusiveness."[56] To confess is not to tell the truth of the self, but to practice failure in order to recognize anew how far out of reach positive knowledge is.

Such inevitable breakdowns of self-knowledge are not opposed to faith. They are its essence. Because one can never know, much less articulate, the full truth of oneself, confession and conversion remain incomplete, imaginative projections. Catholic penitential forms, as Luther and Calvin recognized, in fact threatened a false conclusion to this trial by creating the illusion that accounts had been settled. Although Luther conceded that confession offers "a singular medicine for afflicted consciences," he argued that "any brother or sister," not only clergy, could be an appropriate auditor: "One who has done wrong might lay bare his sin to whomsoever he chooses, and beg absolution, comfort, and Christ's very word from the mouth of his neighbor."[57] This statement does not only strike at the heart of Catholic pastoralism focused on a spiritual master; it also challenges the sequence of confession, penitence, and conversion assumed by Catholic doctrine. The injunction to examine one's conscience is a "hazardous and perverse method" of seeking reconciliation to God, according to Luther, because "we can only know the minor part of our sins; and, further, even our good works are found to be sins."[58] It is more practical and more conducive to faith to let those sins we readily remember stand in synecdochal relation to those we forget: "It is enough if we sorrow for those sins which are actually gnawing at our consciousness, and which can be easily recognized in the mirror of our memory."[59] To assume that scouring the deepest corners of our souls can effect salvation is to fall into the logic of idolatry, for in reality "none of the virtue of penitence is due to the diligence with which we have recollected and enumerated our sins, but only to God's fidelity and to our faith."[60] Contrition, or "fear of his warnings," is a gift from God, not a result of human penitential labor.

Calvin even more strenuously opposes the "ruinous procedure" of the Catholic sacrament of confession.[61] The "dreadful voice . . . always pealing in [believers'] ears, 'Confess all your sins,'" he warns, produces only an excruciating sense of dread and inadequacy. Would-be penitents are tormented by the fear that "'I have not spent enough of time; I have not exerted myself sufficiently: many things I have omitted through negligence: forgetfulness proceeding from want of care is not excusable.'"[62] Even the most devout believer cannot be expected to "collect the sins committed in a single day, seeing every man's experience convinces him that at evening, in examining the faults of that single day, memory gets confused, so great is the number and variety presented."[63] The hypocrite can persuade himself that he has known and spoken the whole truth. But sincere believers "tremble at the thought of that Judge whose knowledge far surpasses our comprehension."[64] Accordingly,

> The surest rule of confession is, to acknowledge and confess our sins to
> be an abyss so great as to exceed our comprehension. . . . When thus rec-
> ognizing himself, the sinner shall have poured out his whole heart before

God, let him seriously and sincerely reflect that a greater number of sins still remains, and that their recesses are too deep for him thoroughly to penetrate [*excutere*]. Accordingly, let him exclaim with David, "Who can understand his errors? cleanse thou me from secret faults" (Ps. 19:12).[65]

The pledge to tell the truth so central to pastoral practices—from Catholic confession to legal proceedings to medical and psychotherapeutic treatments—is understood by Luther and Calvin to be a false and unfulfillable promise. Worse, it compounds sin in that it strives to reclaim precisely the mastery that confession should relinquish. The only "true" confession, from the Augustinian and Reformed point of view, is the confession of opacity.

Donne's writing indicates that he was indeed a "second Austine," but not in the way that Walton meant.[66] Rather, in staging (in Fish's words) "the continual reproduction of a self that can never be the same, that can never be 'its own,'" Donne traces the consequences of Augustinian soteriology for secular eroticism. Rather than write lyrics that fulfill a contractual obligation to tell the truth, Donne's compacted and often inscrutable language renders full disclosure always out of reach. This stance, contrary to both Catholic pastoral models and their modern adaptations, finds apt description in Butler's observation that "any effort to 'give an account of oneself' will have to fail in order to approach being true."[67] The reality that "I can never provide the account of myself that both certain forms of morality and some models of mental health require, namely, that the self deliver itself in coherent narrative form," Butler maintains, reveals not the individual's ethical failure, but the hollowness of the morality and sanity presumed to rest on self-disclosure.[68] Butler argues that we must reimagine the "very meaning of responsibility," turning from the mandate to tell the whole truth and nothing but the truth to the obligation "to avow the limits of any self-understanding, and to establish these limits not only as the condition for the subject but as the predicament of the human community."[69] Butler understands this redefinition of responsibility as a departure from the Christian belief that accounting for desires, unlike acts, will reveal a manageable and coherent identity. But Donne's poetry attests that such a definition is already well established in a Protestant tradition that assumes the fragmented and promiscuous nature of selfhood. Accordingly, if we read

Donne's secular libertine poetry in the context of his religious verse, we can understand it as imagining a form of erotic accountability based not on attachment to identity and fidelity but rather to indifference and adaptation. In dramatizing the failure of "true" love, Donne's libertine lyrics also resist an ideal of a rational, sovereign self that selects its desires rather than being formed, and often deranged, by them.

Exemplary in this regard is "Woman's Constancy," a lyric that offers no empirical means of determining the truth of the self. The poem captures a scene of judgment in which the speaker preemptively accuses the addressee of abandonment. At the very last minute, however, the speaker transforms from a devout supplicant to a confessed libertine:

> Now thou hast loved me one whole day,
> Tomorrow when thou leav'st, what wilt thou say?
> Wilt thou then antedate some new-made vow?
>   Or say that now
> We are not just those persons which we were?
> Or that oaths made in reverential fear
> Of Love and his wrath any may forswear?
> Or, as true deaths true marriages untie,
> So lovers' contracts, images of those,
> Bind but till sleep, death's image, them unloose?
>   Or, your own end to justify,
> For having purposed changes and falsehood, you
> Can have no way but falsehood to be true?
> Vain lunatic! Against these scapes I could
>   Dispute, and conquer, if I would,
>   Which I abstain to do,
> For by tomorrow I may think so too. (1–17)

As in "Oh to vex me," where the "now" of the lyric utterance looks forward to a "tomorrow" in which infidelity will be confirmed, the unpredictability of the future self shapes the experience of present desire. The leaving the speaker anticipates—both a physical departure and a cessation of desire—will happen "Tomorrow," but its very possibility taints the unstable, deictic "Now" with which the poem so abruptly begins. Underscoring the tenuousness of the present, verb tenses slide from future, to present, to past, so that the meaning of the current moment—indeed, the identities of the lovers themselves—is unavailable in isolation. "Tomorrow," in the future, the beloved "wilt" say of both that they "are not just those persons" that they "were" in the earlier "Now," the present in which the poem is set but which the speaker is unable to experience as anything but past. Vows, like the "oaths" and "contracts" evoked in the following lines, are premised on the assumption that we will not be constant of our own accord but must be compelled by something other than desire or affection. The whole purpose of oaths and contracts is to bind people to intentions and feelings that are *expected* to change. Any desire for legalistic assurance assumes, to invert Luther, that formal compliance matters more than what one feels from the bottom of one's heart.

The poem's title announces the indeterminacy of identity: the verses offer no internal evidence by which to decide whether to read this as a man's accusation of his female lover's potential inconstancy or as a woman's confession of her own potential inconstancy.[70] As previous critics have noted, if we read the speaker as male, the poem directly states the same misogynistic male attacks on female constancy as other of Donne's lyrics. If we read the speaker as female, the poem can be read as expressing indirectly the same view through the ethically problematic phenomenon that Elizabeth Harvey has named "transvestite ventriloquism." In Harvey's readings of early modern male authors' ventriloquism of female voices, the act of writing *as* a woman simultaneously erases real women and obscures that erasure, so that male imaginations of female interest and desire replace women's self-representation.[71] Ben Saunders has critiqued the scholarly assumption that the poem's meaning (and its politics) depends on the gender of the speaker, observing that "the final lines actually function in such a way as to make distinctions based on gender *irrelevant*. In other words, *whatever* the gender of the speaker or addressee of the poem, and *whatever* power relation may be implied by that gender dynamic, the last lines work to reverse that relation."[72] I would add that the critical desire to find clear gendered and power relations proceeds from a more general belief that Donne's poems reveal some truth about poetic subjectivity (including the revelation of an unprincipled, manipulative self driven solely by shifting calculations of self-interest). The poem not only shows power relations to be fluid; its indeterminate gender also suggests that the truth of the self is situational rather than absolute. Whether we treat the speaker here as a man or a woman, the poem is less about specifically female constancy or inconstancy than about the speaker's recognition that one's own love, however sincere it may feel in the present moment, might end. The concession that "by tomorrow I may think so too," in its vague summation of the multiple excuses the speaker has just dismissed, is an uncanny recognition of the self in the fantasy of the other as erotic persecutor. Such insight that infidelity may be shared compels the speaker to cede the moral high ground that comes with being betrayed.

Although "Woman's Constancy" initially endeavors to find refuge in the conventional lyric fear of unrequitedness or betrayal, its final lines disclose that the real object of anxiety is not rejection by one's beloved but the volatility of one's own desire, the possibility of its unpredictable end for reasons that one will not be able to fathom or explain. The rapidity with which feelings can change appears in the about-face of the final lines. (In what follows, I use the formulation "they" to emphasize the indeterminacy of the speaker's gender.) Were they so inclined, the speaker insists, they could "Dispute, and conquer" these transparent "scapes" (both attempts to escape commitment and excuses for doing so) with hard logic. Yet logic would not, in actuality, win, for the threatened exposure would reveal that the love of "Now" was never real to begin with, if by "real" we mean permanent, and therefore verifiable only in retrospect. By evaluating love in terms of its endurance, the speaker seeks to transform love and beloved into possessions with no inscrutable, inaccessible inside. By contrast, love entails vulnerability that no logic can "dispute" or "conquer." Such victory may secure guilt or even acquiescence, but not love insofar as it is, in Richard Halpern's term, "autopoetic," or self-inventing and therefore immune to external logic and temporality.[73] Love and the lover—like the deictic "now" that is the time of their existence—are always receding into the past and being reshaped by and as the future.

In response to this realization, the poet abstains from further accusation and dispute, ultimately not out of contempt for the interlocutor, but out of recognition that this has been a potential, even proleptic, confession rather than a preemptive indictment. The poet is, it turns out, the "Vain lunatic" who cannot guarantee that what is said today will remain true tomorrow. Read retrospectively from this endpoint, the poem's initial accusations of infidelity are self-addressed, an acknowledgment that promises do not so much reveal as aspire to a stable subjectivity. As in the Holy Sonnet with which I began, we see in "Woman's Constancy" an admission that "when I would not / I change in vows and in devotion"; or, as Donne puts it in a 1627 sermon, that denunciation of others "is in a great part, self-guiltiness. . . . The calumniator whispers those things, which are true nowhere, but in himself."[74] In accepting that both partners' love may be temporary rather than permanent, the speaker of "Woman's Constancy" evades the "scene of moral judgment" with which the poem, like so many antifeminist lyrics, begins. In such proceedings, as Butler has observed "condemnation can work against self-knowledge, inasmuch as it moralizes a self by disavowing commonality with the judged" in order "to purge and externalize one's own opacity."[75] Rather than persist in such disavowal, Donne's poem breaks down the distinction between the integral, self-knowing masculine subject who may be either speaker or addressee and the fickle, enigmatic feminine subject who may equally play either role in the poem. In refusing to settle these uncertainties, "Woman's Constancy" turns from the affirmation of constant devotion typical of the lyric persona—including other of Donne's speakers—to an acknowledgment of shared guilt, not in act but in the potentiality that is part of human being.

In their humility, the final lines of "Woman's Constancy" depict a worldly version of the divided and self-deceiving soul described by Pauline, Augustinian, and Protestant theology and by Donne's own Holy Sonnets. This about-face is also a shift in ethical orientation from the liberal ideals of autonomy and self-knowledge that critics of Donne have tended to embrace to a disturbing confrontation with the passivity and promiscuity of desire and subjectivity. This is not to treat identity as a matter of giddy or ludic play. Rather, the ethics of promiscuity imagined in Donne's poetry attests that demands for consistency and cohesion can convert "true" love into one more disciplinary mechanism, one that may impair relations with others.

"Woman's Constancy," for all its apparent glibness, stages a scene of absolute forgiveness, in which the addressee is forgiven in advance for a betrayal of which the speaker may prove equally guilty—doing unto others as one would be done to while recognizing that one may also fail in that very empathy and forgiveness. By recognizing a shared propensity to infidelity, the speaker forfeits the conditional forgiveness that requires the sacrifice of the person who has caused pain, who is then reborn as someone who will behave differently in the future. Donne instead both offers and demands the absolute forgiveness that begins from the premise that perfect and permanent fidelity may not be ours to promise. In the insight that we may know ourselves no better than we know others, that none of us may be capable of deserving the love we receive by returning it, we become curiously interchangeable. To offer absolute forgiveness to the other as well as to oneself is to fulfill the law of *caritas*, facetiously to mimic God's indiscriminate love. Insofar as it rejects the morality of the vulnerable and instead assumes the guilt of the persecutor, such promiscuous absolution is also an act of defiance.

Communion and Contagion

Donne's secular lyrics, "Woman's Constancy" among them, are structured by a Pauline-Augustinian-Protestant understanding of selfhood, and this structure refuses normative ideals of monogamous love and subjectivity. These poems thereby allow us to appreciate the queer purposes to which we might put the impossible injunction to confess those parts of the self—the petty, the manipulative, the callous—that we would prefer not to know and that we may genuinely believe to be selfless concern, self-defense, or disinterested moral outrage. In particular, Donne's libertine poetry allow us to perceive how the logic of promiscuity may afford a more ethical, even more faithful, relation to others than that of monogamy. The shift from judgment to anticipatory confession that we see in "Woman's Constancy" puts in secular terms the Pauline and Protestant denial of the efficacy of human works. Paul's Letter to the Romans explains that, soteriologically speaking, God offers *only* absolute forgiveness, only unconditional love, for no human creature deserves grace or salvation. Apparent differences in merit are illusory, "for there is no difference; for all have sinned, and are deprived of the glory of God, and are justified freely by his grace" (GB, Rom. 3:23–24). To deem oneself innocent is to claim love as a right, the position that Donne's speaker relinquishes. Confession, in this view, is an act of imperfect imagination. The ability to picture oneself in the future position of confessing the same crime of which one accuses another erases the distinction between vulnerable lover and injurious beloved. In "Woman's Constancy," the speaker initially seems to fear the beloved's fickleness. At the poem's end, this fear reveals itself to have been based on the dreadful recognition of the speaker's own potential for infidelity, which may render the beloved as fungible as the speaker fears themself to be.

The forbearance envisioned in libertine lyrics such as "Woman's Constancy" might be understood as an expression of *caritas*, that human approximation of divine indifference and generosity. Badiou argues that

> the polemic against "what is due," against the logic of right and duty, lies at the heart of the Pauline refusal of works and law. . . . For Paul, nothing is due. The salvation of the subject cannot take the form of a reward or wage. . . . It pertains to the granting of a gift, *kharisma*. Every subject is initiated on the basis of a charisma; every subject is charismatic.[76]

Taken from the Greek word for "favor" or "gift," "charisma" designates our capacity to attract desire or devotion that we have not, and perhaps cannot, earn. To be charismatic is not, as in modern usages, to possess unique charms or attractions. It is, in the Pauline sense, to be the passive object of undeserved love. Conceding our charisma, we are absorbed into the faceless "all," the creaturely mass "deprived of the glory of God, and are justified freely by his grace." In order for grace to be possible for anyone, it must be possible for everyone: "Only what is absolutely gratuitous can be addressed to all."[77] To hope for grace, we must sacrifice claims of individual difference or merit. "For Paul," Badiou explains, "it is of utmost importance to declare that I am justified only insofar as everyone is. . . . I identify myself in my singularity as subject of the economy of salvation only insofar as this economy is universal."[78] No one is special. Neither grace nor secular love is distributed according to human perceptions of fairness.

To understand love as something free—not paid for, offered "unto all" (GB, Rom. 3:23)—is to grasp toward a *caritas* that radically contradicts, as Freud was well aware, the more common view of love as valuable insofar as it is precious and particular. Discussing the command to love one's neighbor as oneself, Freud objects that "my love is something valuable to me which I ought not to throw away without reflection [*Rechenschaft*]. . . . If I love someone, he must deserve [*verdeinen*] it in some way."[79] In fact, "nothing else runs so strongly counter to the original nature of man" than the injunction to indiscriminate *caritas*.[80] Freud's economic language, especially visible in the German *Rechenschaft* (reckoning, accounting) and *verdeinen* (earn, merit), registers the tension between an erotics based on monogamy and fidelity and a Pauline universalism applied to the secular realm. In imagining a love that is utterly capacious and indiscriminate, in admitting that this is counter to a romantic ideology so deeply entrenched as to appear indistinguishable from "the original nature of man," we might further explore some of the ethical value of promiscuity as that which defies the norms that rest on a truth of desires rather than practices, core identities rather than singular acts.

What Badiou calls a Pauline "indifference to difference" can bring theology into conversation not only with a queer ethics of shared indignity, but also, as I have argued elsewhere, with a posthumanist ethics that denies the exceptional value of humanist definitions of life.[81] One of the objectives that Foucault and Butler share through their interrogation of confessional technologies is to rethink the stability of the Cartesian subject that is set off from other life forms by its ability to know itself as a thinking thing. As distinct from the *bête machine* that simply acts, the *res cogitans* is capable of reflection and therefore of self-determination. In recent decades, this Cartesian picture of the sovereign subject has been contested by a variety of discourses, from poststructuralism and psychoanalysis to new materialist and posthumanist studies that have questioned the exceptional position of human life as such, as well as the racial, gendered, and sexual hierarchies that have been defended through an appeal to humanist reason.[82] In their place, scholars have endorsed what might be understood as an ethics of indifference in which "the human" is no longer an obviously privileged or unique category. Jane Bennett argues that recognizing the "vitality" of matter can "dissipate the onto-theological binaries of life/matter, human/animal, will/determinant, and organic/inorganic."[83] In a discussion of stem-cell research, Bennett proposes that the "free and undetermined agency" of matter shows "secular modernists that while we can surely intervene in the material world, we are not in charge of it, for there are 'foreign' powers about."[84] The "foreign powers" of the material world challenge humanist distinctions between matter as inert and passive, human life as agential and autonomous. In this section, I put posthumanist work, which generally focuses on science studies, into conversation with post-secularist work focused on the political and conceptual imbrication of religiosity and secularity. Bruno Latour famously urges that "a rereading of our history" that rejects a narrative of progressive disenchantment will lead us to "discover that we have never begun to enter the modern era" characterized by scientific rationality as against a premodern thralldom to religious superstition.[85] Posthumanist and new materialist thought provide a useful vantage on what Charles Taylor calls the modern belief in a "buffered" (or "bounded") self as against the "porous self" of premodern, presecular thought, for which "the line between personal agency and impersonal force was not at all clearly drawn."[86] This reorientation entails openness to the past as part of the present rather than its irrelevant precursor. It presumes a recursive, rather than linear, teleology that new materialism, no less than queer theory, has preached but not usually practiced.

Taking seriously the multiplicity of the past—including its religiosity—can help us to rethink many of the categories, both sexual and ontological, that we now take for granted. The premodern archive facilitates, in Henry Turner's view, a "return to a past moment that has never been as human as we thought it was."[87] Although posthuman and new materialist thought avowedly resist a progressively secular and rational view of history, these fields themselves are shaped by a presentist bias that abridges and distorts the philosophic and scientific past. As Andrew Cole explains this contradiction, given that the theoretical consensus is that "after Descartes everything went off the rails in the history of philosophy," it is quite odd that posthumanist scholars "do not focus intensely on the philosophy and thought of the period before Descartes but after the Greeks—a focus that would make instantly visible the medieval mystical discourse upon which such an investigation into objects is founded, discourse that is fundamentally, even beautifully, logocentric."[88] Along with the medieval mysticism flagged by Cole, scholars have shown that a premodern archive makes available a range of perspectives that challenge human exceptionalism.[89] The Aristotelian belief in a tripartite soul, the Galenic insistence on the corporality of thoughts and feelings, and the Lucretian conception of all things as the product of chance combinations of atoms were influential both before and after the publication of Descartes's *Meditations*. They provide an important resource for scholars reassessing a modern dualism that divides culture from nature, mind from body, "humanity" from animal and material other. By understanding life in terms of "vitality," or the sum of organic processes shared by animal and vegetable life, Garrett Sullivan writes, "humoral physiology sutures cognition to embodiment, and thus the rational to the sensitive and vegetative powers."[90] As against Platonic idealism or Cartesian dualism, the Aristotelian and Galenic conviction of the entanglement of physiology with psychology profoundly shaped Christian theology. It also shaped early modern literature, as Andrew Escobedo shows: the trope of personification, in which "figures such as Joy, Fear, Rumor, and War emerge from the agent or from the landscape and take action in the world," registers a more general view that the will is not autonomous from the world, but rather a "complex mixture of activity and passivity."[91] A return to early modern materialism, in which the experience of belief—like secular desire, most frequently attached to the humoral condition of melancholia—was somatic as well as psychic, can usefully contest ideals of romance and chastity as marks of human distinction.[92]

Donne's consciousness of the "subtle knot" of spirit and matter throughout his lyrics is one instance of premodern resistance to Platonic idealism and, later, Cartesian dualism. Insofar as a romanticized ideal of (white) family values and what the anti-abortion movement calls "a culture of life" have been associated with the highest expressions of human rationality and social order as distinct from the indiscriminate rutting of animals—a comparison implicit in Rick Santorum's notorious linking of homosexuality to "man on dog" sex—we can see how designations of species and morality are mutually informative.[93] This work can be put in productive dialogue with Lee Edelman's insistence that queer politics must demand not mere toleration or inclusion within the existing social order, but rather "must insist on disturbing, on queering, social organization as such."[94] Edelman celebrates in queerness "something truly inhuman, something meaningless and mechanistic, that replaces volition and agency with subjection to the drive."[95] Edelman's rejection of a politics of reproductive futurism reminds us how seamlessly ideals of romance, procreation, commitment, and family can morph into a systematic redefinition of "life" in which some persons are understood to possess the human and politically valuable life that, Agamben reminds us, fits the criterion of *bios*, while others cling only to the creaturely, disposable life of *zōe*.[96]

Donne's short, widely anthologized poem "The Flea" is part of an early modern archive that resists a modern, Cartesian distinction between passive body and active mind, intentional human subject and determined nonhuman object. The Augustinian and Lutheran emphasis on the connection between "flesh" and mind is only one instance of a cultural perception of the soul as material and the body as ensouled.[97] Depicting the *corpus Christi* as a bloodsucking insect, "The Flea" breaks down the sacred as well as secular taxonomies that guide normative views of subjectivity and sexuality. The most obvious are those borders between individual bodies and licit and illicit sex. But in what Saunders describes as its "elevation of the trivial and the repulsive to the monumental," this poem more expansively ponders the permeability of other categories on which modern conceptions of proper sexuality are based: between god and beast, human and animal life, procreation and disease, the intentionality and autonomy of "masculine" politics and culture, on the one hand, and the necessity and passivity of "feminine" nature, on the other.[98]

In "The Flea" humanity interacts with other forms of "life" within and without bodily borders in such a way as to undercut human autonomy and sovereignty. Sexual contact is only one instance of what Karen Barad calls a "*congealing of agency*" across, inside, and outside individual bodies.[99] Donne's attention to the irrationality and promiscuity of desire, to the porousness of the self, allows us to rethink the gendered, sexual, and ontological hierarchies that modern thought takes for granted. "The Flea," in particular, offers a premodern, presecular instance of posthumanism's theoretical affordance as Noreen Giffney and Myra Hird describe it: "Recognizing the nonhuman in every trace of the Human also means being cognizant of the exclusive and excluding economy of discourses relating to what it means to be, live, act or occupy the category of the Human."[100] The cynicism about human love and honor that we find in such poems as "The Flea" can be instructive for a queer project of resisting those taxonomies of agency and intentionality that Mel Y. Chen calls "animacy hierarchies" and thereby "veering away from dominant ontologies and the normativities they promulgate."[101] As opposed to an earlier, optimistic generation of work in animal studies and ecocriticism, more recent queer and feminist scholars have emphasized that material-ist thought does not necessarily lead to the warm and fuzzy affect often associated with ecofeminism. This scholarship instead takes a Darwinian perspective in which aggression and competition cannot be wished away, and which brings with it a more sober awareness of a history of politi-cal struggle in which expanding rights to some means denying privilege to others.[102] It thus confronts us with our own impulses to protect the privileges we enjoy at the expense of more expansive social and political justice—or, as I will describe it in the final section of this chapter, the consequences of a choice of an ethics of difference over indifference.[103]

Donne's emphatically materialist vision of human life in "The Flea" is itself inextricable from an indeterminate network of substances: food, flesh, disease, and blood, with all of the latter's connotations of heritage and kinship. This poem gleefully desacralizes conventional social and religious morality, a dismissal that is both familiar and instrumental:

> Mark but this flea, and mark in this,
> How little that which thou deny'st me is:
> Me it sucked first, and now sucks thee,
> And in this flea our two bloods mingled be.
> Confess it! This cannot be said
> A sin, or shame, or loss of maidenhead;
>   Yet this enjoys before it woo,
>   And pampered swells with one blood made of two,
>   And this, alas, is more than we would do.
>
> Oh stay! Three lives in one flea spare
> Where we almost—nay, more than—married are:
> This flea is you and I, and this
> Our marriage-bed and marriage-temple is.
> Though parents grudge, and you, we're met,
> And cloistered in these living walls of jet.
>   Though use make thee apt to kill me,
>   Let not to this self-murder added be,
>   And sacrilege—three sins in killing three.

Cruel and sudden! Hast thou since
Purpled thy nail in blood of innocence?
In what could this flea guilty be,
Except in that drop which it sucked from thee?
Yet thou triumph'st, and say'st that thou
Find'st not thyself nor me the weaker now:
    'Tis true: then learn how false fears be:
    Just so much honour, when thou yield'st to me,
    Will waste, as this flea's death took life from thee. (1–27)

What the coy female addressee is so insistently asked to "mark"—to see, to notice, to assess—is the insignificance of the human honor and religion signified by the poem's references to parents, legal marriage, confession, sin, and sacrilege. The ungendered flea has sucked both speaker and mistress; or, if we indulge the visual joke allowed by the similarity between "s's" and "f's" in seventeenth-century print, fucked both. Promiscuously mingling "two bloods" into "one blood made of two," the flea's sucking/fucking has also performed the mystical office of making speaker and addressee one flesh. They are "almost—nay, more than—married" in the drops of blood that swirl and blend in the insect's small body.

The flea embodies both deficiency and surplus, human and divine agency, the private conjunction of the marriage bed and the public ceremony of the marriage temple. Dispensing with the rhetoric of courtship and biting speaker and addressee openly and unashamedly, the flea has created a material and theological bond both resembling and exceeding that of marriage by mingling their blood with its own. In material terms, the flea evokes premodern understandings of pregnancy as the combination of the parents' blood. In theological terms, the flea's "swelling" with "Three lives"—its own, as well as those would-be lovers whose blood it contains—evokes the "three-personed God" of the Trinity. This trinitarian union, in excess of the procreative couple, relentlessly manifests itself formally: the poem has three stanzas, each made up of three couplets and a final triplet. Constance Furey has argued that relationality in Donne's lyrics is patterned on the Christological union of the seemingly opposite ontologies of deity and humanity. Love therefore holds in tension identity and difference, satisfaction and frustration.[104]

I would add that the flea also draws attention to the communal ingestion of blood that brings all believers together through the mediating body of Christ. Here and elsewhere, as Regina Schwartz has argued, Donne's libertine verses perversely fulfill sacramental longing by treating sex as a Eucharistic ritual.[105] The flea's little body represents on the smallest possible scale the corporate Christendom described by Paul's Letter to the Ephesians. And like the *corpus mysticum* of the Mass, in which all become one, this communal body is notably fluid in its gender: the flea—always "it" or "this," never "he" or "she"—is both penetrative and impregnated.[106] Mimicking in miniature, material form the degendering incorporation of all believers in a mystical *corpus Christi* indifferent to all mere physical differences, "This flea *is* you and I," and the codes of "honor" that legislate sex are worth neither more nor less than the unnoticeable drop of blood "waste[d]" by the flea.

Accordingly, when the mistress crushes the flea, she commits "sacrilege—three sins in killing three." Suicide is inseparable from murder, as she ends a life that no longer properly belongs to any of them because it is shared, their identities no more separable than their mingled blood. This "Cruel and sudden" act, Christopher Warley astutely notices, is unrepresentable, performed in the blank space between stanzas.[107] The uncertain future becomes the unredeemable past, the present disappearing between "Let not" and "Hast thou since." This temporal ellipsis collapses the crushing of the flea into the more distant past of the crucifixion, turning the encounter from Eucharist to Passion Play. In her adherence to the law of parents and state rather than the mysterious grace of sacrifice, the mistress recapitulates the "Jews' impiety" that Donne, no stranger to anti-Semitism, attacks in the Holy Sonnet "Spit in my face, you Jews" (6). The mistress has "purpled" her "nail in blood of innocence," her fingernail performing the same office as did the nails affixing Jesus to the cross. Yet this analogy breaks down just when the mistress "triumph[s]" in proving the previous two stanzas to be nonsense, the couple's individual lives none the poorer for the sacrifice of the flea. It is at this point that the speaker avers that "'Tis true": the flea is just a flea. But this admission brings its own rhetorical triumph in the conclusion that the minuscule drop of blood is a measure of the vanishingly small "honor" that the mistress would yield in having sex. It is here, as Warley points out, that the speaker "offers a competing demystification of ideology: that the very urge to squash the flea as material signifier was a sign of fear, of respect for and complicity with the very idealism that material squashing is supposed to get rid of."[108] Much as the Jews of "Spit in my face" only "killed once an inglorious man," uncomprehending of the resurrection that would turn human desecration into divine glorification, so the mistress's iconoclastic literalism leads her to confuse a single bodily act with a greater "triumph." The speaker's anti-Semitism is instrumental to his appeal to a higher form of honor that cannot be reduced to prescription, beyond the law and the body. Yet in abjuring formal submission to the letter of the law in favor of sincere fulfilment of its spirit, Donne does not so much secularize sex as make its proper sphere the private, interior realm of faith—a logical move, we have seen, shared by Milton—and thereby reveals the secular to be itself a religious formation.

Carrier of infection as well as life, predatory as well as vulnerable, the flea is significant not only because it allegorizes the folly of human ideals of law and honor, but also because it is materially connected to humanity through the blood that both creatures need, and through the bodies that may become pregnant, diseased, itchy, nourishing, dead, and decayed without their consent. Human pretensions to exceptionalism and honor are illusions because "honor"—like the sexual difference, propriety, and normativity that queer studies so devoutly contests—assumes transcendence of the physical existence that connects us to creatures and to matter, including to bodily fluids that never quite stay in place. The ultimate "*failure* of reason" that Saunders detects in "The Flea"—the conspicuous replacement of logical proof with "seductive bullshit"—is what affords "a glimpse of Divine totality" in contrast to which "in both Donne's negative theology and Lacanian psychoanalysis . . . the human being is defined by a failure to comprehend; defined, precisely, as the subject *not* supposed to know."[109]

What Saunders isolates in his comparison of Donne to Lacan, theology to psychoanalysis, is the disavowal of the full implications of one's desire. Donne's trifling poem remains a cultural touchstone for thinking about the permeability not only of bodies and subjectivities, but also of borders between forms of life that are differently valued. Set in a fleabag hotel many centuries later, Alan Jenkins's "Itch (The Flea's Retort)" rewrites Donne's poem from the point of view of a flea observing a couple's loss of innocence:

It must have been their first time—first shared bed,
A hotel off 42nd Street, so sleazy
It had seen stuff that made cockroaches queasy
And even the rats had learned to give head.
But these two were so young, so innocent,
They thought the footsteps that came and went
All night in the corridor, with whispers, meant
Someone was sick, or dead; and so they hid
Their guilty fears by doing what they did,
Three times, then fell asleep. That's when I fed.

Not the kind of place you lie around
And wait for room service in the morning,
Rich on coffee smells. As day was dawning
They scratched their itch again; untangled, found
They were soon scratching at a different one
And this time the scratching was no fun—
In the struggle for survival, I had won
A little victory . . . Inflamed in parts
They'd barely known, with murder in their hearts
They hunted me; but I had gone to ground.

If words could kill me, I would not be here
To tell the tale—they raged, they spat blood libels
On my kind, they hurled their Gideon's Bibles
At specks their maddened vision made appear
On sheets and tiles in that unhappy room.
Did they think it might have been their tomb?—
In a time of plague, the telltale bloom
Of red pinpricks, two bloodstreams joined as one,
Two lifelines cut off in a storm of fear
Before *their* years of bed-hopping had begun! (1–30)

Here, in this "sleazy" "hotel off 42nd Street," an ungendered, unracial-
ized couple discovers that sexual propriety does not inhere so much
in conventional signifiers of spiritual innocence—love, prior virginity,
naiveté so absolute as to misrecognize the genre of their lodging—as

in the material privilege and class hierarchy signified by the availability of "room service," nice "coffee smells," clean sheets, and the absence of vermin. Guilt and horror are occasioned not by sex but by the discovery of fleabites, "the telltale bloom / Of red pinpricks, two bloodstreams joined as one," which in turn prompts the realization that they are in *that* kind of place and therefore have had *that* kind of sex. Both Donne's and Jenkins's poems depict characters who distance themselves from abjected others. Whereas in Donne's poem the flea is depicted as a Christ figure offering eternal life, in Jenkins's sex cannot escape its proximity to death. "In a time of plague," the era of HIV, the sight of blood prompts "a storm of fear / Before *their* years of bed-hopping had begun!" This "first time" between two innocents is not the prelude to living happily ever after in lifelong monogamy, but the beginning of a life of moving from one bed to the other, one that will follow the pattern of the flea's own promiscuous feeding. The flea signifies the stigma of those seedy guests previously sensed only in "whispers" and "footsteps," the fear of contagion exemplified by rats that have learned the human activity of fellatio. Innocence in this poem is itself a sociopolitical privilege, the Gideon's Bible ironically included in the squalid room a useless weapon against the pollution at once material and ideological that comes with creaturely contact and intimacy.

Addressing the ethics of new materialist and posthuman theory, Dana Luciano and Mel Y. Chen ask: Given the overwhelming presence of human misery in the modern world, does not attention to non- or inhuman matter "look away from the already overlooked or advantage the inanimate over the dehumanized?"[110] They respond that "many of queer theory's foundational texts interrogate, implicitly or explicitly, the nature of the 'human' in its relation to the queer, both in their attention to how sexual norms themselves constitute and regulate hierarchies of humanness, and as they work to unsettle those norms and the default forms of humanness they uphold."[111] Contemplating the relations between the human and the non- or inhuman, that is, compels us to reassess the criteria by which we construct hierarchies of "life" and its others, hierarchies that historically have made the "human" a political and rhetorical category, rather than the ontological or biological category it is often assumed to be.[112] In accentuating the material, nonhuman dimension of human sexuality—the bodily as well as social processes that remove sex from the realm of intentionality and spirituality—Donne's and Jenkins's meditations on human-insect intercourse allow us to appreciate the difficulty of drawing a line between virtuous and shameful, human and bestial, sex. The persistence of bare life makes itself known in Aristotle's oft-cited description of humanity as *zōon politikon*, usually translated as "political *animal*"—the life of politics here is not *bios* but *zōe*. To forget that conceptual tension central to human politics is to entertain illusions of autonomy and innocence that creaturely being renders moot.

Caritas (or, Indifference)

The fleas in Donne's and Jenkins's poems encapsulate the revulsion that may be aroused by the indiscriminate love and forgiveness of a God who, according to Paul, never says no: "in him it is always Yes" (2 Cor. 1:19).[113] The beast, no less than the god (or the Freudian unconscious), is profoundly indifferent to human differences, neither attracted nor repulsed in any coherent or justifiable sense. This parody of divine *caritas* appears in human form in Donne's lyric "The Indifferent," a poem that renounces a contractual view of love as a matter of entitlement or desert. Instead, "The Indifferent" depicts desirability as a form of charisma in the sense that Badiou traces: a gift of the one who loves, not a property of the beloved. This definition of love as an act of generosity brings with it the uncomfortable proposition that one cannot be held accountable for *not* loving another as exclusively or intensely as that person would like. This is not an argument for deceit or cruelty, but a validation of intimacy that is nonexclusive, spontaneous, and provisional. In light of the conventional Petrarchan view that unrequitedness itself constitutes persecution (the perspective with which "Woman's Constancy" begins and that a number of Donne's own lyrics sustain), "The Indifferent" probes the limits of what we understand as cruel or callous behavior. Is indifference to what another wants from us—whether in the form of desire or commitment—unethical? Butler rightly observes that "though I might think of the ethical relation as dyadic or, indeed, as presocial, I am caught up not only in the sphere of normativity but in the problematic of power when I pose the ethical question in its directness and simplicity: 'How ought I to treat you?'"[114] In erotic relations, how we treat others encompasses not just how we act toward them, but also how we *feel* toward them. Given that, as Laura Kipnis puts it, "It's generally understood that falling in love means committing to *commitment*," to not want to commit can be interpreted as a form of mistreatment.[115] The equation of love and monogamy almost inevitably implies a "problematic of power" because its coercive normativity disguises its status as a demand for obedience. The desire for commitment never has to be accounted for; the desire for promiscuity always does.

Donne's "The Indifferent" inverts this expectation by accentuating the aggression embedded in the demand for monogamy. "The Indifferent" has often been dismissed as an ironic libertine confection, if not sexist apologia.[116] I propose instead that it constitutes a vital examination of the ethics of the ideals of singularity, superiority, and devotion upon which monogamy is grounded. "The Indifferent" contemplates the ethics of what Tim Dean has called "cruising as a way of life," in which hospitality to strangers *as* strangers offers the possibility of intimacy apart from ideals of classical friendship and modern monogamy: knowledge, sameness, and permanence.[117] This is not to deny the cynical or self-serving dimension of the poem's defense of libertinism, nor is it to claim for the poem a utopian view of radical sexual equality or freedom. Rather, it is to see in the lyric an awareness that idealization of lifelong commitment may be as implicated in cynicism, selfishness, and misogyny as defense of inconstancy.

In the opening stanza, the speaker brags of his ability to be enthusiastically promiscuous in his attachments:

> I can love both fair and brown,
> Her whom abundance melts, and her whom want betrays,
> Her who loves loneness best, and her who masques and plays,
> Her whom the country formed, and whom the town,
>   Her who believes, and her who tries,
>   Her who still weeps with spongy eyes,
> And her who is dry cork, and never cries:
> I can love her and her, and you and you;
> I can love any—so she not be true. (1–9)

The concept of indifference reveals the difficulty of distinguishing between generosity and selfishness, *caritas* and *cupiditas*. Indifference in the early modern period had a range of overlapping meanings. Most familiarly, "indifference" could signify apathy, carelessness, or callousness. But it also carried the more positive valence of impartiality, fairness, or neutrality; and it could mean ambiguity or identity in character, quality, or value. As a substantive noun, indifference could designate one who is impartial and disinterested, neutral, unconcerned, or apathetic. Theologically, "things indifferent," or *adiaphora*, were nonessentials, practices or acts that had no effect on salvation.

The repetition of the formula "her . . . and" ("her" appears eleven times, "and," nine) states the logical extreme of a characteristic that Jeffrey Johnson has observed of Donne's writing more generally: "The matter for Donne is never either/or, but both/and, and therefore all."[118] In his determined indifference, expressed here as promiscuous appetite, the poet refuses to discriminate between or hierarchize "fair and brown" (terms, as we have seen, with decided racial implications in the period), wealth and poverty, introversion and extroversion, provinciality and urbanity, faith and skepticism, sentimentality and stoicism. Rather than elevate one woman above all others, the "indifferent" speaker "can love her and her, and you and you": external qualities of race, class, religion, and affect are nonessentials that exert no pressure on the speaker's offer of love. As in the Pauline doctrine of *adiaphora*, external appearance and behavior grant no entitlement to love. "I can love," a phrase repeated three times, mimics in sexual terms the indifferent grace of God regardless of the merit of the beloved object.

The speaker's stated indifference to the appearance, circumstances, and behavior of those he loves reminds us that to commit is to *choose*, and choice requires discrimination in both its positive and negative senses. To discriminate is to judge, predict, separate, distinguish, differentiate—to make distinctions that are never completely neutral but instead constitute a hierarchy of value. Moroever, Sharon Holland's work on the erotic life of racism, as I discussed in chapters 2 and 3, allows us to appreciate that erotic distinctions are also discriminatory in the sense that they are shaped by the long history of race and colonialism. Such discrimination structures the rhetoric of the conventional Petrarchan lyric, which imagines the fair and chaste beloved as different from and better than all other women. Donne mocks that stance to obscene effect in "The Comparison," where the speaker enumerates differences between two women's bodies, including their sweat and their vaginas, before concluding that the comparisons that would justify erotic devotion themselves are "odious"—both exhibiting and inspiring hatred ("The Comparison," 54). By contrast, the speaker of "The Indifferent" refuses the distinctions that would justify love on the grounds of objective merit. Donne thereby engages with a Petrarchan poetics that, as Heather Dubrow has observed, both struggles to differentiate and mark boundaries and stages the breakdown of the distinctions it draws.[119]

The second stanza of "The Indifferent" charges that the lauded morality of sexual discrimination may itself serve to justify dominance. For although the speaker vows that "I can love any—so she not be true," he does not get the last word. Rather, as this middle stanza demonstrates, fidelity is rarely altruistic or unilateral. It more typically entails an appeal for reciprocity that is also an imposition of debt and a demand for submission:

> Will no other vice content you?
> Will it not serve your turn to do as your mothers?
> Have you old vices spent, and now would find out others?
> Or doth a fear that men are true torment you?
>   Oh we are not, be not thou so:
>   Let me, and do you, twenty know;
> Rob me, but bind me not—and let me go.
> Must I, which came to travail thorough you,
> Grow your fixed subject because you are true? (10–18)

The affect of the plural, female "you" that the speaker addressed in the first stanza here shifts from receptive to prosecutorial. As in "The Flea," something happens between stanzas. In this case, we can infer that the speaker replaces crowing with self-defense in response to an ultimatum that he change and learn to love truly after all. He attributes this demand to everything *but* love. First, he suggests that the pursuit of monogamy is one among many possible "vices." This is not so much an inversion of traditional morality as a literalization of "vice's" etymology in the Latin *vitium*—a flaw, defect, or failing—a generalized sense that was available in the early modern period alongside the more narrowly moralistic meaning. Whether to achieve the thrill of dominance or to assuage guilt, a demand for monogamy can be more vicious than virtuous: "Let me, and do you, twenty know; / Rob me, but bind me not—and let me go." The repetition of "let"—to allow, to relinquish control or ownership of—emphasizes that an unreciprocated wish for monogamy may also be a bid for domination. The confession that men are not "true" offers relief from the debt that commitment constitutes: "Oh we are not, be thou not so."

The stanza's concluding political metaphor extends this logic to suggest that mutual fidelity is not the opposite of hierarchy but may in fact require it. To be the "fixed subject" of a mistress is to be subordinate, to forfeit autonomy. To recall Menon's argument, if the assumption of fixed identity is itself a concession to the disciplinary regimes of normativity, to be "true"—always one and the same—is to become immobile, "fixed" in time and place. We find the strongest expressions of the ideological continuity between sexual possession and imperial dominance in poems where Donne describes the former in colonial terms, as when he compares his mistress to "both Indias of spice and mine"—the spices of the East Indies and the silver of Peru and Mexico—("The Sun Rising," 17) or "my America! My new-found land! / My kingdom, safeliest when with one man manned! / My mine of precious stones! My empery!" ("To His Mistress Going to Bed," 27–29). Because, as Aschah Guibbory has noted, Donne's libertine and romantic verse share many sentiments, these images of brute domination may be understood as admissions that mutual love may itself be founded on force and fraud.[120] We witness this in "The Anniversary." Here, in contrast to a promiscuous afterlife in which "we shall be thoroughly blessed, / But we no more than all the rest" (21–22), the committed couple finds happiness in the exclusivity of its dyad:

> Here upon earth, we're kings, and none but we
> Can be such kings, nor of such subjects be:
> Who is so safe as we? where none can do
> Treason to us, except one of us two. (23–26)

Unlike kings who can be betrayed by multiple subjects, monogamous lovers can be betrayed only by one another. Reassuring as this arrangement might seem, such a state of mutual dependence actually puts the lovers absolutely at one another's mercy. The political metaphor of "treason" underscores the sense of compulsion that enforces mutual fidelity. Treason differs from private betrayal in that it signifies a rebellion against authority, a failure of proper allegiance. What Janet Jakobsen has said of capitalist structures of feeling is also relevant to Donne's insight that equations of virtue, freedom, and fidelity obscure relations of dominance at this moment of nascent capitalism and monogamous marriage: "The independence of the autonomous individual is produced through a hierarchical—a dominative—dependence on others. Thus these others can threaten the self, not just by actively attacking the self but simply by asserting their own autonomy."[121] Promises of loyalty that should foster a sense of security instead provoke anxiety and vulnerability, so that violence against another can be justified as defense of the self.

The final lines of "The Anniversary" acknowledge this danger by redescribing love as charismatic, and therefore dependent not on mutual fidelity but on mutual grace and forgiveness:

> True and false fears let us refrain:
> Let us love nobly and live, and add again
> Years and years unto years, till we attain
> To write threescore. This is the second of our reign. (27–30)

The easy longevity these lines imagine, in which sixty years feels like a second, themselves rest on a deliberate choice to "refrain" from entertaining "True and false fears." Some suspicions may be well-founded even (or especially) in a private world of two. But noblesse oblige: one proves worthy of privilege by practicing magnanimity—or, in Pauline terms, *caritas* that manifests indifference to the particularities of merit.

While they differ in their respective endorsement and repudiation of constancy, "The Anniversary" and "The Indifferent" both demonstrate that a pursuit of monogamous love may authorize an ethically troubling desire to possess and dominate. "The Anniversary" proposes one solution: the selective attention that sustains long-term affection. "The Indifferent" proposes another: rejecting the worldly distinction and domination on which monogamy rests. In this poem's final stanza, the speaker envisions intimacy based on the parity of provisional desire rather than on the subjection of commitment. Here, Venus turns out to be a serendipitous eavesdropper turned *dea ex machina* who rescues the poet from the regime of monogamy:

> Venus heard me sigh this song,
> And by loves sweetest part, variety, she swore,
> She heard not this till now; and it should be no more.
> She went, examined, and returned ere long,
>   And said, "Alas, some two or three
>   Poor heretics in love there be
> Which think t'establish dang'rous constancy.
> But I have told them, 'Since you will be true,
> You shall be true to them, who're false to you.'" (19–27)

At first glance, this decree that monogamy "should be no more" would seem to curtail freedom by making inconstancy the new orthodoxy or norm. This interpretation is supported by the etymology of "heresy" from the Greek αἱρετικός "able to choose." But Venus's decree is actually more flexible. She allows the heresy of monogamy, but with the proviso that it has no power to bind. Those who want to be true are free to do so, but those they love are in turn free to be false. As the response of the "heretics" indicates, this defense of "variety" in fact reveals the limits of the concept of "freedom" in the erotic sphere, where we are dependent on others who may not want the same things we do.

This radical separation of the promise of fidelity from the mandate that it be returned has been interpreted as a punishment, suggesting the difficulty of conceiving of the refusal to commit as anything but a betrayal. Even a Lacanian reader like Saunders, who defends "The Indifferent" as a "fantasy of indiscriminate multiple sexual couplings" made "*equally available to women*," describes this final stanza as acknowledging the "deliberate and painful irony" that "Donne has to push it until *someone*'s happiness is threatened; the poem subsequently and abruptly ends, as if the exuberant boisterous fantasy of shared libertine pleasure runs aground at the point of recognizing the pain that may attend upon loving someone who refuses to be 'true.'"[122] I would argue instead that Donne's point is precisely that absolute autonomy is impossible: because intimacy brings people with different desires and agendas into contact, someone's happiness will *always* be threatened. By denying monogamous love the claim to virtue by which it achieves dominance, Venus makes explicit that a desire for monogamy may be as much an expression of *cupiditas*, or self-serving love, as the promiscuous appetites usually associated with this term. Insofar as it is "establish[ed]"—settled, ordained, instituted—constancy can no longer be an entirely free choice. Constancy is "dang'rous" to the love that Venus allegorizes because it transforms obedience to the passions into obedience to the law, so that monogamy is not a testament of love but an expression of submission and conformity. Venus's determination to allow only *unreciprocated* constancy, to strip monogamy of its moral authority and make it one choice among others, paradoxically makes it a more reliable expression of love by extracting it from an economy of reciprocity and debt. At the same time, Venus accentuates the promiscuity and even superficiality of faith itself, so that the choice of "variety" is no more an index of authenticity than that of commitment.

We might liken Donne's mythological thought experiment here to one proposed by Adam Phillips: "If a law was passed saying that no one was allowed to be monogamous for more than three weeks people would feel under terrible pressure. But pressure to do what exactly? Why would they be suffering? What would they feel deprived of? What would their banners say when they took to the streets?"[123] Silly as it seems, by raising the idea of outlawing monogamy, Phillips allows us to appreciate that those who do not enter legal unions, though no longer specifically criminalized by fornication statutes, continue to be penalized insofar as they are denied access to the legal and economic benefits awarded those in state-sanctioned marriages. In inverting the traditional values of monogamous and promiscuous love, Donne's "The Indifferent" illuminates one underexplored secular interpretation of what Victoria Silver describes as the logic of the Pauline theology that shaped early Protestant writings. Recognizing "a terrible ambivalence and delay between what we are and what we desire to be," Silver writes, "we therefore resist the world's notion of righteousness as an idol and an illusion, since it allows, even encourages, the commission of injustice and the infliction of suffering. . . . In resisting that idea, we imagine and pursue another reality which involves the justification or reform of this one."[124]

To be sure, sixteenth-century Reformers, no less than modern evangelicals, would have been repulsed by Donne's application of this lesson to question the ethics of monogamy. They would have equally supported the suppression of the conjoined antinomianism and sexual promiscuity that Calvin attacked in a pair of pamphlets in which he coined the term "libertine" to designate all free-thinking heretics.[125] Yet, as I have been arguing throughout this book, when we dismiss the queer potential of theology on the grounds that most practicing Christians would disagree, we accord an odd respect to theology's reactionary deployments, many of which are themselves anachronistic and misinformed. We thereby perpetuate the Protestant distinction between secular knowledge and religious faith that makes biblical and theological writing the property of those who believe that it contains truth about an eternal Creator rather than finite creatures. In putting theology and the love lyrics it structures in conversation with contemporary queer, feminist, and critical race theory—indeed, in insisting that theology *is* theory—I have sought to illuminate what it can tell us about ourselves and our ways of being in *this* world, without regard to what Christian believers think comes next. I have thereby tried to expand on the work of previous premodern scholars who, in James Bromley's words, urge that we put past alternatives to the present back in circulation "as persistent reminders, not of a world to which we can or should return, but of the avenues of resistance to dominant ideologies that the circulation of texts opens up."[126] Recognizing that the present was not inevitable gives us hope (faith?) that the future might be lived differently.

Ending with the institution of a counterfactual reality in which monogamy enjoys no moral or legal privileges, Donne's "The Indifferent" presses the concepts of discrimination and fidelity to their logical extremes. This poem thereby illuminates the queer consequences of a Pauline indifference to difference, the promise as well as the vulnerability of a theology of *caritas* that descends impartially on all. Because it exposes the limits of autonomy along with those of commitment, "The Indifferent" provides a fitting end to a study of what discourses of faith can tell us about the ethics of promiscuity. This is neither a systematic nor deliberate ethics for living, nor even an articulable ethos. Promiscuity is not a truth that will set us free. Like the love that is its contrary and its ultimate expression, it is an intimate relation—always itself improvised and irregular—with the humbling, even shaming, compromises that shape our existence as impure creatures in an unjust world.

Coda

The Pressure to Commit: Professionalism, Periodization, Affect

The arc of this book has moved from exploring the necessary failure of faith to the question of our accountability for infidelities that we cannot avoid. By way of conclusion, I consider what the theological structure I have been examining has to tell us about the relation among our intellectual, professional, political, and personal investments as writers and teachers.

It will hardly come as a surprise to most readers that academia is premised on the imperative to commit. Like heterosexuality or marriage, commitment to a field is a compulsory structure disguised as a voluntary, even romantic or passionate, one—indeed, the fact that we are allowed to choose any field at all when we enter graduate school should mean that we do what we do because we love it. We are drawn to a particular period, method, theory, author, genre, language, or national tradition by an excitement, an attraction, an absorption that cannot be calculated or rationalized. But, like fidelity to most things, fidelity to a field eventually becomes its own justification. The further we progress in our educations and, if we are lucky, careers, the harder it becomes to extricate ourselves from a commitment that we make and renew as we write graduate school application statements, enroll in seminars, compose exam lists, select dissertation committees, attend conferences, apply for jobs, teach courses, write articles and books, and serve on exam, dissertation, and professional committees. We prove that our heart is really in this commitment by absorbing ourselves in the primary and secondary material that makes up a given field, and by documenting this absorption in writing that shows how deeply and seriously we have thought about our objects of study. Our inevitable failure to be committed enough awaits exposure by that ubiquitous question at conferences and in reviews: "But what about—?" Latent in queries or critiques regarding what we *haven't* included (the materials we neglected to cite, the debates and histories we abridge, the scholarly debts we fail to acknowledge or even realize we owe) is the charge that we have been glib, sloppy, arrogant, or pretentious—that we have written in bad faith. Local sins of omission are symptomatic of the original scholarly sin: lack of *care*, in the senses of both rigor and love. (And these are not always empty allegations. In all honesty, who among us has not occasionally stood guilty as charged? And who among us has not felt so personally insulted by another's inaccuracy or imprecision that we've itched to cast the first stone?)

In fact, the Pauline distinction between spirit and letter, selfless love and meretricious work, might be in the DNA of academic culture. So might its corollary: that we do truly *good* work only when we do it for the right reasons. This structural affinity should not be surprising, given the historical formation of the Western university. Medieval universities were institutions of papal Christendom; nearly all of the US liberal arts colleges and Ivy League universities now seen as bastions of secular liberalism began as explicitly Protestant establishments.[1] Matthew Arnold's replacement theory, in which love of literature comes to fill the role of religion in modern society, is still felt in the conviction that scholarship should be a higher calling, the more averse to grubby professionalism the better.[2] Stanley Fish noted decades ago that "far from being a stance taken at the margins or the periphery, anti-professionalism is the very center of the professional ethos."[3] As Bruce Robbins parses this stance, "You have to attack the profession in order to assert your own freedom vis-à-vis the profession. And in so doing, you are asserting the ideology of professionalism: freedom, merit, etc."[4] Such freedom is expressed in heartfelt attachment, whether that takes the form of thrilling to the wondrous language of *The Canterbury Tales* or *Finnegan's Wake*; fascination with the material history of ink, paper, manuscripts, and print; enthusiasm about the brave new world of the digital humanities; or dedication to contesting the myriad violences of class, race, gender, and sexuality. The bottom line is that the true scholar *cares* about something beyond getting and keeping a job.

The premium placed on attachment and authenticity, paradoxically, militates against questioning field boundaries or working between fields. This is in part because "field" is defined above all in terms of historical division. Historical periods, aptly deemed "nineteenth-century confections" by Carla Freccero, initially arose to shore up the prestige of literary study, underscoring literature's unique ability to bring bygone eras to life.[5] Tracing this institutional history, Ted Underwood remarks that despite the fact that "different theoretical schools have defined the purpose of literary study in fundamentally different ways," the "organizing grid" of historical periods has survived "repeated, sweeping transformation" of the content—the canons and approaches—of any given period.[6] Eric Hayot argues that the powerful influence of New Historicism on the profession from the 1980s on further

> inculcated a strong unstated theory of *era* as the final goal and subtending force of the intimacies of literary criticism, fixing at the ideological level a powerful theory of periods as social formations. This dominant, new-ish historicism requires a vast expansion of the material necessary to master a single period, and, correspondingly, an increase in the force of institutional and intellectual barriers *between* periods, since crossing them now requires a level of understanding of more than one period as a self-contained whole that cannot be easily acquired.[7]

This is not all bad. Period-specific studies have vastly expanded our knowledge of the complexity of the past and made us aware of how much we don't know; they are indispensable in many respects. But the premium we place on commitment also keeps us in our places, making work that strays across different periods the exception to the professional rule rather than creating broadly applicable patterns for alternative scholarly practices and networks. Along with the examples of scholars not trained in Renaissance studies who have analyzed that period's poetry and whom I mentioned in this book's introduction—Eve Sedgwick, Barbara Johnson, Fred Moten—we might think of the many early modernists who have written extensively across historical periods and the national traditions so often attached to them.[8]

Curiously, fields defined by theoretical perspectives might be more invested in periodization than those organized by historical period. This is surprising, given that borders between periods would seem to protect claims to historical, not theoretical, expertise. But, to take an example close to my own heart, those familiar with recent early modern disputes about the relation between queer and historicist methods of reading will

testify that something different has happened. Debates have waxed polemic, and approaches and styles remain quite different (which can be
a good thing, as I have argued elsewhere).[9] Nonetheless, early modern
scholars have generally concurred in questioning an institutionalization
of queer theory that places, in Valerie Traub's words, "a growing emphasis on the cultural productions of the last century and current moment" with the result that "these temporal frames become the occasion
for theory, while everything prior to the twentieth century increasingly
is positioned as simply history."[10] Indeed, early modern studies as a field
has generally been more hospitable to queer theory than vice versa. As
Madhavi Menon points out, while a number of early modernists engage
with queer theory that analyzes twentieth- and twenty-first-century literature, film, and culture, "the theoretical traffic cannot move in both
directions, because queerness—here conflated with homosexuality—is
a post-nineteenth-century phenomenon." What Menon says of Shakespeare is often true of the conventional perception of premodern materials more generally: "To extend queerness to him is to play fast and loose
with academic credibility."[11]

This credibility, I would add, is not only about expertise, or even about
investment in succession narratives of queer identity. It is also about
an ideal of *political* engagement that must be focused on the present
moment, which marks interest in premodern materials as, in Menon's
words, a "turn away from queer theory."[12] Robyn Wiegman explains it
succinctly when she describes the "twin senses" of professional mastery
as, first, "the mastery of a field, which includes its critical vocabularies,
debates, arguments, impasses, and contexts," and, second, "the mastery
of the *political subjectivity* that is projected onto, sought, and cultivated
within the field."[13] The political subjectivity of queer theory is often
imagined as profoundly different from that of early modern studies. This
distinction partakes of a logic of progress and commitment whereby to
turn one's attention to premodern, presecular literature and culture is
also to indulge an impulse that is at best antiquarian, at worst politically complacent, to divide one's attention and loyalties between a past
we can only study and a present we can change. Consequently, queer
theory as an administrative object of academic teaching and publication tends to reinforce institutional protocols that emphasize the differences between eras and that assign value and relevance in proportion to

proximity to the present. Such logic, as Carolyn Dinshaw points out, is not limited to literary studies, but shapes university structures in which "'hard' sciences (and 'harder' social sciences) continue to be generally cordoned off from other disciplines both intellectually and fiscally" on the grounds that they have immediate and urgent relevance to lives lived now.[14] What Margreta de Grazia has written about periodization provides a more general description of the premium placed on innovation and demonstrable outcomes in the modern university: the distinction of dead past from living present "works less as a historical marker than a massive value judgment, determining what matters and what does not."[15] Periodization, in Kathleen Davis's assessment, is itself a "political technique" that validates particular interests and practices.[16]

One way to think beyond this correlation between periodization and political subjectivity has been proposed by scholars who have endorsed modes of reading variously called "reparative," "uncritical," "surface," "descriptive," "amateur," "postcritical," or "hopeful."[17] The most cited instance of this perspective is Eve Sedgwick's endorsement of reparative reading as a relation to our objects that allows for attachment, vulnerability, and surprise in place of the mastery and distance of the "paranoid" style. Personally, I'm not willing to let go of critique and suspicion entirely (indeed, many of my readings in this book have refused the distinction between surface and symptom, form and content). And I recognize that, as Tim Dean drolly comments, "the reparative often seems a little too convenient as an alibi for masking or denying professional aggressivity" or for warding off criticism of one's own scholarly shortcomings.[18] Still, in this book I have largely sought to practice precisely the openness and amateurism that these theories of reading, along with the critical analyses of modern secularism and science, endorse. Reparative or postcritical reading refuses the "buffered" sense of self that Charles Taylor sees as a product of secular modernity. Insofar as we are buffered, we are "*not* open and porous and vulnerable to a world of spirits and powers"; we also "have confidence in our own powers of moral ordering."[19] Taylor, with his talk of God and religion, has not had a major influence on discussions of reading, but Bruno Latour, another skeptic about secularism, has. Latour notoriously insists that we have never been modern—that is, we have never achieved the cordoning off of mind from world, nature from science, subject from object attributed to modern disenchantment—and maintains that we must resist claiming agency and objectivity in favor of contemplating interactions and networks of variously animate objects.[20] Jane Bennett, likewise, defines "vitality" as "the capacity of things . . . not only to impede or block the will and designs of humans but also to act as quasi agents or forces with trajectories, propensities, or tendencies of their own."[21] Bringing this new materialist work in conversation with the reparative turn, Rita Felski proposes that we treat texts as actors that can affect and change us, forging "cross-temporal networks" that "force us to acknowledge affinity and proximity as well as difference, to grapple with the coevalness and connectedness of past and present."[22] Rather than rely on historical context as the exclusive, or even primary, source of texts' meaning and therefore "stressing their otherness, autonomy, nontransferability," Felski urges us to "point out their portability, mobility, and translatability."[23] Such strategic anachronism can permit the past to attune us to, in Peter Coviello's words, "a scene of broken-off futures, of possibilities skewed toward inarticulacy by time's unfolding," which can alter our current political subjectivities.[24]

In arguing that the presecular past may have agency and significance in the postsecular present, I have taken particular inspiration from the work of medievalists and early modernists who show that valuing attachment and identification could challenge periodization as the ultimate horizon of scholarly commitment. Focused on premodern materials, acknowledging felt connections with writers whom they might not like if they met them on the street *now*—Dinshaw's connection, for instance, with the histrionic medieval Jesus freak Margery Kempe—these scholars model an approach to the past in terms of attraction and fantasy rather than identity or difference, alliance or opposition.[25] This work has also shown how failures of easy comprehension and identification may tell us a lot about ourselves, our desires, our practices: the past, Traub rightly insists, may perform the role of analyst as well as analysand.[26] Taking this insight seriously, I have sought to work through what the presecular perspectives of theologians and poets long past can tell us about the promiscuous tangle of desires and convictions that motivates our erotic, political, and scholarly ways of being.

Queer Faith has been an amateur act, though not quite in the sense that Dinshaw so movingly describes. When I began what I thought would be a project on feminism, queer theory, and love poetry, I did not expect also to write a book about theology, a field in which I feel myself very much an outsider and an amateur. But the structural affinities I kept seeing between religious and secular theories of desire and subjectivity, along with a certain imp of the perverse, ultimately compelled me to think systematically about the translatability of religious writing to queer theory. Having initially been so doubtful myself, it is odd to be in the position of trying to persuade readers from a range of fields—queer theorists, critical race scholars, early modern critics, and theologians—that my promiscuous readings across time and tradition might be productive or pleasurable. In short, this book, like all scholarship, has been a leap of a faith: we both hope and fear that someone will read our imperfect offerings, and we know that the meanings and the uses of our words are not ours to control. Yet, as Edmund Spenser's valediction "Go, little book . . ." captured so well over four hundred years ago, we nonetheless nudge these parts of ourselves out into the world, inviting the promiscuous entanglements by which we strive to convert our readers—and through which we become other to ourselves.

ACKNOWLEDGMENTS

One of the best parts of completing this book is remembering the kindness and generosity of the many people who made it possible for me to start, persist, revise, and finish. Some names appear more than once in recognition of the multiple roles those persons have played in my work and life.

I owe much to the editors of NYU Press's Sexual Cultures Series, Ann Pellegrini, Tavia Nyong'o, and Joshua Takano Chambers-Letson, for supporting this odd project; over the course of writing, conversations with Ann clarified what I was trying to do, and Josh offered feedback and reassurance at just the point that I needed it. The readers for this manuscript, Michael Cobb, Kathryn Schwarz, and a third reader who remained anonymous, provided detailed and rigorous feedback. I hope I have done justice to their generous engagement. Eric Zinner helped me navigate tricky questions of field, audience, and title with patience and humor. Dolma Ombadykow deftly guided this project through its various stages of review and production. Alexia Traganas's scrupulous editing caught errors I would never otherwise noticed.

David Eng, Madhavi Menon, and Will Stockton were my earliest readers and interlocutors for this project, and their enthusiastic engagement at critical junctures gave me the confidence to pursue it. Many friends and colleagues discussed, read, and encouraged me along the way—so many that to recount their contributions in detail might take a book of its own. Ann Coiro, Kim Coles, Heather Dubrow, Carla Freccero, Lowell Gallagher, Achsah Guibbory, Stephen Guy-Bray, Jeffery Knapp, Arthur Little, Gordon Teskey, Ayanna Thompson, and Chris Warley have been particularly generous with their time, advice, and support. For making me think harder, I'm indebted to Sharon Achinstein, John Archer, J. K. Barret, Crystal Bartolovich, Charlene Villaseñor Black, Gina Bloom, Kate Bonnici, Gordon Braden, Jim Bromley, Dympna Callaghan, Joseph Campana, Anne Coldiron, Julie Crawford, Katherine Crawford, John

Curran, Alice Dailey, Drew Daniel, Mario DiGangi, Fran Dolan, Lynn Enterline, Margie Ferguson, John Garrison, Colby Gordon, Catharine Gray, Judith Haber, Graham Hammill, Diana Henderson, Jean Howard, Coppélia Kahn, Victoria Kahn, Aaron Kunin, Russ Leo, Richard Levin, Leah Marcus, Kirsten Mendoza, David Lee Miller, Steve Monte, Erin Murphy, Carol Thomas Neely, Lori Humphrey Newcomb, Sharon O'Dair, Bill Oram, David Orvis, Jonathan Post, Ayesha Ramachandran, Rick Rambuss, Jason Rosenblatt, Colleen Rosenfeld, Kathryn Schwarz, Lauren Silberman, Eric Song, Goran Stanivukovic, Valerie Traub, Harold Veeser, Dan Vitkus, Robert Watson, Will West, and Mary Zaborskis. It was a pleasure getting to know Alan Jenkins a bit amidst the process of securing permission to reprint his wonderful "Itch (the Flea's Retort)."

Audiences at various talks have pushed me on several points to the considerable benefit of this book. I am grateful to those who took the time to attend and engage with me at the University of Illinois Humanities Center; the Columbia University "Futures" conference; Pomona College; the Huntington Library; UCLA; the Johns Hopkins University *ELH* Colloquium; the University of Maryland; the Northeast Shakespeare Seminar at Harvard University; Vanderbilt University; UC Berkeley; the Columbia Shakespeare Seminar; the Northeast Milton Seminar at Rutgers University; Brown University; and the Folger Library Seminar on Race and Gender. Particular thanks for invitations and hospitality go to Catharine Gray, Antoinette Burton, Seth Williams, Colleen Rosenfeld, Ari Friedlander, Will Stockton, Ali Behdad, Jonathan Post, Lowell Gallagher, Arthur Little, Kevin Roberts, Coppélia Kahn, Bill Carroll, Jessie Hock, Leah Marcus, Richard Lee, Jeffrey Knapp, John Staines, Denise Walen, Ann Coiro, Tom Luxon, Tom Fulton, Rick Rambuss, Kim Coles, and Ayanna Thompson.

Closer to home, I have relied for years on the support and intellectual challenges offered by my colleagues at the University of Pennsylvania. This book has profited from the insightful comments of Kevin Brownlee, Rebecca Bushnell, Rita Copeland, David Eng, Jed Esty, Scott Francis, Nancy Hirschmann, Amy Kaplan, Zack Lesser, Ania Loomba, Phyllis Rackin, Peter Stallybrass, David Wallace, and Dag Woubshet. Opportunities to present this work at the following local reading groups and events helped sharpen my thinking: the Gender, Sexuality, and Women's Studies Work-in-Progress group; the Med Ren seminar; the Reading the

Bible in History group; the Shakespeare/Cervantes Conference; the English Department Faculty Colloquium; and the Comparative Liturature Theorizing Seminar. Thanks to Mary Zaborskis and Nancy Hirschmann, Alan Niles and Megan Hall, Drew Starling and Philip Mogen, Zack Lesser and John Pollack, Jed Esty, and Judith Weston and Deanna Cachoian-Schanz for those invitations. Pretty much every idea in this book was worked through in the undergraduate courses and graduate seminars I've taught in recent years: Feminist Theory, Queer Theory, Early Modern Sexualities, the English Proseminar, and Queer Theory and Early Modern Studies. Thanks to those students for the many questions and challenges.

I'm grateful to friends and family who have provided kindness, care, advice, hospitality, and laughter: Geraldine Baer, Emilia Belloni, Lisa Bittel, Toni Bowers, Maya Braguti, Dympna Callaghan, Kim Coles, Rita Copeland, Tim Corrigan, Julie Crawford, Katie Crawford, Jeff Dolven, Remi Dreyfuss, Katherine Eggert, David Eng, Carla Freccero, Marcia Ferguson, Linda Gregerson, Paul Hecht, Victorya Hong, Amy Kaplan, David Kazanjian, Suvir Kaul, James Ker, Ania Loomba, Peter Mancall, Duna Mazza, Erin Murphy, Marissa Nicosia, Helen Oesterheld, Mike Olmi, Greer Olmi-Sanchez, Yolanda Padilla, Jo Park, Pat Parker, Sandro Pozzi, Phyllis Rackin, Clarice Sanchez, Tiffany Sanchez, Kathryn Schwarz, Froukje Slofstra, Will Stockton, Salamishah Tillet, Ayanna Thompson, David Wallace, Chris Warley, Tiffany Werth, Will West, and Chi-ming Yang.

And yet once more, final and biggest thanks go to the family I live with. For two decades now, Chris Diffee has been my toughest and best reader and my beloved and trusted companion. That he still likes me after all of these years is both surprising and humbling. Phineas and Sabine witnessed the composition of just about every word of this book; Clive joined us just in time to help with copyedits and proofs. This book is dedicated, with all of my love, to Quincy Jude Sanchez-Diffee, the First and the Only.

Queer Faith contains portions of the following previously published essays, now considerably revised and dispersed throughout:

"'Modesty or Comeliness': The Predicament of Reform Theology in Spenser's *Amoretti* and *Epithalamion*." This article first appeared in *Renascence* 65, no. 1 (2012): 5–24.

"'In Myself the Smart I Try': Female Promiscuity in *Astrophil and Stella*." ©2012 The Johns Hopkins University Press. This article first appeared in *ELH: English Literary History* 80, no. 1 (2013): 1–27.

"'What Hath Night to Do with Sleep?': Biopolitics in Milton's *Mask*." This article first appeared in *Queer Milton. Early Modern Culture* 10 (2014): 1–21. It was republished in *Queer Milton*, ed. David Orvis, New York: Palgrave MacMillan, 2018.

"Sex and Eroticism in the Renaissance." This essay first appeared in *Edmund Spenser in Context*, edited by Andrew Escobedo, 342–351. Cambridge: Cambridge University Press, 2016.

Alan Jenkins's "Itch (the Flea's Retort)," *White Nights*, Sheep Meadow Press, Copyright © 2018, is reproduced by permission.

NOTES

INTRODUCTION

1 On the sonnet sequence's influence on modern aesthetic forms, see Vickers, "Vital Signs"; Menocal, "We Can't Dance Together" and *Shards of Love*; Johnson, "Muteness Envy"; Freccero, *Queer/Early/Modern*; Moten, *In the Break*, 120.

2 Barrett Browning, *Sonnets from the Portuguese*, 43.11–12.

3 Freccero, *Queer/Early/Modern*, 20.

4 Agamben, "In Praise of Profanation," 23–26.

5 A few instances from across historical fields are Coviello, *Tomorrow's Parties*, 104–128; Dinshaw, *Getting Medieval*; Hanson, *Decadence and Catholicism*; Hollywood, *Sensible Ecstasy*; Luciano, *Arranging Grief*; McGarry, *Ghosts of Futures Past*; Stockton, *Members of His Body*.

6 Rambuss, *Closet Devotions*, 6, 21.

7 Lacan, *Seminar, Book VII*, 83.

8 Lofton, *Consuming Religion*, xii. On the capital needed to acquire the tools and techniques of BDSM, see Weiss, *Techniques of Pleasure*.

9 This is the title phrase of Holland's *The Erotic Life of Racism*, which I discuss in detail in this introduction as well as in chapters 2, 3, and 4.

10 Holland, *The Erotic Life of Racism*, 58, 61.

11 Holland, *The Erotic Life of Racism*, 62; Holland's emphasis.

12 Some predecessors who have particularly influenced my method are Goldberg, *Sodometries*; Dinshaw, *Getting Medieval* and *How Soon Is Now?*; Freccero, *Queer/Early/Modern* and "Tangents (of Desire)"; Gil, *Before Intimacy*; Menon, "Introduction: QueerShakes" and *Indifference to Difference*; Guy-Bray, *Against Reproduction*; Bromley, *Intimacy and Sexuality*; Traub, *Thinking Sex with the Early Moderns*.

13 Goldberg, "After Thoughts," 42.

14 Berlant and Warner, "Sex in Public," 345.

15 Goldberg, "After Thoughts," 36.

16 Jordan, "Religion Trouble," 563.

17 Fradenburg, *Sacrifice Your Love*, 10. See also Caputo, *Prayers and Tears of Jacques Derrida*.

18 Jakobsen and Pellegrini, *Love the Sin*, 12.

19 See Vogel, *James Baldwin and the 1980s*, 93–111; Field, *All Those Strangers*, 82–112; Casanova, "Rethinking Secularization," 20–21; Higginbotham, *Righteous Discontent*; Van Doorn, "Forces of Faith."

20 Buell, "Religion on the American Mind," 32.

21 Scott, *Sex and Secularism*, 122–155.

22 Sutton, *Jerry Falwell and the Rise of the Religious Right*, 119–120.

23 See Vogel, *James Baldwin and the 1980s*, 93–111; Williams, *God's Own Party*; Miller, *The Age of Evangelicalism*.

24 Jakobsen and Pellegrini, *Love the Sin*, 123.

25 Taylor, *Secular Age*, 22, 423–437, 473–504, 573.

26 Cady, "Secularism," 874. More extensively, see Asad, *Formations of the Secular*.

27 The most influential formulation of the secularization thesis is Weber, *Protestant Ethic*. On this background, see Cummings, *Mortal Thoughts*, 1–18. For analysis of secularization's privatizing logic, see Taylor, *Secular Age*, xx; Jakobsen and Pellegrini, *Love the Sin*, 144; Casanova, "Secularization Revisited."

28 On the origination of secularization from within the Latin, then Protestant, Church, see Taylor, *Secular Age*, 25–158; Fessenden, *Culture and Redemption*. Asad and Masuzawa deem the Enlightenment invention of the generic or universalized category of "religion" a Western colonial invention; see Asad, *Genealogies of Religion* and *Formations of the Secular* and Masuzawa, *The Invention of World Religions*.

29 Fessenden, *Culture and Redemption*, 4. See also Casanova, "Secularization Revisited." On the centrality of Protestant election to American mythologies of national destiny and character, see Bercovitch's influential *The Puritan Origins of the American Self*. The essays collected in Fessenden, Radel, and Zaborowska's *The Puritan Origins of American Sex* emphasize the plurality, and often perversity, of Puritan sexual views.

30 See, for instance, Casanova, "The Secular, Secularizations, Secularisms" and "Rethinking Secularism"; Scott, *Sex and Secularism*; Levitt, "Other Moderns, Other Jews." On the influence of Protestantism on US secular culture, see Jakobsen and Pellegrini, *Love the Sin*, 103–127; Jakobsen, "Sex + Freedom = Regulation"; Mahmood, "Sexuality and Secularism" and *Politics of Piety*; McGarry, "Crimes of Moral Turpitude."

31 See Jakobsen and Pellegrini, *Love the Sin*, 106–114, and *Secularisms*; Pellegrini, "Sincerely Held"; Mahmood, "Sexuality and Secularism" and *Politics of Piety*, xiii–xv.

32 On the Enlightenment origins of both secularism and comparative religion, see Baird, "Late Secularism," 162–177. As Scott has shown, the French ban on "conspicuous" display of religious symbols is one instance of a Christian evaluation of religion driving ostensibly secular policy (*Politics of the Veil*).

33 Asad, *Formations of the Secular*, 25.

34 Coviello and Hickman, "Introduction," 647. See also Kaufmann, "The Religious, the Secular, and Literary Studies."

35 As I discuss in chapter 5, this view has affinities with Bruno Latour's well-known critique of the modernist settlement or constitution that partitioned the world into discrete categories that are treated as the marks of modernity (*We Have Never Been Modern*).

36 Sinfield, *Faultlines*, 157.

37 Loomba, *Shakespeare, Race, and Colonialism*, 55–63.

38 See Nyquist, *Arbitrary Rule*; Castronovo, "Enslaving Passions."

39 See Jakobsen and Pellegrini, *Love the Sin*, 47–48; Sweet, *Bodies Politic*, 102–144; Townes, *In a Blaze of Glory*, 89–118.

40 Sweet, *Bodies Politic*, 106; my emphasis.

41 Sweet, *Bodies Politic*, 142. On Spanish constructions of race and religion, see Martínez, *Genealogical Fictions*.

42 As Townes reminds us, even as "Christianity became linked with complexion" in the colonies, the British adopted the Spanish terms "*Negro* and *Indian*" in emergent racial taxonomies (*In a Blaze of Glory*, 94).

43 See, for instance, Bartlett, *The Making of Europe*; Lupton, *Citizen Saints*, esp. 103–124, 159–179; Bartels, *Speaking of the Moor*.

44 Hall, *Things of Darkness*, 255.

45 For discussions of the continued repercussions of early modern literary, racial, and colonial ideologies in contemporary culture, see Daileader, *Racism, Misogyny, and the Othello Myth*; Thompson, *Passing Strange*.

46 Erickson and Hall, "'A New Scholarly Song.'"

47 See, for instance, Loomba, *Shakespeare, Race, and Colonialism* and "Identities and Bodies"; Hall, "Reading What Isn't There" and *Things of Darkness*; Hendricks and Parker, *Women, "Race," and Writing*; Little, *Shakespeare Jungle Fever*; Smith, *Race and Rhetoric*; Eliav-Feldon, Isaac, and Ziegler, *The Origins of Racism*; Nocentelli, *Empires of Love*; Feerick, *Strangers in Blood*; Iyengar, *Shades of Difference*. For primary sources on nonwhite European presence and racialized language, see Habib, *Black Lives in the English Archives*; Loomba and Burton, *Race in Early Modern England*.

48 Loomba, *Shakespeare, Race, and Colonialism*; Thompson, *Performing Race and Torture*; Heng, "The Invention of Race" (both I and II).

49 The work is extensive; for summaries of general guiding principles, see Gates, "Introduction"; Appiah, "Racisms"; Todorov, "'Race,' Writing, and Culture"; Goldberg and Solomos, "Introduction"; Delgado and Stefancic, "Introduction."

50 Balibar, "Is There a 'Neo-Racism'?" 22; Balibar's emphasis.

51 Heng, "Invention of Race" (I), 258. As Loomba notes, premodern religious difference was thought to be expressed through somatic coloration, which encouraged suspicion that conversion could no more alter souls than bodies ("Identities and Bodies"). On the limits that embodied racial difference imposed on Protestant conversion, see Britton, *Becoming Christian*.

52 Medovoi, "Dogma-Line Racism," 45.

53 Medovoi, "Dogma-Line Racism," 66.

54 Greene, *Unrequited Conquests*, 148.

55 Medovoi, "Dogma-Line Racism," 52.

56 On the sexual dimensions of racial differentiation, see Loomba, "Identities and Bodies;" and Burton, "Western Encounters with Sex and Bodies."

57 Puar, *Terrorist Assemblages*, 2. See also Norton, *On the Muslim Question*; Mahmood, *Politics of Piety*; Scott, *Sex and Secularism*, 20–29, 156–183; Farris, *In the Name of Women's Rights*.

58 Puar, *Terrorist Assemblages*, 22–23.

59 I draw here on Tim Dean's proposal that, understood in its broad definition, "promiscuity" can name an ethical disposition toward the stranger that is "mediated by a prior relation to one's own internal otherness" (*Unlimited Intimacy*, 177).

60 Foucault, "On the Genealogy of Ethics" and *Use of Pleasure*. See Goldberg's discussion of these views in an early modern Christian framework (*The Seeds of Things*, 63–121).

61 Lupton, "The Religious Turn," 146. For a summary of the religious turn, see Jackson and Marotti, "The Turn to Religion" and *Shakespeare and Religion*. Work that led the way in exploring the affordances of religion and theology in early modern culture includes Shuger, *Habits of Thought* and *Political Theologies in Shakespeare's England*; Targoff, *Common Prayer*; Knapp, *Shakespeare's Tribe*. On the relation between premodern and modern political theology, see Lupton, *Citizen-Saints* and *Thinking with Shakespeare*; Hammill, *The Mosaic Constitution*; Gallagher, *Sodomscapes*. Against the turn to religion as a system of ethics, Victoria Kahn seeks to recover a purely secular conception of politics and literary creation (*The Future of Illusion*).

62 Hammill and Lupton, "Introduction, 1."

63 See, for instance, Cheng, *Radical Love*, 12–13; Boswell, *Christianity, Social Tolerance, and Homosexuality*.

64 Some examples include Rivera, *Poetics of the Flesh*; Althaus-Reid, *Indecent Theology*; Burras and Keller, *Towards a Theology of Eros*; Martin, *Sex and the Single Savior*; Boisvert and Johnson, *Queer Religion*; Burras, *Saving Shame*; Jordan, *Invention of Sodomy* and *Convulsing Bodies*; Loughlin, *Queer Theology*.

65 Buechel, *That We Might Become God*, 13; Buechel's emphasis.

66 Cornwall, *Controversies*, 2; my emphasis. See also Lofton, "Everything Queer?"; Tonstad, "Ambivalent Loves."

67 Hammill and Lupton, "Introduction," 5; Cornwall, *Controversies*, 186.

68 See, for instance, Lewalski, *Protestant Poetics and the Seventeenth-Century Religious Lyric*; Rambuss, *Closet Devotions*; Schwartz, *Sacramental Poetics at the Dawn of Secularism*; Murray, *The Poetics of Conversion*; Johnson, *Made Flesh*; Furey, *Poetic Relations*.

69 Furey, *Poetic Relations*, 10, 13.

70 Greene, *Unrequited Conquests*, 24.

71 Sedgwick, *Between Men*, 28–48; Johnson, "Muteness Envy"; Moten, *In the Break*, 102–122; Muñoz, "The Sense of Watching Tony Sleep."

72 Freeman, *Time Binds*, xvi–xvii. See also Coviello, who argues that close reading brings errant and oblique habitations of sex and selfhood into relief (*Tomorrow's Parties*, 205–206).

73 I take this term from Robbins, *Secular Vocations*, which explores the contradictions of a field founded on the antiprofessional ideals of Matthew Arnold and Ralph Waldo Emerson.

74 Berlant and Edelman, *Sex*, 113, 115.

CHAPTER 1. THE QUEERNESS OF CHRISTIAN FAITH

1 On the dual meanings of "faith" as oath and credit in the religious and juridico-political senses and the mutual obligations it enjoins, see Agamben, *Time that Remains*, 114–116.

2 Badiou, *Saint Paul*, 93.

3 Bersani and Phillips draw an analogy between the impersonal intimacy of barebacking and sacred love; in their resistance to self-protection, both "are implicit critiques of the multiple forms of ego-driven intimacy" (*Intimacies*, 55).

4 Taking at its word Badiou's depiction of faith as a rupture—an event—that founds its subject, Agamben critiques what he sees as Badiou's consequent vision of unified, universal subjectivity (*Time that Remains*, 51–53). However, Badiou's attention to the labor of faith and to the contradictory impulses of sainthood and priesthood, religious event and political history, in Pauline theology, implicitly recognizes the nonidentity of the self (*Saint Paul*, 39–43, 88–95). On Paul's complex relationship to Judaism, see Taubes, *The Political Theology of Paul*; Boyarin, *A Radical Jew*; Lupton, *Thinking with Shakespeare*, 130–146. Menon aligns Badiou's universalism with Edelman's definition of queerness as the refusal of any substantialization of identity in *No Future*. Yet she strives to extract eventuality from history, describing it not as a singular break but as "a theoretical process of reconsideration that asks questions about what counts as identity and its relation to lived experience" (*Indifference to Difference*, 19–20).

5 See my Note on Translations.

6 Agamben, *Time that Remains*, 7.

7 Hammill, *Sexuality and Form*, 76–88; Goldberg, *Seeds of Things*, 10–25.

8 Burras, Jordan, and MacKendrick, *Seducing Augustine*, 103.

9 Burras, Jordan, and MacKendrick, *Seducing Augustine*, 74.

10 Burras, Jordan, and MacKendrick, *Seducing Augustine*, 78.

11 Hollywood, *Sensible Ecstasy*, 10.

12 See Badiou's distinction of Pauline faith from Jewish prophecy, Greek philosophy, and miraculous glorification (*Saint Paul*, 40–54, esp. 52–53).

13 Coakley, for instance, proposes that a Trinitarian theology that directs desire to God can reconcile the patriarchal structure of Pauline theology with a feminist commitment to worldly equality (*God, Sexuality, and the Self*). For a critique of this position as itself reliant on heterosexual difference, see Tonstad, *God and Difference*, 98–132, esp. 105–108.

14 Žižek, *The Puppet and the Dwarf*, 115.

15 The current consensus is that the Letter to the Ephesians, along with about half of the Pauline Epistles, was written by a follower of Paul of Tarsus rather than the

apostle himself. Nonetheless, because the authorial unity of the "Pauline" corpus was undoubted until the eighteenth century, I use the name "Paul" as a shorthand for the long-presumed coherence of writings circulated and published under that signature, focusing on their impact on subsequent Christian thought rather than their authorship.

16 Badiou, *Saint Paul*, 42–47.

17 Augustine, *Enarrationes in Psalmos*, vol. 1, on Psalm 30, sec 2.

18 On the traditional use of these verses to justify male domination through the "Christian paradox of losing to gain," see Dolan, *Marriage and Violence*, 26–66; 39. Stockton situates these verses at the beginning of a genealogy of biblical marriage that poses the same threat from within religion that the Christian right has usually located in the godless sphere beyond it: a breakdown of "traditional marriage" as a transhistorical, universal ideal (*Members of His Body*).

19 Mills, "Ecce Homo," 162; Mills's emphasis.

20 As Stockton notes, if human marriage is the individual's path to incorporation in the church, heterosexual coupling figuratively gives way to a polygamous membership in the communal flesh of Christ, a "union of the multitude that subsumes and exceeds that of mere same-sex coupling" (*Members of His Body*, 10). Dunning traces the contradictions and inconsistencies of sexual difference in the writings of Paul and his followers (*Specters of Paul*).

21 As Loughlin argues, "one of the queerest things about the Christian church" is that "it celebrates in its symbols what it denies to its members": same-sex union, as imagined not only in the Old Testament representations of Israel as the Bride of Christ (Ezekiel 16:4–9; Song of Songs) and Ruth's commitment to Naomi (Ruth 1:14), but also in the New Testament figure of John (who, Rambuss reminds us, occupied the role of Christ's beloved spouse in the popular Christian imagination at least through the middle of the seventeenth century); see Loughlin, "Introduction: The End of Sex," 2; Rambuss, "Straightest Story." Lochrie argues that biblical imaginations of Christian union render inadequate modern definitions of homoeroticism insofar as they destabilize categories of sex, gender, and sexuality ("Mystical Acts, Queer Tendencies"). Boswell argues that official Catholic homophobia is incongruent with the scarcity of prohibitions of same-sex activity in the New Testament—there is only one: Romans 1:18–32 (*Christianity, Social Tolerance, and Homosexuality*). For the disruptive gendered and sexual dynamics of biblical figurations, see Meeks, "The Image of the Androgyne." On the homoeroticism of Israel as Christ's bride, see Eilberg-Schwartz, *God's Phallus*; Boyarin, *Carnal Israel*.

22 Rambuss, *Closet Devotions*, 50.

23 Rambuss, *Closet Devotions*, 59–60.

24 Dollimore rejects Augustine's conviction that "original sin is really original perversion" to which all human creatures are susceptible on the grounds that it promotes not just internal vigilance but also constant watch against external threats posed by the presence of "*the pervert as the modern incarnation of evil*"

(*Sexual Dissidence*, 147, 143; Dollimore's emphasis). See also Ranke-Heinemann, *Eunuchs for the Kingdom of God*, 75–76; Sorabji, *Emotion and Peace of Mind*, 372–384, 400–417.

25 See Miles, *Desire and Delight*; Hunter, "Augustinian Pessimism?"; Lamberigts, "A Critical Evaluation."

26 Burras, Jordan, and MacKendrick, *Seducing Augustine*, 66–67.

27 All English quotations are from Augustine's *Confessions*, trans. Chadwick, and all Latin quotations are from Augustine's *Confessions*, trans. Hammond; both hereafter cited parenthetically in the text.

28 Harpham, *The Ascetic Imperative*, 61, 43.

29 Brown, *The Body and Society*, 47.

30 See Brown, *The Body and Society*, 65–82, 160–177, 349–386.

31 Brown, *The Body and Society*, xliv, lx.

32 See Foucault, "The Concern for Truth," esp. 261–262.

33 For this view, see Hammill, *Sexuality and Form*, 10–13; Freinkel, *Reading Shakespeare's Will*, 3–45.

34 Unless otherwise noted, English quotations are from *City of God*, trans. Bettenson, and Latin quotations are from *City of God*, trans. Levine; both hereafter cited parenthetically in the text as *CG*.

35 In *City of God*, Augustine repeatedly returns to the figure of synecdoche, noting its use in the statement that the Word became flesh (14.2) and later reaffirming that "*anima* (the soul) and *carne* (the flesh) are parts of a man, and can stand for man in his entirety" (14.4).

36 Luther, "Preface to the Epistle of St. Paul to the Romans" [1522], in *Martin Luther*, trans. Dillenberger, 25; Luther, *Vorrede zum Römerbrief*, 9; hereafter cited parenthetically in the text.

37 Cavadini, "Feeling Right," 200. As James Grantham Turner puts it, living by the flesh is a mode of being that is self-centered rather than God-centered (*One Flesh*, 42).

38 Burras, Jordan, and MacKendrick, *Seducing Augustine*, 16.

39 Badiou, *Saint Paul*, 84.

40 The quotation is from Cicero's *Tuscan Disputations* 3.6.12. On Augustine's rejection of Stoicism, see Cavadini, "Feeling Right"; Bouwsma, "The Two Faces of Humanism."

41 On the recursivity of Augustinian conversion, see Brown, *Augustine of Hippo*, 171; Burras, Jordan, MacKendrick, *Seducing Augustine*, 62–65. Scholars have debated when the real conversion described took place: CE 386, 396, or 410; for a summary of this scholarship, see Burras, Jordan, MacKendrick, *Seducing Augustine*, 9. On Augustine's retrospective imitation of Paul as a claim to theological authority, see Fredriksen, who sees Augustine's appropriation as a "mythic feed-back system" that interprets Paul's conversion through his own and his own through Paul's ("Paul and Augustine," 20–33).

42 Fredriksen argues that while scholars have shown the inaccuracy of the narrative in the Acts, they nonetheless accept Luke's account of a decisive moment of con-

version, one that contrasts with the ongoing struggle alluded to in Paul's letters ("Paul and Augustine," 6–20).

43 Burras, Jordan, MacKendrick, *Seducing Augustine*, 1.

44 Brown, *Augustine of Hippo*, 169.

45 As John Freccero argues, the idolatry and unrequitedness of Petrarchan love lyrics were traditional poses of a long line of poets from the troubadours through Dante; Petrarch's innovation was his conspicuous construction of himself as famous poet through epideictic verse ("The Fig Tree and the Laurel").

46 The narcissism of the Petrarchan tradition more generally is the focus of Braden's *Petrarchan Love*. Scholars who argue that Petrarch conspicuously undercuts himself include Mazzotta, *The Worlds of Petrarch*, esp. 58–79; Dubrow, *Echoes of Desire*.

47 Braden, *Petrarchan Love*, xi. As scholars have noted, "Petrarchism" is itself hardly a single thing. From its earliest reception, the *Rerum vulgarium fragmenta* furnished a multitude of Petrarchs from the penitent cleric to the humanist man of letters to the Neoplatonic Christian to the aggressive misogynist. Out of the many commentaries and imitations, Kennedy writes, "emerges a Petrarch who could be anything and everything to all readers" (*The Site of Petrarchism*, 3). On the circulation and initial reception of Petrarch, see Braden, *Petrarchan Love*, 61–128; Dubrow, *Echoes of Desire*; Greene, *Unrequited Conquests*; Warley, *Sonnet Sequences and Social Distinction*.

48 On Petrarch's admiration for Augustine, see Foster, "Beatrice or Medusa"; Sturm-Maddox, *Petrarch's Metamorphoses*, 95–126, and *Petrarch's Laurels*, 231–276; Quillen, *Reading the Renaissance*; Freinkel, *Reading Shakespeare's Will*, 47–113.

49 Scholars who read Petrarch theologically tend to assume that by the end of the *RVF* his repentance is complete and final. See Roche, *Petrarch and the English Sonnet Sequences*; Greene, *Light in Troy*, esp. 125, 129.

50 Freccero, "The Fig Tree and the Laurel," 34.

51 Halberstam, *Queer Art of Failure*.

52 Dinshaw, *Getting Medieval*, 13; Freccero, "Tangents (of Desire)," 95, 99.

53 See especially Vickers, "Diana Described." Braden goes so far as to state that "[t]he final myth is that of Acteon," erasing the three myths that follow (*Petrarchan Love*, 41).

54 Vickers, "Diana Described," 275. The commonplace that poetry compensates for sexual frustration informs feminist accounts of Petrarch's narcissism. See also Enterline, *Rhetoric of the Body*, 97; Marshall, *The Shattering of the Self*, 67; Kerrigan and Braden, *The Idea of the Renaissance*, 161, 172.

55 Marshall, *The Shattering of the Self*, 56; my emphasis.

56 Bersani, "Is the Rectum a Grave?," 217.

57 Several scholars argue that by the end of the *RVF* Petrarch trades his love for the dead virgin Laura for prayers to *the* Virgin as intercessor; see Chiampi, "Petrarch's Augustinian Excess"; Roche, *Petrarch and the English Sonnet Sequences*; Greene, *Light in Troy*; Foster, *Petrarch: Poet and Humanist*, esp. 73–81. Zak argues that

Petrarch adopts the ancient Stoic principle of "care of the self" and heals his fractured loyalties through "writing as a spiritual technique" (*Petrarch's Humanism*, 10). Strier, though generally at pains to show that Petrarch defends the value of bodily passions, nonetheless describes Petrarch as committed to "Platonized Christianity" and seeking to share with Laura the trust of an old married couple, "his have having been freed from lust by the normal processes of nature" (*Unrepentant Renaissance*, 60–75). Peterson insists on the sequence's underlying coherence (*Petrarch's Fragmenta*).

58 Chiampi, "Petrarch's Augustinian Excess," 17.

59 Langer, "Petrarch's Singular Love Lyric," 66.

60 Goldberg, *Seeds of Things*, 8.

61 As in the French *révolte*, which had acquired this meaning by the late sixteenth century.

62 In this way, the *rivolte* of RVF 118 are part of what Martinez describes as "the wide semantic field comprised by terms like *versare, tornare, rinversare, volgere, voltarre, vivolgere, convertire*—in expressions meaning turn to, turn away, turn back, turn over, turn the page, turn fortune's wheel, but also pour forth words and tears . . . in other words, versify" ("Mourning Laura," 22). Zak sees this dilemma as one of both humanist and religious aspiration, with Petrarch's turns to humanism and Stoicism only exacerbating the self-division they should heal (*Petrarch's Humanism*).

63 Petrarch, *Secretum*, 181, 247; all references are to *Francesco Petrarca: My Secret Book*, trans. Mann. For a different perspective, see Kahn, "The Defense of Poetry in the *Secretum*," 107–108.

64 Thanks to David Wallace for pointing out this pun to me.

65 Just how much of a shift there is between the two parts is up for debate. Numerous critics see RVF 264, the first poem of the *in morte* part, as a real turning point that precedes Laura's death and thereby makes conversion a genuine choice (Hainsworth, "*Rerum vulgarium fragmenta*," 48; Roche, *Petrarch and the English Sonnet Sequences*; Marcozzi, "Making the *Rerum vulgarium fragmenta*," 58; Martinez, "Mourning Laura,"). Wilkins reads RVF 264 as a document of "profound moral conflict" (*The Making of the "Canzoniere,"* 191). Whereas in Wilkins's view the "morality" in question leads to a clear choice of Christianity, I argue that Petrarch more profoundly shows us the contradictions inherent in an Augustinian ideal of faith.

66 As Durling notes, the liturgical celebration of Good Friday did not fall on April 6 in 1327, but Petrarch likely did not expect his readers to notice the discrepancy between historical and liturgical calendars (Introduction to *Petrarch's Lyric Poems*, 7).

67 Vickers, "Diana Described," 275.

68 Petrarch, *Secretum*, 173, 171. Until the end of the sequence, Petrarch repeatedly recalls April 6, which was the date of both his first sight of Laura and that of her death: "One thousand three hundred twenty-seven, exactly at the first hour of the

sixth day of April, I entered the labyrinth" (*RVF* 211.12–14); "at the time which I
first saw her / . . . / It was the April of the year and of my years" (*RVF* 325.11,13);
"'you know that in 1348, on the sixth day of April, at the first hour, that blessed
soul left the body'" (*RVF* 336.12–14).

69 Langer, "Petrarch's Singular Love Lyric," 62–73, 63–64. Mazzotta argues that the
   memory of this life-changing instant also allows Petrarch to imagine the possibility of another new beginning in which everything will change again ("Petrarch's
   Confrontation with Modernity," 234).

70 On Petrarch's revisions of the *RVF*, see Wilkins, *The Making of the "Canzoniere,"*
   150–152, 190–193; Foster, *Petrarch*; Marcozzi, "Making the *Rerum vulgarium*
   fragmenta," 51–62; Hainsworth, "*Rerum vulgarium fragmenta*," 39–40. In contrast
   to more positive views of the poems' dating and order, Hainsworth remarks that
   "beyond registering the crucial event of falling in love, we are quite uncertain how
   to put the poems in any kind of temporal relation to each other" (42).

71 The room the poem leaves for error is at odds with its specificity. There is no
   mention of specific time until poem 30, when we learn that "if I do not err, today
   it is seven years that I go sighing" (*RVF* 30.28–29). The next anniversary poem,
   number 50, is even more approximate, anticipating that it is "very near to the
   tenth year" (50.55); the poem marking the eleventh year is precise and certain:
   "Now turns, my Lord, the eleventh year" (*RVF* 62.9). The fourteenth anniversary
   is celebrated twice, with Petrarch noting "this fourteenth year of sighs" (*RVF* 79.2)
   and, twenty-two poems later, the "seven and seven years" that "desire and reason
   have battled" (*RVF* 101.12–13). Then, in relatively quick succession, Petrarch commemorates the "fifteenth year" (*RVF* 107.7), the "sixteenth year" (*RVF* 118.1), and
   the "seventeen years" (*RVF* 122.1) that have passed. The twentieth anniversary is
   celebrated twice about one hundred poems later (*RVF* 212.12, 221.8). But forty-five
   poems after that he declares that it has been "eighteen years" (*RVF* 266.13), only
   to swing in the very next poem to the news of Laura's death, which occurs on the
   twenty-first anniversary of his first sighting (*RVF* 271.2). The *in morte* poems are
   less attentive to and specific about time; *RVF* 278 notes that it has been "three
   years ago today" (*RVF* 278.14) since Laura's death, and *RVF* 364 marks the end of
   their love as occurring "ten years" after Laura's death.

72 On deixis and on Augustine's views of temporality, see Dinshaw, *How Soon Is
   Now?*, 1–7, 14–16).

73 Mazzotta, reading the *RVF* as a public confession, sees this attention to moral
   ambiguity as a signal of authenticity ("Petrarch's Confrontation with Modernity,"
   228).

74 Strier, *The Unrepentant Renaissance*, 29.

75 Burras, *Saving Shame*, 2, 3.

76 Burras, *Saving Shame*, 2.

77 Agamben, *Time that Remains*, 64–68, 100. On messianic time as a counter to a
   secular temporality assumed to be linear and punctual, see Benjamin, "Theses."

78 A lustrum is a period of five years.

79 As with *RVF* 142, it is hard to fix the exact year of *RVF* 204: the anniversary poems on either side mark the fifteenth (*RVF* 145) and twentieth anniversaries (*RVF* 212), but also disrupt a strict chronology insofar as *RVF* 122 commemorates year seventeen and *RVF* 266 takes us back to year eighteen.

80 Again for *RVF* 264 dating is imprecise even within the fiction: it falls somewhere between the eighteenth anniversary commemorated in *RVF* 266 and Laura's death on the twenty-first anniversary, explicitly marked in *RVF* 271.

81 Sturm-Maddox sees *RVF* 264 as setting the alternatives of Laura and God in newly "lucid opposition" (*Petrarch's Laurels*, 174). While its structural place as the first of the *in morte* series supports this view, there is nothing in the content of *RVF* 264 to distinguish this conversion from previous ones. Braden understands *RVF* 264, in which Petrarch confesses that "I see the better but lay hold of the worse," as a "chilling" assent to "his own damnation" (*Petrarchan Love*, 58).

82 On the sequence's articulation through repetitive words and themes in 1, 264, and 366, see Martinez, "Mourning Laura," 34.

83 Chiampi, "Petrarch's Augustinian Excess," 10.

84 According to the fiction of the sequence, *RVF* 364 is set on April 6, 1358. Petrarch sent an autograph copy of the *RVF* to his friend Pandolfo Maletesta on January 4, 1374 but continued to add to, revise, and rearrange it until just before his death six months later, on July 20, 1374. Wilkins argues (in *The Making of the "Canzoniere"*) that from early on the sequence was divided into two parts, each prefaced with a recantatory poem (poems 1, 264); Foster critiques this view and summarizes Rico's argument for a different timeline for the creation of the final structure (see *Petrarch*, 93–105).

85 Petrarch, *Secretum*, 257.

86 Chiampi rightly maintains that "this, then, is our opening to what we might call Petrarchan irony: if distraction is an essential predicate of attention, then even the later adhesive poems of Petrarch would have a necessary, indeed constitutive, loosening within them that precludes their ever attaching themselves to an object faithfully and prayerfully" ("Petrarch's Augustinian Excess," 17).

87 Feminist critics have emphasized the aggression of Petrarchan love. Vickers argues that the "legacy of fragmentation" encapsulated in the Petrarchan blazon denies the fetishized female body the capacity of speech or writing ("Diana Described," 277). Johnson shows how the Petrarchan pose of victimization legitimates male violence as self-defense ("Muteness Envy"). See also Sturm-Maddox, *Petrarch's Metamorphoses*, 31, 98–99; Estrin, *Laura*, 41–92; Enterline, *The Rhetoric of the Body*, 91–124. For more optimistic readings of the gender dynamics of Petrarchan poetry, see Dubrow, who argues for the fluidity of Petrarchan gender (*Echoes of Desire*, 254) and Marshall, who sees Petrarchan sadomasochism as a challenge to gender fixity (*The Shattering of the Self*, 79–82).

88 Freccero, *Queer/Early/Modern*, 22. See also Durling: "Petrarch = Echo means Laura = Narcissus; if Laura's image = Narcissus' image, Petrarch = Narcissus" (in Petrarch, *Petrarch's Lyric Poems*, 31–32).

89 On the fifteenth- and sixteenth-century formation of an idea of Laura's historical reality, see Cox, "Sixteenth-Century Women Petrarchists," 585–586.

90 Warner, "Tongues Untied," 224, 231.

CHAPTER 2. THE COLOR OF MONOGAMY

1 All references to the sonnets are to *Shakespeare's Sonnets*, ed. Booth; hereafter cited parenthetically in the text.

2 Sedgwick, *Between Men*.

3 Eng, *The Feeling of Kinship*, 12.

4 Examples include Muñoz, *Disidentifications*; Ferguson, *Aberrations in Black*; Eng, Halberstam, and Muñoz, "What's Queer about Queer Theory Now?"; Musser, *Sensational Flesh*.

5 Schweitzer, *Perfecting Friendship*, 53–64. Nyquist has traced the early modern afterlife of Aristotle's conception of liberty in relation to the practice of chattel slavery, which derives from the opposition between "those for whom [political slavery] would represent a demeaning, traumatic loss and those for whom it was supposed to be natural" (*Arbitrary Rule*, 26).

6 Hall, "'These Bastard Signs of Fair.'"

7 On the sixteenth-century semantic shift of "fair" from a synonym for beauty to a description of a light complexion, see Hall, *Things of Darkness*, 1–24.

8 Gil, *Before Intimacy*, 103–135.

9 Foucault, "Friendship as a Way of Life."

10 In the United States in particular, as Cheryl Harris has influentially argued, the legacy of slavery made the rights to intimacy and privacy white properties—rights of exclusion—to be desired and fought for ("Whiteness as Property"). Because only monogamous coupledom is deemed respectable, it is the only relation whose legal status has been granted by courts (in *Loving v. Virginia, Lawrence v. Texas, Obergefell v. Hobbes*). As a result, the "bourgeois intimacy" that monogamy represents is inseparable from racialized hierarchy and privilege (Eng, *Feeling of Kinship*, 48). For critiques of what I am calling the "whiteness of monogamy," see Bergner, *Taboo Subjects*, xiii–xxxii; Ferguson, "Of Our Normative Strivings"; Nyong'o, *The Amalgamation Waltz*, 69–102.

11 Puar, *Terrorist Assemblages*, 1–78.

12 Holland, *The Erotic Life of Racism*, 28.

13 On the varied and brutal suppression of Indigenous American and African forms of kinship, see Goldberg, *Sodometries*, 179–222; Rifkin, *When Did Indians Become Straight?*; Franke, *Wedlocked*.

14 Phillips, *Monogamy*, 10.

15 Bromley and Stockton, "Introduction."

16 Masten, *Queer Philologies*, 77.

17 *OED*, s.v. "monogamy."

18 Derived most immediately from the Middle French *monogamie/monogamie* (first used in the fifteenth century but rare until the late eighteenth), "monogamy" and

"monogamous" come from the Latin "*monogamia/monogamus*" and the Greek
μονογαμία/μονογαμία, both terms for marrying only once in a lifetime (*OED*).

19 Katz, *The Invention of Heterosexuality*.

20 Taverner, *Common Places of Scripture*, ccxii–v.

21 I. B., *Brief and Faythfull Declaracion*, 257.

22 Fulke, *D. Heskins, D. Sanders, and M. Rastel*, n.p.

23 Moryson, *An itinerary*.

24 See, for example, Cohen, "On Saracen Enjoyment"; Traub, "The Psychomorphol-
ogy of the Clitoris," 87–89; di Gangi, *Sexual Types*, 60–87; Loomba and Burton,
Race in Early Modern England, 17–20; Loomba, "Identities and Bodies in Early
Modern Studies."

25 Nocentelli, *Empires of Love*, 94.

26 Puar, *Terrorist Assemblages*, 25.

27 On the imperial underpinnings of universalist LGBTQ rights discourse, see also
Rastegar, "Emotional Attachments and Secular Imaginings."

28 Aristotle, *Politics*, 1.5.

29 For a detailed account of the uneven reimagination of marriage as the height of
friendship, see Luxon, *Single Imperfection*.

30 Bromley, *Intimacy and Sexuality*, 9–13, 27.

31 Miller Gaubert et al., "Supporting Healthy Marriage," 121.

32 Shannon, *Sovereign Amity*, 55–56. For discussions of the centrality of same-sex
friendship to early modern culture, see Smith, *Homosexual Desire in Shakespeare's
England*, 31–77; Goldberg, *Sodometries*, 63–101; Bray, *The Friend*; Traub, *The Renaissance of Lesbianism*, 276–325, and *Thinking Sex with the Early Moderns*, 37–56;
Masten, *Queer Philologies*, 69–105; Garrison, *Friendship and Queer Theory*.

33 Shannon, *Sovereign Amity*, 21.

34 Traub details the gendered exclusion of classical and Renaissance friendship
(*The Renaissance of Lesbianism*, 18–20); Bray argues that even its most seemingly
private expressions of friendship—the letter, the kiss, the shared bed—are inseparable from economic and social aspiration (*The Friend*, esp. 140–176).

35 Puar, *Terrorist Assemblages*, 24.

36 Puar, *Terrorist Assemblages*, 24.

37 Holland, *The Erotic Life of Racism*, 27.

38 Holland, *The Erotic Life of Racism*, 43.

39 Holland, *The Erotic Life of Racism*, 41. Holland here quotes Appiah, "Racisms," 11,
and Levinas, "Meaning and Sense," in *Basic Philosophical Writings*, 52.

40 Holland, *The Erotic Life of Racism*, 42.

41 Greene, *Unrequited Conquests*, 153.

42 Aristotle, *Nichomachean Ethics*, 8.3.6; hereafter cited parenthetically in the text as
NE.

43 On women's natural inequality, see *NE* 8.7.1, 8.12.7, and *Politics* 1.13, which groups
women with children and slaves; see also Cicero, *On Friendship*, in *On Old Age.
On Friendship. On Divination*, 13.46.

44 On the dyadic nature of friendship, see *NE* 9.11.4, where Aristotle deems multiple close friendships as impossible and undesirable as multiple passionate erotic relations.

45 Schweitzer, *Perfecting Friendship*, 39–40.

46 Cicero, *On Friendship*, 21.81, in *On Old Age. On Friendship. On Divination*; all citations to Cicero will be from this edition; hereafter cited parenthetically in the text.

47 Derrida, *Politics of Friendship*, 249.

48 Montaigne, "De l'amitie," *Complete Essays* 211–212, *Essais* 108–109; my emphasis; hereafter cited parenthetically in the text as *Essays*.

49 Derrida, *Politics of Friendship*, 16.

50 Agamben, *Time that Remains*, 128.

51 See Derrida, *Politics of Friendship*, 75–106, 286–288.

52 For this parallel development, see *OED*, s.v. "friend" and "fiend."

53 Derrida, *Politics of Friendship*; Derrida's emphasis.

54 Dean, *Unlimited Intimacy*, 210.

55 Guy-Bray, "Remembering to Forget," 46. For discussions of the young man's infidelities, see Schoenfeldt, "The Sonnets"; Traub, *Thinking Sex with the Early Moderns*, 255.

56 Nirenberg, "Was There Race before Modernity?," 234.

57 On the white slave trade, see Baum, *The Rise and Fall of the Caucasian Race*, 24–57; on the racialization of slavery, see Loomba and Burton, *Race in Early Modern England*, 12–14.

58 John M. Archer, "Right, Duty, and Domination," Modern Language Association Meeting, 2017. Cited, with gratitude, by Archer's permission.

59 See Hall, *Things of Darkness*, 16–22, 226–230. As Habib has shown, the majority of nonwhite persons residing in England were servants, at least some of whom had the legal status of potential chattel for sale (*Black Lives in the English Archives*). See also archival studies by Weissbourd, "'Those in Their Possession'"; Kaufmann, *Black Tudors*.

60 See Derrida, "'Eating Well'"; de Certeau, *Heterologies*, 67–79; Freccero, "Cannibalism, Homophobia, Women."

61 Barthes, *A Lover's Discourse*, 39–40; Barthes's emphasis.

62 Barthes, *A Lover's Discourse*, 40; Barthes's emphasis.

63 Phillips, *On Flirtation*, 55.

64 See especially Schwarz, *What You Will*: "For the early modern period . . . will exemplified the doubled and divided nature of agency: it functions both as a useful tool and as an independent, potentially renegade force" (2). Exploiting this indeterminacy, Shakespeare's attention to the complicity of female will in patriarchal structures of desire undermines any account of power as unidirectional and static (129–153).

65 Freinkel, *Reading Shakespeare's Will*, 224–236. See also Fineman, *Shakespeare's Perjured Eye*, 26, 294–296.

66 On differences between classical friendship and Christian fellowship, see Schweitzer, *Perfecting Friendship*, 43–53.

67 Pellegrini, "Sincerely Held," esp. 74–76, 82.

68 Freinkel, *Reading Shakespeare's Will*, 134.

69 Luther, "Preface to the Epistle of St. Paul to the Romans" [1522], in *Martin Luther*, trans. Dillenberger, 19; Luther, *Vorrede zum Römerbrief*, ed. Krumwiede, 3; hereafter cited parenthetically in the text as "Preface"; pages refer to the English and German editions, respectively.

70 Calvin, *Institutes*, 2.8.39; hereafter cited parenthetically in the text. Latin terms are from *Christianae religionis institutio*.

71 Luther, *Freedom of a Christian*, in *Martin Luther*, trans. Dillenberger, 57.

72 Strier offers a more optimistic reading of Luther and Calvin, claiming that their challenges to Catholic ascetic idealism constitute "powerful defenses of the validity and even the desirability of ordinary hum emotions and passions" (*Unrepentant Renaissance*, 42).

73 Lacan, *Seminar, Book VII*; French references are to *Le Séminaire, livre VII*; page citations hereafter refer to English and French editions, respectively, when both languages are provided.

74 Lacan, *Seminar, Book VII*, 83/101.

75 Lacan, *Seminar, Book VII*, 73/89.

76 Lacan, *Seminar, Book VII*, 81.

77 Lacan, *Seminar, Book VII*, 82.

78 Bersani, "Is the Rectum a Grave?," 215; Bersani's emphasis.

79 Lacan, *Seminar, Book VII*, 170–171/201.

80 Lacan, *Seminar, Book VII*, 187/220.

81 See also Galatians 5:14: "For all the Law is fulfilled in one word, which is this, Thou shalt love thy neighbor as thyself" (GB).

82 Freud, *Civilization and Its Discontents*, 108–109; Freud, *Das Unbehagen in der Kultur*, 268; hereafter pages refer to the English and German editions, respectively, when both languages are provided.

83 Freud, *Civilization and Its Discontents*, 67/239.

84 Freud, *Civilization and Its Discontents*, 67.

85 Freud, *Civilization and Its Discontents*, 109.

86 Althusser, "Ideology," 114.

87 For this tradition, see Wind, *Pagan Mysteries*; Newman, "Love's Arrows"; and Orvis, "Eros and Anteros."

88 Luther, *Freedom of a Christian*, in Martin Luther, trans. Dillenberger, 53.

89 Freud, *Civilization and Its Discontents*, 72–73/243.

90 Derrida, *Politics of Friendship*, 89.

91 Liddell, Scott, and Jones, *Greek-English Lexicon*. Thanks to Gordon Teskey for bringing this term and its meaning to my attention.

92 On the marginalization of Spanish literature as an enduring legacy of propaganda that rendered "Spain biologically (if not visibly) black," see Fuchs, *Exotic*

Nation, 115–138; Martínez, *Genealogical Fictions*, 25–60. On depictions of the Irish as black, see Little, *Shakespeare Jungle Fever*, 122–123; Iyengar, *Shades of Difference*, 86–91. On associations of Indigenous Americans with blackness and sexual pathology, see Goldberg, *Sodometries*, 179–222.

93 Cohen quotes Abelard's comment that "the flesh of a black woman is all the softer to touch though it is less attractive to look at" ("Saracen Enjoyment," 137, n. 11). Iyengar quotes Gerald of Wales' observation that "these Irish people are both of an hotter and moister nature than other nations, we may well conjecture. And this we gather by their wonderfull soft skinne" and notes that early modern writers also associate soft skin with "blake More[s]" and "Negro[s]" (*Shades of Difference*, 92). Kaufmann traces the history of Anne Cobbie, the only African prostitute in sixteenth-century London of whom we have extensive documentary evidence, who was known for her soft skin (*Black Tudors*, 219–242).

94 McEachern, "Hot Protestant Shakespeare," 278.

95 Fineman, *Shakespeare's Perjured Eye*, 18.

96 Dubrow, *Echoes of Desire*, 127. See also de Grazia, "The Scandal of Shakespeare's Sonnets"; Nelles, "Sexing Shakespeare's Sonnets."

97 Traub, *Thinking Sex with the Early Moderns*, 243.

98 Fineman acknowledges that "many features . . . of the dark lady sonnets are operatively present in the young man sonnets as well" (*Shakespeare's Perjured Eye*, 87).

99 Schwarz, *What You Will*, 132.

100 Stockton, *Members of His Body*, 1–14, 25–33.

101 Diehl, "'Infinite Space.'"

102 See the notes to Sonnet 137 in editions by Booth, Kerrigan, and Vendler, 539–42, 563–564.

103 Crewe observes that our approach to these poems might change considerably if "instead of always genteely speaking of Shakespeare's Dark Lady sonnets, we could bring ourselves to call them the Black Woman sonnets," adding in a footnote that taken seriously as depicting what in the nineteenth century would be called "miscegenation," these sonnets "constitute a singularly radical attempt to conceive of the 'other'" (*Trials of Authorship*, 120, 183, n. 4). See also Habib, *Shakespeare and Race*, 21–25. On the race of the mistress, see de Grazia, "The Scandal of Shakespeare's Sonnets"; Hunt, "Be Dark but Not Too Dark." On the term "lady" as an explicit signifier of race as well as class and sexuality—a designation denied to black women as well as white female prostitutes and workers—see Higginbotham, "African-American Women's History," 254, 261–262.

104 Fineman, *Shakespeare's Perjured Eye*, 56, 132; Kerrigan, *The Sonnets*, 59, 61.

105 On the denial of the mistress's promiscuity, see Bell, "Rethinking Shakespeare's Dark Lady," 293–313; Callaghan, *Shakespeare's Sonnets*, 146. For the more general critical attribution of attacks on female promiscuity to male anxieties about dynastic legitimacy, homosocial order, and racial miscegenation, see Gowing, *Domestic Dangers*; Breitenberg, *Anxious Masculinity*.

106 Goldberg, "*Romeo and Juliet*'s Open Rs," 225. See also Halpern's argument that the mistress embodies a "proto-Sadean sublimity . . . that is sodomitical through and through" (*Shakespeare's Perfume*, 31).

107 Traub, "The Sonnets," 288.

108 Traub, *Thinking Sex with the Early Moderns*, 242.

109 Goldberg, *Desiring Women Writing*, 12, 5.

110 Brody, *Impossible Purities*, 43.

111 Dean, *Unlimited Intimacy*, 4.

112 English, Hollibaugh, and Rubin, "Talking Sex," 41.

113 Sanchez, "'Use Me But as Your Spaniel.'"

114 For an essay on the sonnets in which I come to fairly different conclusions, see Sanchez, "The Poetics of Feminine Subjectivity."

115 Muñoz, *Disidentifications*; Ferguson, *Aberrations in Black*, 1–29; Holland, *The Erotic Life of Racism*, 65–93.

116 Anzaldúa, *Borderlands/La Frontera*, esp. 15–23, 77–91.

117 Anzaldúa, *Borderlands/La Frontera*, 79.

118 Anzaldúa describes herself as "queer" in *Borderlands/La Frontera*, 72.

119 Nash, *The Black Body in Ecstasy*, 2.

120 Nash, *The Black Body in Ecstasy*, 3.

121 Musser, *Sensational Flesh*, 22, 26.

122 Miller-Young retheorizes the "illicit eroticism" of black female pornographic actors (*Taste for Brown Sugar*). Fleetwood and Cruz conceptualize BDSM as a mode of accessing and restructuring racialized power; see Fleetwood, "The Case of Rihanna"; Cruz, *The Color of Kink*.

123 Spillers, "Interstices," 83.

124 See Higginbotham, "African-American Women's History"; Hammonds, "Black (W)holes" and "Toward a Genealogy of Black Female Sexuality"; Hine, "Rape and the Inner Lives of Black Women."

125 Booth, *Sonnets*, 491, n. 1–2.

126 Luke 6:31: "And as ye would that men should do to you, so do ye to them likewise" (GB); Matt. 7:12: "Therefore whatsoever ye would that men should do to you, even so do ye to them, for this is the Law and the Prophets" (GB).

127 Freeman, *The Wedding Complex*, xv.

128 Sedgwick, *Between Men*, 31–33.

129 Schwarz, *What You Will*, 152.

CHAPTER 3. THE SHAME OF CONJUGAL SEX

1 Rubin, "Thinking Sex," 278. On the discrimination against sexual and racial minorities following from the legal and economic benefits of marriage, see, for instance, Duggan, "The New Homonormativity" and *Twilight of Equality*, esp. 43–66; Roberts, *Killing the Black Body*, 3–55, 294–312; Cohen, "Punks, Bulldaggers, and Welfare Queens."

2 Warner, *The Trouble with Normal*, 50.

3 For this analysis, see Spivak, *Outside in the Teaching Machine*, 45; Brown, "Suffering the Paradox of Rights."

4 See Franke, *Wedlocked*.

5 This is Rubin's phrase ("Thinking Sex," 281). On the marginalization and pathologization of single persons, see Cobb, *Single*.

6 Luther, *Sermon on the Estate of Marriage*, in *Basic Theological Writings*, ed. Lull, 414; hereafter cited parenthetically in the text as *Sermon*.

7 Warner, *The Trouble with Normal*, 2.

8 Warner, *The Trouble with Normal*, 35–36, Warner's emphasis.

9 Bersani, "Is the Rectum a Grave?," 215; Bersani's emphasis.

10 *Lawrence et. al. v. Texas*, 539 US 558 (2003) at 558; my emphasis.

11 *Obergefell v. Hodges* 135 S. Ct. 2584 (2015) at 2; hereafter cited parenthetically in the text as *Obergefell*.

12 Jakobsen, "Sex + Freedom = Regulation."

13 Edelman, *No Future*, esp. 1–32.

14 Similarly, the 2016 Republican National Committee platform proclaimed: "Traditional marriage and family . . . is [sic] the foundation for a free society and has for millennia been entrusted with rearing children and instilling cultural values" and "Strong families, depending upon God and one another, advance the cause of liberty by lessening the need for government in their daily lives. . . . Marriage remains the greatest antidote to child poverty. . . . Nearly three-quarters of the $450 billion government annually spends on welfare goes to single-parent households" (https://prod-cdn-static.gop.com).

15 Roberts, *Killing the Black Body*; Cohen, "Punks."

16 Warner, *The Trouble with Normal*, 82, 89.

17 Freeman, *Wedding Complex*, esp. 101–177; Jakobsen, "Sex + Freedom = Regulation."

18 Ruskola, "Gay Rights versus Queer Theory," 241.

19 Ruskola, "Gay Rights versus Queer Theory," 243.

20 Ruskola, "Gay Rights versus Queer Theory," 239.

21 Duggan, "The New Homonormativity," 179.

22 Franke, *Wedlocked*, 206.

23 Puar, *Terrorist Assemblages*.

24 Cummings, *Book of Common Prayer*, 434–435; my emphasis.

25 *Book of Common Prayer*, 1928, n.p.; my emphasis.

26 *Book of Common Prayer*, 1979, 423.

27 *Book of Common Prayer*, 1979, 423.

28 Rambuss, "Straightest Story," 545, 548.

29 On this point, see Boswell, *Same-Sex Unions*, 108–161; Martin, "Familiar Idolatry," in *Sex and the Single Savior*; and Loughlin, "Introduction: The End of Sex."

30 See my Note on Translations.

31 Agamben, *Time that Remains*, 69.

32 Edelman, *No Future*, 31.

33 Calvin, *Institutes*, 4.12.24; hereafter cited parenthetically in the text.

34 Discussions of the ascendancy of companionate marriage include Stone, *The Family, Sex, and Marriage*; Belsey, *Shakespeare and the Loss of Eden*, 1–25; Schoenfeldt, *Bodies and Selves in Early Modern England*. On the violent legacy of marriage, see Dolan, *Marriage and Violence*, esp. 67–96.

35 On the centrality of Protestant attacks on clerical celibacy to the formation of modern norms, see Jakobsen "Sex + Freedom = Regulation," 292–298. On Reformation and Counter-Reformation debates on marriage, see Wiesner-Hanks, *Christianity and Sexuality in the Early Modern World*, 21–59, 101–140; Karras, *Sexuality in Medieval Europe*. On the Protestant deployment of antisodomy statutes, see Smith, *Homosexual Desire in Shakespeare's England*, 41–53; Mager, "John Bale."

36 This is Burras's phrase; see her incisive analysis of Augustine's writings on marriage ("'Fleeing the Uxorious Kingdom,'" 4).

37 Quoted in Wiesner-Hanks, *Christianity and Sexuality*, 28.

38 Quoted in Wiesner-Hanks, *Christianity and Sexuality*, 32. See also Brown, *The Body and Society*, 65–82, 160–177, 341–386.

39 Kahn, "Whores and Wives," 248.

40 For the history of the Church's attitudes toward marriage and sexuality, see Wiesner-Hanks, *Christianity and Sexuality*, 38–39; Elliott, *Fallen Bodies*, 81–126; Karras, *Sexuality in Medieval Europe*, 44–45; Olsen, "Progeny, Faithfulness, Sacred Bond" and "Marriage in Barbarian Kingdom."

41 See Crawford, *European Sexualities*, 64–66.

42 Elliott, *Spiritual Marriage*.

43 Payer, *The Bridling of Desire*, 9. For Aquinas's views on marriage and sex, see Supplement (XP): To the Third Part of the *Summa Theologia*, Questions 40–68 (*Summa Theologica*).

44 See Wiesner-Hanks, *Christianity and Sexuality*, 21–59, 101–140; Davies, "'The Sacred Condition of Equality'"; Todd, "Humanists, Puritans, and the Spiritualized Household"; Riddy, "Middle English Romance," 141–145; Pierre, "Marriage, Body, and Sacrament."

45 See Carlson, *Marriage and the English Reformation*; Parish, *Clerical Marriage and the English Reformation*; Shaw, "Reformed and Enlightened Church."

46 See Wiesner-Hanks, *Christianity and Sexuality*, 64, 73.

47 Luther was an Augustinian monk for over a decade, and in the *Institutes* Calvin cites Augustine as an authority four times more than the next most cited nonbiblical source, Calvin's own previous writings, and roughly eight times more than any other theologian or philosopher.

48 Augustine, *Confessions*, 10.30.41.

49 Foucault, "The Battle for Chastity," 231.

50 Brown, *The Body and Society*, 421.

51 Brown, *The Body and Society*, 422, 423. On the suspicion that nocturnal emissions betrayed secret desires, see also Elliott, *Fallen Bodies*, 14–34; Wiesner-Hanks,

Christianity and Sexuality, 23, 35–36; Brown, "Bodies and Minds," 138; Murray, "'The Law of Sin,'" 11, 13.

52 Augustine, *City of God*, trans. Bettenson, 14.23; all citations will be to this edition, hereafter cited parenthetically in the text as *CG* unless otherwise noted.

53 Burras, "'Fleeing the Uxorious Kingdom,'" 8.

54 Wiesner-Hanks, *Christianity and Sexuality*, 61–62.

55 Martin, *Sex and the Single Savior*, 93.

56 Luther, *The Estate of Marriage*, in *Basic Theological Writings*, ed. Lull, 148, 150; hereafter cited parenthetically in the text as *Estate*.

57 As Dubrow shows, English marriage manuals express a similar attraction to life-long virginity for those who are capable of it (*Happier Eden*, 18–20).

58 Edelman, *No Future*, 40.

59 Edelman, *No Future*, 41; Edelman's emphasis.

60 Edelman, *No Future*, 143.

61 Jagose, *Orgasmology*, xiii.

62 On the sonnets' economic language, see Herman, "What's the Use?"; and Callaghan, *Shakespeare's Sonnets*, 37–48, 81–83.

63 Halpern, *Shakespeare's Perfume*, 14, 27.

64 Martin, "Familiar Idolatry," 105.

65 Kunin, "Shakespeare's Preservation Fantasy."

66 Edelman, *No Future*, 3, 31.

67 Kunin, "Shakespeare's Preservation Fantasy," 100–103.

68 For the long critical history of noting aesthetic (re)production in Shakespeare's Sonnets, see Halpern, *Shakespeare's Perfume*, 11–13, 21–22; for a queer challenge to the idealization of male poetic reproduction, see Guy-Bray, *Against Reproduction*.

69 Holland, *The Erotic Life of Racism*, 61.

70 Holland expands on Marlon Ross's work on the genesis of queer critique from sexology, which "casts reproduction for the homosexual as a failed function of *and* a failure to (re)produce the Anglo-Saxon" (*The Erotic Life of Racism*, 75).

71 Holland, *The Erotic Life of Racism*, 75.

72 Hall, "'These Bastard Signs of Fair.'" An oft-cited example of the racialized usage of "fair" appears in the sixteenth-century writer George Best's discussion of the birth of a black child to a mixed-race couple ("an Ethiopian as blacke as a cole" and "a faire English woman") residing in sixteenth-century England: "It seemeth this blacknes proceedeth rather of some natural infection of that man, which was so strong, that neither the nature of the Clime, neither the good complexion of the mother concurring, could anything alter" (Best, *True Discourse*, 5:180–181).

73 Augustine, *St. Augustine, of the Citie of God*, 14.18.

74 The original French edition of Venette's *Tableau de l'amour conjugal* was published in 1696. On the early influence and reception of medical and marital manuals, see Porter, "Spreading Carnal Knowledge"; Fissell, "Hairy Women and Naked Truths."

75 Crooke, *Mikrokosmographia*, n.p. On the relationship between medical manuals, sexology, pornography, and libertine philosophy, see Turner, *Schooling Sex*, esp. 1–71.

76 Vicary, *English-Man's Treasure*, 55; Culpepper, *Directory for Midwives*, 141.

77 *Aristotle's Masterpiece*, 85.

78 Culpepper, *Directory for Midwives*, 3.

79 Venette, *The Mysteries of Conjugal Love*, 14.

80 Traub, "The Nature of Norms in Early Modern England"; and Park, "The Rediscovery of the Clitoris."

81 Crooke, *Mikrokosmographia*, 200, 247.

82 Crooke, *Mikrokosmographia*, 287.

83 Venette, *The Mysteries of Conjugal Love*, 43.

84 See Jordan, *The Invention of Sodomy*, esp. 143–158. Jordan describes sodomy as both a "medieval artifact" for classifying sexual practices and a "judgment" about their value, one that initially encompasses all sex acts but has come to be limited to genital sex between partners of the same gender (1, 9).

85 Culpepper notes that it is only "about the fourth month," when "the child moveth" and "the breasts after that swell with milk," that a woman has the "surest signs" of pregnancy (*Directory for Midwives*, 156, 157).

86 Cohen, "On Saracen Enjoyment."

87 See Haller and Haller, "The Puritan Art of Love"; George and George, *The Protestant Mind*. Turner traces theological and popular views of marriage in *One Flesh*.

88 See, for instance, Lewis, *The Allegory of Love*; Cirillo, "Spenser's Epithalamion"; Johnson, "Gender Fashioning." By contrast, Stapleton stresses the unsublimated, Ovidian desires that structure the *Amoretti* ("Devoid of Guilty Shame").

89 Spenser, *Amoretti* 6.3, 65.14. All references to the *Amoretti* and *Epithalamion* are to the Yale edition, ed. Oram; hereafter cited parenthetically in the text.

90 For the ambivalence and complexity of English Protestant writings on marriage, see Dubrow, *Echoes of Desire*, 10–25. On Spenser's engagement with Reform theology and especially with Calvin, see Hadfield, "Spenser and Religion"; Richey, "The Intimate Other." Kane argues that Spenser's work exposes the fallacy of any ethics directed at complete mastery or final resolution (Kane calls this the "philosophy of administration"), particularly in matters of love (*Spenser's Moral Allegory*, 31–52, 109–137).

91 Kahn, "Whores and Wives," 249.

92 Oram, "Elizabethan Fact and Spenserian Fiction," 635; Johnson, "Gender Fashioning," 505; Stapleton, "Devoid of Guilty Shame," 284.

93 On cultural feminism, see Halley, *Split Decisions*, 59–78.

94 Abelove, "Some Speculations on the History of Sexual Intercourse," 23.

95 English, Hollibaugh, and Rubin, "Talking Sex," 46.

96 Vance, "Pleasure and Danger," 1.

97 MacKinnon, "Feminism, Marxism, Method, and the State," 532.

98 See Sanchez, "Sex and Eroticism."

99 Spenser, *The Faerie Queene*, 4.7.4, 5; hereafter cited parenthetically in the text by book, canto, and stanza number.

100 This is neither the first nor the last time that Spenser associates sexual excess and perversion with foreign locales, religions, and peoples in *The Faerie Queene*. For Lust's hermaphroditism, see Oram, "Elizabethan Fact," 42. For the cannibals' associations with Ireland and the New World, see Cavanagh, "'Licentious Barbarism,'" 273–74; Hamlin, *The Image of America*, 85–87.

101 On Spenser's romanticization of Irish and New World colonization in the *Amoretti*, see Greene, *Unrequited Conquests*, 101–102; Bach, *Colonial Transformations*, 37–66.

102 McCabe, *Edmund Spenser*, 686.

103 Oram argues that the suggestion that "by" means "concerning" is "lexically improbable" (in Spenser, *Shorter Poems*, Yale ed., 634 n.). I would add that reading "to herself" as "*of* herself," which would convey self-assurance rather than self-address, is equally improbable.

104 Luther, *Freedom of a Christian*, in *Martin Luther*, trans. Dillenberger, 57.

105 See Dasenbrock, "The Petrarchan Context"; Johnson, "Gender Fashioning," 518–519; Klein, *The Exemplary Sidney*, 189–192.

106 On this etymology, see Jed, *Chaste Thinking*.

107 See Brown, *The Body and Society*, 168–169; Murray, "'The Law of Sin that Is in My Members,'" 18.

108 Musser, *Sensational Flesh*, 2.

109 MacKinnon, "Feminism, Marxism, Method, and the State," 532.

110 Kahan, *Celibacies*.

111 Catullus, *Poems of Catullus*, 32–35.

112 Scalinger claims that the "name and style" of "Fescennine verses," which he treats as a synonym for epithalamia, "come from the town of Fescennium in Campania or, as others Prefer, in the Sabine region" ("On the Epithalamion," Book II, Chapter 101 of *Poetics*, ed. and trans. by Jackson Bryce, full text reproduced in Dubrow, *Happier Eden*, 271–296; 275, 279–281).

113 Puttenham, *The Arte of English Poesie*, 1.26.

114 Iyengar, *Shades of Difference*, 103–169.

115 Bersani, "Is the Rectum a Grave?," 222; Bersani's emphasis.

CHAPTER 4. THE OPTIMISM OF INFIDELITY

1 Halberstam, "Theorizing Queer Temporalities," 182.

2 The *OED* traces "adultery" as a relational term to the Latin *adultērium*: "conjugal infidelity, blending or mixing of different strains or ingredients, adulteration, contamination, in post-classical Latin also fornication, debauchery, idolatry" (*OED* s.v. "adultery").

3 Lewis, *Allegory of Love*, 12–13, 339–360.

4 Kipnis, *Against Love*, 28.

5 See, for instance, Berlant and Warner, "Sex in Public"; Jakobsen, "Sex + Freedom = Regulation"; Bromley, *Intimacy and Sexuality*.

6 Milton, *Doctrine and Discipline of Divorce*, in *The Complete Prose* 2:347; hereafter cited parenthetically in the text as *DDD*.

7 Calvin, *Institutes* 2.8.43.

8 Stone, *The Road to Divorce*, 302–308. On the history of divorce in England, see also Ingram, *Church Courts, Sex, and Marriage*.

9 Martin, "Familiar Idolatry" and "The Hermeneutics of Divorce" in *Sex and the Single Savior*, esp. 146–147.

10 Luther, "Preface to the Epistle of St. Paul to the Romans," [1522], in *Martin Luther*, trans. Dillenberger, 30.

11 Luther, "Preface to the Epistle of St. Paul to the Romans," 30.

12 Adorno, *Minima Moralia*, 172. Jakobsen traces at length the Protestant roots of this association ("Sex + Freedom = Regulation").

13 Berlant, *Cruel Optimism*, 222.

14 Adorno, *Minima Moralia*, 78.

15 Adorno, *Minima Moralia*, 78.

16 Adorno, *Minima Moralia*, 78.

17 Adorno, *Minima Moralia*, 172.

18 Adorno, *Minima Moralia*, 172.

19 Adorno, *Minima Moralia*, 172.

20 Berlant, *Cruel Optimism*, 51.

21 Berlant, *Cruel Optimism*, 122.

22 Berlant, *Cruel Optimism*, 122.

23 Berlant, *Cruel Optimism*, 123. On reparative reading, see Sedgwick, "Paranoid Reading."

24 Berlant, *Cruel Optimism*, 124.

25 Berlant, *Cruel Optimism*, 227.

26 Berlant, *Cruel Optimism*, 126, 259.

27 Berlant, *Cruel Optimism*, 259, 263; Berlant's emphasis.

28 Jakobsen, "Sex + Freedom = Regulation," 285.

29 For extensive analysis, see Duggan, *The Twilight of Equality*, esp. 67–88.

30 Kipnis, *Against Love*, 197.

31 Kipnis, *Against Love*, 39.

32 *Obergefell v. Hodges* 135 S. Ct. 2584 (2015) at 34.

33 Freeman, *Time Binds*, xxiii.

34 Freeman, *Time Binds*, 4–5. On chronobiopolitics, see Luciano, *Arranging Grief*, esp. 1–24.

35 Freeman, *Time Binds*, 61.

36 D'Emilio and Freedman have seen in the Puritans a "legacy of community regulation of morality" that continues to shape American prudery and heteronormativity (*Intimate Matters*, 52; see, more broadly, 3–52). Goldberg (*Sodometries*, 223–

246) and Warner ("New England Sodom") both trace more nuanced discourses of eroticism, intimacy, and sexuality in early America.

37 Teskey, *Delirious Milton*, 5.

38 For analysis of how Milton's vision of mutual love challenges the "dominant cultural institutions" of marriage and heteronormativity, see Orvis, "Eros and Anteros."

39 Morrissey, "Milton, Modernity," 310.

40 All citations to Milton's prose refer to *The Complete Prose*, vol. 2; hereafter cited parenthetically in the text by title of individual tract.

41 Henry's own divorce was granted by the newly instituted Church of England, not any civil court; he justified it by citing the Catholic ordinance that marriage could be annulled in cases of consanguinity. (Catherine of Aragon had been married to Henry's brother Arthur; Henry married her upon Arthur's death, forming a union that some viewed as incestuous; when Catherine failed to produce a male heir, Henry claimed a case of conscience and sought divorce.)

42 See Stone, *Road to Divorce*.

43 Milton, *Paradise Lost*, in *Complete Poems*, 4.743, 746–747; 9.1013, 1042–1043.

44 Silver, *Imperfect Sense*, 141. Silver incisively argues that the divorce tracts are the most controversial application of the Pauline doctrine of charity (128–143).

45 Phillips, *Monogamy*, Aphorism 62 (n.p.).

46 Orvis, "Eros and Anteros," 17.

47 Orvis, "Eros and Anteros"; Luxon, *Single Imperfection*; Chaplin, "'One Flesh, One Heart, One Soul.'"

48 Calvin, *Institutes* 4.13.18.

49 The ministers Herbert Palmer and Daniel Featley attacked Milton as espousing a dangerous libertinism (see Milton, *Complete Prose* 2:417, 572). For this argument in modern conservative writing, see Wilcox and Dew, "Is Love a Flimsy Foundation?"

50 Unlike modern conservatives, Milton argues that divorce may be better for children than marriage: if children are born of "a former ill-twisted wedlock, begott'n only out of a bestiall necessitie without any true love or contentment, or joy to their parents," marriage "will as little conduce to their sanctifying, as if they had been bastards," so "God therefore knowing how unhappy it would bee for children to bee born in such a family, gives this Law either as a prevention . . . or else as a remedy" (*DDD* 2:259–260; *Tetrachordon* 2:631).

51 On Milton's political radicalism, see Achinstein, "'A Law in This Matter.'"

52 On biography and *Astrophil and Stella*, see Hudson, "Penelope Devereux"; Stillinger, "The Biographical Problem"; Duncan-Jones, "Sidney, Stella, and Lady Rich" and *Sir Philip Sidney*, 238–246; Stewart, *Philip Sidney*, 238–240.

53 On autobiography in Wroth's poetry and fiction, see Roberts, "'The Biographical Problem'"; Carrell, "A Pack of Lies in a Looking Glass"; Salzman, *Literary Culture in Jacobean England*.

54 Sidney, *Astrophil ad Stella* 45.14; Wroth, *Pamphilia to Amphilanthus* F7/P7.33-34.
All quotations from *Astrophil and Stella* will be from Sidney, *The Major Works*;
hereafter cited parenthetically in the text as *AS*.
The print and manuscript history of *Pamphilia to Amphilanthus* is complicated, so citations require a somewhat detailed explanation. *Pamphilia to
Amphilanthus* exists in two distinct editions: a 1621 print version appended to
the *Urania* and an undated manuscript held by the Folger Library. All references to Wroth's poetry in this chapter will be to Salzman's electronic edition,
which includes poems from both (http://wroth.latrobe.edu). Hereafter, I cite
Wroth's poems parenthetically as *PA*, designating them by the number in which
they appear in the Folger manuscript (F) and the print edition (P); those poems
which appear only in the Folger manuscript or print edition are marked only
with an F or a P, respectively.
On the differences between the printed and manuscript *Pamphilia to Amphilanthus*, see Dubrow, "'And Thus Leave Off'"; Hannay, "The 'Ending End'";
Bell, "The Autograph Manuscript of Mary Wroth's *Pamphilia to Amphilanthus*";
Salzman, "Me and My Shadow" and Textual Introduction to *Mary Wroth's
Poetry: An Electronic Edition*.

55 Stillman, "'I am not I.'"

56 Smith, *Homosexual Desire in Shakespeare's England*, 15–17. Smith draws on the
work of Gagnon and Simon; see *Sexual Conduct*, 1–26, and "Sexual Scripts."

57 This is, Smith argues, the myth that maturity and completion are realized only in
heterosexual marriage (*Homosexual Desire*, 64–73).

58 *The Arundel Harington Manuscript*, Fol. 155; reproduced in Hughley, *The Arundel
Harington Manuscript of Tudor Poetry*, 1:254. On Harington's title, see Mitchell,
"Unfolding Verse," 73–84.

59 As Sinfield notes, "enjoy" here has unavoidably sexual connotations ("Sexual
Puns," 349).

60 These are also left out of the unauthorized 1597 edition of *Astrophil and Stella*.

61 For Wroth as for Sidney, the slain Argus embodies the failure of Juno—goddess
of marriage—to prevent Jupiter's infidelity. In *PA* F38/P38, Wroth asks, "How
many eyes poore Love hast thou to guard / Thee, from thy most desired wish, and
end?" only to conclude that "admire / Thee sure wee must, or bee borne without
fire" (*PA* F38/P38.1–2, 13–14). *PA* F30/P65 is even more explicit about the failure
of social stricture to keep lovers from "joy's sports" (*PA* F30/P65.4). Here, Night
replaces Mercury "whose pleasant reede did smite/ All Argus eyes into a deathlike
night / Till they were safe, that non could love reprove"; providing "The shade for
Lovers," darkness makes possible the practice of "joyes right" (*PA* F30/P65.6–8, 2,
10). See also Bell, "Joys Sports," 240–241.

62 See Sanchez, "'In Myself the Smart I Try.'"

63 Just a few examples are Lever, *Elizabethan Love Sonnet*, 81–91; Scanlon, "Sidney's
Astrophil and Stella," 67; de Grazia, "Lost Potential," 35; Roche, *Petrarch and the
English Sonnet Sequences*; Klein, *The Exemplary Sidney*.

64 Sinfield, *Shakespeare, Authority, Sexuality*, 138 (more broadly, 134–140).

65 Feinberg, "The Emergence of Stella," 17–18.

66 Roche, *Petrarch and the English Sonnet Sequences*, 230. See also Sinfield, "Sexual Puns in *Astrophil and Stella*" and "Sidney and Astrophil"; Jones and Stallybrass, "Politics of Astrophil and Stella."

67 Rich and Blount together were godparents to the child of Sidney's brother Robert in 1595 (ten years before Rich's divorce), and Mary Wroth was friends with Isabella Rich, one of the couple's illegitimate daughters. Despite her well-known promiscuity, Penelope Rich remained an influential figure in the Elizabethan court until 1601, when she was expelled for colluding in the treasonous rebellion of her brother, the Earl of Essex. Rich regained her standing at court with the accession of James I in 1603, but both she and Blount were permanently banished in 1605—not for adultery, but for getting married in defiance of canon law that forbade remarriage after divorce. See Wall, "Rich, Penelope"; Hulse, "Stella's Wit"; Ioppolo, "'I Desire to Be Helde.'"

68 Scanlon, "Sidney's *Astrophil and Stella*," 70. See also Sinfield, "Sexual Puns in *Astrophil and Stella*," 342.

69 The phrase is Strycharski's ("Literacy, Education, and Affect," 45). See also de Grazia, "Lost Potential in Grammar and Nature," 30–33; Duncan-Jones, *Sir Philip Sidney*, 206–207; Sinfield, *Shakespeare, Authority, Sexuality*, 136–140.

70 See West, "Equality Theory"; Hasday, "Contest and Consent."

71 See, for instance, Masten, "'Shall I Turne Blabb?'"; Miller, *Changing the Subject*; Bennett, "Playing By and With the Rules," 122.

72 See, for instance, Gil, "The Currency of the Beloved"; Hannay, *Lady Sidney, Mary Wroth*; Bell, "Joys Sports" and "'A too curious secrecie'"; Hecht, "Distortion, Aggression, and Sex"; Kinney, "Turn and Counterturn"; Lamb, "'Can you suspect a change in me?'"

73 Rackin, *Shakespeare and Women*, 11.

74 Jonson, *Conversations*, 39.

75 Hannay, *Lady Sidney*, 108, 131, 251–253, 282–295; Roberts, "'The Knott Never to Bee Untide'" and *The Second Part of the Countess of Montgomeries Urania* (xxi–xxiii).

76 For the view that Wroth signals that the *Urania* is to be read as a fictionalized account of her affair with Pembroke, see Waller, "Mary Wroth and the Sidney Family Romance"; Brennan, Introduction to *Love's Victory*, 4.

77 Lamb, "Women Readers in Mary Wroth's *Urania*," 215. Fienberg describes the *Urania* as "a 558-page prose and poetry 'preface'" to *Pamphilia to Amphilanthus* ("Mary Wroth," 185).

78 Paulissen was the first to notice a pun on the name "Will" here ("The Love Sonnets of Lady Mary Wroth," 48, 152). See also Hannay, "The 'Ending End,'" 5. For poems that appear to pun on the name "Will," see *PA* F7/P7, F15/P15, F102/P40, F55/P55, F74/P71; on "Wroth," see *PA* F15/P15, F/35/P35, F89/84, F101/P94.

79 Bell suggests the opposite: that Wroth sought to conceal any relation between her own relationship with Pembroke and her sonnet sequence; see "Joys Sports" and "'A too curious secrecie.'"

80 Jonson, "A Sonnet, to the Noble Lady, the Lady Mary Wroth," 3–4 (in Jonson, *Complete Poems*). Wroth's poetry was known to Ben Jonson, George Chapman, William Drummond, Dudley Carleton, Edward Conway, Thomas Heywood, and Henry Peacham—some of whom she knew personally, some of whom she had never met—well before the 1621 print edition.

81 Wroth's poetry continued to appear at least through the 1630s, grouped with the work of Sidney, Spenser, Samuel Daniel, and Robert Drayton (see Lewalski, *Writing Women*, 246–247; Hannay, *Lady Sidney*, 151–152, 183, 202, 248, 306–308; Hannay, "The 'Ending End,'" 2–4).

82 For these details, see Hannay, *Lady Sidney*, 131, 203, 228, 249–251, 277, 301–305.

83 Both poems, as well as the longer epistolary exchange between Wroth and Denny, are reproduced in Roberts, *Poems*, 32–35, 237–241. On this exchange, the letters of which were copied and circulated by contemporaries, see Hannay, *Lady Sidney*, 233–242.

84 Letter of March 22, 1622, quoted in Hannay, *Lady Sidney*, 241–242.

85 Wall, *The Imprint of Gender*, 283.

86 See also Masten, "'Shall I Turne Blabb?,'" 84; Walker, *Women Writers*, 175–176; Beilin, *Redeeming Eve*, 211.

87 Hansen, "Boredom and Whoredom," 179, 178; see also Smith, *Sonnets and the English Woman Writer*, 88–92.

88 For her part, Wroth seems to have recognized that airing so much bad behavior was a mistake. She claimed to be the victim of "the strange constructions" that Denny and others had made of purely coincidental resemblances with real persons and events (Letter to Buckingham, December 15, 1621, in Roberts, *Poems*, 236).

89 Lamb, *Gender and Authorship in the Sidney Circle*, 163–167.

90 For Astrophil's flirtations with other women, see sonnets 88, 91, and 97; for Pamphilia's fears of being abandoned, see P60/P59, P62/P61, P101/P94. As a number of Wroth's modern readers have noticed, *Pamphilia to Amphilanthus* dwells on Pamphilia's pain and jealousy at Amphilanthus's (imagined?) infidelities; see, for instance, Kinney, "Mary Wroth's Guilty 'Secrett Art'"; Hannay, "The 'Ending End.'"

91 Rickman, *Love, Lust, and License in Early Modern England*; Bray, *Homosexuality in Renaissance England*; Goldberg, *Sodometries*. On contentions among historians regarding the incidence and perception of adultery, see Ingram, *Church Courts*, 150–167.

92 Rhode, "Why Is Adultery Still a Crime?"

93 Sweeney, "Undead Statutes"; Vasilinda, ""FL: Couples Living Together without Being Married Can Get Arrested."

94 Halberstam, *Female Masculinity*, 53.

95 Braden and Kerrigan, "Milton's Coy Eve."

96 Greene, *Unrequited Conquests*, 176, 180.

97 In the *Symposium*, Socrates famously defines love as "desire for perpetual posses-sion of the good" and therefore a state of perpetual longing and dissatisfaction (Plato, 86).

98 Augustine, *Confessions*, 10.27.38.

99 Bates and Guy-Bray emphasize the centrality of abjection to *Astrophil and Stella*; see Bates, *Masculinity, Gender, and Identity*, 28–88; Guy-Bray, *Against Reproduc-tion*, 91–138.

100 Edelman summarizes this dynamic in which "fantasy, always experienced as the very reality in which we live, installs the law's prohibition as a barrier to protect against jouissance and opens the space of desire to an infinite future of failed pursuit through which desire . . . refuses its satisfaction or enjoyment, prolonging itself by negating the satisfaction at which it aims and only through that negation engaging the enjoyment it refuses to know" (*No Future*, 91).

101 See Freeman, *Time Binds*, 139.

102 Loewenstein deems onanism central to the sequence ("Sidney's Trewant Pen").

103 Goldberg, *Endlesse Work*, vii. See also Parker, *Inescapable Romance*.

104 Beilin, "'The Onely Perfect Vertue,'" 236. See also Dubrow, *Echoes of Desire*, 151–153; Lewalski, *Writing Women*, 258–260; Miller, *Changing the Subject*, 42–43 and 82–87.

105 Rambuss, *Closet Devotions*, 6.

106 Dubrow, *Echoes of Desire*, 36, 135, 152, 156; Dubrow, "'And Thus Leave Off,'" 281–282, 285.

107 Petrarch, *RVF*, 211.12–14.

108 Milton's own translation of 2 Cor. 6:14 differs slightly from those of the Geneva and King James Bibles, which read: "Be not unequally yoked together with the infidels ["unbelievers" in KJB]; for what fellowship hath righteousness with unrighteousness? And what communion hath light with darkness?" On early modern associations of interracial marriage with adultery, see Stockton, *Members of His Body*, 65–72.

109 Milton refers here to biblical verses that treat racial difference as a figure for ir-redeemable sin: "Can the Ethiope change his skin? or the leopard his spots? then may ye also do good, that are accustomed to do evil" (KJB, Jeremiah 13:23). The Geneva translates the first question as "Can the black More change his skin?"

110 According to Sir John Damascene, "They absolutely reject those who marry a second time, and reject the possibility of penance [that is, forgiveness of sins after baptism]" (*Writings*, 125); Milton's mockery is cited by James Mill as evidence for critique of Hindu superstition and idolatry (*History of British India*, 281–283).

111 Bromley, *Intimacy*, 165.

112 Wroth herself had many connections with international Protestantism and English exploration. She was an investor in the East India Company from 1617, had been at court when John Rolfe presented his bride Pocahontas, and was

acquainted with others who had been to the Americas; her cousin and lover, William Herbert, was an investor in the Virginia Company (Hannay, *Lady Sidney*, 50–51, 181, 211–212, 255).

113 See Quilligan, "Completing the Conversation"; Hannay, *Lady Sidney*, 129; Masten, "'Shall I Turne Blabb?,'" 71; Hall, *Things of Darkness*, 106.

114 For many Protestants, the "Black Legend" of Spanish cruelty in the New World was another version of the Roman persecution of the True Church; see Schmidt, *Innocence Abroad*, 1–122; Kuin, "Querre-Muhau."

115 Jonson, *The Masque of Blackness*, 118–119, 150–151. As Hall notes, James I kept Africans at court, and their presence almost certainly influenced the intersecting imperial and aesthetic ideologies of Jonson's masque (*Things of Darkness*, 128–140).

116 For discussion of Wroth's racial and imperial discourse, see Hall, "'I Rather Would Wish to Be a Black-Moor'" and *Things of Darkness*, 177–210; Andrea, "Pamphilia's Cabinet." On Wroth's interest in geography and travel, see Roberts, Introduction to *The First Part of the Urania*, xliv; Cavanagh, *Cherished Torment*.

117 Raman, *Framing "India,"* esp. 83–117.

118 Fuchs, *Mimesis and Empire*; Vitkus, *Turning Turk*, 1–44; Loomba, "Of Gifts, Ambassadors, and Copy-Cats"; Marcus, "Provincializing the Reformation."

119 On romance as a colonial and imperial discourse, see Heng, *Empire of Magic*; Britton, *Becoming Christian*.

CHAPTER 5. ON EROTIC ACCOUNTABILITY

1 Guibbory emphasizes the cohesion of religious and sexual libertinism across Donne's oeuvre ("Reconsidering Donne"). On Donne's ambivalent relation to Petrarchism, see Kerrigan, "What Was Donne Doing?"; Low, *The Reinvention of Love*; Dubrow, *Echoes of Desire*, 205–248; Bell, "Gender Matters"; Saunders, *Desiring Donne*; Kuchar, "Petrarchism and Repentance"; Haskins, "The Love Lyric."

2 Badiou, *Saint Paul*, 98.

3 Menon, *Indifference to Difference*, 2, 15–16.

4 Most influentially, Nygren argues that the great distinction between Lutheran and Catholic (including Augustinian) theology was the definitive separation of divine *agape*, which descends regardless of merit from human *eros*, which always seeks reward or reciprocation (*Agape and Eros*).

5 Milton, *Paradise Lost*, 4.52–53.

6 The Wycliffe, Douay-Rheims, and King James Bibles all translate *caritas* as the more literal "charity." Of fifty-five modern English editions available on Bible Gateway, six translate *agape/caritas* as "charity" and forty-nine translate it as "love" (https://www.biblegateway.com).

7 Butler, *Giving an Account of Oneself*, 108.

8 Butler, *Giving an Account of Oneself*, 83.

9 Butler, *Giving an Account of Oneself*, 42.

10 Butler, *Giving an Account of Oneself*, 42.

11 Butler, *Giving an Account of Oneself*, 42.

12 Butler, *Giving an Account of Oneself*, 102.

13 Butler, *Giving an Account of Oneself*, 101.

14 See Butler, *Giving an Account of Oneself*, 99–108; Levinas, *Otherwise than Being*, esp. chapter 4.

15 Adorno, *Minima Moralia*, 164.

16 Butler, *Giving an Account of Oneself*, 102.

17 Butler, *Giving an Account of Oneself*, 103.

18 Derrida, "On Forgiveness," 35.

19 Derrida, "On Forgiveness," 35.

20 Derrida, "On Forgiveness," 38.

21 Žižek, *The Fragile Absolute*, 127; Žižek's emphasis.

22 Derrida, "On Forgiveness," 34; Derrida's emphasis.

23 Derrida, "On Forgiveness," 39.

24 Derrida, "On Forgiveness," 39.

25 Barthes, *A Lover's Discourse*, 233.

26 Agamben, *Time that Remains*, 116.

27 Derrida, "On Forgiveness," 39.

28 On Donne's emphasis on the predicament of desiring a God who has already made himself available, see Netzley, *Reading, Desire, and the Eucharist*, 106–148.

29 Donne, "Since she whom I loved," 14, in *Complete Poems*, ed. Robbins; all citations to Donne's poetry will be to this edition; hereafter cited parenthetically in the text.

30 Shuger characterizes Donne's subjectivity in the Holy Sonnets as patterned on Mary Magdalene's experience of abandonment and longing (*The Renaissance Bible*, 190); Schoenfeldt sees masculine dominance and female submission as competing desires ("The Gender of Religious Devotion"); Kuchar argues that the Holy Sonnets resist the loss of autonomy that Donne blames on beloved mistress and forbidding God ("Petrarchism and Repentance"); Rambuss underscores the homoeroticism of pleas of a male speaker to be penetrated by a male god (*Closet Devotions*, esp. 49–68).

31 Coles, "The Matter of Belief," 917–918.

32 Donne's doctrinal and confessional views have been a matter of longstanding debate. Some assessments include Lewalski, *Protestant Poetics*, 253–281; Strier, "John Donne Awry and Squint"; Di Pasquale, *Literature and Sacrament*; Cummings, *Literary Culture of the Reformation*, 366–406; Cefalu, *Moral Identity in Early Modern English Literature*; Murray, *Poetics of Conversion*, 69–104; Guibbory, "Reconsidering Donne."

33 For an overview of these comments, see Fish, who takes their moralizing seriously, ("Masculine Persuasive Force," 223), and Saunders, who does not (*Desiring Donne*, 18–19 and 95–97).

34 Conti, *Confessions of Faith*.

35 Carey, *John Donne*.

36 See Marotti, *John Donne*.

37 Goldberg, *James I and the Politics of Literature*, 211.

38 Fish, "Masculine Persuasive Force," 231.

39 Johnson, *Lives of the English Poets*, 16.

40 See Dubrow, *Echoes of Desire*, 207; Guibbory, "Reconsidering Donne"; Carey, *John Donne*; Fish, "Masculine Persuasive Force." Johnson describes Donne's obscurity as part of an early modern poetics in which the "lyric poem becomes a primary cultural site for investigating the capacity of language to manifest presence," an investigation that arises as a result of anxieties about the real presence of Christ in the Eucharist (*Made Flesh*, 6).

41 Quoted by Saunders, *Desiring Donne*, 20, 151.

42 Readers who have described Donne as sexist at best, misogynist at worst include Fish, "Masculine Persuasive Force"; Ricks, "Donne after Love"; Mueller, "Women among the Metaphysicals"; Bach, "(Re)placing John Donne"; and Corthell, *Ideology and Desire*. Defenses of Donne as promoting gendered equality appear in Bell, "The Role of the Lady"; Estrin, *Laura*, 149–226; and Saunders, *Desiring Donne*, 113–146.

43 Quoted by Bald, *John Donne*, 72. For a critique of this developmental narrative, see Dubrow, *Echoes of Desire*, 244–248.

44 Walton, *Life of Donne*, 44; the poem first appeared on the frontispiece of the 1635 edition of Donne's poems.

45 Marcus writes, "In the 1635 edition, the physical space between the covers becomes a measure of temporal duration. The reader's experience of perusing the poems *seriatim* simultaneously recapitulates the poet's life as interpreted by Walton, with the poet's '*Wanton Story*' at the beginning, and his '*Sacrifice and Glory*' as communicated by his sacred verses, at the end" (*Unediting the Renaissance*, 198). Saunders argues that this Augustinian reading was available even in the generically mixed 1633 collection (*Desiring Donne*, 42–50). On these early editions of Donne's poems, see also Marotti, *John Donne*, 250–255.

46 For arguments that Donne's conversion was sincere, see Papazian, *John Donne and the Protestant Reformation*; Targoff, *John Donne, Body and Soul*; and Murray, *Poetics of Conversion*.

47 Foucault, "About the Beginning of the Hermeneutics of the Self," 162, 163.

48 Foucault, *The History of Sexuality*, esp. 17–36.

49 Foucault, "About the Beginning of the Hermeneutics of the Self," 179.

50 Jordan, *Convulsing Bodies*, 138.

51 See Foucault, *The History of Sexuality* and "Afterword: The Subject and Power."

52 Foucault, "On the Government of the Living," 154.

53 Augustine, *Confessions* 10.23.50.

54 Augustine, *Confessions* 7.18.24, 9.13.34.

55 Augustine, *Confessions* 10.5.7.

56 Burras, Jordan, and MacKendrick, *Seducing Augustine*, 13, 14.

57 Luther, "The Pagan Servitude of the Church," in *Martin Luther*, trans. Dillenberger, 321.

58 Luther, "The Pagan Servitude of the Church," 318.

59 Luther, "The Pagan Servitude of the Church," 318.

60 Luther, "The Pagan Servitude of the Church," 318.

61 Calvin, *Institutes*, 3.4.17.

62 Calvin, *Institutes*, 3.4.17.

63 Calvin, *Institutes*, 3.4.17.

64 Calvin, *Institutes*, 3.4.17.

65 Calvin, *Institutes*, 3.4.18.

66 On Augustine's influence on Donne, see Ettenhuber, *Donne's Augustine*.

67 Butler, *Giving an Account of Oneself*, 42.

68 Butler, *Giving an Account of Oneself*, 79.

69 Butler, *Giving an Account of Oneself*, 83.

70 Critics who treat the speaker as male include Docherty, *John Donne, Undone*, 61; and Bald, *John Donne*. Marotti sees the speaker as female (*John Donne*, 73–74). Saunders proposes that the poem functions to make the gender of its speaker irrelevant (*Desiring Donne*, 137).

71 Harvey, *Ventriloquized Voices*, 12–13. See also Corthell, who emphasizes that the "fantasy of a sexually free and active woman is an enduring topos in pornographic discourse" (*Ideology and Desire in Renaissance Poetry*, 66).

72 Saunders, *Desiring Donne*, 135; Saunders's emphasis.

73 Halpern, "The Lyric in the Field of Information."

74 Donne, "From a sermon preached before King Charles (April 1627)," in *Major Works*, 381.

75 Butler, *Giving an Account of Oneself*, 45, 46.

76 Badiou, *Saint Paul*, 77.

77 Badiou, *Saint Paul*, 77.

78 Badiou, *Saint Paul*, 96.

79 Freud, *Civilization and Its Discontents*, 66; Freud, *Das Unbehagen in der Kultur*, 238; page citations hereafter refer to English and German editions, respectively.

80 Freud, *Civilization and Its Discontents*, 70/242.

81 For more expansive discussions of the relation between posthumanism and premodern studies, see Sanchez, "Posthuman Spenser?" and "Antisocial Procreation in *Measure for Measure*."

82 See Wallace, "Literature and Posthumanism."

83 Bennett, *Vibrant Matter*, x. See also Latour, *Reassembling the Social*, esp. 63–86; Alaimo, *Bodily Natures*; Chen, *Animacies*.

84 Bennett, *Vibrant Matter*, 82, 90.

85 Latour, *We Have Never Been Modern*, 46, 47.

86 Taylor, *Secular Age*, 32; more broadly, 29–41.

87 Turner, "Life Science," 14.

88 Cole, "The Call of Things," 115.

89 Along with Cole, some examples include Goldberg, *Seeds of Things*; Nardizzi and Feerick, *The Indistinct Human in Renaissance Literature*; Shannon, *The Accommodated Animal*.

90 Sullivan, *Sleep, Romance, and Human Embodiment*, 7.

91 Escobedo, *Volition's Face*, 3, 5.

92 On the implications of humoral physiology, and particularly melancholy, for both secular and spiritual passions, see Coles, "Matter of Belief"; Schoenfeldt, *Bodies and Selves in Early Modern England* and "Eloquent Blood and Deliberative Bodies"; Trevor, *The Poetics of Melancholy in Early Modern England*; Daniel, *The Melancholy Assemblage*.

93 "Excerpt from Santorum Interview," *USA Today*, April 23, 2003, http://usatoday30.usatoday.com.

94 Edelman, *No Future*, 15–17.

95 Edelman, *No Future*, 56.

96 See Agamben, *Homo Sacer*, 1–11.

97 On the material state of the soul, see Sullivan, *Sleep, Romance, and Human Embodiment*, and Coles, "The Matter of Belief."

98 Saunders, *Desiring Donne*, 150.

99 Barad, *Meeting the Universe Halfway*, 151; Barad's emphasis.

100 Giffney and Hird, "Introduction," 7–8.

101 Chen, *Animacies*, 11, 25–30.

102 Work bringing together feminist, queer, and materialist perspectives includes Hird, "Naturally Queer"; Chen, *Animacies*; Wilson, *Gut Feminism*.

103 On this distinction, see Menon, *Indifference to Difference*.

104 Furey, *Poetic Relations*, 94–106.

105 Schwartz, *Sacramental Poetics*, 88–89, 108–136. See also Di Pasquale, *Literature and Sacrament*, 173–186.

106 On the logic of contagion and individual dissolution in Christian communalism, see Rust, *The Body in Mystery*.

107 Warley, *Reading Class*, 81–82.

108 Warley, *Reading Class*, 82.

109 Saunders, *Desiring Donne*, 150, 155.

110 Luciano and Chen, "Introduction," 184.

111 Luciano and Chen, "Introduction," 186.

112 Luciano and Chen, "Introduction," 196.

113 This is the English Standard Version; the Vulgate gives "non fuit Est et Non, sed Est in illo fuit"; the Geneva and King James, a bit more archaically, translate the full verse as "For the Son of God Jesus Christ . . . was not Yea, and Nay, but in him, was Yea."

114 Butler, *Giving an Account of Oneself*, 25.

115 Kipnis, *Against Love*, 56; Kipnis's emphasis.

116 Marotti, *John Donne*, 76; Mueller, "Women among the Metaphysicals," 145.

117 Dean, *Unlimited Intimacy*, 176–212.

118 Johnson, "Donne, Imperfect," 10.

119 Dubrow, *Echoes of Desire*, 11–12.
120 Guibbory, "Reconsidering Donne." On Petrarchan love and colonial thought, see Greene, *Unrequited Conquests*.
121 Jakobsen, "Sex + Freedom = Regulation," 303.
122 Saunders, *Desiring Donne*, 130–131; Saunders's emphasis.
123 Phillips, *Monogamy*, aphorism 103, n.p.
124 Silver, *Imperfect Sense*, 78.
125 On Calvin's coining of the term "libertine" and its subsequent development in early modern culture, see Guibbory, "Reconsidering Donne," 570–590.
126 Bromley, *Intimacy and Sexuality*, 179.

CODA

1 On this history, see de Ridder-Symoens, *A History of the University in Europe*; Thelin, *A History of American Higher Education*.
2 On Arnold's view of literary study as a replacement for religion, see Robbins, *Secular Vocations*, 16–19, 84–85; Kaufmann, "The Religious, the Secular, and Literary Studies," 614–621.
3 Fish, "Anti-Professionalism," 106.
4 Robbins, *Secular Vocations*, 105.
5 Freccero, "Queer Times," 19.
6 Underwood, *Why Literary Periods Mattered*, 2.
7 Hayot, "Against Periodization," 742; Hayot's emphasis.
8 A partial list includes Dollimore, *Sexual Dissidence*; Sinfield, *Gay and After*; Halpern, *Shakespeare's Perfume*; Freccero, *Queer/Early/Modern*; Goldberg, *The Seeds of Things*; Thompson, *Passing Strange*; Menon, *Indifference to Difference*; Knapp, *Pleasing Everyone*.
9 On these debates, see Sanchez, *Shakespeare and Queer Theory*, chapter 3.
10 Traub, *Thinking Sex with the Early Moderns*, 269.
11 Menon, "Introduction," 5.
12 Menon, "Introduction," 6.
13 Wiegman, "Wishful Thinking," 206–207; Wiegman's emphasis.
14 Dinshaw, *How Soon Is Now?*, 20.
15 De Grazia, "The Modern Divide," 453.
16 Davis, *Periodization and Sovereignty*, 5.
17 See for instance, Sedgwick, "Paranoid Reading"; Warner, "Uncritical Reading"; Best and Marcus, "Surface Reading"; Love, "Close but Not Deep"; Dinshaw, *How Soon Is Now*; Felski, *The Limits of Critique*; Castiglia, *The Practices of Hope*.
18 Dean and Wiegman, "What Does Critique Want?," 115.
19 Taylor, *A Secular Age*, 27.
20 Latour, *We Have Never Been Modern*.
21 Bennett, *Vibrant Matter*, viii.
22 Felski, *The Limits of Critique*, 159. See also Dimock, "A Theory of Resonance."
23 Felski, *The Limits of Critique*, 182.

24 Coviello, *Tomorrow's Parties*, 204.

25 See, for instance, Fradenburg and Freccero, "Introduction"; Dinshaw, *Getting Medieval*; Hammill, *Sexuality and Form*; Lochrie, *Heterosyncrasies*; Fradenburg, *Sacrifice Your Love*; Freccero, *Queer/Early/Modern*; Di Gangi, *Sexual Types*; Harris, *Untimely Matter in the Time of Shakespeare*; Menon, *Indifference to Difference*; Dinshaw, *How Soon Is Now?*; Stockton, *Members of His Body*.

26 Traub, *Thinking Sex with the Early Moderns*, 27. See also Bromley and Stockton, *Sex before Sex*.

BIBLIOGRAPHY

Abelove, Henry. "Some Speculations on the History of Sexual Intercourse during the Long Eighteenth Century in England." In *Deep Gossip*, 21–28. Minneapolis: University of Minnesota Press, 2003.

Achinstein, Sharon. "'A Law in This Matter to Himself': Contextualizing Milton's Divorce Tracts." In *The Oxford Handbook to Milton*, edited by Nicholas MacDowell and Nigel Smith, 174–185. Oxford: Oxford University Press, 2011.

Adorno, Theodor. *Minima Moralia: Reflections from Damaged Life*. 1951. Translated by E. F. N. Jephcott. London: Verso, 1978.

Agamben, Giorgio. "In Praise of Profanation." Translated by Jeff Fort. *Log* 10 (Summer/Fall 2007): 23–32.

———. *The Time That Remains: A Commentary on the Letter to the Romans*. Translated by Patricia Dailey. Palo Alto, CA: Stanford University Press, 2000.

———. *Homo Sacer: Sovereign Power and Bare Life*. 1995. Translated by Daniel Heller-Roazen. Palo Alto, CA: Stanford University Press, 1998.

Alaimo, Stacy. *Bodily Natures: Science, Environment, and the Material Self*. Indianapolis: Indiana University Press, 2010.

Althaus-Reid, Marcella. *Indecent Theology: Theological Perversions in Sex, Gender, and Politics*. New York: Routledge, 2000.

Althusser, Louis. "Ideology and Ideological State Apparatuses." In *Lenin and Philosophy*, translated by Ben Brewster, 85–126. 1968. New York: Monthly Review Press, 2001.

Andrea, Bernadette. "Pamphilia's Cabinet: Gendered Authorship and Empire in Lady Mary Wroth's *Urania*." *ELH: English Literary History* 68, no. 2 (2001): 335–358.

Anzaldúa, Gloria. *Borderlands/La Frontera*. San Francisco: Aunt Lute Books, 1987.

Appiah, Kwame Anthony. "Racisms." In *Anatomy of Racism*, edited by David Theo Goldberg, 3–17. Minneapolis: University of Minnesota Press, 1990.

———. "The Uncompleted Argument: Du Bois and the Illusion of Race." In *"Race," Writing, and Difference*, edited by Henry Louis Gates, Jr., 21–37. Chicago: University of Chicago Press, 1986.

Aquinas, Thomas. *Summa Theologica*, 5 vols. Translated by Fathers of the Dominican Province. 1911. New York: Benziger Brothers, 1948.

Aristotle. *Nichomachean Ethics*, 2nd ed. Translated by and edited by Terence Irwin. Indianapolis: Hackett: 1999.

———. *The Politics and the Constitution of Athens*. Edited by Stephen Everson. Translated by Jonathan Barnes. Cambridge: Cambridge University Press, 1996.

Aristotle's Masterpiece. London, 1698.

Asad, Talal. *Formations of the Secular: Christianity, Islam, Modernity.* Palo Alto, CA: Stanford University Press, 2003.

———. *Genealogies of Religion: Discipline and Reason of Power in Christianity and Islam.* Baltimore, MD: Johns Hopkins University Press, 1993.

Ascoli, Albert Russel, and Unn Falkeid, *The Cambridge Companion to Petrarch.* Cambridge: Cambridge University Press, 2015.

Augustine. *City of God.* Translated by Henry Bettenson. London: Penguin, 1972.

———. *City of God.* Translated by Philip Levine. Loeb Classical Library. Cambridge, MA: Harvard University Press, 1966.

———. *Confessions.* Translated by Henry Chadwick. Oxford: Oxford University Press, 1991.

———. *Confessions.* Translated by Carolyn J. B. Hammond. Loeb Classical Library. Cambridge, MA: Harvard University Press, 2014.

———. *St. Augustine, of the Citie of God: With the Learned Comments of Iohn Lodovico Vives. Englished by J. H.* London, 1610.

———. *Enarrationes in Psalmos,* 2 vols. Edited by E. Dekkers and J. Fraipont. Library of Latin Texts. Turnhout, Belgium: Brepols Press, 2010.

Bach, Rebecca Ann. "(Re)placing John Donne in the History of Sexuality." *ELH: English Literary History* 72, no. 1 (2005): 259–289.

———. *Colonial Transformations: The Cultural Production of the New Atlantic World, 1580–1640.* New York: Palgrave, 2000.

Badiou, Alain. *Saint Paul: The Foundation of Universalism.* Palo Alto, CA: Stanford University Press, 1997.

Baird, Robert J. "Late Secularism." In *Secularisms,* edited by Janet R. Jakobsen and Ann Pellegrini, 162–177. Durham, NC: Duke University Press, 2008.

Bald, R. C. *John Donne: A Life.* Oxford: Oxford University Press, 1970.

Balibar, Étienne, "Is There a 'Neo-Racism'?" In *Race, Nation, Class: Ambiguous Identities,* edited by Etienne Balibar and Emmanuel Wallerstein, translated by Chris Turner, 17–28. London: Verso, 1991.

Barad, Karen. *Meeting the Universe Halfway: Quantum Physics and the Entanglement of Matter and Meaning.* Durham, NC: Duke University Press, 2007.

Barrett Browning, Elizabeth. *Sonnets from the Portuguese.* Edited by Stanley Applebaum. Mineola, NY: Dover Thrift, 1992.

Bartels, Emily C. *Speaking of the Moor: From "Alcazar" to "Othello."* Philadelphia: University of Pennsylvania Press, 2008.

Barthes, Roland. *A Lover's Discourse: Fragments.* 1977. Translated by Richard Howard. New York: Hill and Wang, 1978.

Bartlett, Robert. *The Making of Europe: Conquest, Colonization, and Cultural Change, 950–1350.* Princeton, NJ: Princeton University Press, 1993.

Bates, Catherine. *Masculinity, Gender, and Identity in the English Renaissance Lyric.* Cambridge: Cambridge University Press, 2007.

Baum, Bruce. *The Rise and Fall of the Caucasian Race.* New York: New York University Press, 2006.

Beilin, Elaine. *Redeeming Eve: Women Writers of the English Renaissance*. Princeton, NJ: Princeton University Press, 1987.

———. "'The Onely Perfect Vertue': Constancy in Mary Wroth's *Pamphilia to Amphilanthus*." *Spenser Studies* 2 (1981): 229–245.

Bell, Ilona. "The Autograph Manuscript of Mary Wroth's *Pamphilia to Amphilanthus*." In *Re-Reading Mary Wroth*, edited by Katherine R. Larson and Naomi J. Miller, with Andrew Strycharski, 171–182. New York: Palgrave Macmillan, 2015.

———. "'A too curious secrecie': Wroth's Pastoral Song and 'Urania.'" *Sidney Journal* 31, no. 1 (2013): 23–50.

———. "Joys Sports: The Unexpurgated Text of Mary Wroth's *Pamphilia to Amphilanthus*." *Modern Philology* 111, no. 2 (2013): 231–252.

———. "Gender Matters." In *The Cambridge Companion to John Donne*, edited by Achsah Guibbory, 201–216. Cambridge: Cambridge University Press, 2006.

———. "The Role of the Lady in Donne's Songs and Sonnets." *SEL: Studies in English Literature 1500–1900* 23, no. 1 (1989): 13–29.

———. "Rethinking Shakespeare's Dark Lady." In *A Companion to Shakespeare's Sonnets*, edited by Michael Schoenfeldt, 293–313. Malden, MA: Blackwell, 2007.

Belsey, Catherine. *Shakespeare and the Loss of Eden: The Construction of Family Values in Early Modern Culture*. New Brunswick, NJ: Rutgers University Press, 1999.

Benjamin, Walter. "Theses on the Philosophy of History." In *Illuminations*, edited by Hannah Arendt, translated by Harry Zohn, 253–264. New York: Schocken, 1969.

Bennett, Alexandra G. "Playing by and with the Rules: Genre, Politics, and Perception in Mary Wroth's *Love's Victorie*." In *Women and Culture at the Courts of the Stuart Queens*, edited by Clare McManus, 122–139. London: Palgrave Macmillan, 2003.

Bennett, Jane. *Vibrant Matter: A Political Ecology of Things*. Durham, NC: Duke University Press, 2010.

Bercovitch, Sacvan. *The Puritan Origins of the American Self*. New Haven, CT: Yale University Press, 1975.

Bergner, Gwen. *Taboo Subjects: Race, Sex, and Psychoanalysis*. Minneapolis: University of Minnesota Press, 2005.

Berlant, Lauren. *Cruel Optimism*. Durham, NC: Duke University Press, 2011.

Berlant, Lauren, and Lee Edelman. *Sex, or the Unbearable*. Durham, NC: Duke University Press, 2014.

Berlant, Lauren, and Michael Warner. "Sex in Public." *Critical Inquiry* 24, no. 2 (1998): 547–566.

———. "What Does Queer Theory Teach Us about X?" *PMLA: Publications of the Modern Language Association* 110, no. 3 (1995): 343–349.

Bersani, Leo. "Is the Rectum a Grave?" *October* 43 (Winter 1987): 197–222.

———. *The Freudian Body: Psychoanalysis and Art*. Chicago: University of Chicago Press, 1986.

Bersani, Leo, and Adam Phillips. *Intimacies*. Chicago: University of Chicago Press, 2008.

Best, George. *A True Discourse of the Three Voyages of Discovery.* 1578. Reprinted in Richard Hakluyt, *Principle Navigations.* London, 1600.

Best, Stephen, and Sharon Marcus. "Surface Reading: An Introduction." *Representations* 108, no. 1 (2009): 1–21.

Boisvert, Donald L., and Jay Emerson Johnson, eds. *Queer Religion: LGBT Movements and Queering Religion,* 2 vols. Santa Barbara, CA: Praeger, 2012.

Book of Common Prayer. Published by the Society of Archbishop Justus, 1928, 1979. http://justus.anglican.org/.

Boswell, John. *Same-Sex Unions in Premodern Europe.* 1994. New York: Vintage, 1995.

———. *Christianity, Social Tolerance, and Homosexuality.* Chicago: University of Chicago Press, 1980.

Bouwsma, William J. "The Two Faces of Humanism: Stoicism and Augustinianism in Renaissance Thought." In *A Usable Past: Essays in European Cultural History,* edited by William J. Bouwsma, 19–73. Berkeley: University of California Press, 1990.

Boyarin, Daniel. *A Radical Jew: Paul and the Politics of Identity.* Berkeley: University of California Press, 1994.

———. *Carnal Israel: Reading Sex in Talmudic Culture.* Berkeley: University of California Press, 1993.

Braden, Gordon. *Petrarchan Love and the Continental Renaissance.* New Haven, CT: Yale University Press, 1999.

Braden, Gordon, and William Kerrigan. "Milton's Coy Eve: *Paradise Lost* and Renaissance Love Poetry." *ELH: English Literary History* 53, no. 1 (1986): 27–51.

Bray, Alan. *The Friend.* Chicago: University of Chicago Press, 2002.

———. *Homosexuality in Renaissance England.* Boston: Gay Men's Press, 1982.

Breitenberg, Mark. *Anxious Masculinity in Early Modern England.* Cambridge: Cambridge University Press, 1996.

Brennan, Michael G. Introduction to *Lady Mary Wroth's Love's Victory, The Penshurst Manuscript.* London: The Roxburghe Club, 1988.

Britton, Dennis. *Becoming Christian: Race, Reformation, and Early Modern English Romance.* New York: Fordham University Press, 2014.

Brody, Jennifer. *Impossible Purities: Blackness, Femininity, and Victorian Culture.* Durham, NC: Duke University Press, 1998.

Bromley, James M. *Intimacy and Sexuality in the Age of Shakespeare.* Cambridge: Cambridge University Press, 2012.

Bromley, James M., and Will Stockton. "Introduction: Figuring Early Modern Sex." In *Sex Before "Sex": Figuring the Act in Early Modern England,* edited by James M. Bromley and Will Stockton, 1–23. Minneapolis: University of Minnesota Press, 2013.

Brown, Peter. *The Body and Society: Men, Women, and Sexual Renunciation in Early Christianity.* 1988. New York: Columbia University Press, 2008.

———. "Bodies and Minds: Sexuality and Renunciation in Early Christianity." In *Sexualities in History,* edited by Kim M. Phillips and Berry Raey, 129–140. New York: Routledge, 2002.

———. *Augustine of Hippo.* 1967. Berkeley: University of California Press, 2000.

Brown, Wendy. "Suffering Rights as Paradoxes." *Constellations* 7, no. 2 (2000): 208–229.

Buechel, Andy. *That We Might Become God: The Queerness of Credal Christianity.* Eugene, OR: Cascade Books, 2015.

Buell, Lawrence. "Religion on the American Mind." *American Literary History* 19, no. 1 (2007): 32–55.

Burras, Virginia. "'Fleeing the Uxorious Kingdom': Augustine's Queer Theology of Marriage." *Journal of Early Christian Studies* 19, no. 1 (2011): 1–20.

———. *Saving Shame: Martyrs, Saints, and Other Abject Subjects.* Philadelphia: University of Pennsylvania Press, 2008.

Burras, Virginia, Mark D. Jordan, and Karmen MacKendrick. *Seducing Augustine: Bodies, Desires, Confessions.* New York: Fordham University Press, 2010.

Burras, Virginia, and Catherine Keller, eds. *Towards a Theology of Eros: Transfiguring Passion at the Limits of Discipline.* New York: Fordham University Press, 2006.

Burton, Jonathan. "Western Encounters with Sex and Bodies in Non-European Cultures, 1500–1750." In *The Routledge History of Sex and the Body, 1500 to the Present,* edited by Sarah Toulalan and Kate Fisher, 495–510. New York: Routledge, 2013.

Butler, Judith. *Giving an Account of Oneself.* New York: Fordham University Press, 2005.

Cady, Linell. "Secularism, Secularizing, and Secularization: Reflections on Stout's *Democracy and Tradition*." *Journal of the American Academy of Religion* 73, no. 3 (2005): 871–885.

Callaghan, Dympna. *Shakespeare's Sonnets.* Malden, MA: Blackwell, 2007.

Calvin, John. *Christianae religionis institutio.* 1559. Turnhout, Belgium: Brepols Press, 2017.

———. *Institutes of the Christian Religion.* Translated by Henry Beveridge. Peabody, MA: Hendrickson, 2008.

Caputo, John C. *The Prayers and Tears of Jacques Derrida: Religion without Religion.* Bloomington: Indiana University Press, 1997.

Carey, John. *John Donne: Life, Mind, and Art.* Oxford: Oxford University Press, 1981.

Carlson, Eric. *Marriage and the English Reformation.* London: Wiley-Blackwell, 1994.

Carrell, Jennifer Lee. "A Pack of Lies in a Looking Glass: Lady Mary Wroth's *Urania* and the Magic Mirror of Romance." *SEL: Studies in English Literature 1500–1900* 34, no. 1 (1994): 79–107.

Casanova, José. "The Secular, Secularizations, Secularisms." In *Rethinking Secularism,* edited by Craig Calhoun, Mark Juergensmeyer, and Jonathan VanAntwerpen, 54–74. Oxford: Oxford University Press, 2011.

———. "Rethinking Secularism: A Global Comparative Perspective." *Hedgehog Review* 8 (Spring/Summer 2006): 7–22.

———. "Secularization Revisited: A Reply to Talal Asad." In *Powers of the Secular Modern: Talal Asad and His Interlocutors,* edited by David Scott and Charles Hirschkind, 12–31. Palo Alto, CA: Stanford University Press, 2006.

Castiglia, Christopher. *The Practices of Hope: Literary Criticism in Disenchanted Times.* New York: New York University Press, 2017.

Castronovo, Russ. "Enslaving Passions: White Male Sexuality and the Evasion of Race." In *The Puritan Origins of American Sex: Religion, Sexuality, and National Identity in American Literature,* edited by Tracy Fessenden, Nicholas F. Radel, and Magdalena J. Zaborowska, 145–168. New York: Routledge, 2001.

Catullus. *The Poems of Catullus.* Translated by Charles Martin. Baltimore, MD: Johns Hopkins University Press, 1979.

Cavadini, John C. "Feeling Right: Augustine on the Passions and Sexual Desire." *Augustinian Studies* 36, no. 1 (2005): 195–217.

Cavanagh, Sheila. *Cherished Torment: The Emotional Geography of Lady Mary Wroth's Urania.* Pittsburgh, PA: Duquesne University Press, 2001.

———. "'Licentious Barbarism': Spenser's View of the Irish and *The Faerie Queene*." *Irish University Review* 26, no. 2 (1996): 268–280.

Cefalu, Paul. *Moral Identity in Early Modern English Literature.* Cambridge: Cambridge University Press, 2004.

Chakrabarty, Dipesh. *Provincializing Europe: Postcolonial Thought and Historical Difference.* Princeton, NJ: Princeton University Press, 2000.

Chaplin, Gregory. "'One Flesh, One Heart, One Soul': Renaissance Friendship and Miltonic Marriage." *Modern Philology* 99, no. 2 (2001): 266–292.

Chen, Mel Y. *Animacies: Biopolitics, Racial Mattering, and Queer Affect.* Durham, NC: Duke University Press, 2012.

Cheng, Patrick S. *Radical Love: An Introduction to Queer Theology.* New York: Seabury Books, 2011.

Chiampi, James T. "Petrarch's Augustinian Excess." *Italica* 72, no. 1 (1995): 1–20.

Cicero. *On Old Age. On Friendship. On Divination.* Translated by W. A. Falconer. Loeb Classical Library 154. Cambridge, MA: Harvard University Press, 1923.

Cirillo, A. R. "Spenser's Epithalamion: The Harmonious Universe of Love." *SEL: Studies in English Literature 1500–1900* 8, no. 1 (1968): 19–34.

Coakley, Sarah. *God, Sexuality, and the Self: An Essay "On the Trinity."* Cambridge: Cambridge University Press, 2013.

Cobb, Michael. *Single: Arguments for the Uncoupled.* New York: New York University Press, 2012.

Cohen, Cathy J. "Punks, Bulldaggers, and Welfare Queens." *GLQ: A Journal of Lesbian and Gay Studies* 3, no. 4 (1997): 437–465.

Cohen, Jeffery Jerome. "On Saracen Enjoyment: Some Fantasies of Race in Late Medieval France and England." *Journal of Medieval and Early Modern Studies* 31, no. 1 (2001): 113–146.

Cole, Andrew. "The Call of Things: A Critique of Object-Oriented Ontologies." *minnesota review* 80 (2013): 106–118.

Coles, Kimberley Anne. "The Matter of Belief in John Donne's Holy Sonnets." *Renaissance Quarterly* 68, no. 3 (2015): 899–931.

Conti, Brooke. *Confessions of Faith in Early Modern England.* Philadelphia: University of Pennsylvania Press, 2014.

Cornwall, Susannah. *Controversies in Queer Theology.* London: SCM Press, 2011.

Corthell, Ronald. *Ideology and Desire in Renaissance Poetry: The Subject of Donne.* Detroit, MI: Wayne State University Press, 1997.

Coviello, Peter. *Tomorrow's Parties: Sex and the Untimely in Nineteenth-Century America.* New York: New York University Press, 2013.

Coviello, Peter, and Jared Hickman. "Introduction: After the Postsecular." *American Literature* 86, no. 4 (2014): 645–654.

Cox, Virginia. "Sixteenth-Century Women Petrarchists and the Legacy of Laura." *Journal of Medieval and Early Modern Studies* 35, no. 3 (2005): 583–606.

Crawford, Katherine. *European Sexualities, 1400–1800.* Cambridge: Cambridge University Press, 2007.

Crewe, Jonathan. *Trials of Authorship: Anterior Forms and Poetic Reconstruction from Wyatt to Shakespeare.* Berkeley: University of California Press, 1990.

Crooke, Helkiah. *Mikrokosmographia.* London, 1615.

Cruz, Ariane. *The Color of Kink: Black Women, BDSM, and Pornography.* New York: New York University Press, 2016.

Culpepper, Nicholas. *Directory for Midwives, or, A Guide for Women, the Second Part.* London, 1676.

Cummings, Brian. *Mortal Thoughts: Religion, Secularity, and Identity in Shakespeare and Early Modern Culture.* Oxford: Oxford University Press, 2013.

———. *Literary Culture of the Reformation: Grammar and Grace.* Oxford: Oxford University Press, 2002.

Cummings, Brian, ed. *The Book of Common Prayer: The Texts of 1549, 1559, and 1662.* Oxford: Oxford University Press, 2011.

Daileader, Celia R. *Racism, Misogyny, and the Othello Myth: Inter-Racial Couples from Shakespeare to Spike Lee.* Cambridge: Cambridge University Press, 2005.

Damascene, John. *Writings: The Fount of Knowledge: The Philosophical Chapters, On Heresies, & On the Orthodox Faith,* vol. 37. Edited by Frederic H. Chase Jr. Indianapolis: Ex Fontibus, 2012.

Daniel, Drew. *The Melancholy Assemblage: Affect and Epistemology in the English Renaissance.* New York: Fordham University Press, 2013.

Dasenbrock, Reed Way. "The Petrarchan Context of Spenser's *Amoretti.*" *PMLA: Publications of the Modern Language Association* 100, no. 1 (1985): 38–50.

Davies, Kathleen M. "'The Sacred Condition of Equality'—How Original Were Puritan Doctrines of Marriage?" *Social History* 2, no. 5 (1977): 563–580.

Davis, Kathleen. *Periodization and Sovereignty: How Ideas of Feudalism and Secularization Govern the Politics of Time.* Philadelphia: University of Pennsylvania Press, 2008.

Dean, Tim. *Unlimited Intimacy: Reflections on the Subculture of Barebacking.* Chicago: University of Chicago Press, 2009.

Dean, Tim, and Robyn Wiegman. "What Does Critique Want? A Critical Exchange." *English Language Notes* 51, no. 2 (2013): 107–122.

de Certeau, Michel. *Heterologies*. Minneapolis: University of Minnesota Press, 1986.

de Grazia, Margreta. "The Modern Divide: From Either Side." *Journal of Medieval and Early Modern Studies* 37, no. 3 (2007): 453–467.

———. "The Scandal of Shakespeare's Sonnets." In *Shakespeare's Sonnets: Critical Essays*, edited by James Schiffer, 89–112. New York: Garland, 1999.

———. "Lost Potential in Grammar and Nature: Sidney's *Astrophil and Stella*." *SEL: Studies in English Literature 1500–1900* 21, no. 1 (1981): 21–35.

Delgado, Richard, and Jean Stefancic. "Introduction." In *Critical Race Theory: An Introduction*, 2nd ed., edited by Richard Delgado and Jean Stefancic, 1–18. New York: New York University Press, 2012.

D'Emilio, John, and Estelle B. Freedman. *Intimate Matters: A History of Sexuality in America*, 2nd ed. Chicago: University of Chicago Press, 1997.

Derrida, Jacques. "On Forgiveness." In *On Cosmopolitanism and Forgiveness*, translated by Mark Dooley and Michael Hughes, 25–60. New York: Routledge, 2011.

———. *The Politics of Friendship*. 1994. Translated by George Collins. London: Verso, 1997.

———. "'Eating Well,' or the Calculation of the Subject: An Interview with Jacques Derrida." In *Who Comes after the Subject?*, edited by Eduardo Cadava, Peter Connor, and Jean-Luc Nancy, 96–119. New York: Routledge, 1991.

Diehl, Huston. "'Infinite Space': Representation and Reformation in *Measure for Measure*." *Shakespeare Quarterly* 49, no. 4 (1998): 393–410.

Di Gangi, Mario. *Sexual Types: Embodiment, Agency, and Dramatic Character from Shakespeare to Shirley*. Philadelphia: University of Pennsylvania Press, 2011.

Dimock, Wai Chee. "A Theory of Resonance." *PMLA: Publications of the Modern Language Association* 112, no. 5 (1997): 1060–1071.

Dinshaw, Carolyn. *How Soon Is Now? Medieval Texts, Amateur Readers, and the Queerness of Time*. Durham, NC: Duke University Press, 2012.

———. *Getting Medieval: Sexualities and Communities, Pre- and Postmodern*. Durham, NC: Duke University Press, 1999.

Di Pasquale, Theresa M. *Literature and Sacrament: The Sacred and the Secular in John Donne*. Pittsburgh, PA: Duquesne University Press, 1999.

Docherty, Thomas. *John Donne, Undone*. 1986. New York: Routledge, 2014.

Dolan, Frances E. *Marriage and Violence: The Early Modern Legacy*. Philadelphia: University of Pennsylvania Press, 2008.

Dollimore, Jonathan. *Sexual Dissidence: Augustine to Wilde, Freud to Foucault*. Oxford: Oxford University Press, 1991.

Donne, John. *The Complete Poems of John Donne*. Edited by Robin Robbins. Harlow, UK: Longman, 2008.

———. *The Major Works*. Edited by John Carey. Oxford: Oxford University Press, 1990.

Dubrow, Heather. "'And Thus Leave Off': Reevaluating Mary Wroth's Folger Manuscript, V.a.104." *Tulsa Studies in Women's Literature* 22, no. 2 (2003): 273–291.

———. *Echoes of Desire: English Petrarchism and Its Counterdiscourses*. Ithaca, NY: Cornell University Press, 1995.

———. *A Happier Eden: The Politics of Marriage in the Stuart Epithalamion*. Ithaca, NY: Cornell University Press, 1990.

Duggan, Lisa. *The Twilight of Equality*. Boston: Beacon Press, 2004.

———. "The New Homonormativity: The Sexual Politics of Neoliberalism." In *Materializing Democracy: Toward a Revitalized Cultural Politics*, edited by Russ Castronovo and Dana D. Nelson, 175–194. Durham, NC: Duke University Press, 2002.

Duncan-Jones, Katherine. *Sir Philip Sidney: Courtier Poet*. New Haven, CT: Yale University Press, 1991.

———. "Sidney, Stella, and Lady Rich." In *Sir Philip Sidney: 1586 and the Making of a Legend*, edited by J. A. van Dorsten, Dominic Baker-Smith, and Arthur F. Kinney, 170–192. Leiden: Brill, 1986.

Dunning, Benjamin H. *Specters of Paul: Sexual Difference in Early Christian Thought*. Philadelphia: University of Pennsylvania Press, 2011.

Edelman, Lee. *No Future: Queer Theory and the Death Drive*. Durham, NC: Duke University Press, 2004.

Eilberg-Schwartz, Howard. *God's Phallus: And Other Problems for Men and Monotheism*. Boston: Beacon Press, 1994.

Eliav-Feldon, Miriam, Benjamin Isaac, and Joseph Ziegler, eds. *The Origins of Racism in the West*. Cambridge: Cambridge University Press, 2009.

Elliott, Dyan. *Fallen Bodies: Pollution, Sexuality, and Demonology in the Middle Ages*. Philadelphia: University of Pennsylvania Press, 1999.

———*Spiritual Marriage: Sexual Abstinence in Medieval Wedlock*. Princeton, NJ: Princeton University Press, 1993.

Eng, David L. *The Feeling of Kinship: Queer Liberalism and the Racialization of Intimacy*. Durham, NC: Duke University Press, 2010.

Eng, David L., Jack Halberstam, and José Esteban Muñoz, eds. "What's Queer about Queer Theory Now?" Special issue, *Social Text* 23, nos. 3–4 (2005): 1–18.

English, Deirdre, Amber Hollibaugh, and Gayle Rubin. "Talking Sex: A Conversation on Sexuality and Feminism." *Feminist Review* 11, no. 1 (1982): 40–52.

Enterline, Lynn. *The Rhetoric of the Body from Ovid to Shakespeare*. Cambridge: Cambridge University Press, 2000.

Erickson, Peter, and Kim F. Hall. "'A New Scholarly Song': Rereading Early Modern Race." *Shakespeare Quarterly* 67, no. 1 (2016): 1–13.

Escobedo, Andrew. *Volition's Face: Personification and the Will in Renaissance Literature*. Notre Dame, IN: University of Notre Dame Press, 2017.

Estrin, Barbara L. *Laura: Uncovering Gender and Genre in Wyatt, Donne, and Marvell*. Durham, NC: Duke University Press, 1994.

Ettenhuber, Katrin. *Donne's Augustine: Renaissance Cultures of Interpretation*. Oxford: Oxford University Press, 2011.

Fanon, Franz. "Algeria Unveiled." In *A Dying Colonialism*, translated by Haakon Chevalier. New York: Grove Press, 1965.

Farris, Sara R. *In the Name of Women's Rights: The Rise of Feminonationalism*. Durham, NC: Duke University Press, 2017.

Feerick, Jean. *Strangers in Blood: Relocating Race in the Renaissance*. Toronto: University of Toronto Press, 2010.

Feinberg, Nona. "The Emergence of Stella in Astrophil and Stella." *SEL: Studies in English Literature 1500–1900* 25, no. 1 (1985): 5–19.

Felski, Rita. *The Limits of Critique*. Chicago: University of Chicago Press, 2015.

Ferguson, Roderick A. "Of Our Normative Strivings: African American Studies and the Histories of Sexuality." *Social Text* 23, nos. 3–4 (2005): 85–100.

———. *Aberrations in Black: Toward a Queer of Color Critique*. Minneapolis: University of Minnesota Press, 2004.

Fessenden, Tracy. *Culture and Redemption: Religion, the Secular, and American Literature*. Princeton, NJ: Princeton University Press, 2007.

Fessenden, Tracy, Nicholas F. Radel, and Magdalena J. Zaborowska, eds. *The Puritan Origins of American Sex*. New York: Routledge, 2001.

Field, Douglas. *All Those Strangers: The Art and Lives of James Baldwin*. Oxford: Oxford University Press, 2015.

Fienberg, Nona. "Mary Wroth and the Invention of Female Poetic Subjectivity." In *Reading Mary Wroth*, edited by Naomi Miller and Gary Waller, 175–190. Knoxville: University of Tennessee Press, 1991.

Fineman, Joel. *Shakespeare's Perjured Eye: The Invention of Poetic Subjectivity in the Sonnets*. Berkeley: University of California Press, 1986.

Fish, Stanley. "Masculine Persuasive Force: Donne and Verbal Power." In *Soliciting Interpretation: Literary Theory and Seventeenth-Century English Poetry*, edited by Elizabeth D. Harvey and Katharine Eisaman Maus, 223–252. Chicago: University of Chicago Press, 1990.

———. "Anti-Professionalism." *New Literary History* 17, no. 1 (1985): 89–108.

Fissell, Mary E. "Hairy Women and Naked Truths: Gender and the Politics of Knowledge in 'Aristotle's Masterpiece.'" *William and Mary Quarterly* 60, no. 1 (2003): 43–74.

Fleetwood, Nicole R. "The Case of Rihanna: Erotic Violence and Black Female Desire." *African American Review* 45, no. 3 (2012): 419–435.

Foster, Kenelm. *Petrarch: Poet and Humanist*. Edinburgh: Edinburgh University Press, 1984.

———. "Beatrice or Medusa." In *Italian Studies Presented to E. R. Vincent*, edited by C. P. Brand, Kenelm Foster, and Uberto Limentani, 41–56. Cambridge: Heffer, 1962.

Foucault, Michel. "About the Beginning of the Hermeneutics of the Self." 1980. Transcript by Thomas Keenan and Mark Balsius. In *Religion and Culture*, selected and edited by Jeremy R. Carrette, translated by Richard Townsend, 158–180. London: Routledge, 1999.

———. "On the Government of the Living." 1979–1980. In *Religion and Culture*, selected and edited by Jeremy R. Carrette, translated by Richard Townsend, 154–157. New York: Routledge, 1999.

——. "Friendship as a Way of Life." 1994. In *Ethics: Subjectivity and Truth*, edited by Paul Rabinow, translated by Robert Hurley, 135–140. New York: New Press, 1997.

——. *The History of Sexuality: An Introduction, Volume One*. 1976. Translated by Robert Hurley. New York: Vintage, 1990.

——. *The Use of Pleasure: Volume Two of the History of Sexuality*. 1985. Translated by Robert Hurley. New York, Vintage, 1990.

——. "The Battle for Chastity." 1982. In *Politics, Philosophy, Culture: Interviews and Other Writings, 1977–1984*, edited by Lawrence D. Kritzman, 227–241. New York: Routledge, 1988.

——. "The Concern for Truth." In *Politics, Philosophy, Culture: Interviews and Other Writings, 1977–1984*, edited by Lawrence D. Kritzman, 255–267. New York: Routledge, 1988.

——. "On the Genealogy of Ethics: An Overview of Works in Progress." In *The Foucault Reader*, edited by Paul Rabinow, 440–372. New York: Pantheon, 1984.

——. "Afterword: The Subject and Power." In *Michel Foucault: Beyond Structuralism and Hermeneutics*, edited by Hubert L. Dreyfus and Paul Rainbow, 208–221. Chicago: University of Chicago Press, 1983.

Fradenburg, L. O. Ananye. *Sacrifice Your Love: Psychoanalysis, Historicism, Chaucer.* Minneapolis: University of Minnesota Press, 2002.

Fradenburg, Louise, and Carla Freccero. "Introduction: Caxton, Foucault, and the Pleasures of History." In *Premodern Sexualities*, edited by Louise Fradenburg and Carla Freccero, xiii–xxiv. New York: Routledge, 1996.

Franke, Katherine. *Wedlocked: The Perils of Marriage Equality.* New York: New York University Press, 2015.

Freccero, Carla. "Tangents (of Desire)." *JEMCS: Journal for Early Modern Culture Studies* 16, no. 2 (2016): 91–105.

——. "Queer Times." In *After Sex?: On Writing since Queer Theory*, edited by Janet Halley and Andrew Parker, 17–26. Durham, NC: Duke University Press, 2011.

——. *Queer/Early/Modern.* Durham, NC: Duke University Press, 2006.

——. "Cannibalism, Homophobia, Women: Montaigne's 'Des cannibales' and 'De l'amitié.'" In *Women, "Race," and Writing in the Early Modern Period*, edited by Margo Hendricks and Patricia Parker, 73–83. London: Routledge, 1994.

Freccero, John. "The Fig Tree and the Laurel." *Diacritics* 5, no. 1 (1975): 34–40.

Fredriksen, Paula. "Paul and Augustine: Conversion Narratives, Orthodox Traditions, and the Retrospective Self." *Journal of Theological Studies* n.s. 37, no. 1 (1986): 3–34.

Freeman, Elizabeth. "Still After?" In *After Sex?: On Writing since Queer Theory*, edited by Janet Halley and Andrew Parker, 27–33. Durham, NC: Duke University Press, 2011.

——. "Queer Times." In *After Sex?: On Writing since Queer Theory*, edited by Janet Halley and Andrew Parker, 17–26. Durham, NC: Duke University Press, 2011.

——. *Time Binds: Queer Temporalities, Queer Histories.* Durham, NC: Duke University Press, 2010.

————. *The Wedding Complex: Forms of Belonging in Modern American Culture*. Durham, NC: Duke University Press, 2002.

Freinkel, Lisa. *Reading Shakespeare's Will: The Theology of Figure from Augustine to the Sonnets*. New York: Columbia University Press, 2001.

Freud, Sigmund. *Das Unbehagen in der Kultur [Civilization and Its Discontents]*. In *Studienausgabe, Band IX: Fragen der Gesellschaft Ursprünge der Religion [Study Edition, Volume IX: Questions of Society and the Origins of Religion]*. Frankfurt am Main: Fischer Taschenbuch, 2000.

————. *Civilization and Its Discontents*. 1930. Translated and edited by James Strachey. New York: Norton, 1963.

Fuchs, Barbara. *Exotic Nation: Maurophilia and the Construction of Early Modern Spain*. Philadelphia: University of Pennsylvania Press, 2009.

————. *Mimesis and Empire: The New World, Islam, and European Identities*. Cambridge: Cambridge University Press, 2001.

Fulke, William. *D. Heskins, D. Sanders, and M. Rastel, accounted (among their faction) three pillers and archpatriarches of the popish synagogue: (vtter enemies to the truth of Christes Gospell, and all that syncerely professe the same) ouerthrowne*. Short Title Catalogue 11433. London, 1579.

Furey, Constance. *Poetic Relations: Intimacy and Faith in the English Reformation*. Chicago: University of Chicago Press, 2017.

Gagnon, John H., and William Simon. "Sexual Scripts." *Society* 22, no. 1 (1984): 53–60.

————. *Sexual Conduct: The Social Sources of Human Sexuality*. New Brunswick, NJ: Aldine Press, 1973.

Gallagher, Lowell. *Sodomscapes: Hospitality in the Flesh*. New York: Fordham University Press, 2017.

Garrison, John. *Friendship and Queer Theory in the Renaissance*. New York: Routledge, 2014.

Gates, Henry Louis, Jr. "Introduction: Writing 'Race' and the Difference It Makes." In *"Race," Writing, and Difference*, edited by Henry Louis Gates Jr., 1–20. Chicago: University of Chicago Press, 1986.

Gates, Henry Louis, Jr., ed. *"Race," Writing, and Difference*. Chicago: University of Chicago Press, 1986.

George, Charles H., and Katherine George. *The Protestant Mind of the English Reformation, 1570–1640*. Princeton, NJ: Princeton University Press, 1961.

Giffney, Noreen, and Myra J. Hird. "Introduction: Queering the Non/Human." In *Queering the Non/Human*, edited by Noreen Giffney and Myra J. Hird, 1–16. Aldershot, UK: Ashgate, 2008.

Gil, Daniel Juan. *Before Intimacy: Asocial Sexuality in Early Modern England*. Minneapolis: University of Minnesota Press, 2006.

————. "The Currency of the Beloved and the Authority of Lady Mary Wroth." *Modern Language Studies* 29, no. 2 (1999): 73–92.

Goldberg, David Theo, and John Solomos. "Introduction." In *A Companion to Racial and Ethnic Studies*, edited by David Theo Goldberg and John Solomos, 1–12. Malden, MA: Blackwell, 2002.

Goldberg, Jonathan. "After Thoughts." In *After Sex?: On Writing Since Queer Theory After Sex?*, edited by Janet Halley and Andrew Parker, 34–42. Durham, NC: Duke University Press, 2011.

———. *Sodometries: Renaissance Texts, Modern Sexualities*. 1992. New York: Fordham University Press, 2010.

———. *The Seeds of Things: Theorizing Sexuality and Materiality in Renaissance Representations*. New York: Fordham University Press, 2009.

———. *Desiring Women Writing: English Renaissance Examples*. Palo Alto, CA: Stanford University Press, 1997.

———. "*Romeo and Juliet*'s Open Rs." In *Queering the Renaissance*, edited by Jonathan Goldberg, 218–235. Durham, NC: Duke University Press, 1995.

———. *James I and the Politics of Literature*. Baltimore, MD: Johns Hopkins University Press, 1983.

———. *Endlesse Worke: Spenser and the Structures of Discourse*. Baltimore, MD: Johns Hopkins University Press, 1981.

Gowing, Laura. *Domestic Dangers: Women, Words, and Sex in Early Modern London*. Oxford: Clarendon Press, 1996.

Greene, Roland. *Unrequited Conquests: Love and Empire in the Colonial Americas*. Chicago: University of Chicago Press, 1999.

Greene, Thomas. *The Light in Troy: Imitation and Discovery in Renaissance Poetry*. New Haven, CT: Yale University Press, 1982.

Guibbory, Achsah. "Reconsidering Donne: From Libertine Poetry to Arminian Sermons." *Studies in Philology* 114, no. 3 (2017): 561–590.

Guy-Bray, Stephen. "Remembering to Forget: Shakespeare's Sonnet 35 and Siglo's 'XXXV.'" In *Sexuality and Memory in Early Modern England*, edited by John S. Garrison and Kyle Pivetti, 43–50. New York: Routledge, 2016.

———. *Against Reproduction: Where Renaissance Texts Come From*. Toronto: University of Toronto Press, 2009.

Habib, Imtiaz. *Black Lives in the English Archives, 1500–1677: Imprints of the Invisible*. Aldershot: Ashgate, 2008.

Hadfield, Andrew. "Spenser and Religion—Yet Again." *SEL: Studies in English Literature 1500–1900* 51, no. 1 (2011): 21–46.

Hainsworth, Peter. "*Rerum vulgarium fragmenta*: Structure and Narrative." In *The Cambridge Companion to Petrarch*, edited by Albert Russel Ascoli and Unn Falkeid, 39–40. Cambridge: Cambridge University Press, 2015.

Halberstam, Jack. *The Queer Art of Failure*. Durham, NC: Duke University Press, 2011.

———. "Theorizing Queer Temporalities: A Roundtable Discussion." *GLQ: A Journal of Lesbian and Gay Studies* 13, nos. 2–3 (2007): 177–195.

———. *Female Masculinity*. Durham, NC: Duke University Press, 1998.

Hall, Kim F. "'I Rather Would Wish to Be a Black-Moor': Beauty, Race, and Rank in Lady Mary Wroth's *Urania.*" In *Women, "Race," and Writing in the Early Modern Period,* edited by Margo Henricks and Patricia Parker, 178–194. New York: Routledge, 1994.

———. "'These Bastard Signs of Fair': Literary Whiteness in Shakespeare's Sonnets." In *Post-Colonial Shakespeares,* edited by Ania Loomba and Martin Orkin, 64–83. London: Routledge, 1998.

———. *Things of Darkness: Economies of Race and Gender in Early Modern England.* Ithaca, NY: Cornell University Press, 1996.

———. "Reading What Isn't There: 'Black' Studies in Early Modern England." *Stanford Humanities Review* 3, no. 1 (1993): 23–33.

Haller, William, and Malleville Haller. "The Puritan Art of Love." *Huntington Library Quarterly* 5, no. 2 (1942): 235–272.

Halley, Janet. *Split Decisions: How and Why to Take a Break from Feminism.* Princeton, NJ: Princeton University Press, 2006.

Halley, Janet, and Andrew Parker, ed. *After Sex?: On Writing since Queer Theory.* Durham, NC: Duke University Press, 2011.

Halpern, Richard. *Shakespeare's Perfume: Sodomy and Sublimity in the Sonnets, Wilde, Freud, and Lacan.* Philadelphia: University of Pennsylvania Press, 2002.

———. "The Lyric in the Field of Information: Autopoiesis and History in Donne's *Songs and Sonnets.*" 1993. In *Critical Essays on John Donne,* edited by Arthur F. Marotti, 49–76. London: G. K. Hall, 1994.

Hamlin, William M. *The Image of America in Montaigne, Spenser, and Shakespeare.* New York: St. Martin's Press, 1995.

Hammill, Graham. *The Mosaic Constitution: Political Theology and Imagination from Machiavelli to Milton.* Chicago: University of Chicago Press, 2011.

———. *Sexuality and Form: Caravaggio, Marlowe, and Bacon.* Chicago: University of Chicago Press, 2000.

Hammill, Graham, and Julia Reinhard Lupton, "Introduction." In *Political Theology and Early Modernity,* edited by Graham Hammill and Julia Reinhard Lupton, 1–20. Chicago: University of Chicago Press, 2012.

Hammonds, Evelynn. "Toward a Genealogy of Black Female Sexuality: The Problematic of Silence." In *Feminist Genealogies, Colonial Legacies, Democratic Futures,* edited by J. Alexander and C. T. Mohanty, 170–182. New York: Routledge, 1997.

———. "Black (W)holes and the Geometry of Black Female Sexuality." *differences* 6, nos. 2–3 (1994): 126–145.

Hannay, Margaret. *Lady Sidney, Mary Wroth.* Burlington, VT: Ashgate, 2010.

Hannay, Margaret P. "The 'Ending End' of Lady Mary Wroth's Manuscript of Poems." *Sidney Journal* 31, no. 1 (2013): 1–23.

Hanson, Elizabeth. "Boredom and Whoredom: Reading Renaissance Women's Sonnet Sequences." *Yale Journal of Criticism* 10, no. 1 (1997): 165–191.

Hanson, Ellis. *Decadence and Catholicism.* Cambridge, MA: Harvard University Press, 1997.

Harpham, Geoffrey Galt. *The Ascetic Imperative in Culture and Criticism*. Chicago: University of Chicago Press, 1987.

Harris, Cheryl I. "Whiteness as Property." *Harvard Law Review* 106, no. 8 (1993): 1707–1791.

Harris, Jonathan Gil. *Untimely Matter in the Time of Shakespeare*. Philadelphia: University of Pennsylvania Press, 2008.

Harvey, Elizabeth D. *Ventriloquized Voices: Feminist Theory and English Renaissance Texts*. London: Routledge, 1992.

Hasday, Jill Elaine. "Contest and Consent: A Legal History of Marital Rape." *California Law Review* 88, no. 5 (2000): 1373–1505.

Haskins, Dennis. "The Love Lyric." In *The Oxford Handbook of John Donne*, edited by Jeanne Shami, Dennis Flynn, and M. Thomas Hester, 180–205. Oxford: Oxford University Press, 2011.

Hayot, Eric. "Against Periodization; or, On Institutional Time." *New Literary History* 42, no. 4 (2011): 739–756.

Hecht, Paul J. "Distortion, Aggression, and Sex in Mary Wroth's Sonnets." *SEL: Studies in English Literature 1500–1900* 53, no. 1 (2013): 91–115.

Hendricks, Margo, and Patricia Parker, eds. *Women, "Race," and Writing in the Early Modern Period*. London: Routledge, 1994.

Heng, Geraldine. "The Invention of Race in the European Middle Ages I: Race Studies, Modernity, and the Middle Ages." *Literature Compass* 8, no. 5 (2011): 315–331.

——. "The Invention of Race in the European Middle Ages II: Locations of Medieval Race." *Literature Compass* 8, no. 5 (2011): 332–350.

——. *Empire of Magic: Medieval Romance and the Politics of Cultural Fantasy*. New York: Columbia University Press, 2004.

Herman, Peter C. "What's the Use? Or, the Problematic of Economy in Shakespeare's Procreation Sonnets." In *Shakespeare's Sonnets: Critical Essays*, edited by James Schiffer, 263–283. New York: Garland, 1999.

Higginbotham, Evelyn Brooks. *Righteous Discontent: The Women's Movement in the Black Baptist Church, 1880–1920*. Cambridge, MA: Harvard University Press, 1993.

——. "African-American Women's History and the Metalanguage of Race." *Signs* 17, no. 2 (1992): 251–274.

Hine, Darlene Clark. "Rape and the Inner Lives of Black Women in the Middle West." *Signs* 14, no. 4 (1989): 915–920.

Hird, Myra J. "Naturally Queer." *Feminist Theory* 5, no. 1 (2004): 85–89.

Holland, Sharon Patricia. *The Erotic Life of Racism*. Durham, NC: Duke University Press, 2012.

Hollywood, Amy. *Sensible Ecstasy: Mysticism, Sexual Difference, and the Demands of History*. Chicago: University of Chicago Press, 2002.

Hudson, Hoyt H. "Penelope Devereux as Sidney's Stella." *Huntington Library Bulletin* 7, no. 5 (1935): 89–129.

Hughley, Ruth Willard, ed. *The Arundel Harington Manuscript of Tudor Poetry*, 2 vols. Columbus: Ohio State University Press, 1960.

Hulse, Clark. "Stella's Wit: Penelope Rich as Reader of Sidney's Sonnets." In *Rewriting the Renaissance: The Discourses of Sexual Difference in Early Modern Europe*, edited by Margaret W. Ferguson, Maureen Quilligan, and Nancy J. Vickers, 272–286. Chicago: University of Chicago Press, 1986.

Hunt, Marvin. "Be Dark but Not Too Dark: Shakespeare's Dark Lady as a Sign of Color." In *Shakespeare's Sonnets: Critical Essays*, edited by James Schiffer, 368–389. New York: Garland, 1999.

Hunter, David G. "Augustinian Pessimism? A New Look at Augustine's Teaching on Sex, Marriage, and Celibacy." *Augustinian Studies* 25 (1994): 153–177.

I. B. *A Brife and Faythfull Declaracion of the True Faith of Christ.* London, 1547.

Ingram, Martin. *Church Courts, Sex, and Marriage in England, 1570–1640.* Cambridge: Cambridge University Press, 1990.

Ioppolo, Grace. "'I Desire to Be Helde in Your Memory': Reading Penelope Rich through Her Letters." In *The Impact of Feminism in English Renaissance Studies*, edited by Dympna Callaghan, 299–325. New York: Palgrave, 2007.

Iyengar, Sujata. *Shades of Difference: Mythologies of Skin Color in Early Modern England.* Philadelphia: University of Pennsylvania Press, 2004.

Jackson, Ken, and Arthur F. Marotti. "The Turn to Religion in Early Modern Studies." *Criticism* 46, no. 1 (2004): 167–190.

Jackson, Ken, and Arthur F. Marotti, eds. *Shakespeare and Religion: Early Modern and Postmodern Perspectives.* Notre Dame, IN: Notre Dame University Press, 2011.

Jagose, Annamarie. *Orgasmology.* Durham, NC: Duke University Press, 2013.

Jakobsen, Janet R. "Sex + Freedom = Regulation; Why?" *Social Text* 23, nos. 2–3 (2005): 285–308.

Jakobsen, Janet R., and Ann Pellegrini. "Introduction: Times like These." In *Secularisms*, edited by Janet R. Jakobsen and Ann Pellegrini, 1–38. Durham, NC: Duke University Press, 2008.

Jakobsen, Janet R., and Ann Pellegrini, eds. *Secularisms.* Durham, NC: Duke University Press, 2008.

———. *Love the Sin.* New York: New York University Press, 2003.

Jed, Stephanie. *Chaste Thinking: The Rape of Lucretia and the Birth of Modern Humanism.* Indianapolis: Indiana University Press, 1989.

Johnson, Barbara. "Muteness Envy." 1995. In *The Barbara Johnson Reader: The Surprise of Otherness*, edited by Melissa Feuerstein, Bill Johnson González, Lili Porten, and Keja Valens, 200–215. Durham, NC: Duke University Press, 2014.

Johnson, Jeffrey. "Donne, Imperfect." *John Donne Journal* 27 (2008): 1–20.

Johnson, Kimberley. *Made Flesh: Sacrament and Poetics in Post-Reformation England.* Philadelphia: University of Pennsylvania Press, 2014.

Johnson, Samuel. *Lives of the English Poets.* 1778. Edited by John Mullen and Roger Longsdale. Oxford: Oxford University Press, 2009.

Johnson, William C. "Gender Fashioning and the Dynamics of Mutuality in Spenser's *Amoretti.*" *English Studies* 6 (1993): 503–519.

Jones, Ann Rosalind, and Peter Stallybrass. "The Politics of Astrophil and Stella." *SEL: Studies in English Literature 1500–1900* 24, no. 1 (1984): 53–68.

Jonson, Ben. *The Complete Poems*. Edited by George Parfitt. London: Penguin, 1988.

———. *Conversations of Ben Jonson with William Drummond of Hawthorndon*. Edited by Philip Sidney. London: Gay and Bird, 1906.

———. *The Masque of Blackness*. In *Court Masques: Jacobean and Caroline Entertainments*, edited by David Lindley. Oxford: Oxford University Press, 1995.

Jordan, Mark D. *Convulsing Bodies: Religion and Resistance in Foucault*. Palo Alto, CA: Stanford University Press, 2015.

———. "Religion Trouble." *GLQ: A Journal of Lesbian and Gay Studies* 13, no. 4 (2007): 563–575.

———. *The Invention of Sodomy in Christian Theology*. Chicago: University of Chicago Press, 1998.

Kahan, Benjamin. *Celibacies: American Modernism and Sexual Life*. Durham, NC: Duke University Press, 2013.

Kahn, Coppélia. "Whores and Wives in Jacobean Drama." In *In Another Country: Feminist Perspectives on Renaissance Drama*, edited by Dorothea A. Kehler and Susan Baker, 246–260. London: Scarecrow Press, 1991.

Kahn, Victoria A. "The Defense of Poetry in the *Secretum*." In *The Cambridge Companion to Petrarch*, edited by Albert Russel Ascoli and Unn Falkeid, 100–110. Cambridge: Cambridge University Press, 2015.

———. *The Future of Illusion: Political Theology and Early Modern Texts*. Chicago: University of Chicago Press, 2014.

Kane, Sean. *Spenser's Moral Allegory*. Toronto: University of Toronto Press, 1989.

Karras, Ruth Mazo. *Sexuality in Medieval Europe: Doing unto Others*. London: Routledge, 2005.

Katz, Jonathan Ned. *The Invention of Heterosexuality*. New York: Dutton, 1995.

Kaufmann, Michael. "The Religious, the Secular, and Literary Studies: Rethinking the Secularization Narrative in Histories of the Profession." *New Literary History* 38, no. 4 (2007): 607–627.

Kaufmann, Miranda. *Black Tudors: The Untold Story*. London: Oneworld, 2017.

Kennedy, William. *The Site of Petrarchism: Early Modern National Sentiment in Italy, France, and England*. Baltimore, MD: Johns Hopkins University Press, 2003.

Kerrigan, John, "Introduction." In *The Sonnets and A Lover's Complaint*, edited by John Kerrigan. New York: Viking, 1986.

Kerrigan, William. "What Was Donne Doing?" *South Central Review* 4, no. 2 (1987): 2–15.

Kerrigan, William, and Gordon Braden. *The Idea of the Renaissance*. Baltimore, MD: Johns Hopkins University Press, 1989.

Kinney, Clare R. "Mary Wroth's Guilty 'Secrett Art': The Poetics of Jealousy in *Pamphilia to Amphilanthus*." In *Write or Be Written: Early Modern Women Poets and Cultural Constraints*, edited by Barbara Smith and Ursula Appelt, 69–85. Aldershot, UK: Ashgate, 2001.

———. "Turn and Counterturn: Reappraising Mary Wroth's Poetic Labyrinths." In *Re-Reading Mary Wroth*, edited by Katherine R. Larson and Naomi J. Miller, with Andrew Strycharski, 85–102. New York: Palgrave Macmillan, 2015.

Kipnis, Laura. *Against Love: A Polemic*. New York: Vintage, 2003.

Klein, Lisa M. *The Exemplary Sidney and the Elizabethan Sonneteer*. Wilmington: University of Delaware Press, 1998.

Knapp, Jeffrey. *Pleasing Everyone: Mass Entertainment in Renaissance London and Golden Age Hollywood*. Oxford: Oxford University Press, 2017.

———. *Shakespeare's Tribe: Church, Nation, and Theatre in Renaissance England*. Chicago: University of Chicago Press, 2002.

Kuchar, Gary. "Petrarchism and Repentance in John Donne's Holy Sonnets." *Modern Philology* 105, no. 3 (2008): 535–569.

Kuin, Roger. "Querre-Muhau: Sir Philip Sidney in the New World." *Renaissance Quarterly* 51, no. 2 (1998): 549–585.

Kunin, Aaron. "Shakespeare's Preservation Fantasy." *PMLA: Publications of the Modern Language Association* 124, no. 1 (2009): 92–106.

Lacan, Jacques. *The Seminar of Jacques Lacan, Book VII: The Ethics of Psychoanalysis, 1959–1960*. Edited by Jacques-Alain Miller, translated by Dennis Porter. New York: Norton, 1992.

———. *Le Séminaire, livre VII: L'éthique de la psychanalyse*. Paris: Éditions du Seuil, 1986.

Lamb, Mary Ellen. "'Can you suspect a change in me?': Poems by Mary Wroth and William Herbert, Third Earl of Pembroke." In *Re-Reading Mary Wroth*, edited by Katherine R. Larson and Naomi J. Miller, with Andrew Strycharski, 53–68. New York: Palgrave Macmillan, 2015.

———. "Women Readers in Mary Wroth's *Urania*." In *Reading Mary Wroth*, edited by Naomi J. Miller and Gary Waller, 210–227. Knoxville: University of Tennessee Press, 1991.

———. *Gender and Authorship in the Sidney Circle*. Madison: University of Wisconsin Press, 1990.

Lamberigts, Mathijs. "A Critical Evaluation of Augustine's View of Sexuality." In *Augustine and His Critics*, edited by Robert Dodaro and George Lawless, 176–198. New York: Routledge, 2000.

Langer, Ullrich. "Petrarch's Singular Love Lyric." In *The Cambridge Companion to Petrarch*, edited by Albert Russel Ascoli and Unn Falkeid, 63–73. Cambridge: Cambridge University Press, 2015.

Larson, Katherine R., and Naomi J. Miller, with Andrew Strycharski, eds. *Re-Reading Mary Wroth*. New York: Palgrave Macmillan, 2015.

Latour, Bruno. *Reassembling the Social: An Introduction to Actor-Network Theory*. Oxford: Oxford University Press, 2005.

———. *We Have Never Been Modern*. Translated by Catherine Porter. Cambridge, MA: Harvard University Press, 1993.

Lever, J. W. *The Elizabethan Love Sonnet*. 1956. 2nd ed. London: Methuen, 1966.

Levinas, Emmanuel. *Emmanuel Levinas: Basic Philosophical Writings.* Edited by Adriaan T. Peperzak, Simon Critchley, and Robert Bernasconi. Bloomington: Indiana University Press, 1996.

———. *Otherwise than Being, or beyond Essence.* Translated by Alphonso Lingis. The Hague: Martinus Nijhoff, 1981.

Levitt, Laura. "Other Moderns, Other Jews: Revisiting Jewish Secularism in America." In *Secularisms*, edited by Janet R. Jakobsen and Ann Pellegrini, 107-138. Durham, NC: Duke University Press, 2008.

Lewalski, Barbara K. *Writing Women in Jacobean England.* Cambridge, MA: Harvard University Press, 1993.

———. *Protestant Poetics and the Seventeenth-Century Religious Lyric.* Princeton, NJ: Princeton University Press, 1979.

Lewis, C. S. *The Allegory of Love: A Study in Medieval Tradition.* Oxford: Oxford University Press, 1936.

Liddell, Henry George, Robert Scott, and Henry Stuart Jones. *Greek-English Lexicon*, 9th ed. Oxford: Oxford University Press, 1996.

Little, Arthur L., Jr. *Shakespeare Jungle Fever: National-Imperial Revisions of Race, Rape, and Sacrifice.* Palo Alto, CA: Stanford University Press, 2002.

Lochrie, Karma. *Heterosyncrasies: Female Sexuality when Normal Wasn't.* Minneapolis: University of Minnesota Press, 2005.

———. "Mystical Acts, Queer Tendencies." In *Constructing Medieval Sexuality*, edited by James A. Schultz, Karma Lochrie, and Peggy McCracken, 180–200. Minneapolis: University of Minnesota Press, 1997.

Loewenstein, Joseph. "Sidney's Trewant Pen." *Modern Language Quarterly* 46, no. 1 (1986): 128–142.

Lofton, Kathryn. *Consuming Religion.* Chicago: University of Chicago Press, 2017.

———. "Everything Queer?" In *Queer Christianities: Lived Religion in Transgressive Forms*, edited by Kathleen T. Talvacchia, Michael F. Pettinger, and Mark Larrimore, 195–204. New York: New York University Press, 2015.

Loomba, Ania. "Identities and Bodies in Early Modern Studies." In *The Oxford Handbook of Shakespeare and Embodiment*, edited by Valerie Traub, 228–245. Oxford: Oxford University Press, 2016.

———. "Of Gifts, Ambassadors, and Copy-Cats: Diplomacy, Exchange, and Difference in Early Modern India." In *Emissaries in Early Modern Literature and Culture: Mediation, Transmission, Traffic, 1550–1700*, edited by Brinda Charry and Gitanjali Shahani, 41–75. Aldershot, UK: Ashgate, 2009.

———. *Shakespeare, Race, and Colonialism.* Oxford: Oxford University Press, 2002.

———. *Colonialism/Postcolonialism.* New York: Routledge, 1998.

Loomba, Ania, and Jonathan Burton, eds. *Race in Early Modern England: A Documentary Companion.* New York: Palgrave, 2007.

Loughlin, Gerard. "Introduction: The End of Sex." In *Queer Theology: Rethinking the Western Body*, edited by Gerard Loughlin, 1–34. Oxford: Blackwell, 2007.

Loughlin, Gerard, ed. *Queer Theology: Rethinking the Western Body*. Oxford: Blackwell, 2007.

Love, Heather. "Close but Not Deep: Literary Ethics and the Descriptive Turn." *New Literary History* 41, no. 2 (2010): 371–391.

Low, Anthony. *The Reinvention of Love: Poetry, Politics, and Culture from Sidney to Milton*. Cambridge: Cambridge University Press, 1993.

Luciano, Dana. *Arranging Grief: Sacred Time and the Body in Nineteenth-Century America*. New York: New York University Press, 2007.

Luciano, Dana, and Mel Y. Chen, "Introduction: Has the Queer Ever Been Human?" *GLQ: A Journal of Lesbian and Gay Studies* 21, nos. 2–3 (2015): 183–207.

Lupton, Julia Reinhard. *Thinking with Shakespeare*. Chicago: University of Chicago Press, 2011.

———. "The Religious Turn (to Theory) in Shakespeare Studies." *English Language Notes* 44, no. 1 (2006): 145–149.

———. *Citizen Saints: Shakespeare and Political Theology*. Chicago: University of Chicago Press, 2005.

Luther, Martin. *Martin Luther's Basic Theological Writings*, 2nd ed. Edited by Timothy F. Lull. Minneapolis, MN: Augsberg Fortress, 2005.

———. *Vorrede zum Römerbrief* [*Preface to the Book of Romans*]. Edited by Hans-Walter Krumwiede. Göttingen: Vandenhoeck and Ruprcht, 1982.

———. *Martin Luther: Selections from His Writings*. Translated by John Dillenberger. New York: Anchor, 1962.

Luxon, Thomas H. *Single Imperfection: Milton, Marriage, and Friendship*. Pittsburgh, PA: Duquesne University Press, 2005.

MacKinnon, Catharine A. "Feminism, Marxism, Method, and the State." *Signs* 8, no. 4 (1983): 635–658.

Mager, Donald N. "John Bale and Early Tudor Sodomy Discourse." In *Queering the Renaissance*, edited by Jonathan Goldberg, 141–161. Durham, NC: Duke University Press, 1994.

Mahmood, Saba. "Sexuality and Secularism." In *Religion, the Secular, and the Politics of Sexual Difference*, edited by Tracy E. Linell, 47–58. New York: Columbia University Press, 2013.

———. *Politics of Piety: The Islamic Revival and the Feminist Subject*. Princeton, NJ: Princeton University Press, 2012.

Marcozzi, Luca. "Making the *Rerum vulgarium fragmenta*." In *The Cambridge Companion to Petrarch*, edited by Albert Russel Ascoli and Unn Falkeid, 51–62. Cambridge: Cambridge University Press, 2015.

Marcus, Leah S. "Provincializing the Reformation." *PMLA: Publications of the Modern Language Association* 126, no. 2 (2011): 432–439.

———. *Unediting the Renaissance*. New York: Routledge, 1996.

Marotti, Arthur. *John Donne: Coterie Poet*. Madison: University of Wisconsin Press, 1986.

Marshall, Cynthia. *The Shattering of the Self: Violence, Subjectivity, and Early Modern Texts*. Baltimore, MD: Johns Hopkins University Press, 2002.

Martin, Dale. *Sex and the Single Savior: Gender and Sexuality in Biblical Interpretation.* Louisville, KY: Westminster John Knox Press, 2006.

Martínez, María Elena. *Genealogical Fictions: Limpieza de Sangre, Religion, and Gender in Colonial Mexico.* Palo Alto, CA: Stanford University Press, 2008.

Martinez, Ronald L. "Mourning Laura in the 'Canzoniere': Lessons from Lamentations." *Modern Language Notes* 118, no. 1 (2003): 1–45.

Masten, Jeffrey. *Queer Philologies: Sex, Language, and Affect in Shakespeare's Time.* Philadelphia: University of Pennsylvania Press, 2016.

———. "'Shall I Turne Blabb?': Circulation, Gender, and Subjectivity in Lady Mary Wroth's Sonnets." In *Reading Mary Wroth*, edited by Naomi J. Miller and Gary Waller, 67–87. Knoxville: University of Tennessee Press, 1991.

Masuzawa, Tomoko. *The Invention of World Religions.* Chicago: University of Chicago Press, 2005.

Mazzotta, Giuseppe. "Petrarch's Confrontation with Modernity." In *The Cambridge Companion to Petrarch*, edited by Albert Russel Ascoli and Unn Falkeid, 221–238. Cambridge: Cambridge University Press, 2015.

———. *The Worlds of Petrarch.* Durham, NC: Duke University Press, 1993.

McEachern, Claire. "Hot Protestant Shakespeare." In *The Book in History, the Book as History*, edited by Heidi Brayman, Jesse M. Lander, and Zachary Lesser, 275–300. New Haven, CT: Yale University Press, 2017.

McGarry, Molly. *Ghosts of Futures Past: Spiritualism and the Cultural Politics of Nineteenth-Century America.* Berkeley: University of California Press, 2008.

———. "Crimes of Moral Turpitude: Questions at the Borders of Religion, the Secular, and the U.S. Nation-State." In *Religion, the Secular, and the Politics of Sexual Difference*, edited by Tracy E. Linell, 175–194. New York: Columbia University Press, 2013.

Medovoi, Leerom. "Dogma-Line Racism: Islamaphobia and the Second Axis of Race." *Social Text* 30, no. 2 (2012): 43–74.

Meeks, Wayne. "The Image of the Androgyne: Some Uses of a Symbol in Earliest Christianity." *History of Religions* 13, no. 3 (1974): 165–208.

Menocal, María Rosa. *Shards of Love.* Durham, NC: Duke University Press, 1991.

———. "We Can't Dance Together." *Profession* (1988): 53–58.

Menon, Madhavi. *Indifference to Difference: On Queer Universalism.* Minneapolis: University of Minnesota Press, 2015.

———. "Introduction: QueerShakes." In *Shakesqueer: A Queer Companion to the Complete Works of Shakespeare*, edited by Madhavi Menon, 1–27. Durham, NC: Duke University Press, 2011.

Miles, Margaret R. *Desire and Delight: A New Reading of Augustine's Confessions.* New York: Crossroad, 1992.

Mill, James. *History of British India*, 3 vols. 1817–1818. Cambridge: Cambridge University Press, 2010.

Miller, Naomi J. *Changing the Subject: Mary Wroth and Figurations of Gender in Early Modern England.* Lexington: University of Kentucky Press, 1996.

Miller, Naomi J., and Gary Waller, eds. *Reading Mary Wroth*. Knoxville: University of Tennessee Press, 1991.

Miller, Steven P. *The Age of Evangelicalism: America's Born-Again Years*. Oxford: Oxford University Press, 2014.

Miller Gaubert, Jennifer, Daniel Gubits, Desiree Principe Alderson, and Virginia Knox. *The Supporting Healthy Marriage Evaluation: Final Implementation Findings*. Washington, DC: Office of Planning, Research, Evaluation, Administration for Children and Families, U S Department of Health and Human Services, 2012. www.mdrc.org.

Miller-Young, Mireille. *A Taste for Brown Sugar: Black Women in Pornography*. Durham, NC: Duke University Press, 2014.

Mills, Robert "Ecce Homo." In *Gender and Holiness: Men, Women, and Saints in Late Medieval Europe*, edited by Samantha J. E. Riches and Sarah Salih, 152–173. New York: Routledge, 2002.

Milton, John. *Complete Prose Works of John Milton*, vol. 2, 1644–1645. Edited by Ernest Sirluck. New Haven, CT: Yale University Press, 1962.

———. *John Milton: Complete Poems and Major Prose*. Edited by Merritt Y. Hughes. New York: Macmillan, 1957.

Mitchell, Dianne. "Unfolding Verse: Poetry as Correspondence." PhD diss., University of Pennsylvania, 2017.

Montaigne, Michel de. *The Complete Essays*. Translated by M. A. Screech. Harmondsworth, UK: Penguin, 1987.

———. *Les essais de Michel, Seigneur de Montaigne*. Chez Robert Valentin, 1627.

Morrissey, Lee. "Milton, Modernity, and the Periodization of Politics." *Modern Language Quarterly* 78, no. 3 (2017): 301–319.

Moryson, Fynes. *An itinerary containing his ten yeeres trauell*. London, 1617.

Moten, Fred. *In the Break: The Aesthetics of the Black Radical Tradition*. Minneapolis: University of Minnesota Press, 2003.

Mueller, Janel. "Women among the Metaphysicals: A Case, Mostly, of Being Donne For." *Modern Philology* 87, no. 2 (1989): 142–151.

Muñoz, José Esteban. "The Sense of Watching Tony Sleep." In *After Sex?: On Writing since Queer Theory*, edited by Janet Halley and Andrew Parker, 142–150. Durham, NC: Duke University Press, 2011.

———. *Disidentifications: Queers of Color and the Performance of Politics*. Minneapolis: University of Minnesota Press, 1999.

Murray, Jacqueline. "'The Law of Sin that Is in My Members': The Problem of Male Embodiment." In *Gender and Holiness: Men, Women, and Saints in Late Medieval Europe*, edited by Samantha J. E. Riches and Sarah Salih, 9–22. New York: Routledge, 2002.

Murray, Molly. *The Poetics of Conversion in Early Modern English Literature*. Cambridge: Cambridge University Press, 2009.

Musser, Amber Jamilla. *Sensational Flesh: Race, Power, and Masochism*. New York: New York University Press, 2014.

Nardizzi, Vin, and Jean E. Feerick, eds. *The Indistinct Human in Renaissance Literature*. New York: Palgrave, 2012.

Nash, Jennifer. *The Black Body in Ecstasy: Reading Race, Reading Pornography*. Durham, NC: Duke University Press, 2014.

Nelles, William. "Sexing Shakespeare's Sonnets: Reading beyond Sonnet 20." *English Literary Renaissance* 39, no. 1 (2009): 128–140.

Netzley, Ryan. *Reading, Desire, and the Eucharist in Early Modern Religious Poetry*. Toronto: University of Toronto Press, 2011.

Newman, Barbara. "Love's Arrows: Christ as Cupid in Late Medieval Art and Devotion." In *The Mind's Eye: Art and Theological Argument in the Middle Ages*, edited by Jeffrey F. Hamburger and Anne-Marie Bouché, 263–286. Princeton, NJ: Princeton University Press, 2006.

Nirenberg, David. "Was There Race before Modernity? The Example of 'Jewish' Blood in Late Medieval Spain." In *The Origins of Racism in the West*, edited by Miriam Eliav-Feldon, Benjamin Isaac, and Joseph Ziegler, 239–242. Cambridge: Cambridge University Press, 2009.

Nocentelli, Carmen. *Empires of Love: Europe, Asia, and the Making of Early Modern Identity*. Philadelphia: University of Pennsylvania Press, 2013.

Norton, Anne. *On the Muslim Question*. Princeton, NJ: Princeton University Press, 2013.

Nygren, Anders. *Agape and Eros*. Chicago: University of Chicago Press, 1982.

Nyong'o, Tavia. *The Amalgamation Waltz: Race, Performance, and the Ruses of Memory*. Minneapolis: University of Minnesota Press, 2009.

Nyquist, Mary. *Arbitrary Rule: Slavery, Tyranny, and the Power of Life and Death*. Chicago: University of Chicago Press, 2013.

Olsen, Glenn W. "Marriage in Barbarian Kingdom and Christian Court: Fifth through Eleventh Century." In *Christian Marriage: A Historical Study*, edited by Glenn W. Olsen, 146–212. New York: Crossroad Publishing, 2001.

———. "Progeny, Faithfulness, Sacred Bond: Marriage in the Age of Augustine." In *Christian Marriage: A Historical Study*, edited by Glenn W. Olsen, 101–145. New York: Crossroad Publishing, 2001.

Olsen, Glenn W., ed. *Christian Marriage: A Historical Study*. New York: Crossroad Publishing, 2001.

Oram, William. "Elizabethan Fact and Spenserian Fiction." *Spenser Studies* 4 (1984): 33–48.

Orvis, David L. "Eros and Anteros: Queer Mutuality in Milton's *Doctrine and Discipline of Divorce*." *Early Modern Culture* 10 (2014): n.p.

Papazian, Mary Arshagouni, ed. *John Donne and the Protestant Reformation: New Perspectives*. Detroit, MI: Wayne State University Press, 2003.

Parish, Helen L. *Clerical Marriage and the English Reformation*. Aldershot, UK: Ashgate, 2000.

Park, Katharine. "The Rediscovery of the Clitoris: French Medicine and the Tribade, 1570–1620." In *The Body in Parts*, edited by Carla Mazzio and David Hillman, 171–193. New York: Routledge, 1997.

Parker, Patricia. *Inescapable Romance: Studies in the Poetics of a Mode*. Princeton, NJ: Princeton University Press, 1979.

Paulissen, May N. "The Love Sonnets of Lady Mary Wroth: A Critical Introduction." PhD diss., University of Houston, 1976.

Payer, Pierre J. *The Bridling of Desire: Views of Sex in the Later Middle Ages.* Toronto: University of Toronto Press, 1993.

Pellegrini, Ann. "Sincerely Held; Or, the Pastorate 2.0." *Social Text* 34, no. 4 (2016): 71–85.

Peterson, Thomas E. *Petrarch's Fragmenta: The Narrative and Theological Unity of "Rerum Vulgarium Fragmenta."* Toronto: University of Toronto Press, 2016.

Petrarch, Francesco. *Petrarch's Lyric Poems: The Rime Sparse and Other Lyrics.* Translated and edited by Robert M. Durling. Cambridge, MA: Harvard University Press, 1976.

———. *Francesco Petrarca: My Secret Book.* Translated by Nicholas Mann. I Tatti Renaissance Library. Cambridge, MA: Harvard University Press, 2016.

Phillips, Adam. *Monogamy.* New York: Vintage, 1996.

———. *On Flirtation: Psychoanalytic Essays on the Uncommitted Life.* Cambridge, MA: Harvard University Press, 1994.

Pierre, Teresa Olsen. "Marriage, Body, and Sacrament in the Age of Hugh of St. Victor." In *Christian Marriage: A Historical Study*, edited by Glenn W. Olsen, 213–268. New York: Crossroad Publishing, 2001.

Plato. *The Symposium.* Translated by Walter Hamilton. New York: Penguin, 1951.

Porter, Roy. "Spreading Carnal Knowledge or Selling Dirt Cheap? Nicholas Venette's *Tableau de l'Amour Conjugal* in Eighteenth-Century England." *Journal of European Studies* 14 (1984): 233–255.

Puar, Jasbir. *Terrorist Assemblages: Homonationalism in Queer Times.* Durham, NC: Duke University Press, 2007.

Puttenham, George. *The Arte of English Poesie.* London, 1598.

Quillen, Carol Everhart. *Reading the Renaissance: Petrarch, Augustine, and the Language of Humanism.* Ann Arbor: University of Michigan Press, 1998.

Quilligan, Maureen. "Completing the Conversation." *Shakespeare Studies* 25 (1997): 42–50.

Rackin, Phyllis. *Shakespeare and Women.* Oxford: Oxford University Press, 2005.

Raman, Shankar. *Framing "India": The Colonial Imaginary in Early Modern Culture.* Palo Alto, CA: Stanford University Press, 2001.

Rambuss, Richard. "The Straightest Story Ever Told." *GLQ: A Journal of Lesbian and Gay Studies* 17, no. 4 (2011): 543–573.

———. *Closet Devotions.* Durham, NC: Duke University Press, 1998.

Ranke-Heinemann, Ute. *Eunuchs for the Kingdom of God: Women, Sexuality, and the Catholic Church.* Translated by Peter Heinegg. New York: Doubleday, 1990.

Rastegar, Mitra. "Emotional Attachments and Secular Imaginings: Western LGBTQ Activism on Iran." *GLQ: A Journal of Lesbian and Gay Studies* 19, no. 1 (2012): 1–29.

Rhode, Deborah H. "Why Is Adultery Still a Crime?" *Los Angeles Times*, May 2, 2016. www.latimes.com.

Richey, Esther Gilman. "The Intimate Other: Lutheran Subjectivity in Spenser, Donne, and Herbert." *Modern Philology* 108, no. 3 (2011): 343–374.

Rickman, Johanna. *Love, Lust, and License in Early Modern England: Illicit Sex and the Nobility*. Aldershot, UK: Ashgate, 2008.

Ricks, Christopher. "Donne after Love." In *Literature and the Body: Essays on Populations and Persons*, edited by Elaine Scarry, 33–70. Baltimore, MD: Johns Hopkins University Press, 1988.

Ridder-Symoens, Hilde de, ed. *A History of the University in Europe*, vol. 1. Cambridge: Cambridge University Press, 2003.

Riddy, Felicity. "Middle English Romance: Family, Marriage, Intimacy." In *The Cambridge Companion to Medieval Romance*, edited by Roberta L. Kreuger, 235–252. Cambridge: Cambridge University Press, 2000.

Rifkin, Mark. *When Did Indians Become Straight? Kinship, the History of Sexuality, and Native Sovereignty*. Oxford: Oxford University Press, 2011.

Rivera, Mayra. *Poetics of the Flesh*. Durham, NC: Duke University Press, 2015.

Robbins, Bruce. *Secular Vocations: Intellectuals, Professionalization, Culture*. London: Verso, 1993.

Roberts, Dorothy. *Killing the Black Body: Race, Reproduction, and the Meaning of Liberty*. New York: Random House/Pantheon, 1997.

Roberts, Josephine A. "'The Knott Never to Bee Untide': The Controversy Regarding Marriage in Mary Wroth's *Urania*." In *Reading Mary Wroth*, edited by Naomi J. Miller and Gary Waller, 109–132. Knoxville: University of Tennessee Press, 1991.

———. "The Biographical Problem of Pamphilia to Amphilanthus." *Tulsa Studies in Women's Literature* 1, no. 1 (1982): 43–53.

Roberts, Josephine, ed. *The Second Part of The Countess of Montgomery's Urania*. By Lady Mary Wroth. Binghamton, NY: Center for Medieval and Early Renaissance Studies, State University of New York, 1999.

Roberts, Josephine A., ed. *The First Part of The Countess of Montgomery's Urania*. By Lady Mary Wroth. Binghamton, NY: Center for Medieval and Early Renaissance Studies, State University of New York, 1995.

———, ed. *The Poems of Lady Mary Wroth*. Baton Rouge: Louisiana State University Press, 1983.

Roche, Thomas. *Petrarch and the English Sonnet Sequences*. New York: Abraham's Magazine Service (AMS), 1989.

Rubin, Gayle. "Thinking Sex: Notes for a Radical Theory of the Politics of Sexuality." 1984. In *Exploring Female Sexuality*, 2nd ed., edited by Carol S. Vance, 267–319. London: Pandora, 1992.

Ruskola, Teemu. "Gay Rights versus Queer Theory: What Is Left of Sodomy after *Lawrence v. Texas*?" *Social Text* 23, nos. 3–4 (2005): 235–249.

Rust, Jennifer R. *The Body in Mystery: The Political Theology of the Corpus Mysticum in the Literature of Reformation England*. Evanston, IL: Northwestern University Press, 2014.

Salzman, Paul. "Me and My Shadow: Editing Wroth for the Digital Age." In *Re-Reading Mary Wroth*, edited by Katherine R. Larson and Naomi J. Miller, with Andrew Strycharski, 183–192. New York: Palgrave Macmillan, 2015.

———. *Literary Culture in Jacobean England: Reading 1621.* New York: Palgrave, 2002.

Sanchez, Melissa E. *Shakespeare and Queer Theory.* London: Bloomsbury, 2019.

———. "Antisocial Procreation in *Measure for Measure.*" In *Queer Shakespeare,* edited by Goran Stanivukovic, 263–277. London: Bloomsbury Arden Shakespeare, 2017.

———. "Sex and Eroticism in the Renaissance." In *Edmund Spenser in Context,* edited by Andrew Escobedo, 342–351. Cambridge: Cambridge University Press, 2016.

———. "Posthuman Spenser?" *Spenser Studies* 30 (2015): 19–31.

———. "'In Myself the Smart I Try': Female Promiscuity in *Astrophil and Stella.*" *ELH: English Literary History* 80, no. 1 (2013): 1–27.

———. "The Poetics of Feminine Subjectivity in Shakespeare's Sonnets and 'A Lover's Complaint.'" In *The Oxford Companion to Shakespeare's Poetry,* edited by Jonathan Post, 505–521. Oxford: Oxford University Press, 2013.

———. "'Use Me But as Your Spaniel': Feminism, Queer Theory, and Early Modern Sexualities." *PMLA: Publications of the Modern Language Association* 127, no. 3 (2012): 493–511.

Saunders, Ben. *Desiring Donne.* Cambridge, MA: Harvard University Press, 2006.

Scanlon, James J. "Sidney's *Astrophil and Stella:* 'See What It Is to Love' Sensually!" *SEL: Studies in English Literature 1500–1900* 16, no. 1 (1976): 65–74.

Schiffer, James, ed. *Shakespeare's Sonnets: Critical Essays.* New York: Garland, 1999.

Schmidt, Benjamin. *Innocence Abroad: The Dutch Imagination and the New World, 1570–1670.* Cambridge: Cambridge University Press, 2001.

Schoenfeldt, Michael C. "Eloquent Blood and Deliberative Bodies: The Physiology of Metaphysical Poetry." In *Renaissance Transformations: The Making of English Writing, 1500–1650,* edited by Thomas Healy and Margaret Healy, 145–160. Edinburgh: Edinburgh University Press, 2009.

———. "The Sonnets." In *The Cambridge Companion to Shakespeare's Poetry,* edited by Patrick Cheney, 125–143. Cambridge: Cambridge University Press, 2007.

———. *Bodies and Selves in Early Modern England: Physiology and Inwardness in Spenser, Shakespeare, Herbert, and Milton.* Cambridge: Cambridge University Press, 1999.

———. "The Gender of Religious Devotion: Amelia Lanyer and John Donne." In *Religion and Culture in Renaissance England,* edited by Claire McEachern and Debora K. Shuger, 209–233. Cambridge: Cambridge University Press, 1997.

Schwartz, Regina. *Sacramental Poetics at the Dawn of Secularism: When God Left the World.* Palo Alto, CA: Stanford University Press, 2008.

Schwarz, Kathryn. *What You Will: Gender, Contract, and Shakespearean Social Space.* Philadelphia: University of Pennsylvania Press, 2011.

Schweitzer, Ivy. *Perfecting Friendship: Politics and Affiliation in Early American Literature.* Chapel Hill: University of North Carolina Press, 2006.

Scott, Joan Wallach. *Sex and Secularism.* Princeton, NJ: Princeton University Press, 2018.

———. *The Politics of the Veil.* Princeton, NJ: Princeton University Press, 2010.

Sedgwick, Eve Kosofsky. "Paranoid Reading and Reparative Reading; or, You're So Paranoid, You Probably Think This Essay Is About You." In *Touching Feeling: Affect, Pedagogy, Performativity*, 123–152. Durham, NC: Duke University Press, 2003.

———. *Between Men: English Literature and Male Homosocial Desire*. New York: Columbia University Press, 1985.

Shakespeare, William. *Shakespeare's Sonnets*. Edited by Stephen Booth. New Haven, CT: Yale University Press, 1977.

Shannon, Laurie. *The Accommodated Animal: Cosmopolity in Shakespearean Locales*. Chicago: University of Chicago Press, 2013.

———. *Sovereign Amity: Figures of Friendship in Shakespearean Contexts*. Chicago: University of Chicago Press, 2002.

Shaw, Jane. "Reformed and Enlightened Church." In *Queer Theology: Rethinking the Western Body*, edited by Gerard Loughlin, 215–228. Oxford: Blackwell, 2007.

Shuger, Deborah Kuller. *Political Theologies in Shakespeare's England: The Sacred and the State in "Measure for Measure."* New York: Palgrave, 2001.

———. *The Renaissance Bible: Scholarship, Sacrifice, and Subjectivity*. Berkeley: University of California Press, 1994.

———. *Habits of Thought in the English Renaissance: Religion, Politics, and the Dominant Culture*. Berkeley: University of California Press, 1990.

Sidney, Philip. *The Major Works*. Edited by Katherine Duncan-Jones. Oxford: Oxford University Press, 2002.

Silver, Victoria A. *Imperfect Sense: The Predicament of Milton's Irony*. Princeton, NJ: Princeton University Press, 2001.

Sinfield, Alan. *Shakespeare, Authority, Sexuality: Unfinished Business in Cultural Materialism*. London: Routledge, 2006.

———. *Gay and After: Gender, Culture, Consumption*. London: Serpent's Tail, 1998.

———. *Faultlines: Cultural Materialism and the Politics of Dissident Reading*. Berkeley: University of California Press, 1992.

———. "Sidney and Astrophil." *SEL: Studies in English Literature 1500–1900* 20, no. 1 (1980): 25–41.

———. "Sexual Puns in *Astrophil and Stella*." *Essays in Criticism* 24 (1974): 341–355.

Smith, Bruce. *Homosexual Desire in Shakespeare's England: A Cultural Poetics*. Chicago: University of Chicago Press, 1991.

Smith, Ian. *Race and Rhetoric in the Renaissance: Barbarian Errors*. New York: Palgrave, 2009.

Smith, Rosalind. *Sonnets and the English Woman Writer, 1560–1621: The Politics of Absence*. New York: Palgrave Macmillan, 2005.

Sorabji, Richard. *Emotion and Peace of Mind*. Oxford: Oxford University Press, 2000.

Spenser, Edmund. *The Faerie Queene*. Edited by A. C. Hamilton, Hiroshi Yamashita, and Toshiyuki Suzuki. Harlow: Longman, 2001.

———. *The Yale Edition of the Shorter Poems of Edmund Spenser*. Edited by William A. Oram. New Haven, CT: Yale University Press, 1989.

————. *The Shorter Poems*. Edited by Richard A. McCabe. New York: Penguin, 1999.

Spillers, Hortense J. "Interstices: A Small Drama of Words." In *Pleasure and Danger: Exploring Female Sexuality*, 2nd ed., edited by Carol S. Vance, 73–100. London: Pandora, 1992.

————."Mama's Baby, Papa's Maybe: An American Grammar Book." *diacritics* 17, no. 2 (1987): 64–81.

Spivak, Gayatri Chakravorty. *Outside in the Teaching Machine*. London: Routledge, 1995.

Stapleton, M. L. "Devoid of Guilty Shame: Ovidian Tendencies in Spenser's Erotic Poetry." *Modern Philology* 105, no. 2 (2008): 271–299.

Stewart, Alan. *Philip Sidney: A Double Life*. London: Chatto and Windus, 2000.

Stillinger, Jack. "The Biographical Problem of *Astrophil and Stella*." *Journal of English and German Philology* 59, no. 4 (1960): 617–639.

Stillman, Robert. "'I am not I': Philip Sidney and the Energy of Fiction." *Sidney Journal* 30, no. 1 (2012): 1–26.

Stockton, Will. *Members of His Body: Shakespeare, Paul, and a Theology of Nonmonogamy*. New York: Fordham University Press, 2017.

Stone, Lawrence. *The Family, Sex, and Marriage in England, 1500–1800*. New York: Penguin, 1990.

————. *The Road to Divorce: England, 1530–1987*. Oxford: Oxford University Press, 1990.

Strier, Richard. *The Unrepentant Renaissance*. Chicago: University of Chicago Press, 2011.

————. "John Donne Awry and Squint: The *Holy Sonnets*." *Modern Philology* 86, no. 4 (1989): 357–384.

Strycharski, Andrew. "Literacy, Education, and Affect in *Astrophil and Stella*." *SEL: Studies in English Literature 1500–1900* 48, no. 1 (2008): 45–63.

Sturm-Maddox, Sara. *Petrarch's Laurels*. University Park: Pennsylvania State University Press, 1993.

————. *Petrarch's Metamorphoses: Text and Subtext in the "Rime Sparse."* Columbia: University of Missouri Press, 1985.

Sullivan, Garrett. *Sleep, Romance, and Human Embodiment: Vitality from Spenser to Milton*. Cambridge: Cambridge University Press, 2012.

Sutton, Matthew Avery. *Jerry Falwell and the Rise of the Religious Right: A Brief History with Documents*. Boston: Bedford/St. Martin's, 2013.

Sweeney, JoAnne. "Undead Statutes: The Rise, Fall, and Continuing Uses of Adultery and Fornication Criminal Laws." *Loyola University Chicago Law Review* 46 (2014): 127–173.

Sweet, John Wood. *Bodies Politic: Negotiating Race in the American North, 1730–1830*. Baltimore, MD: Johns Hopkins University Press, 2003.

Targoff, Ramie. *John Donne, Body and Soul*. Chicago: University of Chicago Press, 2008.

————. *Common Prayer: The Language of Public Devotion in Early Modern England*. Chicago: University of Chicago Press, 2001.

Taubes, Jacob. *The Political Theology of Paul.* 1993. Palo Alto, CA: Stanford University Press, 2004.

Taverner, Richard. *Common Places of Scripture . . . by the Right Excellent Clerke Erasmus Sarcerius.* London, 1538.

Taylor, Charles. *A Secular Age.* Cambridge, MA: Harvard University Press, 2007.

Teskey, Gordon. *Delirious Milton.* Cambridge, MA: Harvard University Press, 2006.

Thelin, John R. *A History of American Higher Education.* Baltimore, MD: Johns Hopkins University Press, 2004.

Thompson, Ayanna. *Passing Strange: Shakespeare, Race, and Contemporary America.* Oxford: Oxford University Press, 2011.

———. *Performing Race and Torture on the Early Modern Stage.* New York: Routledge, 2008.

Tilney, Edmund. *A brief and pleasant discourse of duties in Mariage, called the Flower of Friendshippe.* 1568. Edited by Valerie Wayne. Ithaca, NY: Cornell University Press, 1992.

Todd, Margo. "Humanists, Puritans, and the Spiritualized Household." *Church History* 49, no. 1 (1980): 18–34.

Todorov, Tzvetan. "'Race,' Writing, and Culture." In *"Race," Writing, and Difference,* edited by Henry Louis Gates Jr, 370–380. Chicago: University of Chicago Press, 1986.

Tonstad, Linn Marie. "Ambivalent Loves: Christian Theologies, Queer Theologies." *Literature and Theology* 31, no. 4 (2017): 472–489.

———. *God and Difference: The Trinity, Sexuality, and the Transformation of Finitude.* New York: Routledge, 2016.

Townes, Emilie. *In a Blaze of Glory: Womanist Spirituality as Social Witness.* Nashville, TN: Abington Press, 1995.

Traub, Valerie. *Thinking Sex with the Early Moderns.* Philadelphia: University of Pennsylvania Press, 2015.

———. "The Nature of Norms in Early Modern England: Anatomy, Cartography, 'King Lear.'" *South Central Review* 26, no. 1/2 (2009): 42–81.

———. *The Renaissance of Lesbianism in Early Modern England.* Cambridge: Cambridge University Press, 2002.

———. "The Psychomorphology of the Clitoris." *GLQ: A Journal of Lesbian and Gay Studies* 2, nos. 1–2 (1995): 81–113.

Trevor, Douglas. *The Poetics of Melancholy in Early Modern England.* Cambridge: Cambridge University Press, 2004.

Turner, Henry. "Life Science: Rude Mechanicals, Human Mortals, Posthuman Shakespeare." *South Central Review* 26, nos. 1–2 (2009): 197–219.

Turner, James Grantham. *Schooling Sex: Libertine Literature and Erotic Education in Italy, France, and England, 1534–1685.* Oxford: Oxford University Press, 2003.

———. *One Flesh: Paradisal Marriage and Sexual Relations in the Age of Milton.* Oxford: Oxford University Press, 1987.

Underwood, Ted. *Why Literary Periods Mattered: Historical Contrast and the Prestige of English Studies.* Palo Alto, CA: Stanford University Press, 2013.

Vasilinda, Mike. "FL: Couples Living Together without Being Married Can Get Arrested." WCTV, August 31, 2011. www.wctv.tv.

Van Doorn, Niels. "Forces of Faith: Endurance, Flourishing, and the Queer Religious Subject." *GLQ: A Journal of Lesbian and Gay Studies* 21, no. 4 (2015): 635–666.

Vance, Carole S. "Pleasure and Danger: Towards a Politics of Sexuality." In *Pleasure and Danger: Exploring Female Sexuality*, 2nd ed., edited by Carol S. Vance, 1–27. London: Pandora, 1992.

Vance, Carole S., ed. *Pleasure and Danger: Exploring Female Sexuality*, 2nd ed. London: Pandora, 1992.

Vendler, Helen. *The Art of Shakespeare's Sonnets*. Cambridge, MA: Harvard University Press, 1997.

Venette, Nicolas. *The Mysteries of Conjugal Love Reveal'd*, 2nd ed. London, 1707.

Vicary, Thomas. *The English-Man's Treasure*. London, 1586.

Vickers, Nancy. "Vital Signs: Petrarch and Popular Culture." *Romantic Review* 79, no. 1 (1988): 184–195.

———. "Diana Described: Scattered Woman and Scattered Rhyme." *Critical Inquiry* 8, no. 2 (1981): 265–279.

Vitkus, Daniel J. *Turning Turk: English Theater and the Multicultural Mediterranean, 1570–1630*. New York: Palgrave, 2003.

Vogel, Joseph. *James Baldwin and the 1980s: Witnessing the Reagan Era*. Urbana-Champagne: University of Illinois Press, 2018.

Walker, Kim. *Women Writers of the English Renaissance*. New York: Twaine, 1996.

Wall, Alison. "Rich, Penelope." *Oxford Dictionary of National Biography*. Oxford: Oxford University Press, 2004.

Wall, Wendy. *The Imprint of Gender: Authorship and Publication in the English Renaissance*. Ithaca, NY: Cornell University Press, 1993.

Wallace, Jeff. "Literature and Posthumanism." *Literature Compass* 7, no. 8 (2010): 692–701.

Waller, Gary. "Mary Wroth and the Sidney Family Romance: Gender Construction in Early Modern England." In *Reading Mary Wroth*, edited by Naomi J. Miller and Gary Waller, 35–63. Knoxville: University of Tennessee Press, 1991.

Walton, Izaac. *The Life of John Donne*. London, 1658.

Warley, Christopher. *Reading Class through Shakespeare, Donne, and Milton*. Cambridge: Cambridge University Press, 2014.

———. *Sonnet Sequences and Social Distinction in Renaissance England*. Cambridge: Cambridge University Press, 2005.

Warner, Michael. "Uncritical Reading." In *Polemic: Critical or Uncritical*, edited by Jane Gallop. New York: Routledge, 2004.

———. "Tongues Untied: Memoirs of a Pentecostal Boyhood." In *Que(e)rying Religion: A Critical Anthology*, edited by Gary David Comstock and Susan E. Henking, 123–131. New York: Continuum, 1999.

———. *The Trouble with Normal*. New York: Free Press, 1999.

———. "New England Sodom." In *Queering the Renaissance*, edited by Jonathan Goldberg, 330–358. Durham, NC: Duke University Press, 1995.

Weber, Max. *The Protestant Ethic and the Spirit of Capitalism.* 1905. Translated by Talcott Parsons. New York: Scribner's, 1976.

Weiss, Margot. *Techniques of Pleasure: BDSM and the Circuits of Sexuality.* Durham, NC: Duke University Press, 2011.

Weissbourd, Emily. "'Those in Their Possession': Race, Slavery, and Queen Elizabeth's 'Edicts of Expulsion.'" *Huntington Library Quarterly* 78, no. 1 (2015): 1–19.

West, Robin. "Equality Theory, Marital Rape, and the Promise of the Fourteenth Amendment." *University of Florida Law Review* 42 (1990): 45–79.

Wiegman, Robyn. "Wishful Thinking." *Feminist Foundations* 25, no. 3 (2013): 202–213.

Wiesner-Hanks, Merry E. *Christianity and Sexuality in the Early Modern World: Regulating Desire, Reforming Practice.* New York: Routledge, 2000.

Wilcox, W. Bradford, and Jeffrey Dew. "Is Love a Flimsy Foundation?: Soulmate versus Institutional Models of Marriage." *Social Science Research* 39, no. 5 (2010): 687–699.

Wilkins, Ernest Hatch. *The Making of the "Canzoniere" and other Petrarchan Studies.* Rome: Edizioni di Storia e letteratura, 1951.

Williams, Daniel K. *God's Own Party: The Making of the Christian Right.* Oxford: Oxford University Press, 2010.

Wilson, Elizabeth A. *Gut Feminism.* Durham, NC: Duke University Press, 2015.

Wind, Edgar. *Pagan Mysteries in the Renaissance.* New York: Norton, 1958.

Wroth, Mary. *Mary Wroth's Poetry: An Electronic Edition.* Edited by Paul Salzman. Melbourne, Victoria, Australia: La Trobe University, 2012. http://wroth.latrobe.edu.

Zak, Gur. *Petrarch's Humanism and the Care of the Self.* Cambridge: Cambridge University Press, 2010.

Žižek, Slavoj. *The Puppet and the Dwarf: The Perverse Core of Christianity.* Boston: MIT Press, 2003.

———. *The Fragile Absolute, or, Why Is the Christian Legacy Worth Fighting For?* London: Verso, 2000.

INDEX

ABOUT THE AUTHOR

Melissa E. Sanchez is Professor of English, Comparative Literature, and Gender, Sexuality, and Women's Studies at the University of Pennsylvania. She is the author of *Erotic Subjects* (2011) and *Shakespeare and Queer Theory* (2019) and the co-editor of *Rethinking Feminism in Early Modern Studies: Gender, Race, Sexuality* (2016).